IT Strategy & Innovation
Edition 4.0

James D. McKeen
Smith School of Business at Queen's University

Heather A. Smith
Smith School of Business at Queen's University

Prospect Press

Founded in 2014, Prospect Press serves the academic discipline of Information Systems by publishing innovative textbooks across the curriculum including introductory, emerging, and upper-level courses. Prospect Press offers reasonable prices by selling directly to students. Prospect Press provides tight relationships between authors, publisher, and adopters that many larger publishers are unable to offer in today's publishing environment. Based in Burlington, Vermont, Prospect Press distributes titles worldwide. We welcome new authors to send proposals or inquiries to Beth.Golub@ProspectPressVT.com.

Editor: Beth Lang Golub
Production Management: Kathy Bond Borie
Cover Design: Annie Clark

eTextbook
- Edition 4.0
- ISBN: 978-1-943153-43-5
- Available from Redshelf.com and VitalSource.com

Printed Paperback
- Edition 4.0
- ISBN: 978-1-943153-44-2
- Available from Redshelf.com

For more information, visit
http://prospectpressvt.com/titles/mckeen-it-strategy/

Contents

Preface   ix
    What's New in This Edition 4.0?   x
    Key Features of This Book   x
    A Different Approach to Teaching IT Strategy   xi
    Organization of This Book   xii
    Supplementary Materials / Instructor Resources   xvi
    The Genesis of This Book   xvi

About the Authors   xviii

Acknowledgments   xix

SECTION I   DELIVERING VALUE WITH IT   1

Chapter 1   Delivering on the IT Value Proposition   2
    Peeling the Onion: Understanding IT Value   3
    The Three Components of the IT Value Proposition   7
    Five Principles for Delivering Value   12
    Conclusion   14
    Chapter Discussion Questions   14
    References   14

Chapter 2   Developing IT Strategy for Business Value   16
    Business and IT Strategies: Past, Present, and Future   18
    Four Critical Success Factors   20
    The Many Dimensions of IT Strategy   21
    Toward an IT Strategy-Development Process   24
    Challenges for CIOs   26
    Conclusion   27
    Chapter Discussion Questions   27
    References   27

Chapter 3   Advancing a Data Strategy   29
    Why Do We Need a Data Strategy?   30
    What is a Data Strategy?   32

Where Does Data Strategy Fit? 34
The Data Journey 35
Advice to Managers 37
Conclusion 38
Chapter Discussion Questions 38
References 38

Chapter 4 Creating and Evolving a Digital Strategy 39
What is a Digital Strategy? 40
What is the Value of a Digital Strategy? 42
Developing and Implementing a Digital Strategy 43
Supporting Digital Strategy 45
Conclusion 50
Chapter Discussion Questions 50
References 50

Chapter 5 Developing a Cloud Strategy 52
Cloud Computing: The Current Reality 53
Developing a Cloud Strategy 55
Cloud Computing Challenges 56
Cloud Vendor Selection and Management 59
Recommendations for Managers 62
Conclusion 63
Chapter Discussion Questions 63
References 63
Appendix A 64

Section I Mini Cases 66
Global Logistics and the Maritime Transport Ecosystem 66
IT Planning at ModMeters 73
IT Investment at North American Financial 77

SECTION II IT–BUSINESS PARTNERSHIP 82

Chapter 6 Governance for a Redefined IT 83
The Increasing Importance of Governance 84
Elements of Effective IT Governance 85
IT Governance Evolution 87
Promoting Effective IT Governance 89
Conclusion 91
Chapter Discussion Questions 91
References 91

Chapter 7   The IT Budgeting Process   **92**
Key Concepts in IT Budgeting   93
The Importance of Budgets   95
The IT Planning and Budget Process   97
IT Budgeting Practices That Deliver Value   102
Conclusion   104
Chapter Discussion Questions   104
References   104

Chapter 8   Managing IT-Based Risk   **106**
A Holistic View of IT-Based Risk   107
Holistic Risk Management: A Portrait   110
Developing a Risk Management Framework   112
Improving Risk Management Capabilities   115
Conclusion   116
Chapter Discussion Questions   117
References   117
Appendix A   118

Chapter 9   Building a Strong Relationship with the Business   **120**
The Nature of the Business–IT Relationship   121
The Foundation of a Strong Business–IT Relationship   123
Conclusion   131
Chapter Discussion Questions   131
References   131
Appendix A   133
Appendix B   134

Chapter 10   Enabling Collaboration with IT   **136**
Why Collaborate?   137
Characteristics of Collaboration   141
Components of Successful Collaboration   143
The Role of IT in Collaboration   146
First Steps for Facilitating Effective Collaboration   148
Conclusion   151
Chapter Discussion Questions   151
References   151

Section II Mini Cases   **154**
Enterprise Architecture at Nationstate Insurance   154
Transforming IT at Global Digital Imaging   160
Delivering Business Value with IT at Hefty Hardware   167

SECTION III   IT–ENABLED INNOVATION   172

Chapter 11   Developing Thought Leaders in IT   173
What is a Thought Leader?   174
Thought Leadership and IT   175
Characteristics of an IT Thought Leader   177
Fostering Thought Leaders in IT   179
Conclusion   181
Chapter Discussion Questions   181
References   182

Chapter 12   Managing Disruption in IT   184
Disruption in Organizations   185
Disruption and IT   187
Disruption and the Future of IT   188
Managing Disruption in IT   190
First Steps for IT Managers   192
Conclusion   193
Chapter Discussion Questions   194
References   194

Chapter 13   IT's Role in a Culture of Experimentation   196
What is Experimentation?   197
Experimentation and IT   199
The Experimentation Life Cycle   202
Getting Started with Experimentation   205
Conclusion   207
Chapter Discussion Questions   207
References   207

Chapter 14   Improving the Customer Experience: An IT Perspective 209
Customer Experience and Business value   210
The Many Dimensions of Customer Experience   212
The Role of Technology in Customer Experience   214
Customer Experience Essentials for IT   215
First Steps to Improving Customer Experience   218
Conclusion   219
Chapter Discussion Questions   220
References   220

Chapter 15   Moving Towards an API Economy   222
What is an API?   223
The Value of APIs   225
The API Economy   226

A Framework for Thinking about APIs   227
Getting Started with APIs   230
Conclusion   233
Chapter Discussion Questions   234
References   234

Chapter 16   Preparing for Artificial Intelligence   **236**
What is AI?   237
What Are Organizations Doing About AI?   238
Dimensions of AI Management   240
Recommendations for Managers   242
Conclusion   244
Chapter Discussion Questions   245
References   245

Section III Mini Cases   **246**
Enterprise Transformation at Trustworthy Insurance   246
Innovation at International Foods   253
Consumerization of Technology at IFG   259

SECTION IV IT PORTFOLIO DEVELOPMENT AND MANAGEMENT   **264**

Chapter 17   Managing Emerging Technologies   **265**
Emerging Technologies in Business Today   265
Identifying Emerging Technologies   267
Assessing Emerging Technologies   267
Addressing Uncertainty   269
Managing Emerging Technologies   270
Recommendations for Getting Started in ET Management   272
Conclusion   273
Chapter Discussion Questions   273
References   273

Chapter 18   Enhancing Development Productivity   **275**
The Problem with System Development   276
Trends in System Development   277
Obstacles to Improving System Development Productivity   280
Improving System Development Productivity: What We
    Know that Works   282
Next Steps to Improving System Development Productivity   286
Conclusion   287
Chapter Discussion Questions   288
References   288

Chapter 19   Transforming to DevOps   **290**
What Problem is DevOps Solving?   291
What is DevOps?   292
DevOps Challenges   295
Getting Started with DevOps   298
Conclusion   300
Chapter Discussion Questions   300
References   300

Chapter 20   Managing IT Demand   **302**
Understanding IT Demand   303
The Economics of Demand Management   305
Three Tools for Demand Management   305
Key Organizational Enablers for Effective Demand Management   307
Conclusion   314
Chapter Discussion Questions   314
References   314

Chapter 21   Application Portfolio Management   **316**
The Applications Quagmire   317
The Benefits of a Portfolio Perspective   318
Making APM Happen   322
Key Lessons Learned   329
Conclusion   330
Chapter Discussion Questions   331
References   331
Appendix A   331

Section IV Mini Cases   **336**
Project Management at MM   336
Working Smarter at Continental Furniture International   341
Introducing Agile Development at American Attire   347

Index   **354**

Preface

Today information technology (IT) functions in organizations have finally achieved a long-sought goal; that is, to be considered as a strategic business partner. No longer is IT relegated to the "back room" or expected to be order-takers. Today's IT organizations are driving business transformation, developing business intelligence and analytics, enabling 24/7 global operations, and creating innovative digital products, services, and business models. With this new status come new expectations. First, IT leaders must not simply manage IT, they must use IT to deliver business value. Second, they must think and act strategically not only with overall IT strategy, but also in collaborating with business strategy development. As one CIO explained to us, "We can no longer deliver business solutions in our company without using technology so IT and business strategy must constantly interact with each other." Third, IT must deliver more than traditional systems. Modern IT organizations are responsible for developing external partnerships to leverage their own internal IT resources, curating data and enabling anywhere, anytime access to it, developing apps and APIs to facilitate new types of products and services, and doing all this faster and more responsively than ever before. And finally, IT leaders are the protectors of the organization's information capital, evaluating risk, and ensuring privacy and security. This responsibility colors all that IT does and is frequently at odds with IT's other roles. Thus today's IT leaders are no longer simply managers or technology leaders, they are essential business leaders who must educate, guide, envision, and execute on an organization's potential. Effective IT leadership is therefore about more than technology; it must marry strategy with execution; protection with innovation; and quality with time-to-market. This book tackles these real-life IT management issues and reflects both the opportunities and the challenges involved in being an effective IT leader.

All too often, in our efforts to prepare future executives to deal effectively with the issues of IT strategy and management, we lead them into a foreign country where they encounter a different language, different culture, and different customs. Acronyms (e.g., SOA, FTP/IP, SDLC, ITIL, ERP), buzzwords (e.g., asymmetric encryption, proxy servers, agile, enterprise service bus), and the widely adopted practice of abstraction (e.g., Is a software monitor a person, place, or thing?) present formidable "barriers to entry" to the technologically uninitiated. But more importantly, they obscure the importance of teaching students how to make *business* decisions about a key organizational resource. By taking a critical issues perspective, *IT Strategy &*

Innovation 4.0 treats IT not as a study by itself but as a tool to be leveraged to save and/or make money or transform an organization.

As in the first three editions of this book, this Edition 4.0 combines the experiences and insights of senior IT managers from leading-edge organizations with thorough academic research to bring important issues in IT management to life and demonstrate how IT strategy is put into action in contemporary businesses. This new edition has been designed around an enhanced set of critical real-world issues in IT management, such as thought leadership with IT, digital transformation, enhancing customer experience, and strategizing for business intelligence. It introduces students to the challenges of making IT decisions that have significant impacts on how businesses function and deliver value to stakeholders.

What's New in This Edition 4.0?

- A new title, in recognition of a new section devoted to innovation;
- A new section focusing on the IT-business partnership;
- Eleven new chapters reflecting IT's evolving strategic, innovation, and execution responsibilities, including: advancing a data strategy; creating and evolving a digital strategy; developing a cloud strategy; governance for a redefined IT; developing thought leaders in IT; managing disruption in IT; experimentation in IT; moving to an API economy; preparing for artificial intelligence; managing emerging technologies; and transforming to DevOps.
- Three new mini cases based on real companies and real IT leadership situations, including: Global Logistics and the Maritime Transport Ecosystem, Enterprise Transformation at Trustworthy Insurance, and Introducing Agile Development at American Attire;
- Retention of the replaced chapters and mini cases on our Web site: http://www. prospectpressvt.com/titles/mckeen-it-strategy/.

IT Strategy & Innovation focuses on how IT is changing and will continue to change organizations as we now know them. However, rather than learning concepts "free of context," students are introduced to the complex decisions facing real organizations by means of a number of mini cases. These provide an opportunity to apply the models/ theories/frameworks presented and help students integrate and assimilate this material. By the end of the book, students will have the confidence and ability to tackle the tough issues regarding IT management and strategy and a clear understanding of their importance in delivering business value.

Key Features of This Book

- A focus on IT management issues as opposed to technology issues;
- Critical IT issues explored within their organizational contexts;
- Readily applicable models and frameworks for implementing IT strategies;

- Mini cases to animate issues and focus classroom discussions on real-world decisions, enabling problem-based learning;
- Proven strategies and best practices from leading-edge organizations;
- Useful and practical advice and guidelines for delivering value with IT;
- Extensive teaching notes for all mini cases.

A Different Approach to Teaching IT Strategy

The majority of management information systems (MIS) textbooks are organized by system category (e.g., supply chain, customer relationship management, enterprise resource planning), by system component (e.g., hardware, software, networks), by system function (e.g., marketing, financial, human resources), by system type (e.g., transactional, decisional, strategic), or by a combination of these. Unfortunately, these approaches do not promote an understanding of IT management in practice.

The real world of IT consists of critical issues such as the following:

- How do we know if we are getting value from our IT investment?
- How can we innovate with IT?
- What specific IT functions should we seek from external providers?
- How do we build an IT leadership team that is a trusted partner with the business?
- How should we evolve IT capabilities?
- What is IT's role in creating an intelligent business?
- How can we best take advantage of new technologies in our business and develop strategies for them?
- How can we manage IT risk?

IT Strategy & Innovation tackles the real-world challenges of IT management. By focusing the text as well as the twelve mini cases on today's critical issues, the book naturally reinforces problem-based learning. The mini cases are each based on a real company presented anonymously and are not simply abbreviated versions of standard, full-length business cases. They differ in two significant ways:

1. *A horizontal perspective.* Unlike standard cases that develop a single issue within an organizational setting (i.e., a "vertical" slice of organizational life), mini cases take a "horizontal" slice through a number of coexistent issues. Rather than looking for a solution to a specific problem as in a standard case, students analyzing a mini case must first identify and prioritize the issues embedded within the case. This mimics real life in organizations where the challenge lies in "knowing where to start" as opposed to "solving a predefined problem."

2. *Highly relevant information.* Mini cases are densely written. Unlike standard cases, which intermix irrelevant information, in a mini case each sentence exists for a reason and reflects relevant information. As a result, students must analyze each case very carefully so as not to miss critical aspects of the situation.

Teaching with mini cases is thus very different than teaching with standard cases. With mini cases students must determine what is really going on within the organization. What first appears as a straightforward "technology" problem or opportunity may in fact be a political challenge, a strategic approach, or one of five other "technology" issues. Detective work is, therefore, required. The problem identification and prioritization skills needed are essential skills for future managers to learn for the simple reason that it is not possible for organizations to tackle all of their problems concurrently. Mini cases help teach these skills to students and can balance the problem-solving skills learned in other classes. Best of all, detective work is fun and promotes lively classroom discussion.

To assist instructors, extensive teaching notes are available for all mini cases. Developed by the authors and based on tried and true in-class experience, these notes include case summaries and they identify the key issues within each case, present ancillary information about the company/industry represented in the case, and offer guidelines for organizing the classroom discussion. Because of the structure of these mini cases and their embedded issues, it is common for teaching notes to exceed the length of the actual mini case!

This book is most appropriate for MIS courses where the goal is to understand how IT delivers organizational value. These courses are frequently labeled "IT Strategy" or "IT Management" and are offered within undergraduate as well as master's and MBA programs. For undergraduate juniors and seniors in business and commerce programs, this is usually the "capstone" MIS course. For master's-level students, this course may be the compulsory core course in MIS, or it may be an elective course.

Each chapter and mini case in this book has been thoroughly tested in a variety of undergraduate, graduate, and executive programs at the Smith School of Business.[1] These materials have proven highly successful within all programs because we adapt how the material is presented according to the level of the students. Whereas undergraduate students "learn" about critical business issues from the book and mini cases for the first time, graduate students are able to "relate" to these same critical issues based on their previous business experience. As a result, graduate students are able to introduce personal experiences into the discussion of these critical IT issues.

Organization of This Book

One of the advantages of an issues-focused structure is that chapters can be approached in any order because they do not build on one another. Chapter order is immaterial; that is, one does not need to read the first three chapters to understand the fourth.

[1] The Smith School of Business at Queen's University is one of the world's premier business schools, with a faculty team renowned for its business experience and academic credentials. The School has earned international recognition for its innovative approaches to team-based and experiential learning. In addition to its highly acclaimed MBA programs, the Smith School of Business is also home to Canada's most prestigious undergraduate business program and several outstanding graduate programs. As well, the School is one of the world's largest and most respected providers of executive education.

This provides an instructor with maximum flexibility to organize a course as he or she sees fit. Thus within different courses/programs, the order of topics can be changed to focus on different IT concepts.

Furthermore, because each mini case includes multiple issues, they too can be used to serve different purposes. For example, the mini case "Enterprise Transformation at Trustworthy Insurance" could be used to discuss innovation and thought leadership, improving the customer experience, delivering value with IT, or developing various IT strategies. The result is a rich set of instructional materials that lends itself well to a variety of pedagogical applications, particularly problem-based learning, and that clearly illustrates the reality of IT strategy in action.

The book is organized into four sections, each emphasizing a key component of developing and delivering effective IT strategy:

- **Section I: Delivering Value with IT** is designed to examine the complex ways that IT and business value are related. Over the past twenty years, researchers and practitioners have come to understand that "business value" can mean many different things when applied to IT. Chapter 1 (Delivering on the IT Value Proposition) explores these concepts in depth. Unlike the simplistic value propositions often used when implementing IT in organizations, this chapter presents "value" as a multilayered business construct that must be effectively managed at several levels if technology is to achieve the benefits expected. Chapter 2 (Developing IT Strategy for Business Value) examines the dynamic interrelationship between business and IT strategy and looks at the processes and critical success factors used by organizations to ensure that both are well aligned. Chapter 3 (Advancing a Data Strategy) examines *why* a company needs a data strategy and what might be included in one; discusses *where* a data strategy fits in relation to all other data and corporate activities; and identifies realistic and achievable stages of data strategy maturity. Chapter 4 (Creating and Evolving a Digital Strategy) discusses the value of having a separate digital strategy and how to best develop and evolve one over time. Chapter 5 (Developing a Cloud Strategy) explores how and where to manage and deploy cloud computing as part of a company's overall business and technology strategies.

  In the mini cases associated with this section, the concepts of delivering value with IT are explored in a number of different ways. In "Global Logistics and the Maritime Transport Ecosystem," informatics specialist Murray Johnson searches for ways data from various stakeholders could be used to make the Maritime Transport Ecosystem more competitive as a whole while at the same time benefitting the individual stakeholders. The "IT Planning at ModMeters" mini case follows CIO Brian Smith's efforts to create a strategic IT plan that aligns with business strategy, keeps IT running, and does not increase IT's budget. In "IT Investment at North American Financial," CIO Carolyn Weese wrestles with how to allocate limited IT resources to strike an effective balance between the needs of individual lines of business and the overall enterprise.

- **Section II: IT–Business Partnership** explores key concepts in how the IT organization is structured and managed to work with business to deliver IT products and services to the organization. Chapter 6 (Governance for a Redefined IT) discusses the system of structures, processes, and roles that collectively *oversee* how decisions about what IT work is done (i.e., strategy) and how it is done (i.e., execution), and how best to balance the needs of the enterprise (i.e., common processes, architecture, data, and controls) with responsiveness to and alignment with the business. Chapter 7 (The IT Budgeting Process) describes the "evil twin" of IT planning, discussing how budgeting mechanisms can significantly undermine effective business strategies and suggesting practices for addressing this problem while maintaining traditional fiscal accountability. Chapter 8 (Managing IT-Based Risk) describes how many IT organizations have been given the responsibility of not only managing risk in their own activities (i.e., project development, operations, and delivering business strategy) but also of managing IT-based risk in *all* company activities (e.g., mobile computing, file sharing, and online access to information and software) and the need for a holistic framework to understand and deal with risk effectively. Chapter 9 (Building a Strong Relationship with the Business) examines the nature of the business–IT relationship and the characteristics of an effective relationship that delivers real value to the enterprise. Chapter 10 (Enabling Collaboration with IT) identifies the principal forms of collaboration used in organizations, the primary business drivers involved in them, how their business value is measured, and the roles of IT and the business in enabling collaboration.

    The mini cases in this section examine how companies manage complex IT issues when they intersect substantially with important business issues. In "Enterprise Architecture at Nationstate Insurance," CIO Jane Denton endeavors to make IT more flexible and agile, while incorporating new and emerging technologies into its strategy. In "Transforming IT at Global Digital Imaging," we see the challenges for IT during a divestiture and how CIO Ben Perry uses vision and governance to transform a traditional IT function into a more effective and collaborative unit better aligned with its new business. In "Delivering Business Value with IT at Hefty Hardware," we see business and IT executives grappling with multiple priorities and perspectives and determining how best to work together to achieve the company's strategy.

- **Section III: IT-Enabled Innovation** discusses a variety of ways IT leadership is transforming organizations. Chapter 11 (Developing Thought Leaders in IT) explores the nature of thought leadership and how it fits with IT's mandate, and describes some of the characteristics of an effective IT thought leader and how IT functions can foster thought leadership successfully. Chapter 12 (Managing Disruption in IT) discusses the concept of disruption within IT functions and how to effectively deal with it. Chapter 13 (IT's Role in a Culture of Experimentation) examines why an organization would choose to experiment and how experimentation fits into the IT organization and IT's delivery mechanisms. Chapter 14 (Improving the

Customer Experience: An IT Perspective) explores the IT function's role in creating and improving an organization's customer experiences and the role of technology in helping companies to understand and learn from their customers' experiences. Chapter 15 (Moving Towards an API Economy) discusses how organizations are approaching the opportunities and challenges of using Application Programming Interfaces (APIs) to deliver value and how these will lead to economic transformation. Chapter 16 (Preparing for Artificial Intelligence) looks at IT's role in selecting, designing, implementing, and managing AI and where it fits with other types of technology in use in organizations.

The mini cases in this section focus on the key issues companies must address in innovating with IT. "Enterprise Transformation at Trustworthy Insurance" looks at a successful digital initiative and explores how the lessons learned in implementing the "Sonnet" project can be applied to transforming the enterprise as a whole. "Innovation at International Foods" contrasts the need for process and control in corporate IT with the strong push to innovate with technology and the clash of style and culture that must be addressed. "Consumerization of Technology at IFG" looks at how organizations must balance new systems of engagement with traditional systems of record and the need for bimodal IT organizations.

• *Section IV: IT Portfolio Development and Management* looks at how the IT function must transform itself to be able to deliver business value faster and more effectively in the future. Chapter 17 (Managing Emerging Technologies) describes the ways organizations identify and assess emerging technologies, and then energize their organizations around imagining their possibilities. Chapter 18 (Enhancing Development Productivity) explores how system development practices are changing and how managers can create an environment to promote improved development productivity. Chapter 19 (Transforming to DevOps) examines the newest practices for speeding up IT delivery and the claims that DevOps can improve deployment frequency, leading to faster times to market, lower failure rates of new releases, and faster mean times to recovery. Chapter 20 (Managing IT Demand) looks at the often neglected issue of demand management (as opposed to supply management), explores the root causes of demand for IT services, and identifies a number of tools and enablers to facilitate more effective demand management. Chapter 21 (Application Portfolio Management) describes the ongoing management process of categorizing, assessing, and rationalizing the IT application portfolio.

The mini cases associated with this section describe many of these themes embedded within real organizational contexts. The "Project Management at MM" mini case shows how a top-priority, strategic project can take a wrong turn when project management skills are ineffective. The "Working Smarter at Continental Furniture International" mini case follows an initiative to improve the company's analytics so it can reduce its environmental impact. The mini case "Introducing Agile Development at American Attire" shows some of the benefits and challenges of implementing new agile development methods.

Supplementary Materials / Instructor Resources

The following supplements are available online to adopting instructors:
- Powerpoint Lecture Notes
- Mini Case Teaching Notes
- A test bank
- Additional chapters addressing: linking IT to business metrics, communicating with business managers, building better IT leaders, creating IT shared services, IT sourcing, information management, innovation with IT, big data and social computing, building business intelligence, creating and evolving a technology roadmap, and information delivery.

To access the supplements, please visit our web site:

http://www.prospectpressvt.com/titles/mckeen-it-strategy/instructor-resources/

The Genesis of This Book

Since 1990 we have been meeting quarterly with a group of senior IT managers from a number of leading-edge organizations (e.g., BMO, IBM, CIBC, Bell Canada, McDonalds, Bank of Nova Scotia, and Sun Life) to identify and discuss critical IT management issues. This focus group represents a wide variety of industry sectors (e.g., retail, manufacturing, pharmaceutical, banking, telecommunications, insurance, media, food processing, government, and automotive). Originally, it was established to meet the companies' needs for well-balanced, thoughtful, yet practical information on emerging IT management topics, about which little or no research was available. However, we soon recognized the value of this premise for our own research in the rapidly evolving field of IT management. As a result, it quickly became a full-scale research program in which we were able to use the focus group as an "early warning system" to document new IT management issues, develop case studies around them, and explore more collaborative approaches to identifying trends, challenges, and effective practices in each topic area. As we shared our materials with our business students, we realized that this issues-based approach resonated strongly with them, and we began to incorporate more of our research into the classroom. This book is the result of our many years of work with senior IT managers, in organizations, and with students in the classroom.

Each issue in this book has been selected collaboratively by the focus group after debate and discussion. As facilitators, our job has been to keep the group's focus on IT management issues, not technology per se. In preparation for each meeting, focus group members research the topic within their own organization, often involving a number of members of their senior IT management team as well as subject matter experts in the process. To guide them, we provide a series of questions about the issue, although members are always free to explore it as they see fit. This approach provides both structure for the ensuing discussion and flexibility for those members whose organizations are approaching the issue in a different fashion.

The focus group then meets in a full-day session where the members discuss all aspects of the issue. Many also share corporate documents with the group. We facilitate the discussion, in particular pushing the group to achieve a common understanding of the dimensions of the issue and seeking examples, best practices, and guidelines for dealing with the challenges involved. Following each session, we write a report based on the discussion, incorporating relevant academic and practitioner materials where these are available. (Because some topics are "bleeding edge," there is often little traditional IT research available.)

Each report has three parts:

1. A description of the issue and the challenges it presents for both business and IT managers.

2. Models and concepts derived from the literature to position the issue within a contextual framework.

3. Near-term strategies (i.e., those that can be implemented immediately) that have proven successful within organizations for dealing with the specific issue.

For the purposes of this book, these individual reports are transformed into chapters, each highlighting a critical IT issue. We have learned over the years that the issues themselves vary little across industries and organizations, even in enterprises with unique IT strategies. However, each organization tackles the same issue somewhat differently. It is this diversity that provides the richness of insight in this book. Our collaborative research approach is based on our belief that, when dealing with complex and leading-edge issues, "everyone has part of the solution." Every focus group, therefore, provides us an opportunity to explore a topic from a variety of perspectives and to integrate different experiences (both successful and otherwise) so that, collectively, a thorough understanding of each issue can be developed and strategies for how it can be managed most successfully can be identified.

About the Authors

James D. McKeen is Professor Emeritus at the Smith School of Business at Queen's University. He has worked in the IT field for many years as a practitioner, researcher, and consultant. In 2011 he was named the "IT Educator of the Year" by Computer World Canada. Jim has taught at universities in Canada, New Zealand, United Kingdom, France, Germany, Ukraine, and the United States. His research is widely published in a number of leading journals, and he is the coauthor (with Heather Smith) of eight books on IT strategy and management. Their previous book—*IT Strategy: Issues and Practices 3rd ed.* (2015)—is currently the best-selling IT strategy text in the United States.

Heather A. Smith has been named the most-published researcher on IT management issues in two successive studies (2006, 2009). A senior research associate with Smith School of Business at Queen's University, she is the author of eight books, the most recent being *IT Strategy: Issues and Practices 3rd ed.* (2015). She is also a senior research associate with the American Society for Information Management's Advanced Practices Council. A former senior IT manager, she is co-director of the IT Management Forum (www.itmgmtforum.ca) and the CIO Brief (https://smith.queensu.ca/ciobrief/) that facilitate interorganizational learning among senior IT executives. Heather consults and collaborates with organizations worldwide.

Acknowledgments

The work contained in this book is based on numerous meetings with many senior IT managers. We would like to acknowledge our indebtedness to the following individuals who willingly shared their insights based on their experiences "earned the hard way":

Michele Baughman, Nastaran Bisheban, Peter Borden, Lindsay Cartwright, Ryan Coleman, Michael East, Doug Gerhart, Erin Golding, Chris Harvison, Richard Hayward, Sherman Lam, Ron McKelvie, Sean O'Farrell, Kashif Parvaiz, Brian Patton, Ashish Saxena, Raymond Smolskis, Kartik Subramani, Bruce Thompson, Joseph Trohak, and Julia Zhu.

We would also like to recognize the contribution of the Smith School of Business at Queen's University to this work. The school has facilitated and supported our vision of better integrating academic research and practice and has helped make our collaborative approach to the study of IT management and strategy an effective model for interorganizational learning.

James D. McKeen
Heather A. Smith
Smith School of Business at Queen's University
Kingston, Ontario
April 2018

SECTION I

Delivering Value with IT

Chapter 1: Delivering on the IT Value Proposition
Chapter 2: Developing IT Strategy for Business Value
Chapter 3: Advancing a Data Strategy
Chapter 4: Creating and Evolving a Digital Strategy
Chapter 5: Developing a Cloud Strategy

Mini Cases for Section I:
- Global Logistics and the Maritime Transport Ecosystem
- IT Planning at ModMeters
- IT Investment at North American Financial

CHAPTER 1

Delivering on the IT Value Proposition[1]

It's déjà vu all over again. For at least twenty years, business leaders have been trying to figure out exactly how and where IT can be of value in their organizations. And IT managers have been trying to learn how to deliver this value. When IT was used mainly as a productivity improvement tool in small areas of a business, this was a relatively straightforward process. Value was measured by reduced head counts—usually in clerical areas—and/or the ability to process more transactions per person. However, as systems grew in scope and complexity, unfortunately, so did the risks. Very few companies escaped this period without making at least a few disastrous investments in systems that didn't work or didn't deliver the bottom-line benefits executives thought they would. Naturally, fingers were pointed at IT.

With the advent of the strategic use of IT in business, it became even more difficult to isolate and deliver on the IT value proposition. It was often hard to tell if an investment had paid off. Who could say how many competitors had been deterred or how many customers had been attracted by a particular IT initiative? More recently, many companies have been left with a substantial investment in e-business and little to show for it. Although over the years there have been many improvements in where and how IT investments are made, and good controls have been established to limit time and cost overruns, we are still not able to accurately articulate and deliver on a value proposition for IT when it comes to anything other than simple productivity improvements or cost savings.

Problems in delivering IT value can lie with how a value proposition is conceived or in what is done to actually implement an idea—that is, selecting the right project and doing the project right (Cooper et al. 2000; McKeen and Smith 2003). In addition, although most firms attempt to calculate the expected payback of an IT investment before making it, few actually follow up to ensure that value has been achieved or to question what needs to be done to make sure that value will be delivered.

[1] Excerpted from "Developing and Delivering on the IT Value Proposition," *Communications of the Association for Information Systems* 11 (April 2003): 438–50 by H. A. Smith and J. D. McKeen. Used with permission from the Association for Information Systems, Atlanta, GA: 404-413-7444; www.aisnet.org. All rights reserved.

In this chapter we first look at the nature of IT value and "peel the onion" into its different layers. Then we examine the three components of delivering IT value: value identification, conversion, and value realization. Finally, we identify five general principles for ensuring IT value will be achieved.

Peeling the Onion: Understanding IT Value

Thirty years ago the IT value proposition was seen as a simple equation: deliver the right technology to the organization, and financial benefits will follow (Cronk and Fitzgerald 1999; Marchand et al. 2000). In the early days of IT, when computers were most often used as direct substitutes for people, this equation was understandable, even if it rarely worked this simply. It was easy to compute a bottom-line benefit where "technology" dollars replaced "salary" dollars.

Problems with this simplistic view quickly arose when technology came to be used as a productivity support tool and as a strategic tool. Under these conditions, managers had to decide if an IT investment was worth making if it saved people time, helped them make better decisions, or improved service. Thus other factors, such as how well technology was used by people or how IT and business processes worked together, became important considerations in how much value was realized from an IT investment. These issues have long confounded our understanding of the IT value proposition, leading to a plethora of opinions (many negative) about how and where technology has actually contributed to business value over the past fifteen years. Stephen Roach (1989) made headlines with his macroeconomic analysis showing that IT had had absolutely no impact on productivity in the services sector. More recently, many companies feel they have been sold a bill of goods by the promise of e-business and have been lured into spending millions on Web sites and online shopping with very little payback (Earle and Keen 2000).

These perceptions, plus ever-increasing IT expenditures, have meant business managers are taking a closer look at how and where IT delivers value to an organization (Ginzberg 2001). As they do this, they are beginning to change their understanding of the IT value proposition. Although, unfortunately, "silver bullet thinking" (i.e., plug in technology and deliver bottom-line impact) still predominates, IT value is increasingly seen as a multilayered concept, far more complex than it first appeared. This suggests that before an IT value proposition can be identified and delivered, it is essential that managers first "peel the onion" and understand more about the nature of IT value itself (see Figure 1.1).

What Is IT Value?

Value is defined as the worth or desirability of a thing (Cronk and Fitzgerald 1999). It is a subjective assessment. Although many believe this is not so, the value of IT depends very much on how a business and its individual managers choose to view it. Different companies and even different executives will define it quite differently.

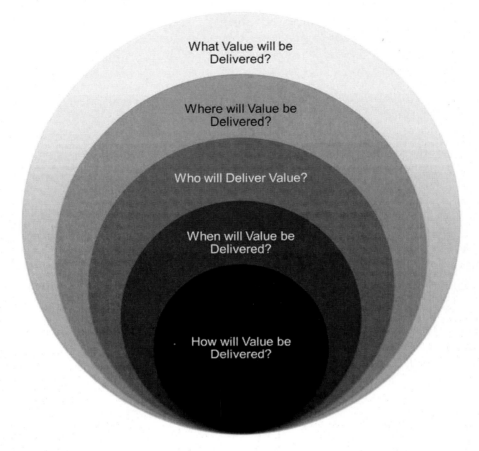

Figure 1.1 Value is a many-layered concept.

Strategic positioning, increased productivity, improved decision-making, cost savings, or improved service are all ways value could be defined. Today most businesses define value broadly and loosely, not simply as a financial concept (Ginzberg 2001). Ideally, it is tied to the organization's business model because adding value with IT should enable a firm to do its business better. In the focus group (see the Preface), one company sees value resulting from all parts of the organization having the same processes; another defines value by return on investment (ROI); still another measures it by a composite of key performance indicators. In short, there is no single agreed-on measure of IT value. As a result, misunderstandings about the definition of value either between IT and the business or among business managers themselves can lead to feelings that value has not been delivered. Therefore, a prerequisite of any IT value proposition is that everyone involved in an IT initiative agree on what value they are trying to deliver and how they will recognize it.

Where Is IT Value?

Value may also vary according to where one looks for it (Davern and Kauffman 2000). For example, value to an enterprise may not be perceived as value in a work group or by an individual. In fact, delivering value at one level in an organization may actually conflict with optimizing value at another level. Decisions about IT value are often made to optimize firm or business process value, even if they cause difficulties for business units or individuals. As one manager explained, "At the senior levels, our bottom-line drivers of value are cost savings, cash flow, customer satisfaction, and revenue. These are not always visible at the lower levels of the organization." Failure to consider value implications at all levels can lead to a value proposition that is counterproductive and may not deliver the value that is anticipated. Many executives take a hard line with these value conflicts. However, it is far more desirable to aim for value that is not a win–lose proposition but a win–win at all levels. This can leverage overall value many times over (Chan 2000).

Who Delivers IT Value?

Increasingly, managers are realizing that it is the interaction of people, information, and technology that delivers value, not IT alone.[2] Studies have confirmed that strong IT practices alone do not deliver superior performance. It is only the combination of these IT practices with an organization's skills at managing information and people's behaviors and beliefs that leads to real value (Ginzberg 2001; Marchand et al. 2000). In the past, IT has borne most of the responsibility for delivering IT value. Today, however, business managers exhibit a growing willingness to share responsibility with IT to ensure value is realized from the organization's investments in technology. Most companies now expect to have an executive sponsor for any IT initiative and some business participation in the development team. However, many IT projects still do not have the degree of support or commitment from the business that IT managers feel is necessary to deliver fully on a value proposition (Thorp 1999).

When is IT Value Realized?

Value also has a time dimension. It has long been known that the benefits of technology take time to be realized (Chan 2000). People must be trained, organizations and processes must adapt to new ways of working, information must be compiled, and customers must realize what new products and services are being offered. Companies are often unprepared for the time it takes an investment to pay off. Typically, full payback can take between three and five years and can have at least two spikes as a business adapts to the deployment of technology. Figure 1.2 shows this "W" effect—named for the way the chart looks—for a single IT project.

---

[2] These interactions in a structured form are known as *processes*. Processes are often the focus of much organizational effort in the belief that streamlining and reengineering them will deliver value. In fact, new research shows that without attention to information and people, very little value is delivered (Segars and Chatterjee 2010). In addition, attention to processes in organizations often ignores the informal processes that contribute to value.

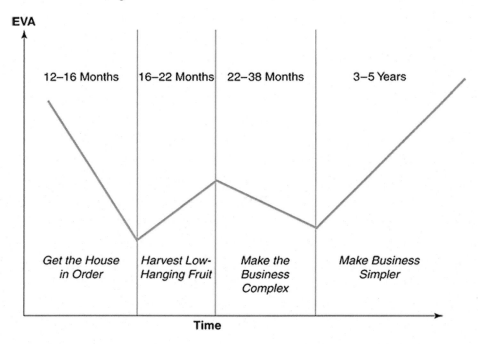

Figure 1.2 The "W" effect in delivering IT value (Segars and Chatterjee, 2010)

Initially, companies spend a considerable amount in deploying a new technology. During this twelve-to-sixteen-month period, no benefits occur. Following implementation, some value is realized as companies achieve initial efficiencies. This period lasts for about six months. However, as use increases, complexities also grow. Information overload can occur and costs can increase. At this stage, many can lose faith in the initiative. This is a dangerous period. The final set of benefits can occur only by making the business simpler and applying technology, information, and people more effectively. If a business can manage to do this, it can achieve sustainable, long-term value from its IT investment (Segars and Chatterjee 2010). If it can't, value from technology can be offset by increased complexity.

Time also changes perceptions of value. Many IT managers have stories of how an initiative was vilified as having little or no value when first implemented, only to have people say they couldn't imagine running the business without it a few years later. Similarly, most managers can identify projects where time has led to a clearer understanding of the potential value of a project. Unfortunately, in cases where anticipated value declines or disappears, projects don't always get killed (Cooper et al. 2000).

Clarifying and agreeing on these different layers of IT value is the first step involved in developing and delivering on the IT value proposition. All too often, this work is forgotten or given short shrift in the organization's haste to answer this question: How will IT value be delivered? (See next section.) As a result, misunderstandings arise and technology projects do not fulfill their expected promises. It will be next to impossible to do a good job developing and delivering IT value unless and until the concepts involved in IT value are clearly understood and agreed on by both business and IT managers.

Best Practices in Understanding IT Value

- Link IT value directly to your business model.
- Recognize value is subjective, and manage perceptions accordingly.
- Aim for a value "win–win" across processes, work units, and individuals.
- Seek business commitment to all IT projects.
- Manage value over time.

The Three Components of the IT Value Proposition

Developing and delivering an IT value proposition involves addressing three components. First, potential opportunities for adding value must be identified. Next, these opportunities must be converted into effective applications of technology. Finally, value must be realized by the organization. Together, these components comprise the fundamentals of any value proposition (see Figure 1.3).

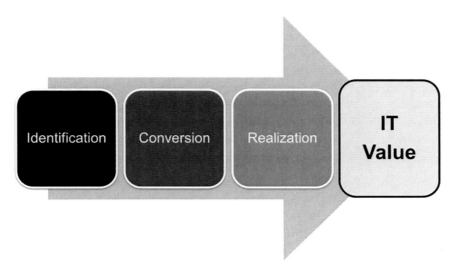

Figure 1.3 Three components of the IT value proposition

Identification of Potential Value

Identifying opportunities for making IT investments has typically been a fairly informal activity in most organizations. Very few companies have a well-organized means of doing research into new technologies or strategizing about where these technologies can be used (McKeen and Smith 2010). More companies have mechanisms for identifying opportunities within business units. Sometimes a senior IT manager will be designated as a "relationship manager" for a particular unit, with responsibility for working with business management to identify opportunities where IT could add value (Agarwal and Sambamurthy 2002). Many other companies, however, still leave it up to business managers to identify where they want to use IT. There is growing evidence that relegating the IT organization to a passive role in developing systems according to business instructions is unlikely to lead to high IT value. Research shows that involving IT in business planning can have a direct and positive influence on the development of successful business strategies using IT (Ginzberg 2001; Marchand et al. 2000). This suggests that organizations should establish joint business–IT mechanisms to identify and evaluate both business and technical opportunities where IT can add value.

Once opportunities have been identified, companies must then make decisions about where they want to focus their dollars to achieve optimal value. Selecting the right projects for an organization always involves balancing three fundamental factors: cash, timing, and risk (Luehrman 1997). In principle, every company wants to undertake only high-return projects. In reality, project selection is based on many different factors. For example, pet or political projects or those mandated by the government or competitors are often part of a company's IT portfolio (Carte et al. 2001). Disagreement at senior levels about which projects to undertake can arise because of a lack of a coherent and consistent mechanism for assessing project value. All organizations need some formal mechanism for prioritizing projects. Without one, it is very likely that project selection will become highly politicized and, hence, ineffective at delivering value. There are a variety of means to do this, ranging from using strictly bottom-line metrics, to comparing balanced scorecards, to adopting a formal value-assessment methodology. Although these methods help to weed out higher cost–lower return projects, they do not constitute a foolproof means of selecting the right projects for an organization. Using strict financial selection criteria, for example, can exclude potentially high-value strategic projects that have less well-defined returns, longer payback periods, and more risk (Cooper et al. 2000). Similarly, it can be difficult getting important infrastructure initiatives funded even though these may be fundamental to improving organizational capabilities (Byrd 2001).

Therefore, organizations are increasingly taking a portfolio approach to project selection. This approach allocates resources and funding to different types of projects, enabling each type of opportunity to be evaluated according to different criteria (McKeen and Smith 2003). One company has identified three different classes of IT—infrastructure, common systems, and business unit applications—and funds them in different proportions. In other companies, funding for strategic initiatives is allocated in stages so their potential value can be reassessed as more information about them becomes known (Luehrman 1997). Almost all companies have found it necessary to justify infrastructure initiatives separately. In fact, some remove these types of projects from the selection process altogether and fund them with a "tax" on all other development (McKeen and Smith 2003). Other companies allocate a fixed percentage of their IT budgets to a technology renewal fund.

Organizations have come a long way in formalizing where and how they choose to invest their IT dollars. Nevertheless, there is still considerable room for judgment based on solid business and technical knowledge. It is, therefore, essential that all executives involved have the ability to think strategically and systematically as well as financially about project identification and selection.

Best Practices in Identifying Potential Value

- Joint business–IT structures to recognize and evaluate opportunities;
- A means of comparing value across projects;
- A portfolio approach to project selection;
- A funding mechanism for infrastructure.

Effective Conversion

"Conversion" from idea/opportunity to reality is what IT organizations have been about since their inception. A huge amount of effort has gone into this central component of the IT value proposition. As a result, many IT organizations have become very good at developing and delivering projects on time and on budget. Excellent project management, effective execution, and reliable operations are a critical part of IT value. However, they are not, in and of themselves, sufficient to convert a good idea into value or to deliver value to an organization.

Today, both managers and researchers are recognizing that more is involved in effective conversion than good IT practices. Organizations can set themselves up for failure by not providing adequate and qualified resources. Many companies start more projects than they can effectively deliver with the resources they have available. Not having enough time or resources to do the job means that people are spread too thin and end up taking shortcuts that are potentially damaging to value (Cooper et al. 2000). Resource limitations on the business side of a project team can be as damaging to conversion as a lack of technical resources. "[Value is about] far more than just sophisticated managerial visions …. Training and other efforts … to obtain value from IT investments are often hamstrung by insufficient resources" (Chircu and Kauffman 2000). Inadequate business resources can lead to poor communication and ineffective problem solving on a project (Ginzberg 2001). Companies are beginning to recognize that the number and quality of the staff assigned to an IT project can make a difference to its eventual outcome. They are insisting that the organization's best IT and businesspeople be assigned to critical projects.

Other significant barriers to conversion that are becoming more apparent now that IT has improved its own internal practices include the following:

- **Organizational barriers.** The effective implementation of IT frequently requires the extensive redesign of current business processes (Chircu and Kauffman 2000). However, organizations are often reluctant to make the difficult complementary business changes and investments that are required (Carte et al. 2001). "When new IT is implemented, everyone expects to see costs come down," explained one manager. "However, most projects involve both business and IT deliverables. We, therefore, need to take a multifunctional approach to driving business value." In recognition of this fact, some companies are beginning to put formal change management programs in place to help businesses prepare for the changes involved with IT projects and to adapt and simplify as they learn how to take advantage of new technology.
- **Knowledge barriers.** Most often new technology and processes require employees to work differently, learn new skills, and have new understanding of how and where information, people, and technologies fit together (Chircu and Kauffman 2000). Although training has long been part of new IT implementations, more recently businesses are recognizing that delivering value from technology requires a broader and more coordinated learning effort (Smith et al. 2010). Lasting value comes from people and technology working *together* as a system rather than as discrete entities. Recent research confirms that high-performing organizations have not only strong IT practices but also people who use good information management practices and who are able to effectively use the information they receive (Marchand et al. 2000).

Best Practices in Conversion

- Availability of adequate and qualified IT and business resources;
- Training in business goals and processes;
- Multifunctional change management;
- Emphasis on higher-level learning and knowledge management.

Realizing Value

The final component of the IT value proposition has been the most frequently ignored. This is the work involved in actually realizing value *after* technology has been implemented. Value realization is a proactive and long-term process for any major initiative (Thorp 1999). All too often, after an intense implementation period, a development team is disbanded to work on other projects, and the business areas affected by new technology are left to sink or swim. As a result, a project's benefits can be jeopardized. Technology must be used extensively if it is to deliver value. Poorly designed technology can lead to high levels of frustration, resistance to change, and low levels of use (Chircu and Kauffman 2000).

Resistance to change can have its root cause in an assumption or an action that doesn't make sense in the everyday work people do. Sometimes this means challenging workers' understanding of work expectations or information flows. At other times it means doing better analysis of where and how a new process is causing bottlenecks, overwork, or overload. As one manager put it, "If value is not being delivered, we need to understand the root causes and do something about it." His company takes the unusual position that it is important to keep a team working on a project until the expected benefits have been realized. This approach is ideal but can also be very costly and must be carefully managed. Some companies try to short-circuit the value management process by simply taking anticipated cost savings out of a business unit's budget once technology has been implemented, thereby forcing it to do more with less, whether or not the technology has been as beneficial as anticipated. Unfortunately, many organizations do little or no follow-up to determine whether or not benefits have been achieved.

Measurement is a key component of value realization (Thorp 1999). After implementation, it is essential that all stakeholders systematically compare outcomes against expected value and take appropriate actions to achieve benefits. In addition to monitoring metrics, a thorough and ongoing assessment of value and information flows must also be undertaken at all levels of analysis: individual, team, work unit, and enterprise. Efforts must be taken to understand and improve aspects of process, information, and technology that are acting as barriers to achieving value.

A significant problem with not paying attention to value recognition is that areas of unexpected value or opportunity are also ignored. This is unfortunate because it is only after technology has been installed that many businesspeople can see how it could be leveraged in other parts of their work. Realizing value should, therefore, also include provisions to evaluate new opportunities arising through serendipity.

Best Practices in Realizing Value

- Plan a value-realization phase for all IT projects.
- Measure outcomes against expected results.
- Look for and eliminate root causes of problems.
- Assess value realization at all levels in the organization.
- Have provisions for acting on new opportunities to leverage value.

Five Principles for Delivering Value

In addition to clearly understanding what value means in a particular organization and ensuring that the three components of the IT value proposition are addressed by every project, five principles have been identified that are central to developing and delivering value in every organization.

Principle 1. Have a Clearly Defined Portfolio Value Management Process

Every organization should have a common process for managing the overall value being delivered to the organization from its IT portfolio. This would begin as a means of identifying and prioritizing IT opportunities by potential value relative to each other. It would also include mechanisms to optimize *enterprise* value (e.g., through tactical, strategic, and infrastructure projects) according to a rubric of how the organization wants to allocate its resources.

A portfolio value management process should continue to track projects as they are being developed. It should ensure not only that projects are meeting schedule and budget milestones but also that other elements of conversion effectiveness are being addressed (e.g., business process redesign, training, change management, information management, and usability). A key barrier to achieving value can be an organization's unwillingness to revisit the decisions made about its portfolio (Carte et al. 2001). Yet this is critically important for strategic and infrastructure initiatives in particular. Companies may have to approve investments in these types of projects based on imperfect information in an uncertain environment. As they develop, improved information can lead to better decision-making about an investment. In some cases this might lead to a decision to kill a project; in others, to speed it up or to reshape it as a value proposition becomes clearer.

Finally, a portfolio value management process should include an ongoing means of ensuring that value is realized from an investment. Management must monitor expected outcomes at appropriate times following implementation and hold someone in the organization accountable for delivering benefits (Thorp 1999).

Principle 2. Aim for Chunks of Value

Much value can be squandered by spreading IT investments over too many projects (Marchand et al. 2000). Focusing on a few key areas and designing a set of complementary projects that will really make a difference is one way companies are trying to address this concern. Many companies are undertaking larger and larger technology initiatives that will have a significant transformational and/or strategic impact on the organization. However, unlike earlier efforts that often took years to complete and ended up having questionable value, these initiatives are aiming to deliver major value through a series of small, focused projects that, linked together, will result in both short-term impact and long-term strategic value. For example, one company has about 300–400 projects underway linked to one of a dozen major initiatives.

Principle 3. Adopt a Holistic Orientation to Technology Value

Because value comes from the effective interaction of people, information, and technology, it is critical that organizations aim to optimize their ability to manage and use them together (Marchand et al. 2000). Adopting a systemic approach to value, where technology is not viewed in isolation and interactions and impacts are anticipated and planned, has been demonstrated to contribute to perceived business value (Ginzberg 2001). Managers should aim to incorporate technology as an integral part of an overall program of business change rather than dealing with people and information management as afterthoughts to technology (Thorp 1999). One company has done this by taking a single business objective (e.g., "increase market penetration by 15 percent over five years") and designing a program around it that includes a number of bundled technology projects.

Principle 4. Aim for Joint Ownership of Technology Initiatives

This principle covers a lot of territory. It includes the necessity for strong executive sponsorship of all IT projects. "Without an executive sponsor for a project, we simply won't start it," explained one manager. It also emphasizes that all people involved in a project must feel they are responsible for the results. Said another manager, "These days it is very hard to isolate the impact of technology, therefore there must be a 'we' mentality." This perspective is reinforced by research that has found that the quality of the IT-business relationship is central to the delivery of IT value. Mutual trust, visible business support for IT and its staff, and IT staff who consider themselves to be part of a business problem-solving team all make a significant difference in how much value technology is perceived to deliver (Ginzberg 2001).

Principle 5. Experiment More Often

The growing complexity of technology, the range of options available, and the uncertainty of the business environment have each made it considerably more difficult to determine where and how technology investments can most effectively be made. Executives naturally object to the risks involved in investing heavily in possible business scenarios or technical gambles that may or may not realize value. As a result, many companies are looking for ways to firm up their understanding of the value proposition for a particular opportunity without incurring too much risk. Undertaking pilot studies is one way of doing this (Thomke 2001). Such experiments can prove the value of an idea, uncover new opportunities, and identify more about what will be needed to make an idea successful. They provide senior managers with a greater number of options in managing a project and an overall technology portfolio. They also enable potential value to be reassessed and investments in a particular project to be more frequently reevaluated and rebalanced against other opportunities. In short, experimentation enables technology investments to be made in chunks and makes "go/no go" decisions at key milestones much easier to make.

Conclusion

In this chapter we have explored the concepts and activities involved in developing and delivering IT value to an organization. In their efforts to use technology to deliver business value, IT managers should keep clearly in mind the maxim "Value is in the eye of the beholder." Because there is no single, agreed-on notion of business value, it is important to make sure that both business and IT managers are working toward a common goal. This could be traditional cost reduction, process efficiencies, new business capabilities, improved communication, or a host of other objectives. Although each organization or business unit approaches value differently, increasingly this goal includes much more than the simple delivery of technology to a business unit. Today, technology is being used as a catalyst to drive many different types of organizational transformation and strategy. IT value can no longer be viewed in isolation from other parts of the business, namely people and information. Thus it is no longer adequate to focus simply on the development and delivery of IT projects in order to deliver value. Delivering IT value means managing the entire process, from conception to cash.

Chapter Discussion Questions

1. Describe a situation where value at one level of the enterprise may not be seen as valuable at another level.
2. Explain how lack of business support can cause an IT project to fail to deliver value.

References

Agarwal, R., and V. Sambamurthy. "Organizing the IT Function for Business Innovation Leadership." Society for Information Management Advanced Practices Council Report, Chicago, September 2002.

Byrd, T. A. "Information Technology, Core Competencies, and Sustained Competitive Advantage." *Information Resources Management Journal* 14, no. 2 (April–June 2001): 27–36.

Carte, T., D. Ghosh, and R. Zmud. "The Influence of IT Budgeting Practices on the Return Derived from IT Investments." CMISS White Paper, November 2001.

Chan, Y. "IT Value: The Great Divide Between Qualitative and Quantitative and Individual and Organizational Measures." *Journal of Management Information Systems* 16, no. 4 (Spring 2000): 225–61.

Chircu, A., and R. J. Kauffman. "Limits to Value in Electronic Commerce-Related IT Investments." *Journal of Management Information Systems* 17, no. 2 (Fall 2000): 59–80.

Cooper, R., S. Edgett, and E. Kleinschmidt. "New Problems, New Solutions: Making Portfolio Management More Effective." *Research Technology Management* 43, no. 2 (March/April 2000): 18–33.

Cronk, M., and E. Fitzgerald. "Understanding 'IS Business Value': Derivation of Dimensions." *Logistics Information Management* 12, no. 1–2 (1999): 40–49.

Davern, M., and R. Kauffman. "Discovering Potential and Realizing Value from Information Technology Investments." *Journal of Management Information Systems* 16, no. 4 (Spring 2000): 121–43.

Earle, N., and P. Keen. *From .com to .profit: Inventing Business Models That Deliver Value and Profit.* San Francisco: Jossey-Bass, 2000.

Ginzberg, M. "Achieving Business Value Through Information Technology: The Nature of High Business Value IT Organizations." Society for Information Management Advanced Practices Council Report, Chicago, November 2001.

Luehrman, T. A. "What's It Worth? A General Manager's Guide to Valuation." *Harvard Business Review* (May–June 1997): 131–41.

Marchand, D., W. Kettinger, and J. Rollins. "Information Orientation: People, Technology and the Bottom Line." *Sloan Management Review* (Summer 2000): 69–80.

McKeen, J. D., and H. A. Smith. *Making IT Happen.* Chichester, England: John Wiley & Sons, 2003.

McKeen, J. D., and H. A. Smith. "Application Portfolio Management." *Communications for the Association of Information Systems* 26, Article 9 (March 2010): 157–70.

Roach, S. "The Case of the Missing Technology Payback." Presentation at the Tenth International Conference on Information Systems, Boston, December 1989.

Segars, A. H., and D. Chatterjee. "Diets That Don't Work: Where Enterprise Resource Planning Goes Wrong." *Wall Street Journal*, August 23, 2010. online.wsj.com/article/SB10001424052748703514404574588060852535906.html.

Smith, H. A., J. D. McKeen, and S. Singh. "Creating the KM Mindset." *Knowledge Management Research and Practice* 8, no. 2 (June 2010): 112–20.

Thomke, S. "Enlightened Experimentation: The New Imperative for Innovation." *Harvard Business Review* (February 2001): 67–75.

Thorp, J. "Computing the Payoff from IT." *Journal of Business Strategy* 20, no. 3 (May/June 1999): 35–39.

CHAPTER 2

Developing IT Strategy for Business Value[1]

Suddenly, it seems, executives are "getting" the strategic potential of IT. Instead of being relegated to the back rooms of the enterprise, IT is now being invited into the boardrooms and is expected to play a leading role in delivering topline value and business transformation (Venkatramen and Henderson 1998). Thus it can no longer be assumed that business strategy will naturally drive IT strategy, as has traditionally been the case. Instead, different approaches to strategy development are now possible and sometimes desirable. For example, the capabilities of new technologies could shape the strategic direction of a firm (e.g., e-business, wireless). IT could enable new competencies that would then make new business strategies possible (e.g., just-in-time inventory). New options for governance using IT could also change how a company works with other firms (think Walmart). Today, new technologies coevolve with new business strategies and new behaviors and structures (see Figure 2.1). If IT is to deliver business value, IT strategy must always be closely linked with sound business strategy.

Ideally, therefore, business and IT strategies should complement and support each other relative to the business environment. Strategy development should be a two-way process between the business and IT. Yet, unfortunately, poor alignment between them remains a perennial problem (Frohman 1982; McKeen and Smith 1996; Rivard et al. 2004). Research has already identified many organizational challenges to effective strategic alignment. For example, if their strategy-development processes are not compatible (e.g., if they take place at different times or involve different levels of the business), it is unlikely that the business and IT will be working toward the same goals at the same time (Frohman 1982). Aligning with individual business units can lead to initiatives that suboptimize the effectiveness of corporate strategies (McKeen and Smith 1996). Strategy implementation must also be carefully aligned to ensure

---

[1] H. A. Smith, J. D. McKeen, and S. Singh, "Developing IT Strategy for Business Value," *Journal of Information Technology Management* 18, no. 1 (June 2007). Reproduced by permission of the Association of Management.

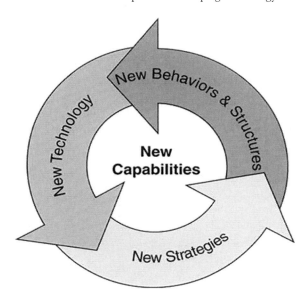

Figure 2.1 Business and IT strategies co-evolve to create new capabilities

the integration of business and IT efforts. Finally, companies often try to address too many priorities, leading to an inadequate focus on key strategic goals.

Strategic *alignment* is only one problem facing IT managers when they develop IT strategy. With IT becoming so much more central to the development and delivery of business strategy, much more attention is now being paid to strategy *development* than in the past. What businesses want to accomplish with their IT, and how IT shapes its own delivery strategy are increasingly vital to the success of an enterprise.

In this chapter we explore how organizations are working to improve IT strategy development and its relationship with business strategy. We first look at how our understanding of business and IT strategies has changed over time and at the forces that will drive even further changes in the future. Then we discuss some critical success factors for IT strategy development about which there is general consensus. Next we look at the different dimensions of the strategic use of IT that IT management must address. Finally, we examine how some organizations are beginning to evolve a more formal IT strategy-development process and some of the challenges they are facing in doing so.

Business and IT Strategies: Past, Present, and Future

At the highest level, a strategy is an approach to doing business (Gebauer 1997). Traditionally, a competitive business strategy has involved performing different activities than those of competitors or performing similar activities in different ways (Porter 1996). Ideally, these activities were difficult or expensive for others to copy and, therefore, resulted in a long-term competitive advantage (Gebauer 1997). They enabled firms to charge a premium for their products and services.

Until recently, the job of an IT function was to understand the business's strategy and create a plan to support it. However, all too often IT's strategic contribution was inhibited by IT managers' limited understanding of business strategy and by business managers' poor understanding of IT's potential. Therefore, most *formal* IT plans were focused on the more tactical and tangible line of business needs or opportunities for operational integration rather than on supporting enterprise strategy (Burgelman and Doz 2001). Furthermore, projects were selected based largely on their abilities to affect the short-term bottom line rather than on delivering topline business value. "In the past IT had to be a strategic incubator because businesspeople simply didn't recognize the potential of technology," said a member of the focus group (see the Preface).

As a result, instead of looking for ways to be different, in the past much business strategy became a relentless race to compete on efficiencies, with IT as the primary means of doing so (Hitt et al. 1998; Porter 1996). In many industries, companies' improved information-processing capabilities have been used to drive down transaction costs to near zero, threatening traditional value propositions and shaving profit margins. This is leading to considerable disruption because business models (i.e., the way companies add value) are under attack by new, technology-enabled approaches to delivering products and services (e.g., the music industry, bookselling). Therefore:

> Strategists [have to] honestly face the many weaknesses inherent in [the] industrial-age ways of doing things. They [must] redesign, build upon and reconfigure their components to radically transform the value proposition. (Tapscott 1996)

Such new business strategies are inconceivable without the use of IT. Other factors, also facilitated by IT, are further influencing the relationship between the business and IT strategy. Increasingly, globalization is altering the economic playing field. As countries and companies become more deeply interrelated, instability is amplified. Instead of being generals plotting out a structured campaign, business leaders are now more likely to be participating in guerilla warfare (Eisenhardt 2002). Flexibility, speed, and innovation are, therefore, becoming the watchwords of competition, and they must be incorporated into any business or IT strategy-development process (Hitt et al. 1998).

These conditions have dramatically elevated a business's attention to the value of IT strategy (Ross and Beath 2002). As a result, business executives recognize that it was a mistake to consider technology projects to be solely the responsibility of IT. There is a much greater understanding that business executives have to take leadership in making technology investments in ways that will shape and/or complement business strategy. There is also recognition at the top levels of most organizations that problems with IT strategy implementation are largely the fault of leaders who "failed to realize that adopting … systems posed a business—not just a technological—challenge" and didn't take responsibility for the organizational and process changes that would deliver business value.

Changing value models and the development of integrated, cross-functional systems have elevated the importance of both a corporate strategy and a technology strategy that crosses traditional lines of business. Many participants remarked that their executive teams at last understand the potential of IT to affect the top line. "IT recently added some new distribution channels, and our business has just exploded," stated one manager. Others are finding that there is a much greater emphasis on IT's ability to grow revenues, and this has affected how IT budgets are allocated and projects prioritized. "Our executives have finally recognized that business strategy is not only enabled by IT, but that it can provide new business opportunities as well," said another manager. This is reflected in the changing position of the CIO in many organizations over the past decade. "Today our CIO sits on the executive team and takes part in all business strategy discussions because IT has credibility," said a group member. "Our executives now want to work closely with IT and understand the implications of technology decisions," said another. "It's not the same as it was even five years ago." Today CIOs are valued for their insight into business opportunities, their perspective across the entire organization, and their ability to take the long view.

However, this does not mean that organizations have become good at developing strategy or at effectively integrating business and IT strategies. "There are many inconsistencies and problems with strategy development," said a participant. Organizations have to develop new strategy-making capabilities to cope in the future competitive environment. This will mean changing their current top-down method of developing and implementing strategy. If there's one thing that leading academics agree on, it's that future strategy development will have to become a more dynamic and continuous process (Eisenhardt 2002; Kanter 2002; Prahalad and Krishnan 2002; Quinn 2002; Weill et al. 2002). Instead of business strategy being a well-crafted plan of action for the next three to five years, from which IT can devise an appropriate and supportive technology strategy, business strategy must become more and more evolutionary and interactive with IT. IT strategy development must, therefore, become more dynamic itself and focused on developing strategic capabilities that will support a variety of changing business objectives. In the future, managers will not align business strategy and IT at particular points in time but will participate in an organic process that will address the need to continually evolve IT and business plans in concert with each other (Prahalad and Krishnan 2002).

Four Critical Success Factors

Each focus group member had a different approach to developing IT strategy, but there was general agreement that four factors had to be in place for strategy development to be effective.

1. *Revisit your business model.* The worlds of business and IT have traditionally been isolated from each other, leading to misaligned and sometimes conflicting strategies. Although there is now a greater willingness among business managers to understand the implications of technology in their world, it is still IT that must translate their ideas and concepts into business language. "IT must absolutely understand and focus on the business," said a participant.

   Similarly, it is essential that all managers thoroughly understand how their business as a whole works. Although this sounds like a truism, almost any IT manager can tell war stories of business managers who have very different visions of what they think their enterprise should look like. Business models and strategies are often confused with each other (Ross and Beath 2002). A business model explains how the different pieces of a business fit together. It ensures that everyone in an organization is focused on the kind of value a company wants to create. Only when the business model is clear can strategies be developed to articulate how a company will deliver that value in a unique way that others cannot easily duplicate (Ross and Beath 2002).

2. *Have strategic themes.* IT strategy used to be about individual projects. Now it is about carefully crafted programs that focus on developing specific business capabilities. Each program consists of many smaller, interrelated business and IT initiatives cutting across several functional areas. These are designed to be adapted, reconfigured, accelerated, or canceled as the strategic program evolves. Themes give both business and IT leaders a broad yet focused topic of interest that challenges them to move beyond current operations (Kanter 2002). For example, one retail company decided it wanted to be "a great place to work." A bank selected e-banking as a critical differentiator. Both firms used a theme to engage the imaginations of their employees and mobilize a variety of ideas and actions around a broad strategic direction. By grouping IT and business programs around a few key themes, managers find it easier to track and direct important strategic threads in an organization's development and to visualize the synergies and interdependencies involved across a variety of projects spread out across the organization and over time.

3. *Get the right people involved.* One of the most important distinguishing factors between companies that get high business value from their IT investment and those that don't is that senior managers in high-performing companies take a leadership role in IT decision-making. Abdication of this responsibility is a recipe for disaster (Ross and Weill 2002). "In the past it was very hard to get the right people involved," said a focus group member. "Now it's easier." Another

noted, "You don't send a minion to an IT strategy meeting anymore; it's just not done." In this type of organization, the CIO typically meets regularly with the president and senior business leaders to discuss both business and IT strategies.

Getting the right people involved also means getting business managers and other key stakeholders involved in strategy as well. To do this, many companies have established "account manager" positions in IT to work with and learn about the business and bring opportunities for using technology to the table. Research shows that the best strategies often stem from grassroots innovations, and it is therefore critical that organizations take steps to ensure that good ideas are nurtured and not filtered out by different layers of management (Kanter 2002). "We have two levels of strategy development in our organization," said a focus group participant. "Our account managers work with functional managers, and our CIO with our business unit presidents on the IT steering committee." This company also looks for cross-functional synergies and strategic dependencies by holding regular meetings of IT account managers and between account managers and infrastructure managers.

4. ***Work in partnership with the business.*** Successful strategy demands a true *partnership* between IT and the business, not just the use of the term. Strategy decisions are best made with input from both business and IT executives (Ross and Weill 2002). The focus group agreed. "Our partnerships are key to our success," stated a manager. "It's not the same as it was a few years ago. People now work very closely together." Partnership is not just a matter of "involving" business leaders in IT strategy or vice versa, or "aligning" business and IT strategies. Effective strategizing is about continuous and dynamic synchronization of capabilities (Prahalad and Krishnan 2002). "Our IT programs need synchronizing with business strategy—not only at a high level, but right down to the individual projects and the business changes that are necessary to implement them properly," explained another participant.

The Many Dimensions of IT Strategy

One of the many challenges of developing effective IT strategy is the fact that technology can be used in so many different ways. The opportunities are practically limitless. Unfortunately, the available resources are not. Thus a key element of IT strategy is determining how best to allocate the IT budget. This issue is complicated by the fact that most businesses today require significant IT services just to operate. Utility and basic support costs eat up between 30 and 70 percent of the focus group members' budgets. That's just the cost of "keeping the lights on"—running existing applications, fixing problems, and dealing with mandatory changes (e.g., new legislation). IT strategy, therefore, has two components: how to do more with less (i.e., driving down fixed costs) and how to allocate the remaining budget toward those projects that will support and further the organization's business strategy.

With occasional exceptions, CIOs and their teams are mostly left alone to determine the most cost-effective way of providing the IT utility. This has led to a variety of IT-led initiatives to save money, including outsourcing, shared services, use of software-as-a-service (SaaS), global sourcing, and partnerships. However, it is the way that IT spends the rest of its budget that has captured the attention of business strategists. "It used to be that every line of business had an IT budget and that we would work with each one to determine the most effective way to spend it," said a manager. "Now there is much more recognition that the big opportunities are at the enterprise level and cut across lines of business."

Focus group members explained that implementing a strategic program in IT will usually involve five types of initiatives. Determining what the balance among them will be is a significant component of how IT strategy delivers business value. Too much or too little emphasis on one type of project can mean a failure to derive maximum value from a particular strategic business theme.

1. *Business improvement.* These projects are probably the easiest to agree on because they stress relatively low-risk investments with a tangible short-to-medium-term payback. These are often reengineering initiatives to help organizations streamline their processes and save substantial amounts of money by eliminating unnecessary or duplicate activities or empowering customers/suppliers to self-manage transactions with a company. Easy to justify with a business case, these types of projects have traditionally formed the bulk of IT's discretionary spending. "Cost-reduction projects have and always will be important to our company," stated one member. "However, it is important to balance what we do in this area with other types of equally important projects that have often been given short shrift."

2. *Business enabling.* These projects extend or transform how a company does business. As a result, they are more focused on the topline or revenue-growing aspects of an enterprise. For example, a data warehouse could enable different parts of a company to "mine" transaction information to improve customer service, assist target marketing, better understand buying patterns, or identify new business opportunities. Adding a new Web-based channel could make it easier for customers to buy more or to attract new customers. A customer information file could make it more enjoyable for a customer to do business with a company (e.g., only one address change) and also facilitate new ways of doing business. Often the return on these types of projects is less clear, and as a result it has been harder to get them on the IT priority list. Yet many of these initiatives represent the foundations on which future business strategy will be built. For example, one CIO described the creation of a customer information file as "a key enabler for many different business units. ... It has helped us build bench strength and move to a new level of service that other companies cannot match" (Smith 2003).

3. ***Business opportunities.*** These are small-scale, experimental initiatives designed to test the viability of new concepts or technologies. In the past, these types of projects have not received funding by traditional methods because of their high-risk nature. Often, it has been left up to the CIO to scrounge money for such "skunkworks." There is a growing recognition of the potential value of strategic experiments in helping companies to learn about and prepare for the future. In some companies the CEO and CFO have freed up seed money to finance a number of these initiatives. However, although there is considerably more acceptance for such projects, there is still significant organizational resistance to financing projects for which the end results are unpredictable (Quinn 2002). In fact, it typically requires discipline to support and encourage experiments, which, by definition, will have a high number of false starts and wrong moves (Kanter 2002). The group agreed that the key to benefiting from experiments is to design them for learning, incorporate feedback from a variety of sources, and make quick corrections of direction.

4. ***Opportunity leverage.*** A neglected but important type of IT project is one that operationalizes, scales up, or leverages successful strategic experiments or prototypes. "We are having a great deal of success taking advantage of what we have learned earlier," said one manager. Coming up with a new strategic or technological idea needs a different set of skills than is required to take full advantage of it in the marketplace (Charitou and Markides 2003). Some companies actually use their ability to leverage others' ideas to their strategic advantage. "We can't compete in coming up with new ideas," said the manager of a medium-sized company, "but we can copy other peoples' ideas and do them better."

5. ***Infrastructure.*** This final type of IT initiative is one that often falls between the cracks when business and IT strategies are developed. However, it is clear that the hardware, software, middleware, communications, and data available will affect an organization's capacity to build new capabilities and respond to change. One study found that most companies feel their legacy infrastructure can be an impediment to what they want to do (Prahalad and Krishnan 2002). Research also shows that leading companies have a framework for making targeted investments in their IT infrastructure that will further their overall strategic direction (Weill et al. 2002). Unfortunately, investing in infrastructure is rarely seen as strategic. As a result, many companies struggle with how to justify and appropriately fund it.

Although each type of project delivers a different type of business value, typically IT strategy has stressed only those initiatives with strong business cases. Others are shelved or must struggle for a very small piece of the pie. However, there was a general recognition in the group that this approach to investment leads to an IT strategy with a heavy emphasis on the bottom line. As a result, all participating companies were looking at new ways to build a strategy-development process that reflects a more appropriate balance of all dimensions of IT strategy.

Toward an IT Strategy-Development Process

Strategy is still very much an art, not a science, explained the focus group. And it is likely to remain so, according to strategy experts. Strategy will never again be a coherent, long-term plan with predictable outcomes—if it ever was. "Leaders can't predict which combinations [of strategic elements] will succeed [and] they can't drive their organizations towards predetermined positions" (Quinn 2002). This situation only exacerbates the problem that has long faced IT strategists—that is, it is difficult to build systems, information, and infrastructure when a business's direction is continually changing. Yet this degree of flexibility is exactly what businesses are demanding (Prahalad and Krishnan 2002). Traditional IT planning and budgeting mechanisms done once a year simply don't work in today's fast-paced business environment. "We always seem to lag behind the business, no matter how hard we try," said a manager.

Clearly, organizations need to be developing strategy differently. How to do this is not always apparent, but several companies are trying ways to more dynamically link IT strategy with that of the business. Although no one company in the focus group claimed to have the answer, they did identify several practices that are moving them closer to this goal:

- *"Rolling" planning and budget cycles.* All participants agreed that IT plans and budgets need attention more frequently than once a year. One company has created an eighteen-month rolling plan that is reviewed and updated quarterly with the business to maintain currency.
- *An enterprise architecture.* This is an integrated blueprint for the development of the enterprise—both the business and IT. "Our enterprise architecture includes business processes, applications, infrastructure, and data," said a member. "Our EA function has to approve all business and IT projects and is helpful in identifying duplicate solutions." In some companies this architecture is IT initiated and business validated; in others, it is a joint initiative. However, participants warned that an architecture has the potential to be a corporate bottleneck if it becomes too bureaucratic.
- *Different funding "buckets."* Balancing short-term returns with the company's longer-term interests is a continual challenge. As noted earlier, all five types of IT projects (business improvement, business enabling, business opportunities, opportunity leverage, and infrastructure) are necessary for an effective IT strategy. In order to ensure that each different type of IT initiative is appropriately funded, many companies are allocating predetermined percentages of their IT budget to different types of projects (Ross and Beath 2002). This helps keep continual pressure on IT to reduce its "utility costs" to free up more resources for other types of projects. "Since we implemented this method of budgeting, we've gone from spending 70 percent of our revenues on mandatory and support projects to spending 70 percent on discretionary and strategic ones," said a manager. This is also an effective way to ensure

that IT infrastructure is continually enhanced. Leading companies build their infrastructures not through a few large investments but gradually through incremental, modular investments that build IT capabilities (Weill et al. 2002).

- *Account or relationship managers.* There is no substitute for a deep and rich understanding of the business. This is why many companies have appointed IT account managers to work closely with key lines of business. These managers help business leaders to observe their environments systematically and identify new opportunities for which IT could be effective. Furthermore, account managers can work together to identify synergies and interdependencies among lines of business. One organization holds both intra and interfunctional strategy sessions on a regular basis with business managers to understand future needs, develop programs, and design specific roadmaps for reaching business goals. "Our account managers have been a significant factor in synchronizing IT and business strategies," said its manager.

- *A prioritization rubric.* "We don't do prioritization well," said one participant. IT managers have long complained that it is extremely difficult to justify certain types of initiatives using the traditional business case method of prioritization. This has led to an overrepresentation of business improvement projects in the IT portfolio and has inhibited more strategic investments in general capabilities and business opportunities. This problem is leading some companies to adopt multiple approaches to justifying IT projects (Ross and Beath 2002). For example, business-enabling projects must be sponsored at a cross-functional level on the basis of the capabilities they will provide the enterprise as a whole. Senior management must then take responsibility to ensure that these capabilities are fully leveraged over time. Infrastructure priorities are often left up to IT to determine once a budget is set. One IT department does this by holding strategy sessions with its account and utility managers to align infrastructure spending with the organization's strategic needs. Unfortunately, no one has yet figured out a way to prioritize business opportunity experiments. At present this is typically left to the "enthusiasms and intuitions" of the sponsoring managers, either in IT or in the business (Ross and Beath 2002). "Overall," said a manager, "we need to do a better job of thinking through the key performance indicators we'd like to use for each type of project."

Although it is unlikely that strategy development will ever become a completely formalized process, there is a clear need to add more structure to how it is done. A greater understanding of how strategy is developed will ensure that all stakeholders are involved and a broader range of IT investments are considered. The outcomes of strategy will always be uncertain, but the process of identifying new opportunities and how they should be funded must become more systematic if a business is going to realize optimum value from its IT resources.

Challenges for CIOs

As often happens in organizations, recognition of a need precedes the ability to put it into place. IT leaders are now making significant strides in articulating IT strategy and linking it more effectively with business strategy. Business leaders are also more open to a more integrated process. Nevertheless, some important organizational barriers that inhibit strategy development remain.

A supportive governance structure is frequently lacking. "Now that so many strategies are enterprise-wide, we need a better way to manage them," explained one manager. Often there are no formal structures to identify and manage interdependencies between business functions and processes. "It used to be that everything was aligned around organizational boundaries, but strategy is now more complex since we're working on programs with broader organizational scope," said another. Similarly, current managerial control systems and incentives are often designed to reward thinking that is aligned to a line of business, not to the greater organizational good. Enterprise-wide funding models are also lacking. "Everything we do now requires negotiation for funding between the lines of business who control the resources," a third stated. Even within IT, the group suggested it is not always clear who in the organization is responsible for taking IT strategies and turning them into detailed IT plans.

Traditional planning and budgetary practices are a further challenge. This is an often-neglected element of IT strategy. "Our business and IT strategies are not always done in parallel or even around the same time," said a participant. As a result, it is not easy to stay aligned or to integrate the two sets of plans. Another commented, "Our business plans change constantly. It is, therefore, common for IT strategies to grow [further and further] apart over time." Similarly, an annual budgeting process tends to lock an organization into fixed expenditures that may not be practical in a rapidly changing environment. IT organizations, therefore, need both a longer-term view of their resourcing practices and the opportunity to make changes to it more frequently. Even though rolling budgets are becoming more acceptable, they are by no means common in either IT or the business world today.

Both business and IT leaders need to develop better skills in strategizing. "We've gotten really good at implementing projects," said an IT manager. "Strategy and innovation are our least developed capabilities." IT is pushing the business toward better articulation of its goals. "Right now, in many areas of our business, strategy is not well thought through," said another manager. "IT is having to play the devil's advocate and get them to think beyond generalities such as 'We are going to grow the business by 20 percent this year.'" With more attention to the process, it is almost certain to get better, but managers' rudimentary skills in this area limit the quality of strategy development.

Over and over, the group stressed that IT strategy is mainly about getting the right balance between conflicting strategic imperatives. "It's always a balancing act between our tactical and operational commitments and the work that builds our long-term capabilities," said a participant. Deciding how to make the trade-offs between the different types of IT work is the essence of effective strategy. Unfortunately, few businesses do this very well (Burgelman and Doz 2001). According to the focus group, traditional business thinking tends to favor short-term profitability, while IT leaders tend to take a longer-term view. Making sure some types of IT work (e.g., infrastructure, new business opportunities) are not underfunded while others (e.g., utility, business improvement) are not overfunded is a continual challenge for all IT and business leaders.

Barriers to Effective IT Strategy Development
- Lack of a governance structure for enterprise-wide projects;
- Inadequate enterprise-wide funding models;
- Poorly integrated processes for developing IT and business strategies;
- Traditional budget cycles;
- Unbalanced strategic and tactical initiatives;
- Weak strategizing skills.

Conclusion

Effective strategy development is becoming vital for organizations. As the impact of IT has grown in companies, IT strategy is finally getting the attention it deserves in business. Nevertheless, most organizations are still at the earliest stages of learning how to develop an effective IT strategy and synchronize it with an overall business strategy. Effectively addressing the many different ways IT can be used to affect a business is a constant challenge for leaders and one on which they do not always agree. Although there is, as yet, no generally-accepted IT strategy-development process, there appears to be general agreement on certain critical success factors and the key elements involved. Over time, these will likely be refined and better integrated with overall business strategy development. Those who learn to do this well without locking the enterprise into inflexible technical solutions are likely to win big in our rapidly evolving business environment.

Chapter Discussion Questions

1. Think of a new technology (e.g., blockchain) and a traditional business (e.g., Walmart). Create a strategy for how Walmart might use blockchain to gain competitive advantage.

2. What success measures should business leaders at Walmart use to evaluate their blockchain strategy?

References

Burgelman, R., and Y. Doz. "The Power of Strategic Integration." *MIT Sloan Management Review* 42, no. 3 (Spring 2001): 28–38.

Charitou, C., and C. Markides. "Responses to Disruptive Strategic Innovation." *MIT Sloan Management Review* (Winter 2003): 55–63.

Eisenhardt, K. "Has Strategy Changed?" *MIT Sloan Management Review* 43, no. 2 (Winter 2002): 88–91.

Frohman, A. "Technology as a Competitive Weapon." *Harvard Business Review* (January–February 1982): 80–94.

Gebauer, J. "Virtual Organizations from an Economic Perspective." *Communications of the ACM* 40 (September 1997): 91–103.

Hitt, M., B. Keats, and S. DeMarire. "Navigating in the New Competitive Landscape: Building Strategic Flexibility." *Academy of Management Executive* 12, no. 4 (1998): 22–42.

Kanter, R. "Strategy as Improvisational Theater." *MIT Sloan Management Review* (Winter 2002): 76–81.

McKeen, J. D., and H. A. Smith. *Management Challenges in IS: Successful Strategies and Appropriate Action.* Chichester, England: John Wiley & Sons, 1996.

Porter, M. "What Is Strategy?" *Harvard Business Review* (November–December 1996): 61–78.

Prahalad, C., and M. Krishnan. "The Dynamic Synchronization of Strategy and Information Technology." *MIT Sloan Management Review* (Summer 2002): 24–33.

Quinn, J. "Strategy, Science, and Management." *MIT Sloan Management Review* (Summer 2002): 96.

Rivard, S., B. Aubert, M. Patry, G. Pare, and H. Smith. *Information Technology and Organizational Transformation: Solving the Management Puzzle.* New York: Butterworth Heinemann, 2004.

Ross, J., and C. Beath. "Beyond the Business Case: New Approaches to IT Investment." *MIT Sloan Management Review* (Winter 2002): 51–59.

Smith, H. A. "The Best of the Best: Part II." *CIO Canada*, October 1, 2003.

Tapscott, D. *The Digital Economy: Promise and Peril in the Age of Networked Intelligence.* New York: McGraw-Hill, 1996.

Venkatramen, N., and J. Henderson. "Real Strategies for Virtual Organizing." *Sloan Management Review* 40, no. 33 (Fall 1998).

Weill, P., M. Subramani, and M. Broadbent. "Building IT Infrastructure for Strategic Agility." *MIT Sloan Management Review* (Fall 2002): 57–65.

CHAPTER 3

Advancing a Data Strategy

In many ways organizations seem to be making a full circle from data processing (DP) to information systems (IS) to information technology (IT) and then back to a new focus on data processing. Data, and the information and knowledge that can be derived from it, is one of the biggest challenges facing organizations today (Chen et al. 2012). There are a number of reasons for this. First, data is integral to both the work of business and IT, but whereas business units want data and processes to stay stable and primarily support their individual functions, IT has an interest in standardizing much of it at an enterprise level to achieve synergies and create new opportunities. Second, we have come to recognize that how we manage data in both business and IT will significantly affect our capabilities, products, and services and thus our business and technology strategy. Therefore, data is no longer considered a subset of a system, but important and valuable in its own right. Third, we now recognize that data is both a corporate asset and a corporate vulnerability that needs to be protected and developed. And, finally, data is booming. New types and amounts of data are already swamping organizations, and IT managers realize that they are only on the tip of a very large data iceberg. For these reasons and others, IT managers believe developing a data strategy is crucial.

This is easier said than done. Although much has been written about business and technology strategy, data strategy is very much an undeveloped field that is complementary to both. Many organizations have found the task of developing "an intergalactic data model" daunting in the extreme, and most have failed, and this doesn't even begin to address data *strategy*. Today, it is fair to say that organizations are all over the map when it comes to developing a data strategy, but most are finding the lack of one to be limiting to what they want or need to do.

Delivering the right information to the right person at the right time requires a plan of what an organization wants to accomplish with data and how it proposes to derive business value from it (Shim et al. 2015). This chapter first articulates *why* a company needs a data strategy in the first place and outlines what might be included in one. It then shows *where* a data strategy fits in relation to all other data and corporate activities, such as master data, big data, and architecture. Finally, it discusses lessons learned from previous failures, describes realistic and achievable stages towards data strategy maturity, and identifies actionable steps for getting started on this journey.

Why Do We Need a Data Strategy?

A strategy of any type—be it business, technical, data, or otherwise—is a plan to help an organization succeed. There are two ways an organization can do this (Porter 1996, 2001; Smith et al. 2010):

1. *Develop new capabilities.* With this approach, strategies are designed to help organizations become more flexible and responsive to changing markets and competition. Here, the emphasis is on improvisation, adaptation, and reinvention throughout the organization. Companies focus on their core competencies (e.g., key resources and capabilities), best practices, and benchmarking to keep ahead of (or level with) their competitors. Advantage comes from continual reinvention and lots of experimentation.

2. *Create a uniquely competitive position.* More traditionally, strategies are designed to perform activities that are different from those of their competitors or to do them in different ways. These stress tailoring a company's activities to address its chosen position in the marketplace, and designing them so they reinforce each other in a coherent fashion. Competitive advantage and the ability to sustain it arise from integration across all activities. This approach to strategy is not to be confused with performing similar activities better than competitors, which is operational effectiveness and which should be considered part of an organization's everyday activities.

Data strategy, like other strategies, co-evolves with new technologies, new capabilities, and new behaviors and structures. These elements must reinforce each other in order to achieve a company's strategic goal. Although a company's position relative to its business environment must always be paramount in all strategy development, business opportunities can come from any of these elements, and business value can only be derived from all of them working in concert.

Ideally, the "strategy" of an organization is further detailed in specific business and technology strategies that are consistent and aligned across the enterprise. Until recently, data issues have been addressed within technology strategy and in piecemeal ways, such as plans for storage, databases, a data warehouse, or master data. Developing a separate data strategy that would complement both business and technology strategy has not been a priority for business or IT leaders (Dayley et al. 2014). Now several factors are changing this:

• *New analytical technologies.* These new tools enable large quantities of data from a variety of sources to be integrated and analyzed in order to accomplish new activities not possible previously. These include: developing new and more detailed insights into current company practices (e.g., by particular demographics or products); better and more quickly measuring the impact of new strategies on the market; and using the information derived from it to create new products or services.

- *New types of data.* Companies are being flooded with data and are therefore seeking ways to take advantage of it while managing the volume, variety, and velocity of data involved. Organizing and managing data before the Internet and other forms of external data were available was challenging enough. Companies have long struggled with data accuracy, integrity, and delivery issues (Ferguson 2014; Redman 2013). Now, with so many new types of data being created and made available and much of it external to the organization (e.g., social media, sensor, unstructured data), companies are recognizing that they need to "up their game" in utilizing it.

- *New risk and compliance concerns.* Increasingly, governments are enacting laws to require that companies provide accurate information on their performance in a number of areas. In addition, high-profile security breaches are showing business leaders firsthand some of the market downside of failing to protect their data. This is driving demands for new policies and practices concerning data usage and handling, such as retention, security, privacy, and access.

- *New competition.* New products and services are emerging in different industries that demonstrate the market value of using data for competitive advantage. Stories of companies that have effectively done this (e.g., UPS) abound, as do stories of companies that have literally changed the marketspace (e.g., Amazon) for products and services. The explosion of data-intensive devices that are all connected is creating new ways of working, playing, and living that are not only changing the types of data being generated but also driving new customer needs for data didn't exist previously (e.g., Fitbit).

- *New value.* Companies are discovering that considerable business value can be achieved by incorporating data into their strategies. From a productivity point of view, researchers have found that knowledge workers can spend up to 50 percent of their time hunting for data, identifying and correcting errors, and seeking confirmatory sources for data they do not trust (Redman 2013). Another study found that up to 14 percent of a company's revenue is lost when enterprises do not manage and analyze their data (Bowen and Smith 2014). There is greater awareness that data can be used to improve productivity and effectiveness.

Many in the focus group believe it is time to take a more comprehensive and strategic look at how data are used in their organizations. "The demand for data is so strong in our company," said one manager, "that if we're not out in front with a data strategy for the business, it will run ahead of us." Another pointed out, "Our game is being upped with the introduction of analytical power." "Because we're so data dependent, we are implicitly driving a data strategy, but this needs to be better aligned with our business and technology strategies," said a third.

They agreed that a new model of strategy development should incorporate business, technology, and data strategies, and that each of these must not only work in concert with the others but also be open to external competitive forces and new possibilities created by new technologies and new types of data.

What is a Data Strategy?

Although there is a clear need for companies to strategize about data, there is little agreement about what actually constitutes a data strategy. Focus group members were all in the early stages of thinking about or developing one. They agreed that it is important to conceive of a data strategy as a "living" plan. Although there are many good reasons to have a data strategy in place, they noted that there is little appetite in the business for overly constraining approaches that cost a lot and deliver nothing but data models in a few years' time. Leaving this comprehensive approach aside, the companies in the focus group presented a range of philosophies about what a data strategy should be that trace a maturity path from data chaos to managed agility:

1. *Pragmatic.* "Our data strategy must be flexible and iterative," said one manager. "We're changing so fast, we need pragmatic data solutions that we can use to enable business results asap." He compared this approach to feudalism in that it serves local needs in the lines of business, rather than the enterprise as a whole. Another explained how this approach functioned in her organization. "There's no data that we don't have, but only a few people can tell you where it is."

2. *Action-oriented.* "We are trying to understand what critical business needs we should be addressing with data, and organize our data strategy around it," said another manager. This approach could be compared with early industrialization where design practices were beginning to be introduced.

3. *Risk-oriented.* Companies begin to move into more enterprise-wide approaches when they recognize the risks associated with data. "We're trying to manage our legal exposure, appropriate uses of data, use of data to make erroneous business decisions, and operational exposures related to loss of privacy and security," said one manager. "We consider ourselves stewards of data and we need to understand the boundaries of control, risk, and regulation that we must operate within. Then we need to ask ourselves, what are we doing within these boundaries to better manage and use data?"

4. *Post-industrial.* Although none of the focus group companies is at this point, the vision for a future data strategy is quite clear. Here, good quality data is available to appropriate users, along with useful metadata, such as when it was created and who created it, and standard definitions, and it is organized in ways that enable it to be easily found, accessed, and utilized. Also, appropriate tools are available to support analytics, information creation, and delivery. "This strategy supports a 'pick what you need' model," explained one manager.

In addition to understanding what an organization wants from its data strategy, it is also essential to understand what data it wants to include in its strategy. The managers in the focus group stressed that tackling too much all at once can be a recipe for failure. "We tried to develop a complete information architecture a decade ago and it wasn't successful," said one manager. "Then a few years later we tried to articulate a comprehensive strategy but it was too polarizing in the organization. Now we are taking a more staged and pragmatic approach to strategy development."

Participants have tried a variety of ways to determine what data to focus on. This includes limiting their attention to one or all of the following types of data:

- Enterprise-level data;
- Data subject to any sort of compliance or regulatory need;
- Data needed for competitive purposes;
- Metadata to identify authoritative sources and content owners;
- Foundational data (i.e., data that is central to the business), also known as the book of record;
- External data to improve business functionality or to develop new opportunities.

Finally, a data strategy must address a number of other business and technical issues about data once a general direction and scope has been articulated. There are four major sets of issues related to data: policy, operations, stewardship, and standards. Each of these will guide the decisions that are made about data, and must in turn be informed by a specific strategic approach and focus that is set at a high level in the organization.

- *Policy* provides the basis for developing the processes, standards, and guidelines needed to manage data assets throughout the organization. It directs the development of more detailed practices related to accountabilities, quality, protection, risk tolerance, compliance, creation of new assets, acquisition, retention, integration, analytics, and records management. Because of the large number of stakeholders affected, it should be developed by a multidisciplinary team, including IT, key lines of business, and the legal, HR, audit, privacy, and compliance functions.
- *Operations* includes specific practices that need to be put in place in order for a strategy to be successful. These practices will vary depending on the strategy involved but should address: governance, planning, technology and architecture, education and behavior, and processes for each of the areas outlined in the data policy.
- *Stewardship* specifically describes the roles and responsibilities associated with data management and distinguishes between business and technical responsibilities. Data management is a boundary-spanning activity. Data owners are typically business people, although there appears to be a general lack of interest for this role in the business. Owners define data and determine who should have access to it, and are accountable for its accuracy, integrity, currency, and meaning. Technology roles are both custodial (i.e., determining how retained data will be stored and accessed, mapping which systems use which data) and strategic (i.e., developing

a technology foundation that supports appropriate data architecture, multi-purpose access, and protection, as well as creating a data dictionary and acquisition of appropriate analytic tools).

• **Standards** enable the organization to develop enterprise-wide solutions, better integrate evolving new technologies, implement partnerships, and create innovative solutions (Palem 2014). As noted above, there is ongoing tension in many organizations between IT, which wants to promote the adoption of standards, and the lines of business, which tend to prefer to use data in their individualized context. Many focus group organizations have made considerable progress in this area. Most have established master data for key customer and corporate records. Several are using compliance requirements to move forward with standardization of key data assets. Nevertheless, standards continue to be a divisive issue that needs to be pursued with caution.

Where Does Data Strategy Fit?

A significant challenge for any organization is determining where data strategy fits in the organizational structure. Is it a business or an IT function? At what level in the organization should it report? On the one hand, it is the business that must decide which data are important and how to use this data to deliver business value. On the other, IT has the responsibility for the data life cycle from acquisition through organization, processing, maintenance, and retention. The majority of focus group companies now have a senior data role in their IT organizations, with titles such as Director Data Services, AVP Data Strategy, or Chief Data Officer. Only one had positioned this role outside of IT. As with other boundary-spanning initiatives, IT is often called upon to bring its enterprise perspective to the table. However, in doing so, there is a danger that the business could see data strategy as "just another technical initiative."

The focus group stressed that technology should not be the sole driver of data strategy or it will be doomed to failure. Multidisciplinary governance is essential to providing the sponsorship and guidance to make it effective (Laney and Beyer 2013; Daley et al. 2014). Most of the group's participants had created data governance councils to provide the necessary direction to both IT and business regarding data strategy and its implementation. This council focuses on key data assets, and ensures that data strategy is consistent with (and complementary to) business and technology strategy, and that new opportunities for leveraging data are addressed. It also determines how fast to move with implementing data architecture, standards, roles, and activities, and acts as mediator in the event of disagreements over the management of shared assets.

A second challenge for data strategists is: Where does it fit with the rest of the "data ecosystem"? Today, there is considerable confusion among business and IT leaders regarding both the variety of data an organization must cope with and the number of different ongoing initiatives associated with some type of data. This problem is

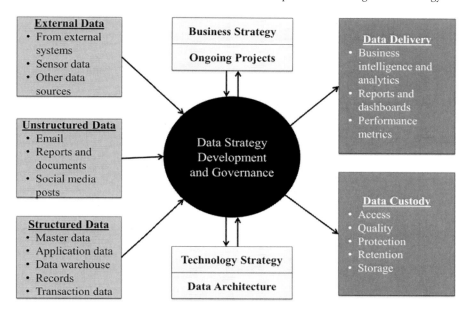

Figure 3.1 A data ecosystem

further exacerbated by the fact that the data ecosystem is also changing rapidly with new types and sources of data being developed on a regular basis, and new forms of competition evolving through the use of data analytics. The result is a rather fuzzy picture where some pieces overlap and where there are significant gaps, making it difficult to articulate a clear data strategy.

A key prerequisite to developing an effective data strategy is therefore understanding and clarifying an organization's data ecosystem and putting in place ongoing activities to further clarify it and fill in gaps (see Figure 3.1). A company's data ecosystem consists of both data and the activities that utilize it. As this figure shows, a good starting point for data strategists is taking an inventory of all types of data currently available in their organizations; ongoing projects that use data or create new information; current data delivery and custody practices; and technology strategy, architecture, and tools. "It's unlikely that we will be addressing the full ecosystem with our new data strategy initiative, but we want to make informed decisions based on our knowledge of it," said a manager.

The Data Journey

The focus group stressed that developing an effective data strategy is a journey, not a one-time activity. "We're maturing in our data management practices," explained a manager, "and hoping that, as we demonstrate the value of data, we can enhance and extend our data strategy." Thus, in addition to understanding the big picture of data strategy, there are several practices that will develop organizational readiness to become more strategic about data. These include:

- **Improving data quality.** Data quality problems "plague every department, every industry, at every level for every type of information," and employees routinely work around or correct errors in their daily work (Redman 2013). Poor data quality costs the organization—in unnecessary work, in driving poor decisions, and in generating distrust in data-based decisions. High-quality data enhances trust in what it's saying and encourages people to rely more fully on it (Ferguson 2014; Bowen and Smith 2014) and is a key factor in improving the information orientation of an organization that has been shown to have a strong relationship with performance (Davenport 2007; Marchand and Kettinger 2000). Focus group members stressed that data quality problems should not inhibit the development of a data strategy, and efforts to improve quality should address the root causes of poor data, rather than "fix" it at a later data. To do this, best practices include improving communication between the creators and users of the data, and developing data quality metrics to monitor improvements (Redman 2013). In some cases, the growing size of the data sets available may make errors less important to correct as well.

- **Working on data definitions.** Common definitions of key data elements, including their attributes, are a fundamental component of data integrity; that is, data that consistently means the same thing everywhere in the organization (Bowen and Smith 2014; Lewis 2012). "We suffer from different data definitions," said one manager. "Everyone agrees that we should have a common definition but wants to use their own version." Appointing data stewards to "own" key data elements and work with stakeholders to define them appears to be the best practice for making headway in this area. But members warned that it can be a frustrating and time-consuming activity unless there's a direct value motivation. One company is using advanced tools to assist this work, such as a semantic database that links similar concepts with different names, and automated introspection searches that pull out linked data to make it easier to develop common definitions. "Tools can make this problem more tractable," said the manager involved, "but in the end the only way to achieve common definitions and ensure these aren't changed is [by] having a data owner."

- **Developing engagement.** Many companies are seeking to demonstrate the potential value of a data strategy by engaging people with data. "The more we can provide self-serve analytics, the greater the value we can deliver to the business," said one manager. "We are trying to deliver pragmatic data solutions that will enable business results asap and show how data can make us competitive," said another. Although many business managers are beginning to recognize data as a business asset to be protected, most are still constrained by their experience and need more insights into what new opportunities might be possible with data. Generating excitement and engagement around small data initiatives is a key way to obtain funding for more significant data initiatives.

- **Setting priorities.** All companies in the focus group had a number of clear data priorities, even if they did not have a formal data strategy. These tended to be more technical than business-oriented, reflecting the areas in which IT has control. "Wherever possible, we do foundational work with data," said a manager. This includes: decoupling data from tools and applications to make it more accessible, storing data in its rawest form so that it can be used for a variety of purposes, and developing metadata to ensure consistency.

Advice to Managers

Moving forward with a data strategy is challenging. Funding, skills, and resources are in short supply. Working with different business units with differing business strategies, priorities, and timelines can mean that progress is patchy at best. And generating business interest and appetite for foundational data work can be a struggle. Focus group managers had several recommendations for others who are finding it difficult to make progress with their data strategy:

- **Put someone in charge.** It is more likely that progress will be made if someone is paying attention to developing a data strategy and making it a priority.
- **Have a vision and set priorities.** All members of the focus group knew what their top data priorities were and why. Some were working on obtaining an enterprise mandate for data, others on data architecture and standards; and many were trying to provide easier access to data. Having a big picture vision enables IT to undertake smaller projects of more practical value to business that still make a contribution to achieving a broader data strategy.
- **Keep it pragmatic.** Even with a mandate, it is important to continually show real business value from data. "We are more likely to get support for and understanding of data as a business asset if we can deliver business value with it," said a manager. A corollary to this is that no organization should attempt to implement a data strategy in a "big bang." "This approach has consistently proven ineffective," said a manager.
- **Educate the business.** Simple proof of concept initiatives can help the business see the opportunities for using data more effectively and highlight the value of how a clear data strategy can support and enhance a business strategy.
- **Measure progress.** People pay attention to what is measured. Therefore, several participants have added data metrics to their enterprise scorecards. "We have scorecard metrics around data quality and data governance," said a manager. It is also important to know what success looks like, especially in the early days of strategy development. "We believe that success is any result that leads to more demand for data delivery work that can, in turn, fund foundational data work," a manager explained.

Conclusion

Developing a data strategy is not for the faint of heart. It can mean stirring up a hornet's nest of territorialism and politics. It can also feel like a thankless task that garners very little support or appreciation from business. Moving down this path involves knowing where you are at present and where you want to be, and then developing a business appetite for improving data strategy through such activities as education and proof-of-concept initiatives. As with many other organizational changes over the years, IT is anticipating the future, and it's all about data. IT's challenge is to implement an effective data strategy that will not only deliver immediate value to the business, but also put the pieces in place to more fully enable new business strategies in the future.

Chapter Discussion Questions

1. At GM, how might data be used to develop cars of the future?
2. Discuss the relationship between GM's business strategy and their data strategy to improve the company's competitive position.

References

Bowen, R., and A. Smith. "Developing an Enterprise Data Strategy." *Healthcare Financial Management* 68, no. 4 (April 2014): 86–89.

Chen, H., R. Chiang, and V. Storey. "Business Intelligence and Analytics: From Big Data to Big Impact." *MIS Quarterly* 36, no. 4 (2012): 1165–188.

Davenport, T., and J. Harris. *Competing on Analytics: The New Science of Winning.* Boston: Harvard Business School Press, 2007.

Dayley, A., D. Logan, and G. Landers. "Best Practices for Data Retention and Policy Creation will Lower Costs and Reduce Risks." Gartner Research Report, ID: G00262827, April 2014.

Ferguson, R. "Elevating Data, Analytics to the C-Suite." *MIT Sloan Management Review*, Reprint no. 55401, March 25, 2014.

Laney, D., and M. Beyer. "Big Data Essentials for Business and IT." *Financial Times*, August 2, 2013.

Lewis, N. "Six Ways Healthcare Can Assess Data Strategy." *Information Week*, April 16, 2012.

Marchand, D., W. Kettinger, and J. Rollins. "Information Orientation: People, Technology and the Bottom Line." *Sloan Management Review* (Summer 2000): 69–81.

Palem, G. "Formulating an Executive Strategy for Big Data Analytics." *Technology Innovation Management Review* (March 2014): 25–34.

Porter, M. "What is Strategy?" *Harvard Business Review* (November–December 1996).

Porter, M. "Strategy and the Internet." *Harvard Business Review* (March 2001): 62–78.

Redman, T. "Data's Credibility Problem." *Harvard Business Review* (December 2013).

Shim, J., A. French, C. Guo, and J. Jablonski. "Big Data and Analytics: Issues, Solutions, and ROI." *Communications of the Association for Information Systems* 37, Article 39.

Smith, H., J. D. McKeen, and S. Singh. "Developing and Aligning a KM Strategy." *Journal of Information Science & Technology* 7, no. 1 (June 2010): 40–60.

CHAPTER 4

Creating and Evolving a Digital Strategy

The word "digital" appears everywhere today, and there is a growing consensus that the world as we know it is in transition from our "old" ways of doing business and using technology, to "new" ways of thinking about, living with, and working with technology. "The change is different in scale because it's also a disruptive change in how society works," said one IT manager. "There's a lot of hype about digital but there's also a lot at stake." "We've seen an unbelievable shift in the past five years," said another, "and in the past six months 'digital' is a given."

There are a lot of reasons why organizations are feeling a sense of urgency about "going digital" and the pressure to change. Buying patterns are evolving because more customers are shopping online and comparing prices, products, and service levels. Companies are therefore more concerned with customer experience and differentiating themselves to consumers (Baggi 2014; Willmott 2014; Press 2016a; Hirt and Willmott 2014). The cost of delivering IT solutions is also changing. What would have been very expensive and time-consuming to develop in the past can now be delivered in just weeks or months, by combining apps and off-the-shelf and cloud-based solutions (Willmott 2014). In conjunction with "plug-and-play" dynamics, new competitors can now attack specific areas of a company's value chain without needing to develop the whole thing themselves (Digital Strategy Conference 2015). This lowers barriers to entry and enables entrepreneurs to cherry-pick subcategories of products and undercut pricing (Hirt and Willmott 2014). In turn, these factors (lower costs, faster delivery, new dynamics, lower barriers to entry) are changing the competitive landscape, undermining established business models, and putting pressure on business and IT alike to change rapidly. "There's a real sense of fear in our organizations that it can't be business as usual, and concern that we won't be able to keep up," said one manager.

These elements have already profoundly changed the strategic context of business (Hirt and Willmott 2014), and this is driving companies to look at more holistic ways to respond to it. "We've had lots of individual strategies in the past but never an overarching one," said one manager. "In this environment, most strategies only have a shelf life of about five minutes." Nevertheless, companies are pushing forward to deal more comprehensively with the inevitable changes that are coming. Most are still struggling to develop a coherent digital strategy, while about a quarter are lagging in this regard, and another quarter are more mature (Kane et al. 2015b). All recognize that the move to digital will place a huge burden on IT to change. One study estimated that by 2018, 35 percent of IT resources will be spent on supporting the creation of new digital revenue streams and that this will grow to 50 percent by 2020 (Press 2016a). IT staff skills will also need to change to incorporate new technologies, new ways of working, a new focus on data, and an increased emphasis on risk, security, and compliance (Press 2016a). Thus, creating a successful digital strategy and an organization to support it is now a top priority for both business and IT management (Iyengar and Mok 2014).

In this chapter we first examine the meaning of the term "digital strategy." Then we explore the value of having a digital strategy as part of a company's business and IT strategies. We describe how to go about developing a digital strategy. Finally, we look at the broader implications of digitization for the organization and what further changes will be needed to support a successful strategy in an enterprise.

What is a Digital Strategy?

"Few terms have created as much confusion or have as many completely different definitions as a digital strategy," wrote one researcher (McGee 2015). In the focus group everyone agreed that there is no commonly understood definition of the concept. Some members pointed out that "everything is digital," so it's just an evolutionary development of traditional IT strategy. Others strongly disagreed. In the end, all recognized that digital strategy is an evolving concept and that "where you're going, depends on your industry and where you're starting from." Researchers corroborate this and suggest that "depending on your sector and industry, the perception and role of digital changes radically" (Digital Strategy Conference 2015).

Regardless of the starting point, there is broad acceptance that digital strategy is different from traditional business and IT strategy in several key areas:

- *The unknown.* Businesses are changing dramatically in very short periods of time as a result of applying new technologies to traditional business models. Unlike traditional strategies, which were longer term and based on well-established business models and competitive landscapes, digital strategy is dynamic, with business and IT leaders working together to guess what the future will be and revise their strategies on the fly (Kane et al. 2015a).
- *Complexity.* Digital strategy can involve every part of the organization—functions, processes, products, services, data, technology, and employees—as well as partners, suppliers, customers, the value chain, and competitors. It seeks "methods to employ information and IT in new ways to create new value with new products, services, business practices, or even new business models" (McGee 2015).

- **Holistic.** Companies usually start off with isolated digital initiatives, but as their understanding and capabilities mature, they realize that the true value of a digital strategy lies in its ability to present a coherent and integrated approach to connecting people, processes, and things, and to enable them to communicate with each other via the Internet in ways that have never been possible before (Lopez 2015).
- **Exploration.** Unlike traditional strategy that seeks certainty about what to do, digital strategy stresses innovation, experimentation, and exploration. This requires different ways of thinking and working that incorporate both new ideas and tools with a supportive and flexible IT infrastructure and a disciplined and practical approach to development, implementation, and evaluation (Press 2016b).
- **Scope.** Although traditional business and IT strategies were designed to bring about change, they were always focused within a traditional business model. Mature digital strategies, on the other hand, seek business transformation by incorporating three key trends—big data and analytics, the internet of things, and artificial intelligence—to create new business designs that connect and/or integrate business assets (people, processes, and things) beyond the IT function and beyond the control of any one company (Press 2016a; Lopez 2015).

In short, a digital strategy is only the first step in a new approach to using business and technology. It outlines a map of what a company wants to become. Simply deploying a "digital something" will not automatically accomplish this or change mindsets, cultures, or work practices. Therefore, a company needs to be able to clearly articulate what it wants to accomplish and how it wants to operate as a digital business (Press 2016a, Baggi 2014). Failing to do this is a major barrier to progress and is now a concern reaching up to board level in organizations (Kiron et al. 2013b) (see box).

The Importance of Digital Strategy*

"In a stunning decision [a Toronto based retailer replaced its CEO] with [a person] best suited to deal with the myriad challenges of a rapidly changing, uncertain retail environment ... [The] board was concerned the company's digital retail strategy was inadequate in the face of fast-moving competitors ... The company's immediate priorities are finding and implementing the right strategy ... Every day customers are demanding more control of their shopping experience ... [The board is concerned about] ... 1) the appropriate digital strategy, 2) the pace of its implementation, [and] 3) the role of acquisitions in implementing the company's digital strategy.... The change in the CEO reflect[s] that traditional retailing paradigms are under stress and must evolve."

* *Globe and Mail*, July 14, 2016

After reflecting on how these dimensions change the nature of strategy, the focus group came up with the following definition:

> A digital strategy is a means of embracing new and different technologies in ways that challenge operational and value assumptions and which integrate them with existing technologies to deliver new products, services, business models, revenue streams and/or customer/stakeholder experiences.

What is the Value of a Digital Strategy?

A digital strategy serves as a tool for communicating these concepts to the organization and answers the following strategic questions:

1. Where will we choose to play?
2. How will we win?
3. What are the unconventional insights that matter?
4. What new concepts can we design and test?
5. What experiences do we want to create?

It helps both business and IT leaders to think about the true value of digital early on and identify both new opportunities and potential threats, so they can come up with the right balance of attack and defend positions (Willmott 2014).

In addition, there are a number of other benefits to having a well-thought-out and clearly communicated digital strategy, such as:

- *A mechanism for thinking about new directions for business.* The focus group felt that, if nothing else, the hype about and pressure to become more digital would be a catalyst for IT and business leaders to re-evaluate all aspects of their business model, from revenue streams, products, services, and channels to more mundane matters such as new practices and ways of working to save money, improve productivity, and create value.
- *An overarching view of multichannel business.* Focus group members stressed that old channels don't go away in this new digital world. New channels such as mobile and sensors supplement existing physical, telecommunications, and web channels. Ideally, together these create a richer experience where the channels complement and reinforce each other. However, if channel strategies are developed and implemented separately by different organizational silos, this opportunity will be lost.
- *The ability to mutually reinforce the physical and digital experience.* One company with a more advanced digital strategy found that although online is very important, bricks and mortar are not going away. "It's about both," said the manager. "There has to be a shared e-commerce model because physical touch is still important for much shopping. There is a lot of power in the combination of digital and physical. The proof is in the sales figures," he said.

- *An organizing metaphor for change.* Whereas in the past, IT work was grouped into projects, a digital strategy provides a more comprehensive roadmap for change with technology. It also makes it easier to track and adapt to changes in a particular industry and clarifies digital's impact on a business.
- *Improved connection with internal and external audiences.* A digital strategy ensures that a customer's overall experience with a company and all forms of customer engagement are considered by leaders, according to the focus group. Digital channels can also be used to enhance interactions with suppliers, stakeholders, and employees, and lower the cost of transactions. "This connectivity highlights the fact that a digital strategy is a two-way concept," said a manager. "With it, companies can now learn from their customers and others and even from their products in real time."
- *Improved integration.* When all the pieces in a process or an experience work together in a holistic way, companies can accomplish amazing things. Done well, this results in better leveraging of company assets (Kane et al. 2015b).
- *Improved innovation.* With a clear vision in place, innovation can be more focused and guided by both digital strategy and ongoing feedback. This facilitates continuous improvement and the development of new business and revenue models.
- *Improved business decision-making.* Real-time feedback from customers, suppliers, and employees, as well as from the big data collected by various types of digital technologies enables leaders to make improved decisions and reduce operational risk.
- *Improved employee engagement.* One unanticipated side-effect of the implementation of a successful digital strategy is a positive cultural shift in which employees feel more connected to the company, engaged with its brand, and aware of its strategy (Kane et al. 2015b).

"Our digital strategy will evolve," said an IT manager, "but we are excited that it will help to shape new directions for our business in ways that we haven't been able to achieve before." A digital strategy therefore represents a new way for business and IT leaders to work together to achieve new types of value with new technologies in new ways.

Developing and Implementing a Digital Strategy

As noted above, developing and implementing a digital strategy is a continuous process of ideation, experimentation, and evaluation. "It's a journey, not a destination" (Shen 2015). Simply providing some tools and praying that they will be used is not a recipe for success (Kiron et al. 2013b). Although it is true that digital strategy is akin to guessing at the future, there are ways to guide and structure these guesses. Developing and implementing a digital strategy takes both vision and discipline, said the focus group. They identified several practices that can assist leaders in narrowing and focusing their efforts:

- ***Seek broad community engagement.*** It is important to recognize that ideas and complementary skills can come from anywhere in the world (Press 2016a, Baggi 2014). Advice and input should be sought from leaders in a wide variety of industries (Baggi 2014). In some cases, organizations that have been competitors can potentially be collaborators (Willmott 2014). In addition, IT leaders must seek to ensure their staff is thoroughly engaged with the business and also with vendors, partners, and even customers. "A big challenge for IT leaders is that, while they have a good view of the overall organization, they are not experts in it," said one manager. "They should therefore explore where the knowledge lies in their organizations and plant seeds, even if they don't get the credit for the new ideas. It's a pioneering role."
- ***Think backwards and then focus.*** Since the future is unknown, organizations have the opportunity to create it for themselves. Experts recommend starting with a long-term vision of where the business needs to go and then reverse engineering from there, identifying the capabilities needed and then setting priorities (Kane et al. 2015a, Kane 2015). Following this, a small number of focused first steps can be identified. "Start small," one manager advised. "Set the stage and then help move change along with small milestones."
- ***Nurture new ideas.*** Companies need to cultivate new ideas in a systematic way. There are many ways to do this, such as internal crowdsourcing, innovation jams, or establishing a process for identifying and evaluating new ideas. However a company chooses to do this, it is most important that its leaders endorse and model their support for new approaches, experiments, and collaborative processes. In addition, companies must understand the innovation life cycle, its role, key transition points, and the different types of people needed at different points in the cycle, said the group.
- ***Consider the role of the CIO.*** Although some companies are creating Chief Digital Officers to lead the development and implementation of digital strategy, others believe this is the CIO's responsibility. "CIOs should be leading innovation because technology is driving serious change in our organizations," said one manager. Regardless of who leads, all senior leaders need to be actively involved, including the C-suite, line of business heads, the board, and finance (Kiron et al. 2013b). Ideally, the CIO should aim to catalyze innovation in the business, said the focus group, by asking business leaders, "Have you thought about this?"

  CIOs are also best equipped to understand the cutting edge, said the group. They can bring innovators and opportunities into the organization and then translate these into organizational language. CIOs and other IT leaders should therefore aim to be connectors, catalysts, pioneers, and incubators of change. In turn, they will need to be supported by two sets of people in IT: idea generators and solution generators.
- ***Communicate constantly.*** As with any major change, leaders need to invest time and effort in explaining what they are planning to do and what new ways of working will be involved and expected (Kane et al. 2015a; Kiron et al. 2015b). A digital

strategy needs to be clearly communicated to all levels of the organization and all stakeholders. The better leaders can communicate their strategy, the more engaged the staff will be (Kane et al. 2015a,b).

• *Establish a digital business structure.* There is no "right" way to do this, said the group, but there is widespread agreement that however digital initiatives are structured, they need to be composed of cross-functional teams at all levels. Some companies are creating separate digital organizations, sometimes in separate premises, in order to break away from traditional cultures and work practices. Others place it in the marketing organization since many digital initiatives are customer-facing. Still others centralize strategy and decision-making while distributing teams where most appropriate (Kiron et al. 2013a,b; Hirt and Willmott 2014). The most important elements of any structure are an agreed-on strategy, involvement of both business and IT, strong support for new ways of working, and continual evaluation of future directions.

A mature digital strategy will also include:

1. *A digital experience design.* This outlines a long-term vision for the customer experience, including estimates of benefits, customer personas, a customer story map, app features, wireframes of key processes, and detailed user stories.

2. *A digital operating model.* This assesses the options, criteria, and path that will assist selection of the technology required. It includes evaluation of the current architecture and required web services, a list of integrations required, and proposed solution architecture.

3. *A digital platform assessment.* This outlines the timing, effort, and costs required for the organization to deliver multiple releases.

4. *Delivery plans for specific solutions.* These plans should include: creative concepts and designs, developer-ready requirements, prototypes for testing, deployed mobile apps, change and communication plans and support, and assistance in promoting and marketing apps and determining and measuring business value.

Supporting Digital Strategy

A successful digital strategy requires more than "dreaming in Technicolor." The ability to develop, implement, and evolve an effective digital strategy is fostered and supported by a number of new organizational capabilities and components, which in turn will be guided by the evolution of an organization's digital strategy. Focus group members and experts both agree that the success of a particular strategy depends less on the technologies involved and more on the ability to implement them innovatively by rethinking strategy, culture, and talent (Kane et al. 2015a; Kiron et al. 2013a). As one researcher explained, "It's not about acquiring technology, but reconfiguring your business to take advantage of the information new technologies enable.

Digital technologies must be integrated across people, processes, and functions to achieve an important business advantage" (Press 2016a).

The focus group identified eight capabilities and components which, although not digital strategy per se, need to be in place and interacting with digital strategy in order for it to be a success:

1. *A data and analytics strategy.* Data and analytics are essential to digital strategy for two reasons. First, they support informed decision-making, improved customer experience, and process improvement (Wade 2016; Wixom 2016). Second, the data created by digital initiatives enable new opportunities that will guide the evolution of a digital strategy. As we have noted elsewhere, there are four major sets of issues related to data that must be addressed: policy, operations, stewardship, and standards. Each of these will guide the decisions that are made about data and must in turn be informed by a specific strategic approach and focus that is set at a high level in the organization. Like digital strategy, a data and analytics strategy is a journey, not a one-off project, which grows and evolves with the direction of the company. A healthy respect for data and the ability to use it well at all levels of the organization has long been shown to contribute to organization performance (Marchand et al. 2000). However, a data and analytics strategy is essential not only to delivering immediate value to the business, but also to putting the pieces in place that will enable new digital business strategies in the future.

2. *Pervasive relationship management.* Digital technologies are putting pressure on companies to provide a unified global customer experience, which in turn helps them engage with the world no matter where they're located (Hirt and Willmott 2014; Press 2016b). Because of this, companies need to rethink their network of business relationships and how they incorporate partnerships to create value. Furthermore, digital business also increases the interconnections between people, organizations, and devices to enable new products, services, and business models (Blosch and Burton 2016). To take advantage of these new opportunities, companies need to create and reach out to their business ecosystems—organizations, people, and technology platforms—for ideas, information, skills, and delivery assistance.

   There are many different ways companies can connect with their broader community, such as (Blosch and Burton 2016):
   - *Platform ecosystems* that provide a foundational platform for other ecosystem members to develop complementary products and services.
   - *Innovation ecosystems* that access capabilities and talents from outside the organization, often from unexpected fields.
   - *Interest ecosystems* that create interest around a company's products and services and that can also serve as a source of new ideas.
   - *Commercial ecosystems* that are formed by complementary organizations to deliver products and services.

- *Device ecosystems* that connect consumers and organizations. It is essential that a company understand, build, and manage these ecosystems in order to deliver its desired digital future.

3. **Supportive culture.** Digital strategy involves significant business transformation and that means supporting new ways of thinking, working, and leading, said focus group members. Typically, digital strategies require high levels of collaboration across organizational silos and especially between business and IT. Often organizations are risk intolerant and so they shy away from some of the recommended digital implementation activities, such as rapid development and implementation, or experimentation (Kane et al. 2015b). Cultural change is notoriously difficult to achieve in traditional organizational structures and therefore requires significant and focused efforts to incent desired behaviors (Kane et al. 2015a). This starts with leadership, said the focus group. Often the biggest cultural problems arise at the top levels of the organization. Leaders can fail to keep up with new technologies and trends because these lie outside their personal comfort zones. As a result, many employees believe that their leaders don't have the skills and abilities to lead digital change (Kane et al. 2015a) and that few leaders are alert to the threats and opportunities of a changing digital environment (Wade 2016). The focus group stressed that education and clear communication are essential to changing culture. Attention should also be paid to processes and incentives that inhibit collaboration, experimentation, and risk-taking, as well as data sharing and usage. In short, if cultural change is to be realized, people must understand the new corporate strategy, what the new expectations of their behavior will be, and how changes will be rewarded.

4. **New capabilities.** There is widespread agreement that digital capabilities will increasingly determine which companies create value and which ones lose value (Hirt and Willmott 2014). Companies have begun to recognize that they will need a new set of competencies to develop and deliver on a digital agenda. Most of these competencies require an understanding of both business and technology, and the ability to bridge the gaps between the two that often plague organizations. There is no clear agreement about where these skills should reside, only that they are needed. First and foremost, companies need people who can understand and conceptualize how digital technologies can affect current business models (Kane et al. 2015a). These people need to cultivate "hyperawareness" of their industry, business, and technical environment as well as listen for new ideas from employees, partners, customers, and ecosystems (Kiron et al. 2013a; Wade 2016). Second, organizations need to upgrade their HR practices to identify and acquire the new capabilities they will need both internally and externally. "We are not clear about what exactly we will be doing in the future," said a manager, "but we can plan to have the skills available to take advantage of them." Many of the skills organizations will need are "soft" skills rather

than specific knowledge or technical skills. These include: ability to collaborate and share; willingness to experiment and take risks; ability to work in a fast-paced, distributed environment; and ability to be both flexible and disciplined. Third, organizations must increase efforts to cross-pollinate staff skills in order to expand their awareness of context and broaden their skill set (Press 2016a). For example, IT staff could go on sales calls and interact with customers; and business people could go on vendor visits. Developing these new capabilities will be crucial to the success of any digital strategy, concluded the focus group.

5. *Support for experimentation.* Since there is considerable uncertainty about the potential of digital technology to drive all sorts of business transformation, organizations are being urged to develop practices that would enable them to quickly absorb, test, and adopt emerging technologies (Press 2016a). This is a complex challenge that few companies do well. It involves establishing a mechanism to cultivate, evaluate, and integrate innovation (both business and technical) that addresses three key questions: What is desirable for users? What is viable in the marketplace? and What is possible with technology? Furthermore, it requires that IT is competent to explore emerging technologies with an eye to asking, What is their future potential? One of the best ways of accomplishing this is through the design, development, and implementation of experiments or prototypes, which are specifically focused on answering one or all of these questions. Experiments require a radical change in organizational philosophy in order to accept failures, learn from mistakes, and quickly pivot, as well as a radical change in IT practices to deliver rapidly and to be flexible.

6. *Flexible architecture.* Architecture is usually the function in IT that is charged with assessing emerging technologies and providing the infrastructure that will support experiments (Smith and Watson 2015). It has traditionally been responsible for ensuring a stable infrastructure and promoting standardization that can enable improved security, privacy, and integration, while reducing costly maintenance and outages. However, in the digital world many business users, tired of waiting for IT to deliver, simply use their credit cards to buy the software and technology they want, thereby circumventing architectural plans. As well, many new technologies are now delivered through the cloud, apps, sensors, and mobile, which have their own infrastructure and standards. Increased flexibility is required for enterprise architects to anticipate and plan for the larger architectural implications of new technologies (Kiron et al. 2013b) as well as for finding ways to ensure that integration and stability are still a focus (Kane et al. 2015b).

7. *Rapid development and implementation.* IT development work is currently undergoing a sea change to accommodate digital technologies, new ways of exploring their value, and new business and customer expectations, said the

focus group. This is because the ability to develop and implement new products and services on an iterative basis is essential to the success of any digital strategy (Press 2016a,b). Many IT organizations are now using agile development methodologies, which involve developing deliverable pieces of functionality in short intervals and require active business participation. However, as development productivity improved, a new bottleneck—implementation—has emerged. It now appears that operations functions also need to adopt agile processes to facilitate the rapid introduction of iterative products and services and incorporate experiments. Known as DevOps, this new set of practices incorporates operations staff into a development team to ensure the speedy transition of new development output into implementation. Taken together, agile development and DevOps will result in IT organizations that work more productively and flexibly than the IT organizations of the past.

8. *Improved measurement.* Measurement of the impact of the different components of a digital strategy is a challenge (Kiron et al. 2013b). Nevertheless, it is incumbent on business and technical leaders to begin to design measures that will provide them with positive or negative feedback on their digital initiatives as soon as possible, said the focus group. Members stressed that the metrics involved should be business measures for which both business and IT are held accountable, not technical ones. And with digital initiatives, daily or weekly metrics are most important, rather than the more traditional monthly or quarterly measures (Baggi 2014). The group recommended identifying a small number of metrics and then evaluating and evolving them over time. A key starting point for focusing initial efforts is to ask the key "value questions": What value will be delivered? Where will value be delivered? Who will deliver value? When will value be delivered? How will value be delivered?

Taken together, these new practices and components that are required to successfully execute a digital strategy underscore the scope and nature of the transformation that will be involved with a digital strategy, particularly in IT. Clearly, such significant changes will be difficult to accomplish while at the same time continuing to sustain "business as usual"—something akin to changing the engine of an airplane while in midair, said the focus group. Nevertheless, this is precisely what is being asked of today's organizations.

The challenges are immense, the group agreed. "The field is moving so fast, you can't keep up," said one. "It's very hard to get a shared vision of change," said another, "and piecemeal approaches miss the mark." However, others noted that their organizations have capabilities that they're not taking advantage of. "Our biggest problem is that we need skills to integrate what we already have," said a manager. All participants believed that their organizations must be responsive to the new digital world. "We can't stay where we are," said a manager. "We cannot lead or influence if we are focused on traditional business applications and operations and ways of working."

Conclusion

Organizations have suddenly moved from "IT doesn't matter" to an awareness that digital business will likely disrupt every industry (Lopez 2015; Carr 2003). The radical changes required and the uncertainties involved have created a sense of unease in even well-established businesses. There is no doubt that technology will be at the center of whatever happens in a digital strategy. The question is, where will IT be? In the past, IT functions have been guilty of dragging their heels when radical changes are proposed. Today there is a huge opportunity for IT to demonstrate its value to the organization and to become a true business partner in leading and catalyzing the business. IT leaders and staff must rise to the challenge with vision, education, business awareness, and significant internal change.

Chapter Discussion Questions

1. Should a company's digital strategy differ from its business/IT strategy?
2. What types of business value does a digital strategy enable?

References

Baggi, S. "The Revolution will be Digitized." *Journal of Direct, Data, and Digital Marketing Practices* 16, no. 2 (2014): 86–91.

Blosch, M. and B. Burton. "Five Business Ecosystem Strategies Drive Digital Innovation." Gartner Research Report, ID: G00291298, January 12, 2016.

Carr, N. "IT Doesn't Matter." *Harvard Business Review* (May 2003). Digital Strategy Conference Blog. "Defining Digital Strategy: Finding Common Ground." http://www.digitalstrategyconference.com/blog/digitalstrategy/what-is-digital-strategy/, @dstrategycon2015 (accessed July 22, 2016).

Hirt, M. and P. Willmott. "Strategic Principles for Competing in the Digital Age." *McKinsey Quarterly*, May 2014.

Iyengar, P. and L. Mok. "Transform Eight Critical Capabilities to Succeed in a Digital World." Gartner Research Report, ID: G00259971, August 8, 2014.

Kane, G. "How Digital Transformation is Making Health Care Safer, Faster and Cheaper." *Sloan Management Review Digital*, 2015.

Kane, G., D. Palmer, A. N. Phillips, and D. Kiron (a). "Is Your Business Ready for a Digital Future?" *MIT Sloan Management Review* 54, no. 4 (Summer 2015).

Kane, G., D. Palmer, A. N. Phillips, D. Kiron, and N. Buckley (b). "Strategy, Not Technology Drives Digital Transformation." *MIT Sloan Management Review* and *Deloitte University Press*, July 2015.

Kiron, D., D. Palmer, A. N. Phillips, and R. Berkman (a). "Social Business: Shifting Out of First Gear." *MIT Sloan Management Review Research Report 2013*. http://www.sloanreview.mit.edu.

Kiron, D., D. Palmer, A. N. Phillips, and R. Berkman (b). "The Executive's Role in Social Business." *MIT Sloan Management Review* 54, no. 4 (Summer 2013).

Lopez, J., J. Tully, P. Meehan, M. Burkett, and D. Scheibenrif. "Agenda Overview for Digital Business, 2015." Gartner Research Report, ID: G00270684, January 5, 2015.

Marchand, D., W. Kettinger, and J. Rollins. *Information Orientation: The Link to Business Performance*. Toronto: Oxford University Press, 2000.

McGee, K. "Definitional Confusion Slows CIOs' Development of Meaningful Digital Strategies." Gartner Research Report, ID: G00271712, January 29, 2015.

Press, G. (a). "Six Predictions About The Future of Digital Transformation." *Forbes.com*, December 6, 2015.

Press, G. (b). "Six IT Transformation Moves for a Successful Digital Transformation." *Forbes.com*, November 23, 2015.

Shen, S. "How to Develop a Digital Commerce Strategy." Gartner Research Report, ID: G00290525, November 2, 2015.

Smith, H. A., and R. T. Watson. "The Jewel in the Crown: Enterprise Architecture at Chubb." *MIS Quarterly Executive* 14, no. 4 (December 2015).

Wade, M. "The Personalization Paradox." Presentation to the Society for Information Management Advanced Practices Council, May 3–4, 2016.

Willmott, P. "Digital Strategy." Interview. https://www.mckinsey.com/insights/business_technology/digital_strategy, May 2014.

Wixom, B. "Generating Business Value from Data." Presentation to the Society for Information Management Advanced Practices Council, May 3–4, 2016.

CHAPTER 5

Developing a Cloud Strategy

Infrastructure, applications, and data are migrating to the "cloud" with astonishing rapidity. Like many other radical innovations in IT, cloud computing promises to radically reduce prices, increase flexibility, and provide new benefits to users. However, some would suggest that cloud computing's rapid adoption is also outstripping plans to manage it effectively and appropriately. As always happens with emerging types of IT, confusion abounds and best practices are few (Nelson 2014). Because "cloud" can refer to many different elements of this new technology—what it is, how it is deployed, and what it does—confusion is understandable. In addition, since "cloud" is the newest hot topic in IT, many things are also being "cloud-washed"; that is, called "cloud" when they are not (Smith 2014). And it doesn't help when CEOs and senior business executives demand cloud computing and expect it to be a panacea for all their IT woes.

There is no end to the predictions that cloud computing is going to dramatically change IT and how organizations use technology:

> [Cloud computing is] a sea change—a deep and permanent shift in how computing power is generated and consumed. It's as inevitable and irreversible as the shift from steam to electric power in manufacturing.... And just as that transition brought many benefits and opened up new possibilities ... so too will the cloud confer advantage to its adopters. (McAfee 2011)

> Cloud computing is creating a shift in the economics of IT. It will have an evolutionary impact on IT architecture, sourcing, and service delivery and a revolutionary impact on business strategy. (Deloitte 2011)

Although everyone knows what's coming, as with other significant technological changes the challenge for IT leaders with cloud computing will be understanding the change in all its dimensions and learning how and where to utilize it appropriately. Such cloud computing strategies will evolve as our understanding of and trust in these new models of computing grows and as part of companies' overall business and technology strategies. However, there is now enough experience with cloud computing in organizations that IT leaders can begin to manage and deploy cloud technologies in a much more strategic fashion than they have in the past.

Cloud Computing: The Current Reality

Cloud computing is being used in organizations far more than most IT leaders believe (Skyhigh 2015). A 2014 study, based on actual usage data, showed that when both sanctioned and unsanctioned use of cloud services is counted, the average company now uses 897 cloud services, up 43 percent from 2013. Many of these are adopted by employees on their own and include: file sharing, content sharing, social media, collaboration (e.g., Gmail), and development services.

This study found that the average *employee* now uses 27 different cloud services at work including: six collaboration services, four social media applications, and three file-sharing services. The average *company* uses: 45 file-sharing services and 139 collaboration services (e.g., Office 365, Google docs, Skype). It is clear from this diversity that the market for cloud services is still maturing as new players enter the market, existing companies are acquired, and companies invest in new capabilities, and that a single dominant player has yet to emerge in any major category (Skyhigh 2015).

All companies in the focus group recognized that they are using a number of cloud services already and that this number is growing. However, with one exception, none had a formal strategy for how and where cloud computing could and should be used in their organizations. One manager described the typical situation in the focus group companies: "We have no cohesive strategy as yet. It's being addressed by the individual business groups. To date, we have grown organically in this area and been driven by a need for point-in-time solutions. As a result, we have siloed uses of cloud, such as many different versions of Salesforce."

The group recognized that there was a need to tie the acquisition of cloud services to a larger vision or strategy that would provide consistency, address concerns, and ensure the decisions being made about cloud computing are in the best interests of the enterprise. But most companies had not gone beyond articulating the need for a strategy and identifying a few criteria for vendor selection. "We are open to exploring cloud," said a manager, "but we need policy approval for each application because of our concerns about data residency." "We would like to use cloud for development and quality assurance," said another "but will not use it with production data." "We believe the first step is data vaulting and archiving," said a third.

All participants stated that IT is feeling pressure to move to the cloud more quickly than they would like. This comes from many sources:

- **Business.** In many focus group companies, the business, not IT, is the leading driver of cloud adoption. "The business has gone and gotten cloud services on its own, so we are being compelled to develop a cloud strategy," said a manager.

- **Vendors.** Vendors are eliminating their on-premise versions of software and strongly promoting cloud-based versions. "We've run out of options with vendors," said another manager. "We're being pushed to adopt cloud and don't have a choice."
- **Mobility.** Mobile apps are easier to implement with cloud services and run faster with them.
- **Value.** Cloud computing is perceived by many business leaders as being more flexible and easier to implement. As a result, some IT organizations have been told that they must use cloud for new applications. Members of the focus group agreed that there is real value to be achieved in some cloud services. For example, they provide access to considerable functionality: "We couldn't build Salesforce on our own."
- **Cost.** Cloud solutions are perceived to cost much less than in-house solutions. "Our IT managers want to go slowly and steadily," said one "but the cost differentials are keeping the pressure up."

Strategically, companies are beginning to incorporate cloud computing into architecture and technology roadmaps. "Developing a cloud strategy is no longer a choice," said a manager. "With such widespread adoption, we need to address gaps and breakpoints in services," said another. "We want a consistent cloud architecture where we can extend existing services and resolve key gaps while retaining our differentiating capabilities and protecting our data," said a third.

The wide variety of ways cloud computing can be deployed leads to challenges in developing a coherent cloud strategy. These include:

1. **Infrastructure-as-a-service (IaaS).** This gives companies access to the computing power they need on a virtual and dynamic basis. Through IaaS, companies can access the servers, storage, and networking functionality they need on an as-needed basis.

2. **Platform-as-a-service (PaaS).** These cloud computing services provide a platform allowing customers to develop, run, and manage Web applications without the complexity of building and maintaining the infrastructure typically associated with them (Wikipedia 2015). It also provides operations management specialists with a range of services, such as spam filtering and software that can be used to develop private cloud services.

3. **Software-as-a-service (SaaS).** SaaS provides shared software functionality through the cloud. It is browser-based and runs in a logical and virtual environment that is automatically upgraded and maintained. Because SaaS applications are based on standardized, consistent code, they can be very economical and easy to implement, enabling companies to obtain access to software quickly, pay only for the services that are used, and to scale up or down as needed.

4. **Business-process-as-a-service (BaaS).** Some providers offer specific business processes through the cloud. Examples of these include: employee benefits management, procurement, business travel, and industry-specific processes.

In addition, organizations that are concerned about the risks of public cloud sharing can create a private cloud that enables IT capabilities to be delivered internally "as a service" over an intranet and behind their firewall.

Developing a Cloud Strategy

Organizations are adopting cloud services and creating cloud architectures but are often late in building cloud strategies. Too often these strategies are developed by architecture groups or infrastructure leaders alone, without business input (Bittman 2014). The problem with this approach is that cloud does not have a single value proposition. As shown above, cloud computing may be adopted in organizations in many different ways and for many different reasons, so any cloud computing strategy must clarify which are appropriate and which are not. Furthermore, the underlying reason for adopting any type of cloud computing must be how and why it addresses business goals and what business value can be achieved by using it. "We can't look at cloud strategy on its own," said a manager. "We must look at what the business needs and whether it can or should be delivered by the cloud." An effective strategy means beginning with business goals and mapping potential benefits (Smith 2014).

One of the worst ways to implement any type of cloud computing is to send a process or a service that is an internal mess to the cloud. "Right now, companies don't even know what problems they are trying to solve. Their first approach is usually to replicate in the cloud what they currently have in order to save money. But cloud computing also offers the opportunity to rethink how we do business," said a manager. It is therefore important to work both with business users and internal IT stakeholders to better understand their needs and then explore cloud computing options to see what is possible.

Following this understanding, "a strategy for the use of cloud should have clear goals and objectives; establish a repeatable approach for identifying and assessing actionable opportunities and cloud readiness; and create a standardized framework for cloud transition planning, a cloud target architecture, and a transition roadmap," said a manager. Although only one member of the focus group had such a comprehensive strategy for using cloud, most were beginning to establish a framework for where and how they will adopt it, at least initially, using one of several starting points:

1. *Cloud for infrastructure.* "We are using cloud to extend our capabilities," said a manager. "In our analysis, infrastructure is becoming highly commoditized and so we are using it for flexibility and load balancing of our computing capabilities." "This is inevitable," said another. "No one cares where commodity services come from."

2. *Cloud for development support.* "We are using cloud for our development groups and for quality assurance," said a manager. "This enables us to scale up and down more flexibly for these purposes."

3. ***Cloud for usage management.*** "We have a seasonal business," said one manager. "Cloud enables us to better manage spikes or bursts of usage."

4. ***Cloud for data storage.*** "We have huge amounts of data. Using cloud as a data vault for archival data helps us contain our data center footprint and costs."

5. ***Cloud for business innovation.*** The "rental model" of cloud software makes it relatively easy to quickly implement stand-alone solutions for exploring new business opportunities, and many business functions in the focus group's companies had done just this—with or without IT's approval.

6. ***Cloud for integration.*** "We prefer to buy into cloud ecosystems or platforms, rather than use cloud as a point solution. This enables us to expand our digital offering much more quickly, as all software is integrated and works together," said a manager.

7. ***Cloud for expertise.*** "We're new at this," said a manager. "Cloud solutions give us access to many new technologies and applications and the necessary resources and expertise on an as-needed basis, at least while we're learning."

8. ***Cloud for cost saving.*** Although this is not the primary reason mentioned by the focus group, cost is a consideration for everyone—to contain costs, reduce costs, or smooth out the cost of new development.

Cloud Computing Challenges

In spite of its potential, the risks and challenges of cloud computing loom large for the group's managers and must be assessed and mitigated in any cloud strategy (Proctor et al. 2015). There are two broad categories of risk:

1. ***External risks.*** These relate almost entirely to the vendor selection and management process and are linked to the reduced control IT leaders have when turning over large chunks of data and functionality to another company. Several external risks were identified by the focus group:

   Data risk. Many companies are required to ensure that data is physically resident in a particular geographic region or country. This is particularly true of regulated industries and government organizations, but is of concern to most companies because they perceive they would lose credibility with their customers if personal data were exposed or used in another country. Moreover, some companies simply do not want some types of data or intellectual property to reside in the cloud.

   Compliance and regulatory risk. Some organizations may have further restrictions due to legal (e.g., privacy) or contractual requirements, so moving to the cloud involves assessing such matters and determining where some cloud computing could be inhibited. Focus group members added that cloud vendor contracts must accommodate the same restrictions as those that apply to their companies, and vendors must also enforce the restrictions with any third parties with which they sub-contract.

Lack of agility. "Cloud salespeople tend to promise a great deal more than their service can actually deliver," said a manager. Every vendor therefore needs to be assessed on its ability to actually deliver the features, functions, and levels of service that are needed to meet business needs. Network latency can be problematic, as can availability. "'High availability' can mean different things," said another manager. "It can be 99.5 percent in each service but in a multi-cloud environment, taken together, availability can be significantly lower."

Supplier risk. Cloud computing is still maturing as an industry and many service providers are financially fragile. As a result, business failures have occurred on short notice, causing serious problems (Proctor et al. 2015; Smith David and Lee 2011).

Security breaches. These are by far the biggest concern of most business and IT managers (Nelson 2014). The good news is that cloud service providers have listened to their customers and are investing heavily in security and certifications (see box). However, the bad news is that many of the most popular services (e.g., Paypal and Gmail) still store sensitive, personally identifiable information as unencrypted data. And in 2014 more software vulnerabilities were discovered and more data breaches occurred than in any previous year. The same study found that 92 percent of companies have users with compromised identities. As these statistics show, IT leaders need to recognize that security breaches will happen with cloud services and plan what to do when they happen.

Cloud Security Statistics*

In 2014, 1,459 services (17 percent) provided multi-factor authentication (705 in 2013); 533 (5 percent) were ISO 270001 certified (188 in 2013); and 1,082 encrypted data (11 percent) compared with 470 in 2013.

* www.skyhigh.com

2. *Internal risks.* Although the external risks of using cloud are better known, companies are learning that there are also significant internal risks that arise with cloud computing. Several were discussed in the focus group:

Increased cost. Although perceived to be cost efficient due to a lower cost of entry, cloud services may actually be more expensive from the perspective of total cost of ownership. The risk is higher future charges. Coupling less-than-transparent cost structures with the ease of ramping up cloud usage leads to false economies. Several companies in the focus group noted that ramping down or turning off these services is not so easy, and additional costs may be hidden (e.g., compliance regulations, backup, restore, disaster recovery, and problem solving). "There's a perception that software-as-a-service is cheap, but it can be a money pit," said one manager.

Lack of cloud readiness. Focus group members agreed that some workflows and processes are more cloud-ready than others. "Cloud works for the machine processes but not the people," said one manager. "To use cloud effectively, we must develop industry standard integration and a candidacy pipeline management process internally," said another. As a result, one company was developing a set of cloud readiness principles.

IT governance. Cloud computing is essentially a powerful platform operating across the enterprise incorporating both IT and business units. This new layer of IT adds to IT governance. To incorporate adopting cloud computing platforms and services, organizations will need to redefine their existing processes and standards and add different types of expertise to these processes (such as legal). At present, none of the companies in the focus group had changed their governance processes to accommodate cloud, although they were each addressing individual elements.

Loss of control. Although cloud may be cheaper, the cost of losing control for some parts of a business is too high. With cloud service providers dictating the pace of technical innovation, an under-investment in new technology denies client flexibility while an over-investment leaves organizations dealing with more upgrades than they'd like, and often at a time they don't like. Moreover, cloud computing does not provide the ability to customize software, so for core competencies especially, this can be a significant drawback to using cloud. Finally, it is often difficult and expensive to move data between vendors, resulting in locking a company into one provider.

Third-party applications. As cloud "ecosystems" become larger, they are adding other related services to their offerings. However, it is not widely known that these can be of two types: native applications that are certified by the ecosystem vendor; and composite applications, which are integrated into the ecosystem but not guaranteed by the vendor, creating a hidden, but significant, security risk.

Integration challenges. The focus group noted that integration with equipment hosted in other data centers is still difficult to achieve. Peripherals such as printers and local security IT equipment (e.g., access systems) can be difficult to integrate, as well as USB devices, smart phones, groupware, and email systems. In addition, existing systems may need to be redesigned to be compatible with a cloud environment. This may involve additional expenditure, which business users may be unwilling to incur. "One shouldn't underestimate what it takes to integrate your internal systems to work with a cloud solution," said a manager. "It's a lot more complex than we thought." "Most of us underestimated the exponential complexity of cloud platforms," said another.

Adjustments in IT practices. IT organizations will need to adjust architecture and design principles and practices for new and current systems to incorporate the advantages of cloud technology. Maintenance models and IT costing models will also need to be reassessed. Participants pointed out that it is not widely recognized that changing from traditional software to cloud computing can involve significant investment. Thus an organization which has invested significantly in its own storage and security systems may have a difficult time justifying the decision to migrate to a cloud environment.

Changes in IT knowledge and skills. New IT skills and knowledge will be needed to use cloud computing effectively, such as implementing and managing cloud service contracts. Moreover, since all knowledge about how the cloud works (e.g., hardware, software, virtualization, and deployment) is concentrated at the cloud service provider, it will be important to determine what technical, hardware, and software skills will need to be developed and retained in-house.

Cloud Vendor Selection and Management

Migrating services to the cloud is a big move for an organization, and selecting one or more appropriate cloud vendors is critical to its success. The cloud computing market is still evolving rapidly, so there is a great deal of confusion in the market. Every cloud vendor has its own set of pricing, billing, flexibility, support, contracting practices, and other important parameters in their service model. Focus group members noted that companies need new criteria for selecting and managing vendors to ensure that the risks they've identified are properly mitigated and they get the services they expect.

"In many ways, vendor selection is the same process as outsourcing," one manager noted, "but there are some subtleties that make it more challenging." The group identified a three-phase process to use when looking for a cloud computing vendor:

1. ***Maintain a competitive environment*** by exploring a variety of options. Focus group members noted that because cloud solutions are inexpensive and easy to install, more than one alternative can be implemented as prototypes so that an organization can actually try them out before committing to them. One company has a deliberate strategy of creating vendor tension by using more than one vendor for its infrastructure cloud services. "We use a variety of vendors for these commodity services," the manager said. "We don't want to get locked in." Vendors should be compared on the basis of several parameters, such as their technology stack, alignment with requirements, and security and compliance. (Appendix A provides a more thorough set of comparative criteria.)

Vendor lock-in and loss of data are two important criteria to discuss with vendors at this stage. It is often difficult to move data between vendors or to recover it easily in the event that a vendor goes out of business. "We believe ease of integration with a company's technology plus vendor support should be major selection criteria," said a manager. "In the past, when companies have used cloud services on a stand-alone basis, this wasn't a concern, but now that cloud is moving more into mainstream IT, it is becoming increasingly critical." As with other forms of purchased technology, companies must consider whether buying "best of breed" technology is more desirable than buying into an integrated suite of technologies. Both have their merits and their disadvantages. Understanding these can help a company make an effective choice.

2. ***Prepare*** by developing skill levels, establishing a process for deciding, and determining needs and exact requirements. Following this, companies must prepare for contract negotiations, assemble a negotiating team, determine a negotiation strategy, and acquire vendor knowledge. "Don't underestimate the importance of being prepared," said a manager. "We need better governance, improved legal expertise, and contract negotiation skills, as well as business and IT education about what's involved." Clarity about the costs involved is particularly important to ensure that proper comparisons between internal services and various cloud offerings are made appropriately.

   It is also essential to understand the data issues involved, not only data security and residency, but also what data are being used and created by the proposed service. Many companies have strict policies about the type of data they will allow to leave their organization, so data classification practices are a must for software-as-a-service and process-as-a-service offerings. Finally, the benefits the company expects should be articulated, including cost savings, new functionality, and flexibility.

3. ***Insist on negotiation*** with potential vendors. This can be an extremely difficult process. "Most cloud service providers are not interested in negotiating," said the managers. "The contracts they offer are usually very inflexible." Nevertheless, most experts recommend persisting in negotiations. Cloud computing contract terms should clearly define each party's rights and responsibilities in order to facilitate a more effective relationship between the institution and the service provider. An institution's leverage is typically strongest prior to signing the initial contract and making the initial payment, so it is important to codify in advance the terms under which the institution can continue using the service, as well as those under which it can change or terminate the service.

   One of the challenges of structuring cloud computing contracts is designing clear service level agreements (SLAs). Negotiating teams need to understand how to evaluate performance in a cloud environment. Some measures include: cost, reliability, agility, and business owner satisfaction. Procedures must be developed to collect and aggregate these data, evaluate them against

SLA expectations, and distribute results to the business (Smith David and Lee 2011). Because there are typically so many players involved, it is often hard to determine who should be responsible for delivering a particular SLA. "If you make one party responsible, make sure that they can deliver what you are asking and that they have control over the other parties involved. Most people don't know how to do this, and lawyers often don't understand the nature of this business," one manager noted.

Standard cloud SLAs offered by a provider are often complex and difficult to understand. Some of the key issues a customer should clarify with a provider are:

- *Outages and uptime.* Many businesses do not need extremely high levels of uptime even though these are often specified in SLAs. High uptimes are only achievable if network, storage, and computer designs have significant redundancy. These are not cheap so if SLA requirements are set too high, they will increase the price of cloud services.

- *Backup and recovery services.* Customers with virtual machines in the cloud rarely have access to their own backup processes. Instead, they have to rely on the backup processes of the provider. This potentially means that they could be in a queue behind other customers waiting for backup to be completed. Contracts may also stipulate that if data loss occurs, the customer will have to pay to get data back within a certain amount of time. In addition, companies should explore the granularity of a provider's disaster recovery. Cloud providers may bring back the data, but it may not be consistent or have the needed level of granularity to replicate what was lost.

- *Price caps.* Because vendors attract clients with lower initial buy-in costs, to protect future interests it is essential that a contract specify the cost of continuing to use the service after the initial purchase period and volume. Also, before signing a contract, costs for any expansion of the initial volume or usage should be negotiated so that they are equal to or less than the cost per unit of the initial purchase.

- *Functionality.* An often-overlooked clause is a description of the functionality of the services being acquired. Many contracts simply state a product's name without clarifying what it does. The constantly evolving nature of cloud computing services, however, means that a cloud service provider could update its underlying infrastructure at any time, including adding or deleting functionality. A deleted function could be one that a company depends on, so a cloud computing contract should include a clause requiring the vendor to provide notice prior to discontinuing a feature or functionality of its service.

- *Vendor management.* After contracting for a cloud service, an organization should manage the contract, seek to optimize vendor performance, control difficult vendors, and direct the long-term relationship. "We need a different type of vendor management," said one focus group participant. "We need to adapt our practices and find a balance between our different vendors that works. Furthermore, we need to manage the business's relationship with vendors. Most in our business don't understand the SLAs we need to contract for, and the vendors are not going to tell them." Because cloud computing is still maturing, management should monitor the marketplace and a company's cloud vendors' financial health regularly to ensure that changes, such as buyouts, partnerships, and acquisitions, are not putting the company at risk.

Recommendations for Managers

The focus group is still learning how best to implement cloud but they have already gained much practical wisdom from their companies' initial forays. They offered the following recommendations for other IT managers:

- *Define what you need up front.* First and foremost, a cloud computing strategy should address a business need, and any cloud solution should not contravene company policies or regulations.
- *Educate your business.* Since many areas of the business are involved in purchasing and using cloud services, it is important to educate all parties about some of the issues associated with adopting them. At minimum, guidelines for reviewing vendors and ensuring that effort is not duplicated need to be developed. These are especially important if a company doesn't have a well-developed cloud computing strategy that would prevent non-compliant purchases.
- *Look for certified vendors.* Any potential vendors should be expected to: use internationally certified practices (such as ISO 27001 and ISO 27017—see box), enable audits of the cloud provider, offer data encryption both in transit and at rest, and address your business compliance needs.
- *Classify your data.* "For certain data, cloud computing would be unthinkable," a manager stated. Managers must understand the sensitivity of each data item that is potentially to be stored or created in the cloud.
- *Prototype.* This is a relatively inexpensive and easy way to test a variety of offerings and vendors.
- *Test backup and data recovery.* It is essential to ensure that vendor promises in this area will be delivered in the event of a disaster or a vendor going out of business.
- *Establish the criteria for "yes."* In spite of the many IT concerns related to cloud computing, all managers in the focus group recognized that it is a very significant new form of computing that is here to stay. IT cannot hold back the inevitable or become the "police" of the organization. It is far better to establish the criteria for saying "yes" to cloud computing rather than constantly saying "no."

Conclusion

There is no question that cloud computing is a dramatically new way to deliver IT services to a company. Today's IT managers recognize and accept its potential to both change existing cost structures and enable new business products and services that

ISO 27001 and 27017*

ISO27001 specifies an information security management system (ISMS); that is, a systematic approach to managing sensitive company information so that it remains secure. It includes people, processes, and IT systems by applying a risk management process.

ISO27017 (in draft form) provides guidance on the information security elements of cloud computing, recommending and assisting with the implementation of cloud-specific information security controls.

* http://en.wikipedia.org/wiki/ISO/IEC_27001:2013; http://www.iso.org/iso/home/standards/management-standards/iso27001.htm; http://www.iso27001security.com/html/27017.html

haven't previously been possible. However, at the same time, they are leery of the hype surrounding cloud computing, and mindful of its costs and risks as well as its opportunities. The key to the effective use of cloud computing is to carefully select where and how to use the cloud. This involves adopting internal decision-making practices to incorporate cloud services as potential options and using a rigorous assessment process to determine the appropriateness of a cloud solution and its potential benefits. Once this key decision has been made, companies should carefully evaluate cloud service providers from several perspectives and then actively manage the creation and implementation of cloud service contracts. This will require the development of new skills and knowledge within IT, as well as actively engaging existing IT and business stakeholders in all parts of the development and implementation of an effective cloud strategy.

Chapter Discussion Questions

1. In what ways does a cloud strategy change the skills IT needs?
2. What types of applications might a company choose *not* to move to the cloud?

References

Bittman, T. "The Three Rationales Behind Cloud Computing Strategies." Gartner Research Report, ID: G00270141, October 10, 2014.

Deloitte Consulting. "Tech Trends 2011: The Natural Convergence of Business and IT." Technology Trends Discussion A4, May 17, 2011.

Nelson, J. "Businesses Can Get Ahead in the Cloud." *The Globe and Mail*, October 29, 2014.

McAfee, A. "What Every CEO Needs to Know About the Cloud." *Harvard Business Review*, November 30, 2011.

Mell, P., and T. Grance. "The NIST Definition of Cloud Computing." NIST Special Publication 80-145, September 2011.

Proctor, P., D. Plummer, and J. Heiser. "A Public Cloud Risk Model: Accepting Cloud Risk is OK, Ignoring Cloud Risk is Tragic." Gartner Research Report, ID: G00261246, January 6, 2015.

Skyhigh Networks. "Cloud Adoption and Risk Report Q4 2014." https://www.sky-highnetworks.com/ (accessed 2015).

Smith David, J., and M. Lee. "SAAS and Integration: An Update." Presentation to the Society for Information Management Advanced Practices Council, Mount Laurel, NJ, January 18–19, 2011.

Smith, D. "Technology Building Blocks for a Successful Cloud Deployment." Gartner Research Note, ID: G00269969, October 16, 2014.

Wikipedia. "Platform as a Service." *Wikipedia*, http://en.wikipedia.org/wiki/Platform_as_a_service (accessed March 6, 2015).

APPENDIX A
An Evaluation Framework for Cloud Services Providers

1. Meets your current requirements and future roadmap
   - Does the vendor provide a range of cloud-hosting capabilities to meet your requirements today and in the future?
   - What cloud types are supported (public, private, hybrid, all)?
   - Does it have a broad range of options that fit your requirements, e.g., operating and hardware?
   - Does it offer Identity and Authorization Management (IAM) to allow secure and controlled access to services and resources with existing corporate identities?
   - What ability does it have to scale quickly and cost effectively—both up and down?
   - What service tools are available (ease of use, number and quality)?
   - Does the customer get complete control and ownership of provisioned resources (e.g., transparent privacy policy, security, updates)?
   - Does it allow use of an enterprise SW license, if desired?
   - What languages are supported?
   - What data bases are supported?
   - Are there data limitations?

2. Already serving enterprises like yours
   - Does the vendor have related work experience, i.e., is it deployed in a wide range of industries?
   - Is the vendor already serving customers like us?

3. Strong technology stack
   - What ecosystems and partnerships exist or are likely to develop in the future?

- Does it use the technology stack most likely to win in the marketplace?
- Does it support the latest versions of a wide range of operating systems and databases?

4. Security and compliance
   - What information security and IT compliance features does it offer?
   - Do data security methodologies integrate with existing security and identity management technologies?
   - What encryption and virus protection standards are used?
   - How are infrastructure monitoring, fault detection, and notification handled?
   - Where would data be stored?
   - How is our data backed up and by whom?
   - Who has access to our data?
   - How can our auditors observe compliance?

5. Meeting your service-level agreements (SLAs)
   - Availability: What are the vendors' availability levels?
   - Disaster recovery: Does the solution deploy and manage antivirus, spam, backup, and disaster recovery?
   - Does it support disaster recovery architectures and multiple data centers?
   - Performance: Are performance metrics acceptable, e.g., latency, throughput, downtime, and load balancing?
   - Backup: Does it have redundant storage in multiple physical locations in the same availability zone?
   - Maintenance: Are upgrades applied transparently with visible schedules?
   - Patriot Act: Is the company bound by the U.S. Patriot Act?
   - Lock-in: How can we recover our data if we choose not to renew our contract or if vendor goes out of business?

6. Responsiveness
   - Does the vendor provide 24/7 customer support and operations (call center)?
   - Does it have a global presence—worldwide data center locations?
   - What is the vendor's engagement model (e.g., dedicated team, escalation, QBRs, highly flexible)?

7. Change management process
   - Are migration strategy and planning support available?

8. Reporting and monitoring
   - What reporting and monitoring capabilities are available?

9. Pricing
   - What pricing options are available (e.g., prepaid options, special payment services)?

Global Logistics and the Maritime Transport Ecosystem

Carlos Fernandez, COO of Global Logistics (GL), punched a button on his phone to summon his secretary, Alice. "Get me that new guy we just hired, what's his name?" "Murray Johnson," she supplied. "Yes, get him here asap!"

Five minutes later Murray Johnson rushed in, hastily tightening his tie and running his fingers through his rumpled hair. "Have a seat," Carlos invited him. "How are you getting on at GL? What do you think of our little operation?" The "little operation" was in fact a global freight forwarding company responsible for handling the supply chain logistics of hundreds of major companies who shipped everything from the smallest widgets to large, heavy construction machines and materials everywhere in the world.

After a few minutes of chat, he got down to business. "Murray, I understand you're a smart guy—with a PhD in informatics no less." Murray inclined his head modestly. "I have an important job for you." Murray looked up with interest. "Here's the problem we have …." Carlos quickly sketched out how difficult it was to get information about their customers' overseas cargo shipments—whether coming from China or going to Europe or North America.

"Our job is to integrate the whole process of shipping for our customers," he explained in his soft Spanish accent. "We need to track every detail from pick-up to delivery. We need cargo information, land transport information, port and terminal information, and ship information, and then port and terminal information, land transport information and cargo information on the other end of the shipment. We need to crunch this information for *every* shipment and then add in business information to calculate our bill. It's challenging because there are so many steps, types of information, and systems involved, particularly in the maritime transport portion.

"We want to provide our customers with end-to-end service but, with overseas shipping, it's currently impossible to track their shipments and they're getting increasing frustrated. I've had four irate customer calls this month asking why they can't simply track their overseas shipments like they do with FedEx. This could be a real business opportunity for us. We need a fresh perspective so see what you can come up with. I'll introduce you to Reggie who can give you an overview of how thing work."

Reggie Finch, one of GL's shipping agents, grinned when he heard what Carlos wanted Murray to do. "The first thing I have to do when someone has a cargo to ship is to understand the cargo and how it is to be transported. We usually start about six months in advance to determine the nature and dimensions of the cargo, where it's going, and what our options are for transportation. Although we can often choose between rail and truck for land transportation, shipping is usually the only choice for intercontinental travel for larger cargos. I call around to see what's available and then, depending on the nature of the cargo, where it's going, and how fast it has to get there, we will charter a ship or a place on a container ship. This means negotiating a contract with the ship owner or charterer that will cover all aspects of the voyage from where, when, and how the cargo will be picked up to where, when, and how it will be delivered and everything in between."

"Then we negotiate with the shipper, the receiver, and the transporters to set the terms of the shipment and get agreement on the costs involved...." Murray's eyes and mind wandered to the panoramic view out the windows of the office to the port spread out almost as far as he could see. To his far right were the tall multi-storied Ro-Ro ships with their rows and rows of cars. Just beneath him was the container terminal with fields of full and empty containers, train tracks leading into it, and lines of trucks entering and departing—some with containers and some without. Giant automated cranes busily moved up and down the rows, selecting and loading containers according to a predetermined loading plan. To his left, a few general cargo ships were at berth and to his far left was the oil terminal where giant tankers glided into pumping stations.

"It's my job to keep track of every piece of data related to a shipment so we can calculate the costs involved," continued Reggie. "That also includes any customs charges, penalties levied, and fairway dues for going through narrow straits. And that's just the business information that relates to the cost of transporting the cargo that we pick up, carry, and deliver. There's a lot more!"

Reggie went to the white board and quickly sketched some slightly intersecting ovals. "The stuff I've just told you about is the information we need for business and financial purposes. That's how we figure out what to charge our customers and what to pay to the various entities that transport their cargo, or process it, or allow it to move through their territory ... whatever. It's the beginning and the end of the transportation chain."

Reggie continued, "As you can see, some of this data intersects with what's used in other parts of maritime transport so it's important to be clear about what *information* you need because the data exists in various systems and databases. It would be great if it were all in one place but it's not. And much of this information is paper- or email-based, which means that it's not easy to look up with a computer."

"Let's look at a supply chain that most people know about." Reggie went on to explain that when shipping a parcel by courier, each package is assigned a bar code making tracking relatively straightforward because the code can be scanned at all way points—when it reaches a sorting station, when it reaches its regional destination, when it is loaded on the truck for delivery, and finally when it is delivered. This allows customers to track their package along its route.

"We do something similar for containers and other bulk shipments when they go by land," Reggie said. "Each one gets a bar code we can scan at different points of its journey … pickup at the factory, delivery to the terminal, loading on the ship, unloading from the ship, pickup from the terminal, and delivery to the buyer. But once it is on the ship, we can't track the shipment itself, we have to track the ship."

"So, what's the problem? Can't you track the ship?" asked Murray.

"Let me show you, rather than tell you," Reggie replied. They went down some back stairs, through a security gate, and up the gangway of a medium-sized cargo ship, the *Eleni*. The mate recognized Reggie and walked them to a small office adjacent to the bridge. Captain Anders Haraldson was at his computer surrounded by stacks of paper. Reggie introduced Murray. "Murray's on a mission to find out how he can get information about GL's shipments. I thought you might be a good person to explain how you use information on a ship and what information you provide to others. Could I leave him here with you for an hour?

Captain Haraldson grabbed a pile of papers from the office's sole visitor's chair and invited Murray to sit. "You've taken on a big job," he commented. "Nothing in this business is streamlined or designed for sharing, and your information need, while important, is not the only factor I have to balance when doing my job. As captain, safety of the ship, crew, and cargo is of paramount concern. And it's foundational to almost every aspect of the maritime transport ecosystem. No one wants to see lives lost, pollution, collisions, groundings, and cargo destroyed."

"So, I plan my route with safety in mind, as well as getting to my next port as quickly and efficiently as possible. I consult navigational charts, both online and paper, and meteorological data—weather, tides, icebergs—from a variety of sources: online from our subscription services, from regional radio broadcasts that give me coastal warnings, and from VTS (Vessel Traffic Service) in busy areas. Then I plan my route and update it as the voyage progresses. This works reasonably well for me but because my route data isn't shared with anyone, it can't be accessed by other ships, our next port, the cargo owner, not even the ship's owner. It's an informational dead end."

"So if no one knows your route, how do they know where you are or when you plan to get to port?" asked Murray.

"There are several ways," Anders explained. "First, all medium-large ships have an Automated Identification System or AIS, that contains the ship's ID number, destination, and expected time of arrival (ETA), as well as other information about it. You can use this to see all the other ships in your immediate vicinity." He turned to his computer and in a few clicks found the *Eleni* and a map of all the other ships in port at this time.

"So, what's wrong with AIS?" Murray wondered.

"It's good as far as it goes," replied Anders. "A lot of us use it to identify and contact other ships and VTS uses it to monitor ships in their coastal waters. In fact, anyone can log in and monitor how ships are moving around. But it's another informational dead end. The data is collected and put in a database somewhere, but it doesn't connect to anything else. So I can see it if I want or VTS can, but to track your cargo, you have to know what ship it's on and go looking for it. It doesn't update some real-time tracking system somewhere. And while it gives a destination port, it doesn't show the route the ship has planned, so I still pretty much have to rely on calling the ships around us to find out whether we're going to cross paths. It's not like Air Traffic Control where everyone files a flight plan and then controllers approve and monitor all the traffic. Here, you're pretty much on your own, at least until you get to a congested fairway or a port."

"If AIS is a dead end, how do I get your data to track our customer's cargo?" asked Murray frowning.

"Don't laugh," said Anders, "but every day at noon, I send a report to the ship's owners. It acts as an official history of the voyage and helps us determine what supplies we need at port. I'm also in communication with our agent at the next port—at least 72 hours out—and he in turn informs charterers, the cargo owners, the port authority, and various other agencies about my ETA. I'm not sure who they all are, but Reggie can fill you in. So if you're tracking cargo on my ship, you could always watch for my emails!"

"Well, that's not a very efficient way to do it!" said Murray. "With our numerous cargos, it would be an incredibly time-consuming job!"

"It's even worse than that," said Reggie, who had just popped back into the office. "Every port and state has a myriad of different forms and systems. Although there are common laws and regulations set by the International Maritime Organization, each country interprets and applies them differently. The result is a situation where every port and state has set up systems, data, and procedures in a way that works for *them* but it doesn't work for the captain or for the transport system as a whole. There are so many stakeholders with their own systems, they don't see the forest for the trees! We are basically drowning in paperwork and data and have no information!"

Haraldson continued, "We need to get everyone together to look at the maritime transport ecosystem as a whole and see where efficiencies in paperwork and data sharing could benefit everyone. The way I see it is that much of the same data is replicated over and over—to ports, agents, terminals, freight forwarders, VTS, owners and port services. It's not just the captains who would benefit from this type of sharing; everyone would!"

Murray was thoughtful as he walked back to Reggie's office with him. "So there's no one who has an overview of the whole process from end-to-end!" he muttered. "And nothing talks to anything else, though most of the data is the same."

"That's pretty much right," agreed Reggie. "If we had that overview and everyone could access the data they needed just-in-time, the way they do with land transport, there would be a lot better collaboration between everyone. Today, if a vessel is late or early, service providers and freight forwarders will only know that if the captain or the agent tells them."

"The way I understand it is that cargo shippers and planners, port authorities, ship captains and owners, and other shore-based services like berths, tugs, and pilots, all need a similar understanding of the status of the voyage with slightly different information," said Murray. "But even though the data is out there, it's not getting out to the right people in the right format. There are so many information dead ends and we're creating the same data over and over."

"That's true, but it's also worse than that because any confusion can cause delays and loss of revenue," said Reggie. "For example, at this port, when a ship sends me an ETA, I send the vessel's information to the Maritime Authority and the State Authority and to the Directorate of Merchant Shipping. Then I have to report it to the Port Authority and the port will assign a berth and send me a berthing authorization, with a copy to the State Authority. The Port Authority also sends the information to Customs. Every time a document is sent, its receipt has to be acknowledged. So everything Captain Haraldson sends me, I have to send off to the proper authority and get a receipt. I do the same with port services, such as pilotage, tugs, waste removal, electricity, water supply, and any other services they need. The berth authorization is given to the pilots, who then contact the captain by radio. VTS and the coast guard are also in touch regarding weather conditions, traffic, and vessel coordination because there are some conditions under which we won't let certain ships into our harbor. And now with increased security concerns, there's a whole new set of document exchanges! If there's a slip-up, there can be a domino effect of misunderstandings that cost time and money. Plus, because every country—even every port—does things a little differently, we don't have the option of developing systems with straightforward flow-through processes. And no one wants to change how they're collecting data to create more useful information for other stakeholders in the ecosystem."

When they reached his office, Reggie pulled out the diagram he'd drawn of the different sets of data involved in transporting GL's cargo across the ocean. "I think we've covered it all," he said. "Financial and business information needs, navigational and nautical information, ship information, port information, state and regulatory information, and cargo information. These are mostly separate worlds that intersect only minimally and with a lot of manual processes, but for your purposes, you need some data from each of these areas, and so do a lot of others working in maritime transport—port services, VTS, other ships, and terminals—just to name a few."

"The problem is," Reggie continued, "that shipping has evolved over hundreds of years without coordination. Air transport started off being coordinated less than a century ago. And in land transport, the coordinated systems have also evolved with the industry. Both air and land use technology in a much more integrated and standard fashion than maritime transport."

"So is *nothing* being done to improve this situation?" Murray asked. "It's hard to believe that smart people aren't trying to do something about this."

Reggie scratched his head. "Well, the EU is trying to help. I know we'll soon be able to file some documents electronically. The problem is it takes years to implement these types of things. Even then compliance can be spotty, especially in some countries and some smaller ports. And that's just to do with after-the-fact reporting. It doesn't address some of the real-time information you and others are looking for. I know that some of the major shipping companies and cruise lines are fed up with the slow pace of change and are trying to do something. Those guys have much better systems than the small and medium operators, but they're just looking at their own needs and not the needs of the whole ecosystem. Imagine if British Airways optimized its own flights and didn't worry about anything else in the air!"

Murray thanked Reggie for his help and headed back to his cubicle. There *had* to be a way to get better data sharing across the different parts of the maritime transport ecosystem without forcing everyone to buy and install an expensive system that would force them all to work in the same way (something he now realized would be impossible, given all the entities involved). With all the new technology out there, surely there would be a way to utilize what ships and ports and freight forwarders were *already* producing without adding *further* administrative burdens on them. In fact, there should be a way to make this burden *less* onerous. He thought about his PhD thesis in energy informatics, where he had installed sensors that passively collected energy usage from thousands of homes and then informed each study participant about their patterns of consumption and compared it with their (anonymized) neighbors. Was there a similar model that could be used here?

Looking back at Reggie's diagram, Murray realized that his challenge boiled down to connecting the circles on the diagram. What if there was a service that could access AIS and other ship data, cargo data, and route data and then provide it securely in the format needed when requested by an authorized user? What if captains and freight forwarders and port services could obtain this information in real time to make decisions? What if port services and agents could be dynamically informed of the progress of every ship headed into and out of their ports to improve traffic flow and services planning and coordination? What if each state and each port could also get the information they needed, in the format they needed, when they needed it? The data was already there. All it would take would be some standard data sharing and access protocols (much like AIS already provides) and agreement that it could be shared as needed.

"That's it!" he thought excitedly. "It could work! I know it! I can't wait to tell Carlos about this. It's a great business opportunity for us! It could be a win-win-win for everyone in maritime transport."

Discussion Questions

1. Identify all the stakeholders in this ecosystem and their individual goals.
2. Describe the business opportunity you think Murray sees. What other opportunities are there for the non-business stakeholders?
3. Propose a potential solution to the problems in this ecosystem. In your proposal, be sure to address the following questions:
   - What would motivate the stakeholders to adopt your solution?
   - Who would cover the costs of your solution?
   - What role would GL play?

IT Planning at ModMeters

Brian Smith, CIO of ModMeters, groaned inwardly as he listened to CEO John Johnson wrapping up his remarks. "So our executive team thinks there are real business opportunities for us in developing these two new strategic thrusts. But before I go to the board for final approval next month, I need to know that our IT, marketing, and sales plans will support us all the way," Johnson concluded.

Brian mentally calculated the impact these new initiatives would have on his organization. He had heard rumors from his boss, the COO, that something big was coming down. He had even been asked his opinion about whether these strategies were technically doable, *theoretically*. But *both* at once? Resources—people, time, and money—were tight, as usual. ModMeters was making a reasonable profit, but the CFO, Stan Abrams, had always kept the lid screwed down tightly on IT spending. Brian had to fight for every dime. How he was going to find the wherewithal to support not one but *two* new strategic initiatives, he didn't know.

The other VPs at this strategy presentation were smiling. Taking ModMeters global from a North American operation seemed to be a logical next step for the company. Its products, metering components of all types, were highly specialized and in great demand from such diverse customers as utility companies, manufacturers, and a host of other industries. Originally founded as Modern Meters, the firm had grown steadily as demand for its metering expertise and components had grown over the past century or so. Today ModMeters was the largest producer of metering components in the world with a full range of both mechanical and now digital products. Expanding into meter assembly with plants in Asia and Eastern Europe was a good plan, thought Brian, but he wasn't exactly sure how he was going to get the infrastructure in place to support it. "Many of these countries simply don't have the telecommunications and equipment we are going to need, and the training and new systems we have to put in place are going to be substantial," he said.

But it was the second strategic thrust that was going to give him nightmares, he predicted. How on earth did they expect him to put direct-to-customer sales in place so they could sell "green" electric meters to individual users? His attention was jerked back to the present by a flashy new logo on an easel that the CEO had just unveiled.

"In keeping with our updated strategy, may I present our new name—MM!" Johnson announced portentously.

"Oh, this is just great," thought Brian. "Now I have to go into every single application and every single document this company produces and change our name!"

Because of its age and scientific orientation, ModMeters (as he still preferred to call it) had been in the IT business a long time. Starting back in the early 1960s, the company had gradually automated almost every aspect of its business from finance and accounting to supply chain management. About the only thing it didn't have was a fancy Web site for consumers, although even *that* was about to change. ModMeters currently had systems reflecting just about every era of computers from punch cards to PCs. Unfortunately, the company never seemed to have the resources to invest in reengineering its existing systems. It just layered more systems on top of the others. A diagram of all the interactions among systems looked like a plate of spaghetti. There was *no way* they were going to be able to support two new strategic thrusts with their current budget levels, he thought as he applauded the new design along with the others. "Next week's IT budget meeting is going to be a doozy!"

Sure enough, the following week found them all, except for the CEO, back in the same meeting room, ready to do battle. Holding his fire, Brian waited until all the VPs had presented their essential IT initiatives. In addition to what needed to be done to support the new business strategies, each division had a full laundry list of essentials for maintaining the *current* business of the firm. Even Stan had gotten into the act this year because of new legislation that gave the firm's outside auditors immense scope to peer into the inner workings of every financial and governance process the organization had.

After listening carefully to each speaker in turn, Brian stood up. "As many of you know, we have always been cautious about how we spend our IT budget. We have been given a budget that is equal to 2 percent of revenues, which seriously limits what we in IT have been able to do for the company. Every year we spend a lot of time paring our project list down to bare bones, and every year we make do with a patchwork of infrastructure investments. We are now at the point where 80 percent of our budget in IT is fixed. Here's how we spend our money." Brian clicked on a PowerPoint presentation showing a multicolored pie chart.

"This large chunk in blue is just about half our budget," he stated. "This is simply the cost of keeping the lights on—running our systems and replacing a bare minimum of equipment. The red chunk is about 30 percent of the pie. This is the stuff we *have* to do—fixing errors, dealing with changes mandated by government and our own industry, and providing essential services like the help desk. How we divide up the remainder of the pie is what this meeting is all about."

Brian clicked to a second slide showing a second pie chart. "As you know, we have typically divided up the remaining IT budget proportionately, according to who has the biggest overall operating budget. This large pink chunk is you, Fred." Brian gestured at Fred Tompkins, head of manufacturing and the most powerful executive in the room. It was his division that made the firm's profit. The pink chunk easily took up more than half of the pie. Tompkins smiled. Brian went on, pointing out the slice that each part of the firm had been allotted in the previous year. "Finally, we come to

Harriet and Brenda," he said with a smile. Harriet Simpson and Brenda Barnes were the VPs of human resources and marketing, respectively. Their tiny slivers were barely visible—just a few percent of the total budget.

"This approach to divvying up our IT budget may have served us well over the years" (Brian didn't think it had but he wasn't going to fight past battles), "however, we all heard what John said last week, and this approach to budgeting doesn't give us *any* room to develop our new strategies *or* cover our new infrastructure or staffing needs. Although we might get a little more money to obtain some new applications and buy some more computers"—Abrams nodded slightly—"it won't get us where we need to go in the future."

A third graph went up on the screen, showing the next five years. "If we don't do something *now* to address our IT challenges, within five years our entire IT budget will be eaten up by just operations and maintenance. In the past we have paid minimal attention to our infrastructure or our information and technology architecture or to reengineering our existing systems and processes." A diagram of the "spaghetti" flashed on. "This is what you're asking me to manage in a cost-effective manner. It isn't pretty. We need a better plan for making our systems more robust and flexible. The foundation just isn't there for us to be moving in new directions with this firm. Stan, you *should* be worried that we won't be able to give our auditors what they ask for. But you should also be worried about our risk exposure if one of these systems fails and about how we are going to integrate two new business ventures into this mess."

Tompkins looked up from his papers. It was clear he wasn't pleased with where this presentation was headed. "Well, I for one *need* everything I've asked for on my list," he stated flatly. "You can't expect me to be the cash cow of the organization and not enable me to make the money we need to invest elsewhere."

Brian was conciliatory. "I'm not saying that you don't, Fred. I'm just saying that we've been given a new strategic direction from the top and that some things are going to have to change to enable IT to support the whole enterprise better. For example, until now we have always prioritized divisional IT projects on the basis of ROI. How should we prioritize these new strategic initiatives? Furthermore, these new ventures will require a *lot* of additional infrastructure, so we need to figure out a way to afford this. Right now our systems don't 'talk' to the ones running in other divisions because they don't use the same terminology. But in the future, if we're going to have systems that won't cost increasing amounts of our budget, we are going to have to simplify and integrate them better.

Tompkins clearly hadn't considered the enterprise's needs at all. He scowled but said nothing. Brian continued, "We are being asked to do some new things in the company. Obviously, John hopes there's going to be a payback, but it may take a while. New strategies don't always bear fruit right away." Now looking at Stan, he said pointedly, "There's more to IT value than short-term profit. Part of our business strategy is to *make* new markets for our company. That requires investment, not only in equipment and product, but also in the underlying processes and information we need to manage and monitor that investment."

Harriet Simpson spoke for the first time. "It's like when we hire someone new in R&D. We hire for quality because we want their ideas and innovation, not just a warm body. I think we need to better understand how we are going to translate our five key corporate objectives into IT projects. Yes, we need to make a profit, but Stan needs to satisfy regulators and Brenda's going to be on the hot seat when we start marketing to individuals. And we haven't even spoken about Ted's needs." As the VP of R&D, Ted Kwok was tasked with keeping one or more steps ahead of the competition. New types of products and customer needs would mean expansion in his area as well.

Stan cleared his throat. "*All* of you are right. As I see it, we are going to have to keep the cash flowing from Fred's area while we expand. But Brian's got a point. We may be being penny wise and pound foolish if we don't think things through more carefully. We've put a lot of effort into developing this new strategy, and there *will* be some extra money for IT but not enough to do that plus everything all of you want. We need to retrench and regroup *and* move forward at the same time."

There was silence in the room. Stan had an annoying way of stating the obvious without really helping to move the ball forward. Brian spoke again. "The way I see it, we have to understand two things before we can really make a new budget. First, we need to figure out how each of the IT projects we've got on the table contributes to one of our key corporate objectives. Second, we need to figure out a way to determine the *value* of each to ModMeters so that we can prioritize it. Then I need to incorporate a reasonable amount of IT regeneration so that we can continue to do new projects at all."

Everyone was nodding now. Brian breathed a small sigh of relief. That was step one accomplished. But step two was going to be harder. "We have a month to get back to the board with our assurances that the IT plan can incorporate the new strategies and what we're going to need in terms of extra funds to do this. As I said earlier, this is *not* just a matter of throwing money at the problem. What we need is a *process* for IT planning and budgeting that will serve us well over the next few years. This process will need to accomplish a number of things: It will need to take an *enterprise* perspective on IT. We're all in these new strategies together. It will have to incorporate all types of IT initiatives—our new strategies, the needs of Fred and others for the new IT to operate and improve our existing business, Stan's new auditing needs, and our operations and maintenance needs. In addition, we *must* find some way of allocating some of the budget to fixing the mess we have in IT right now. It must provide a better way to connect new IT work with our corporate objectives. It must help us prioritize projects with different types of value. Finally, it must ensure we have the business *and* IT resources in place to deliver that value."

Looking at each of his colleagues in turn, he asked, "Now how are we going to do this?"

Discussion Question

Develop an IT planning process for ModMeters to accomplish the demands as set out above.

IT Investment at North American Financial[1]

Caroline Weese checked her makeup and then glanced at her watch for the tenth time. Almost 10:45. Showtime. As North American Financial's (NAF) first female CIO, she knew she had to be better than good when she met with the company's senior executives for the first time to justify her IT budget. They had shown their faith in her three months ago by giving her this position, when NAF's long-serving senior vice president of IT had had to retire early due to ill health. But women were just beginning to crack the "glass ceiling" at the bank, and she knew there was a lot more riding on this presentation than just this budget.

That said, the budget situation wasn't great. As she well knew from her earlier experience in more subordinate roles, the CIO had the unenviable task of justifying the company's $500M budget to a group of executives who only saw the expense of IT, not its value. This was especially frustrating because NAF's IT management was excellent, when looked at by any standard. NAF's IT group consisted of almost 7,000 professionals who followed all the recommended standards, such as CMM, CMMI, ISO9001, and ITIL, to ensure that its IT processes were efficient, cost effective, and on par with, if not higher than, industry standards. It had been certified at a minimum Level 3 CMMI and was an industry leader in delivering projects on time, on budget, and in scope. But in the past few years, NAF executives had implemented rigorous cost containment measures for IT, leaving the CIO to struggle to be all things to all people.

"They want innovation, they need reliability and stability, and we're required by law to meet ever more stringent government regulations, but they're still nickel-and-diming us!" Caroline thought indignantly. She envied the bank's business units that could clearly show profit-and-loss statements, and their ability to make strategic decisions about what to do with the excess capital they often had. In her world, business strategies changed regularly and thus IT's goals had to as well. But strategies

---

[1] H. A. Smith and J. D. McKeen, "IT Investment at North American Financial," #1-L09-1-001. Smith School of Business at Queen's University, October 2009. Reproduced by permission of Queen's University, Smith School of Business, Kingston, Ontario, Canada.

were not linked to budgets, which were typically set six to nine months in advance. As a result, IT was always struggling to keep up and find the resources to be flexible.

She squared her shoulders, took a deep breath, pasted a smile on her face, and pushed open the door to the executive conference room to face her colleagues and her future. The room was full of "suits"—a few females here and there, but mostly tough, middle-age males who expected answers and action. Following a few pleasantries about how she was adjusting to her new role, they got down to business. "The thing we're most concerned about, Caroline," said Bill Harris, NAF's CEO, "is we simply don't see where we're getting value from our IT investments. There's no proof in the bottom line." Matt Harper, NAF's CFO added, "Every year we approve hundreds of millions of dollars for IT projects, which are supposedly based on sound cost–benefit analyses, but the benefits never materialize." Heads around the room began nodding.

Caroline's mind was whirling. What did they really want from her? Pulling her thoughts together quickly, she responded. "If you're looking for IT to tell you which projects will deliver the most business value, or if you want me to monitor the business units after the projects they asked for are implemented to see if they are delivering value, you're asking me to do something that's well beyond IT's scope of expertise. We're not the experts in your business case, and it shouldn't be up to us to monitor how you use the technology we give you. I'll take full responsibility for the quality of our work, its timely delivery, and its cost, but we really have to work together to ensure we're investing in the right projects and delivering benefits."

"What do you recommend then?" asked Sam Patel, head of Retail Banking. "I think we need an IT Investment Committee that I would co-lead jointly with you, Matt," Caroline said while looking pointedly at the CFO. "We need a strong partnership to explore what can be done and who should be responsible for doing it. Finance is the only place where all the money comes together in this organization. Although I have to pull together an IT budget every year, it's really contingent on what each business unit wants to spend. We don't really have an enterprise IT budgeting process that looks across our business silos to see if what we're spending is good for NAF as a whole." Matt looked thoughtful. "You could be on to something here, Caroline. Let's see if we can figure this out together."

The rest of the meeting passed in a blur, and before Caroline knew it, she and Matt were trying to identify who they should assign to help them look at their IT investment challenges. These were significant. First, there was inconsistent alignment of the total IT development budget with enterprise strategies. "We have enterprise strategies but no way of linking them to enterprise spending," Caroline pointed out. IT budgets were allocated according to the size of the business unit. Smaller lines of business had smaller IT budgets than larger ones. "For some small business units like ours, government mandatory projects eat up our entire IT budget," complained Cathy Benson, senior vice president of Business Banking Product Management. This made it extremely difficult to allocate IT resources strategically—say, for example, to grow a smaller business unit into a larger one.

Second, project approvals were made by business units without addressing cross-unit synergies. Looking at the projects IT had underway revealed that the company had eighteen separate projects in different parts of the business to comply with anti–money laundering regulations. "We've got to be reinventing the wheel with some of these," complained Ian Ha, senior director of NAF's Risk and Compliance department.

Third, although business cases were required for all major projects, their formats were inconsistent, and the data provided to justify the costs lacked rigor. "There seems to be a lot of gaming going on here," observed Michael Cranston, director of Financial Strategy. "A lot of these numbers don't make sense. How come we've never asked the business sponsors of these projects to take ownership for the business benefits they claim when they ask for the money in the first place?"

Fourth, once a project was approved, everyone focused on on-time, on-budget delivery. No one ever asked whether a project was still necessary or was still on track to deliver the benefits anticipated. "Do we ever stop projects once they've started or review the business case 'in-flight'?" mused Matt. Finally, no one appeared to be accountable for delivering these benefits once an IT project was developed and implemented; rather, everyone just heaved a great sigh of relief and moved on to the next project.

Because the total IT budget for new development work was allocated by business unit, the result was a prioritization process that worked reasonably well at the business unit level but not for NAF as a whole. Enterprise executives created enterprise strategies, but they didn't get involved in implementing them in the business units, which left the business unit heads to prioritize initiatives within their own silo. In prioritization meetings, leaders would argue passionately for their own particular cause, focusing on their own needs, not on NAF's overall strategies. "We really need to align this process with our enterprise priorities," said Caroline. Matt agreed. "There's got to be a process to bring all our investment decisions for new projects together so we can compare them across business units and adjust our resourcing accordingly."

Looking deeper into these matters revealed that there was more to IT spending than simply prioritizing projects, however. Almost 60 percent of the bank's IT budget was spent not on strategic new development projects but on maintaining existing systems, interfaces, and data. Another 20 percent was work that had to be done to meet the demands of government legislation or the bank's regulators. "How is this possible?" asked Sam. "No wonder we're not getting much 'bang for our buck,'" Caroline exclaimed. "Every time we develop or acquire a new system without getting rid of something else, we add to our 'application clutter.' When we continually add new systems while holding IT budgets and head counts relatively flat, more and more of our resources have to be devoted to supporting these systems." New systems meant new interfaces between and among existing systems, additional data and dependencies, and increasing risk that something could go wrong. "We've tried to get the business units interested in sponsoring an initiative to reduce duplication and simplify our applications portfolio, but they're not interested in what they call 'IT housekeeping.'

They don't see how dealing with this will help them in the long run. I guess we haven't explained it to them very well."

Brenda Liu, senior director of IT Infrastructure, added, "We also have to keep our IT environment up to date. Vendors are continually making upgrades to software, and there are also license fees to consider. And, as you know, we have to build in extra reliability and redundancy for our critical systems and data, as well as privacy protection for our banking customers. It's an expensive process." "I get all this," said Cathy, "but why can't you explain it to us properly? How can you just expect us to accept that 80 percent of your budget is a 'black box' that doesn't need justification? Although every dime you spend may be critical to this company, the fact remains that IT's lack of transparency is damaging its internal credibility with the business."

Round and round the issues they went. Over the next two months, Caroline, Matt, and their team hammered away trying to solve them. Eventually, they came up with a set of five principles on which their new IT investment process would be based:

1. Alignment of the IT development portfolio with enterprise strategies;

2. Rigor and common standards around IT planning and business casing;

3. Accountability in both business and IT for delivering value;

4. Transparency at all levels and stages of development;

5. Collaboration and cross-group synergies in all IT work.

In their team update to the bank's executive committee, Caroline and Matt wrote, "Our vision is for a holistic view of our IT spending that will allow us to direct our resources where they will have the greatest impact. We propose to increase rigor and discipline in business casing and benefits tracking so NAF can invest with confidence in IT. The result will be strategic partnerships between IT and business units based on trust, leading us to surprise and delight our customers and employees and amaze our competitors."

With the executive committee's blessing, the IT Investment Office was created to design and implement a detailed investment optimization process that could be implemented throughout the bank in time for the next budget cycle. Cathy Benson was named its new director, reporting to Matt. Speaking to her staff after the announcement, Caroline stated, "I really believe that getting this work out of IT and into the business will be critical for this process. We need to make the decision-making process clearer and more collaborative. This will help us learn how to jointly make better decisions for the enterprise."

With the hand-off from IT officially in place, Cathy and Matt knew they had to move quickly. "We've got three months before the next budget cycle begins," said Matt. "You've got to make it real by then. I'll back you all the way, but you're going to have to find some way to deal with the business unit heads. They're not going to like having their autonomy for decision-making taken away from them. And you have to remember they need some flexibility to do work that's important to them." Cathy nodded. She had already heard some of the negative rumors about the process and knew she was going to have to be tough if it was going to be successful and not torpedoed during its implementation.

Calling her project team together for its first meeting, she summarized their challenge. "We have to design and implement three interrelated practices: a thorough and rigorous method of project categorization and prioritization, comprehensive and holistic governance of IT spending and benefits delivery at all levels, and an annual IT planning process that provides transparency and accountability for all types of IT spending and which creates an integrated and strategically aligned development portfolio. Then we have to roll it out across the organization. The change management is going to be massive. Now, who has any ideas about what to do next?"

Discussion Questions

Cathy Benson, the director of the newly created IT Investment Office, is tasked with the "design and implementation of a detailed investment optimization process to be implemented throughout the bank in time for the next budget cycle." She has three months to do this and it must be in accordance with the five established principles to guide the bank's IT investment process. Your task is to design and implement the following:

1. A thorough and rigorous method of project categorization and prioritization;

2. A comprehensive and holistic governance of IT spending and benefits delivery at all levels;

3. An annual IT planning process that provides transparency and accountability for all types of IT spending and that creates an integrated and strategically aligned development portfolio.

SECTION II

IT–Business Partnership

Chapter 6: Governance for a Redefined IT
Chapter 7: The IT Budgeting Process
Chapter 8: Managing IT-Based Risk
Chapter 9: Building a Strong Relationship with the Business
Chapter 10: Enabling Collaboration with IT

Mini Cases for Section II:
• Enterprise Architecture at Nationstate Insurance
• Transforming IT at Global Digital Imaging
• Delivering Business Value with IT at Hefty Hardware

CHAPTER 6

Governance for a Redefined IT

IT is facing many new pressures to deliver faster, deliver different products and services, and work differently at all levels of the organization and with vendors, partners, and even customers. As a result, there is broad recognition that IT needs to redefine itself to be more effective for the future. Change is not optional for today's IT organizations. The major challenge for IT leaders is therefore deciding what to change and how fast to do it.[1]

As this quote makes clear, the pressure is on IT to deliver faster and this means working differently. IT managers are in general agreement with this goal but also feel a responsibility to protect the organization and its data. Many of IT's so-called "bureaucratic processes" were put in place for good reasons, such as to ensure quality, interoperability, and cost-efficacy. And in many highly regulated industries, such as finance and health care, laws and risk-aversion govern much of what can and cannot be done by IT. Nevertheless, there is a need to reconcile these competing priorities and rethink how IT works.

IT work involves two major components: 1) making decisions about what work to do (i.e., strategy), and 2) delivering the work (i.e., execution). IT governance is the system of structures, processes, and roles that collectively *oversee* these two major components of IT work. Championing the needs of the enterprise (i.e., common processes, architecture, data, and controls) favors more centralized forms of governance just as championing responsiveness to the business favors more decentralized (or perhaps hybrid) forms of governance. Balancing these is at the nub of the challenge for today's IT leaders: the need to act faster and in closer alignment with the business while still protecting the organization's overarching interests.

---

[1] H. A. Smith and J. D. McKeen, "It's time to redefine IT," IT Management Forum 2013, https://smith.queensu.ca/it-forum/index.php.

The Increasing Importance of Governance

IT governance is a framework of processes and structures that specify who makes decisions about and who is accountable for the IT function and its work. It also determines who should have input to issues, how disputes should be settled, and how decisions should be made, implemented, and managed (Weill and Ross 2005). It is *not* about what specific decisions are made or how groups are organized and led. Effective IT governance is designed to encourage desirable behavior in the use of IT that is consistent with an organization's mission, strategy, and culture (Weill 2004).

Research shows that effective governance has a significant influence on the benefits an organization receives from its IT investments. Value is achieved by ensuring "that the right groups are making the key IT decisions so that those decisions enable the desired goals and behaviors of the enterprise" (Weill 2004). Although it does not point to a single best governance model, effective governance is carefully designed to link to an organization's particular performance goals (Weill and Ross 2005).

A significant reason for an organization's ability to derive value from IT is that its governance provides senior leaders with a clear understanding of how IT decisions are made, thus helping to: 1) clarify business strategies and IT's role in achieving them, 2) measure and manage IT investments, 3) design organizational practices to align IT and business strategies, 4) assign accountability for change, and 5) learn (Weill 2004). Therefore, it is unfortunate that IT governance has all too often been found to be a mystery to key decision-makers at most companies (Weill and Ross 2005).

Although getting value from IT is an important reason for leaders to design for effective governance, in recent years a number of other factors have also become drivers for senior managers to focus on it. These include:

- **Ensuring privacy and security.** Concerns about security have now reached the board level. More and more, CIOs are being asked to present their IT security plans to directors, who recognize that a security breach could at minimum embarrass their company, and potentially cause significant losses. Recent accounts of major customer information losses due to security lapses have heightened attention to the need to have effective governance of security practices even in the most insignificant areas.
- **Compliance with laws and regulations.** There was general agreement in the focus group that there is a growing amount of legislation affecting governance, that regulators in specific industries are becoming more demanding, and that both internal and external auditors are becoming more intrusive and prescriptive in their reports. "This all results in more process and additional work," said a manager. While not all industries are regulated, many are. In this focus group, companies from the finance, insurance, healthcare, travel, and food industries all noted the increasingly onerous burden of regulation. And all companies are feeling the pressure of new legislation and more detailed audits. In addition, international or global companies must comply with a variety of individual country regulations, such as separating data or management oversight.

- *Improving risk management.* IT work has become more complex and is less often under direct management control. Today's IT service offerings typically include third-party software developed by outsourced staff (often not even in the same country) and rely on a rapidly evolving ecosystem of service providers in emerging industries (e.g., cloud, software-as-a-service). Under these circumstances, it is all the more important for governance to recognize and address the additional vulnerabilities involved.
- *Improving alignment between strategy and execution.* Often organizations have misaligned governance structures—one for innovation and strategic projects and another for execution and operations. If actions in one ignore governance requirements in the other, such as when putting new changes into operational systems or circumventing existing architecture, then governance is undermined to the detriment of the company as a whole.
- *Increasing customer involvement.* As technology touches the lives of end customers more often and is more visible, corporate reputations are increasingly at risk. As one manager put it: "It's important that we use customer information to interact with our customers appropriately or it could be embarrassing or worse."

Group members commented that with so many competing dynamics, it is especially difficult to design governance without adding significant extra work for IT staff. "Our goal is to design governance that is *enabling*," said a member. "If everyone understands their roles and responsibilities, when they need permission, and the right people have the right tools, then this is possible. Not everyone will like it but at least it is clear." Another added, "Our goal is to make effective governance a part of our culture. We want to build integrity into everything we do."

It is clear that governance is more of a challenge the larger a company gets, and it's a greater challenge in some industries or countries than in others. Regardless of the company, the need for effective IT governance has never been more evident, and companies are scrambling to keep up as IT itself changes and the interaction between these drivers evolves.

Elements of Effective IT Governance

Effective governance is not attained by a single committee or set of rules, except perhaps in very small organizations. Instead, it is achieved through an integrated framework of organizational groups that provide oversight in different areas, standards, and practices founded on industry best practices, legal and compliance requirements, and policy guidelines that direct how work is to be accomplished. Governance should be designed to provide clarity and consistency to IT work and focus IT decisions on what is most important to the organization. It should also ensure that governance practices support each other, rather than work at cross-purposes.

A governance framework most often operates at three levels, although this may vary according to size and geographic needs:

- **Board governance.** While board level governance involves more than IT, boards are increasingly aware of their responsibility to become better informed about the IT decisions made in their organizations. Boards are responsible to their shareholders for managing both the finances of their companies and the risks they undertake, as well as their reputation and brands. In addition, a board is responsible for ensuring that its organization is compliant with all regulatory requirements and reporting, and for addressing all issues raised by its internal and external auditors. Each of these can now be significantly affected by IT strategy and execution. One need only pick up a newspaper these days to see how damaging it is for a board to fail in its oversight of one or more of these areas. Thus many boards now have technology committees or at least members who have some technology background, and IT matters are being more frequently questioned at this level. This is a positive change according to the focus group, as it raises the profile of serious IT concerns to the highest echelons in the firm.

- **Enterprise IT governance.** This is a level of governance that is growing considerably as IT leaders realize the value that good governance can deliver. As Figure 6.1 shows, enterprise IT governance provides detailed integration of factors affecting IT decision-making in several areas including:

  Architecture. This sets current and future technology strategy, ensuring it is consistent with overall business strategy. It identifies best practices and industry standards for use in IT and provides oversight and approvals for all technology initiatives to ensure that the company is both protected and positioned well for the future.

  Security and privacy. This provides oversight and guidance on all security matters to ensure that the organization's information assets and infrastructure are protected and to proactively and continuously address security risks. It also oversees access management practices.

  Operations. This ensures that all technology implementations and changes follow proper procedures and standards, and provides oversight of all ongoing operations. It also reviews and reports on ongoing service levels and seeks to ensure that risks are mitigated and issues resolved.

  Strategic projects. This oversees the processes designed to ensure that the most strategically valuable projects are properly and expeditiously resourced and funded. It also tracks project progress to ensure that all standards are followed and risks identified and mitigated.

  IT capabilities. This ensures that IT has the necessary capabilities to carry out its mandate, whether internal or external, and also oversees the organization's relationship with its vendors and service providers, ensuring they meet all standards and contractual responsibilities.

  Data. This is the newest component of IT governance, responsible for managing data as a strategic asset, building a common framework and definitions for key corporate data, and developing effective data management practices and accountabilities.

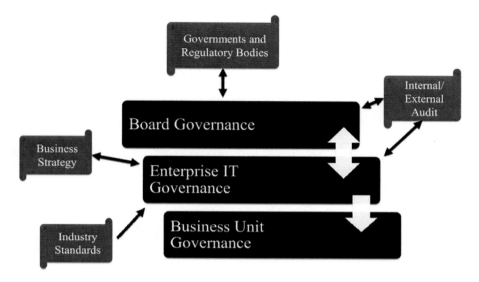

Figure 6.1 IT governance integrates many components.

• *Local (business unit) governance.* Most organizational governance frameworks also allow for some discretionary IT decision-making. This involves making decisions about smaller-scale, lower-cost, new applications and prioritizing changes to existing IT applications to be made in the business units. In general, organizations try to limit business unit IT decisions in order to focus the vast majority of IT spending on higher-value, strategic initiatives. And most recognize the need for this level of decision-making to support local flexibility. Enterprise IT provides oversight for and input to this level of governance, ensuring it follows appropriate practices and standards for development, testing, and implementation.

IT Governance Evolution

Once designed, IT governance should not need to be rethought simply because of changes in the economy or adjustments to strategy (Weill 2004). Circumstances under which governance should be completely re-evaluated include a major change in strategy or a merger. Within these two extremes, however, lies the area of "practical governance," which involves enhancing, extending, or tweaking governance models to provide more clarity or to adapt to changing IT practices. "We have evolved our current governance model over the past six or seven years," said one manager, "and we still have areas that we need to address more fully."

Evolving areas of governance usually lie in new areas of IT work where best practices and standards are not well understood, such as:

- **Third party vendors/outsourcers.** Many companies have found gaps in governance and assumptions about decision-making when work is subcontracted out to third parties, who may in turn subcontract out some work. This can lead to any number of problems from a legal, audit, compliance, security, or privacy perspective. For example, "We thought we could outsource application development to get it done more quickly, but then we found we had to retrofit these applications to meet our security criteria. This was very painful," said a manager. "Because IT still has accountability for products developed in this way, we've found it necessary to add extra layers of due diligence when dealing with third parties," said another. Although it introduces additional complexity, there was general agreement in the group that with a good governance framework in place, and if vendors understand it well, shifting IT work to third parties can be successful.
- **Cloud services providers.** "With cloud software-as-a-service, we at first naively assumed we could impose our own controls, but with these large cloud vendors, *you* have to adapt," said one manager. Under these circumstances, companies must be extra vigilant to ensure that cloud vendors meet all corporate, regulatory, and government criteria, such as where data is located. Many countries explicitly prohibit their data from virtually or physically leaving their borders. In these cases, companies must evaluate their own processes and policies as well as those of their vendors to both adjust their internal governance practices and ensure that certain minimum standards are adhered to by their provider. "If these can't be met, you shouldn't be doing business with them," said a manager.
- **Mobility and other new technologies.** Although new technologies do not affect governance *per se*, there are at least three reasons why governance needs to be reconsidered when they are introduced. First, the technologies themselves may contain new vulnerabilities that have never been considered. For example, company tablets may contain confidential information or customer data that could be stolen or hacked due to immature protections on these devices. Second, in the rush to implement new technology and innovative applications, a company may be pressured to short circuit tried-and-true practices that could cause anything from operational issues to simple malfunctions to occur. Many companies are experimenting with new technologies these days and so developing ways to explore potential opportunities safely without circumventing existing governance practices is a challenge for IT leaders. One company in the focus group has a "fast track" approval process that enables strategically desirable projects to jump the queue in the prioritization process, while still following the standard review procedures afterward; another has developed a "governance-lite" approach for pilots, with the understanding that if the decision is made to scale these up into production, they will follow all proper procedures. Third, new technologies typically have immature and rapidly changing standards that make it difficult to integrate into a technical architecture. An IT nightmare can occur if different projects select similar new technology that operates in different ways. Good governance prevents this from occurring.

- **Data.** The most challenging area of governance at present for many companies is data, and it is often a political hot potato. "Data has been a very painful journey," sighed one manager. "We've tried to do it many times before. We're now confident we have the commitment and the roles, responsibilities, accountabilities, and processes clear, but we are still meeting bi-weekly to figure out what's not working and who's not engaged so that we can deal with it. Otherwise, we'd be wasting our time." Good data governance requires consistent standards for each piece of data, but without clarity about who owns what, who produces it and who uses it, the information produced can be inaccurate or conflicting. One company learned a hard lesson when its CFO asked for integrated revenue data only to learn that different business units had different mechanisms for calculating this figure, which made the information highly suspect. "We needed to start top down and determine who owned which data and who had a mandate for changing it," said the manager involved. "We had a good data architecture for sourcing data but needed governance. We are now looking to develop data standards and good management practices."

In these new areas, governance best practices are not yet mature, and companies are trying to adapt their existing governance models to fit the need. Managers in the focus group stressed the importance of monitoring new governance practices as they evolve to ensure they are working well and doing what they are supposed to do. Without this attention, governance models can fall into disuse or become so bureaucratic that a company is seriously impeded in its work. "Good governance should help everyone understand the rules and make sure that the right levels have the right tools and responsibilities. We should never lose sight of this when designing governance," said a manager.

Promoting Effective IT Governance

Focus group members had several recommendations for managers seeking to redesign or improve their IT governance practices:

1. **Make fact-based decisions.** "Ideally, all decisions should be based on facts, not gut feel," said a manager. "But we still have some way to go in this area." The group agreed that the more facts that are brought to bear on a decision, the better that decision will be. Facts improve clarity and consistency and create trust in the decisions that are made. As a result, they also encourage people to play by the rules and reduce "politicking."

2. **Work from the premise that one size does not fit all.** Governance in any company should be as simple as possible with a limited number of goals (Weill 2004). However, the group emphasized that governance will vary according to the industry, size of company, and geographical makeup of the organization. Thus a global financial company will need a more complex governance model than a small firm in a less-regulated industry. Many companies have been successful

with different governance models (Wade and Buttchel 2013). "Small companies and large ones have the same set of issues, but they need to deal with them differently," said one manager. Similarly, centralization is not necessarily better than decentralization. "We should aim for the right model for the right types of decisions," said a manager. "We shouldn't centralize simply for the sake of centralizing," added another.

3. *Monitor and iterate.* Although governance models should be carefully designed to reinforce an organization's goals, they are not easy to get correct the first time. The group stressed the importance of monitoring how a model works in practice and making adjustments to ensure all processes integrate smoothly and efficiently. "It is especially important to align strategy and execution governance," said a manager. There can also be resistance to governance that is perceived to be inhibiting. The group stressed understanding where governance is not working and why, adapting it in some cases and reinforcing the rules in others. "At some point, you have to say 'these are the rules' but you also need to make sure that the culture is aligned top-down to meet these goals or governance will be perceived as intolerably bureaucratic," said a manager.

4. *Communicate from the top.* It is essential that the CIO and senior leadership team communicate strategy clearly throughout the organization and educate all levels of personnel about the rationale for key governance mechanisms. Ideally, governance should be able to be communicated on a single page and education should be used to better align the culture with organizational objectives. "Often we see that our VPs are aligned with our goals but this doesn't filter down to other levels where our projects are actually implemented. We therefore need a much heavier focus on communication and education to reinforce governance," said a manager.

5. *Clarify strategies and principles for staff augmentation.* With so much IT work now being done by vendors, it is critically important to ensure that an organization has clear strategies and principles for how staff augmentation is to be handled. Organizations need to ensure that vendors comply with their governance practices and that staff is fully trained in what is expected. "This is especially important when dealing with offshore companies who may have different assumptions from our own. We've learned that we have to select vendors very carefully and hold them to very high standards. In our company, we rigorously review all outsourced work to ensure staff has followed our practices," said a manager.

6. *Include release valves.* Even the best designed governance model needs an exception process to handle justifiable deviations from best practices, said the group. "Standards are black and white," said a manager. "We need to have ways to exempt projects from them if there's a good reason, such as a compelling business opportunity." However, exemptions should only be made after a clear

consideration of the potential impact and risks, and often for a limited time period. This might be the case if a project wants to use a new and untried technology or if a competitor has come out with a new product or service that has rapidly become "table stakes."

Conclusion

Effective IT governance is an essential element of delivering IT value. Designed well, it can facilitate alignment with corporate strategy and performance objectives and enable best practices in risk management, security and privacy protection, auditability, and information management. It ensures that the right decisions are made by the right people at the right time and provides guidelines for how best to address redefining IT. Designed poorly, it can be a roadblock to innovation, hinder performance, encourage non-compliance with the rules, and wrap the organization up in red tape. CIOs play a very clear role in setting the right tone at the top, promoting education about the role of governance, and creating transparent processes based on facts. There are many excellent governance guidelines available for IT leaders to use as a starting point, but they must also make the time to ensure that their governance actually works in practice and make adjustments where needed.

Chapter Discussion Questions

1. Under what conditions would a decentralized governance model be more effective than a centralized one?
2. What problems might you expect to see if IT governance is *not* working well?

References

Wade, M., and B. Buttchel. "Anchored Agility: How to Effectively Manage the Balance Between Local Flexibility and Global Efficiency." *SIM Advanced Practices Council Research Report*, January 22, 2013, http://www.simnet.org.

Weill, P. "Don't Just Lead, Govern: How Top-performing Firms Govern IT." *MIS Quarterly Executive* 3, no. 1 (March 2004).

Weill, P., and J. Ross. "A Matrixed Approach to Designing IT Governance." *MIT Sloan Management Review* 46, no. 2 (Winter 2004).

CHAPTER 7

The IT Budgeting Process

Forget about trying to contact an IT manager in September because you won't get very far. September is budget month for most companies, and that means that most managers are hunkered down over a spreadsheet or in all-day meetings trying to "make the numbers work." "Budgeting is a very negative process at our firm," one IT manager told us. "And it takes way too long." Asking many IT managers about budgeting elicits much caustic comment. Apparently, significant difficulties with IT budgeting lead to widespread disenchantment among IT leaders, who feel much of the work involved is both artificial and overly time-consuming.

Others agree. While there has been little research done on IT budgeting per se (Hu and Quan 2006; Kobelsky et al. 2006), there appears to be broad, general consensus that the budgeting processes of many corporations are broken and need to be fixed (Buytendijk 2004; Hope and Fraser 2003; Jensen 2001). There are many problems. First, budgeting takes too long and consumes too much managerial time. One study found that budgeting is a protracted process taking at least four months and consuming about 30 percent of management's time (Hope and Fraser 2003). Second, most budgeting processes are no longer effective or efficient. They have become slow and expensive and disconnected from business objectives (Buytendijk 2004). Third, rigid adherence to these annual plans has been found to stifle innovation and discourage frontline staff from taking responsibility for performance (Hope and Fraser 2003; Norton 2006). And fourth, although many researchers have studied how organizations choose among strategic investment opportunities, studies show that the budgeting process frequently undercuts management's strategic intentions, causing significant frustration among managers at all levels (Norton 2006; Steele and Albright 2004).

Finally, the annual planning cycle can cast spending plans "in concrete" at a time when the business needs to be flexible and agile. This is particularly true in IT. "Over time ... IT budgeting processes become institutionalized. As a result, IT investments become less about creating competitive advantages for firms [and] more about following organizational routine and creating legitimacy for management as well as organizations" (Hu and Quan 2006). Now that senior business leaders recognize the strategic importance of IT and IT has become many firms' largest capital expenditure (Koch 2006), a hard look at how IT budgets are created is clearly merited.

In this chapter we first look at key concepts in IT budgeting to establish what they mean for IT managers and how they can differ among IT organizations. Then we explore why budgets are an important part of the management process. Next we examine the elements of the IT budget cycle. Lastly, we identify some recommended practices for improving IT budgeting.

Key Concepts in IT Budgeting

Before looking at how budgeting is actually practiced in IT organizations, it is important to understand what a budget is and why an effective IT budgeting process is so important, both within IT and for the enterprise as a whole. Current organizational budgeting practices emerged in the 1920s as a tool for managing costs and cash flows. Present-day annual fixed plans and budgets were established in the 1970s to drive performance improvements (Hope and Fraser 2003). Since then, most organizations have adhered rigidly to the ideals of this process, in spite of much evidence of their negative influence on innovation and flexibility (Hope and Fraser 2003). These problems are clearly illustrated by the impact this larger corporate fiscal management process has on IT budgeting and the problems IT managers experience in trying to make their budget processes work effectively. The concepts and practices of the corporate fiscal world bear little similarity to how IT actually works. As a result, there are clear discontinuities between these two worlds.

These gaps are especially apparent in the differences between the fiscal view of IT and the functional one. *Fiscal IT budgets* (i.e., those prepared for the CFO) are broken down into two major categories: *capital expenditures* and *operating expenses*, although what expenditures go into each is highly variable across firms. In accounting, capital budgets are utilized to spread large expenses (e.g., buying a building) over several years, and operating expenses cover the annual cost of running the business. The distinction between these two concepts gets very fuzzy, however, when it comes to IT.

Generally speaking, all IT organizations want to capitalize as much of their spending as possible because it makes their annual costs look smaller. However, CIOs are limited by both organizational and tax policies as to the types of IT expenditures they can capitalize. It is the CFO who, through corporate financial strategy, establishes what may be capitalized, and this, in turn, determines what IT can capitalize in its fiscal budget and what it must consider as an operating expense. As a result, some firms capitalize project development, infrastructure, consulting fees, some cloud computing costs, and full-time staff, whereas others capitalize only major technology purchases.

How capital budgets are determined and the degree to which they are scrutinized also vary widely. Some firms allocate and prioritize IT capital expenses out of a corporate "pot"; others manage IT capital separately. Typically, capital expenses appear to be more carefully scrutinized than operating expenses, but not always. It is surprising to learn how different types of expenses are handled by different firms and the wide degree of latitude allowed for IT costs under generally accepted accounting principles. In fact, there are few generally accepted accounting principles when it comes to IT spending (Koch 2006). As a result, researchers should use caution in relying on measures of the amount of capital spent on IT in firms or industries.

It is within this rather fuzzy fiscal context that the structure and purpose of *functional IT budgets* (i.e., those used by IT managers as spending plans) must be understood because these accounting concepts do not usually correspond exactly with how IT managers view IT work and how they plan and budget for it. In contrast to how fiscal IT budgets are designed, IT managers plan their spending using two somewhat different categories: *operations costs* and *strategic investments*.

- **Operations costs.** This category consists of what it costs to "keep the lights on" in IT. These are the expenses involved in running IT like a utility. Operations involves the cost of maintenance, computing and peripheral functions (e.g., storage, network), and support, regardless of how it is delivered (i.e., in-house or outsourced). This category can therefore include both operating and capital costs. Between 50 and 90 percent of a firm's IT budget (average of 76 percent) is spent in this area, so the spending involved is significant (Gruman 2006). In most firms there is continual pressure on the CIO to reduce operations costs year after year (Smith and McKeen 2006).
- **Strategic investments.** The balance of the IT budget consists of the "new" spending—that is, spending on initiatives and technology designed to deliver new business value and achieve the enterprise's strategic objectives. Because of the interactive nature of IT and business strategy, this part of the IT budget can include a number of different types of spending, such as business improvement initiatives to streamline processes and cut costs, business-enabling initiatives to extend or transform how a company does business, business opportunity projects to test the viability of new concepts or technologies and scale them up, and sometimes infrastructure (Smith et al. 2007). Because spending in this area can include many different kinds of expense (e.g., full-time and contract staff, software and hardware), some parts of the strategic investment budget may be considered capital expenses whereas others are classified as operating expenses.

Another fuzzy fiscal budgeting concept is *cost allocation*—the process of allocating the cost of the services IT provides to others' budgets. The cost of IT can be viewed as a corporate expense, a business unit expense, or a combination of both, and the way in which IT costs are allocated can have a significant impact on what is spent for IT. For example, a majority of companies allocate their IT operating expenses to their business units' operating budgets—usually using a formula based on factors such as the size and previous year's spending of the business unit. Similarly, strategic expenses are typically allocated on the basis of which business unit will benefit from the investment. In today's IT environment, these approaches are not always effective for a number of reasons.

Many strategic IT investments involve the participation of more than one business unit, but budgeting systems still tend to be designed around the structure of the organization (Norton 2006). This leads to considerable artificiality in allocating development resources to projects, which in turn can lead to dysfunctional behavior, such as lobbying, games, nonsupportive cross-functional work, and the inability to successfully implement strategy (Buytendijk 2004; Norton 2006). "We don't fund corporate projects very well," admitted one manager whose company allocates all costs to individual business units.

Allocations can also lead to operational inefficiencies. "The different allocation models tend to lead to 'gaming' between our business units," said another participant. "Our business unit managers have no control over their percentage of operating costs," explained a third. "This is very frustrating for them and tends to be a real problem for some of our smaller units." Because of these allocations, some business units may not be willing to share in the cost of new hardware, software, or processes that would lead to reduced enterprise costs in the longer term. This is one of the primary reasons so many IT organizations end up supporting several different applications all doing the same thing. Furthermore, sometimes, when senior managers get disgruntled with their IT expenses, this method of allocating operations costs can lead to their cutting their IT operational spending in ways that have little to do with running a cost-effective IT organization. For example, one company cut back on its budget for hardware and software upgrades, which meant that a significant percentage of IT staff then had to be redeployed to testing, modifying, and maintaining new systems so they would run on the old machines. Although IT managers have done some work educating their CEOs and CFOs about what constitutes effective cost cutting (e.g., appropriate sourcing, adjusting service levels), the fact remains that most business executives still do not understand or appreciate the factors that contribute to the overall cost of IT. As a result, allocations can lead to a great deal of angst for IT managers at budget time as they try to justify each expense while business managers try to "nickel and dime" each expense category (Koch 2006).

As a result of all this fuzziness, modern IT budgeting practices do little to give business leaders confidence that IT spending is both effective and efficient (Gruman 2006). And the challenges IT managers face in making IT spending fit into contemporary corporate budgeting practices are significant.

The Importance of Budgets

Ideally, budgets are a key component of corporate performance management. "If done well, a budget is the operational translation of an enterprise's strategy into costs and planned revenue" (Buytendijk 2004). Budgets are also a subset of good governance processes in that they enable management to understand and communicate what is being spent and where. Ideally, therefore, a budget is more than a math exercise; it is "a blueprint for fiscally sound IT and business success" (Overby 2004). Effective IT budgeting is important for many reasons, but two of the most important are as follows:

1. *Fiscal discipline.* As overall IT spending has been rising, senior business leaders have been paying much closer attention to what IT costs and how its budgets are spent. In many organizations a great deal of skepticism remains that IT budgets are used wisely, so reducing spending, or at least the operations portion of the budget, is now considered a key way for a CIO to build trust with the executive team (Gruman 2006). Demonstrating an understanding and appreciation of the realities of business finance has become a significant part of IT leadership (Goldberg 2004), and the ability to create and monitor a budget is therefore "table stakes" for a CIO (Overby 2004).

    It is clear that senior executives are using the budgeting process to enforce tougher rules on how IT dollars are spent. Some organizations have centralized IT budgeting in an effort to better understand what is being spent; others are making the link between reducing operations spending and increasing investment in IT a reason for introducing new operations disciplines (e.g., limiting maintenance, establishing appropriate support levels). Still others have established tighter requirements for business cases and for monitoring returns on investment. Organizations also use their IT budgets to manage and limit demand. "Our IT budget is capped by our CEO," stated one manager. "And it's always less than the demand." Using budgets in this way, although likely effective for the enterprise, can cause problems for CIOs in that they must in turn enforce spending disciplines on business unit leaders.

    Finally, budgets and performance against budgets are key ways of holding IT management accountable for what it spends, both internally to the leadership of the organization and externally to shareholders and regulatory bodies. Improperly used, budgets can distort reality and encourage inappropriate behavior (Hope and Fraser 2003; Jensen 2001). When used responsibly they can be "a basis for clear understanding between organizational levels and can help executives maintain control over divisions and the business" (Hope and Fraser 2003). Research is beginning to show a positive relationship between good IT budgeting practices (i.e., using IT budgets to manage demand, make investment decisions, and govern IT) and overall company performance (Kobelsky et al. 2006; Overby 2004).

2. *Strategy implementation.* Budgets are also the means to implement IT strategy, linking the long-term goals of the organization and short-term goal execution through the allocation of resources to activities. Unfortunately, research shows that the majority of organizations do not link their strategies to their budgets, which is why so many have difficulty making strategic changes (Norton 2006). This is particularly true in IT. As one manager complained, "No one knows

what we're doing in the future. Therefore, our goals change regularly and at random." Another noted, "The lines of business pay little attention to IT resources when they're establishing their strategic plans. They just expect IT to make it happen."

Budgets can affect IT strategy implementation in a number of ways. First, *where* IT dollars are spent determines the impact IT can have on corporate performance. Clearly, if 80 percent of IT expenditures is going to operations and maintenance, IT can have less strategic impact than if this percentage is lower. Second, *how* discretionary IT dollars are spent is important. For example, some companies decide to invest in infrastructure and others do not; some will choose to "bet the company" on a single, large IT initiative, and others will choose more focused projects. In short, the outcome of how a company chooses among investment opportunities is reflected in its budgets (Steele and Albright 2004).

Third, the budgeting process itself reflects and reinforces the ability of strategic decision-making to have an impact. Norton (2006) states that because budget processes are inherently biased toward the short term, operational needs will systematically preempt strategic ones. In IT the common practice of routinely allocating a fixed percentage of the IT strategic budget to individual business units makes it almost impossible to easily reallocate resources to higher-priority projects at the enterprise level or in other business units. In addition, siloed budgeting processes make it difficult to manage the cross-business costs of strategic IT decisions.

Overall, budgets are a critical element of most managerial decisions and processes and are used to accomplish a number of different purposes in IT: compliance, fiscal accountability, cost reduction, business unit and enterprise strategy implementation, internal customer service, delivering business value, and operational excellence, to name just a few. This, in a nutshell, is the reason IT budgeting is such a complex and challenging process.

The IT Planning and Budget Process

Given that IT budgets are used in so many different ways and serve so many stakeholders, it is no wonder that the whole process of IT budgeting is "painful," "artificial," and in need of some serious improvement. Figure 7.1 illustrates a generic and simplified IT planning and budgeting process. This section outlines the steps involved in putting together an IT budget utilizing some of the key concepts presented earlier.

Corporate Processes

The following three activities set the corporate context within which IT plans and budgets are created.

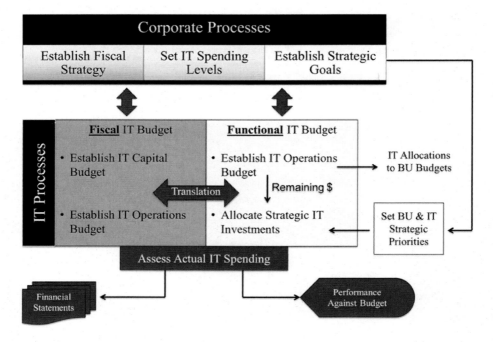

Figure 7.1 A generic IT planning and budgeting process

1. ***Establish corporate fiscal policy.*** This process is usually so far removed from the annual budget cycle that IT leaders may not even be aware of its influence or the wide number of options in the choices that are made (particularly around capitalization). Corporate fiscal policies are not created with IT spending in mind but, as noted above, can significantly impact how a fiscal IT budget is created and the levels of scrutiny under which certain kinds of expenses are placed. A more direct way that corporate fiscal policies affect IT is in company expectations around the return on investment for IT projects. Most companies now have an explicit expected return rate for all new projects that is closely monitored.

2. ***Establish strategic goals.*** Conversely, IT budgeting is directly and continuously affected by many corporate strategic goals. The process of establishing IT and business unit strategies occurs within the context of these overall goals. In some organizations there is tight integration between enterprise, business unit, and IT strategic planning; in others these elements are more loosely coupled, informal, and iterative. What is truly rare is a provision for enterprise funding for enterprise IT initiatives. Rather, corporate strategic goals are typically broken down into business unit budgets. As one manager explained, "First our executives decide our profits and then the business units decide how to achieve

them, and then IT develops a plan with the business unit.... We still don't do many corporate projects."

3. ***Set IT spending levels.*** Establishing how much to spend on IT is the area that has been most closely studied by researchers. This is a complex process, influenced by many external and internal factors. Externally, firms look to others in their industry to determine the level of their spending (Hu and Quan 2006). In particular, companies frequently use benchmarks with similar firms to identify a percentage of revenue to spend on IT (Koch 2006). Unfortunately, this approach can be dangerous for a number of reasons. First, it can be a strong driver in inhibiting competitive advantage and leading to greater similarities among firms in an industry (Hu and Quan 2006). Second, this metric tells management nothing about how well its money is being spent (Koch 2006). Third, it does not address IT's ability to use IT strategically (Kobelsky et al. 2006).

A second and increasingly strong external driver of IT spending is the regulatory environment within which a firm operates. Legislation, standards, and professional practices all affect what IT can and cannot do and how its work is done (Smith and McKeen 2006). These in turn affect how much is spent on IT and where it is spent (Hu and Quan 2006). Other external factors that have been shown to affect how much money is spent on IT include the following:

- ***Number of competitors.*** More concentration in an industry reduces the amount spent.
- ***Uncertainty.*** More uncertainty in a business's external environment leads to larger IT budgets.
- ***Diversification of products and services.*** Firms competing in more markets will tend to spend more on IT (Kobelsky et al. 2006).

Internal factors affecting the size of the IT budget include the following:

- ***Affordability.*** A firm's overall performance and cash flow will influence how much discretion it has to spend on IT.
- ***Growth.*** Growing firms tend to invest relatively more in IT than mature firms.
- ***Previous year's spending.*** Firm spending on IT is unlikely to deviate significantly year to year (Hu and Quan 2006; Kobelsky et al. 2006).

IT Processes

These are multilevel and complex and frequently occur in parallel with each other.

1. ***Set the functional IT budget.*** This budget documents spending as it relates to how IT organizations *work*—that is, what is to be spent on IT operations and how much is available to be spent on strategic investments. As noted above, the operations budget is relatively fixed and contains the lion's share of the dollars. In spite of this, IT managers must go through a number of machinations annually to justify this expenditure. Most IT organizations are still seen as

cost centers, so obtaining budget approvals is often a delicate, ongoing exercise of relationship building and education to prevent inappropriate cost cutting (Koch 2006). Once the overall IT operations budget has been established, the challenge of allocating it to the individual business units remains, which, given the complexity of today's shared technical environment, is often a fixed or negotiated percentage of the total. Business units can resent these allocations over which they have no control, and at best they are viewed as a "necessary evil." In organizations where the IT operations budget is centralized, IT managers have greater opportunity to reduce expenses year by year by introducing standards, streamlining hardware and software, and sharing services. But in many companies, operations budgets are decentralized into the business units and aggregated up into the overall IT budget. This approach makes it considerably more difficult for IT managers to implement effective cost-reduction measures. Even in those firms that are highly effective and efficient, the relentless pressure from executives to do more with less makes this part of the annual budgeting process a highly stressful activity.

Allocating the funds remaining to strategic investments is a completely separate process in which potential new IT projects are prioritized and their costs justified. Companies have many different ways of doing this, and most appear to be in a transition phase between methods of prioritization. Traditionally, IT organizations have been designed to parallel the organization structure, and new development funds have been allocated to business units on the basis of some rule of thumb. For example, each business unit might be allotted a certain number of IT staff and dollars to spend on new development (based on percentage of overall revenue) that would remain relatively stable over time. More recently, however, with greater integration of technology, systems, and data, there has been recognition of the cross-business costs of new development and of the need for more enterprise spending to address these. Increasingly organizations are moving to prioritize some or all new development at the enterprise level, thereby removing fixed allocations of new development resources from the business units.

However it is determined, the strategic portion of the functional IT budget also involves staffing the initiatives. This introduces yet another level of complexity in that, even if the dollars are available, appropriate IT resources must also be available to be assigned to particular projects. Thus undertaking a new project not only involves cost justification and prioritization but also requires the availability of the right mix of skills and types of staff. Although some firms use fixed percentages of full-time, contract, and offshore staff in their projects, most use a more variable mix of employees and contract staff in their development projects in order to keep overhead costs low. As a result, creating new IT development budgets often involves a complementary exercise in staff planning.

2. *Set the fiscal IT budget.* A second, parallel stream of IT budgeting involves establishing the *fiscal* IT budget, which the CFO uses to implement the company's fiscal strategy and provide financial reports to shareholders and regulatory and tax authorities. This is seen largely by IT managers as a "translation" exercise where the functional IT budget is reconstituted into the operating and capital spending buckets. Nevertheless, it represents an additional "hoop" through which IT managers must jump before their budgets can be approved. In some companies capital funding is difficult to obtain and must be justified against an additional set of financial criteria. Some organizations require that IT capital expenditures be prioritized against all other corporate capital expenses (e.g., buildings, trucks), which can be a very challenging exercise. In other firms CFOs are more concerned about increasing operating expenses. In either case this is an area where many IT managers set themselves up for failure by failing to "speak the language of finance" (Girard 2004). Because most IT managers think of their work in terms of operations and strategic investments, they are not mindful of some of the larger drivers of fiscal strategy such as investor value and earnings per share. To get more "traction" for their budgets, it is important for IT leaders to better translate what IT can do for the company into monetary terms (Girard 2004). To this end, many companies have begun working more closely with their internal finance staff and are seeing greater acceptance of their budgets as a result.

Assess Actual IT Spending

At the other end of the budgeting process is the need to assess actual IT spending and performance. A new focus on financial accountability has meant that results are more rigorously tracked than in the past. In many companies finance staff now monitor business cases for all new IT projects, thus relieving IT of having to prove the business returns on what is delivered. Often the challenge of finding the right resources for a project or unexpected delays means that the entire available development budget is not spent within a given fiscal year. "We typically tend to spend about 85 percent of our available development budget because of delays or resourcing problems," said one manager. Hitting budget targets exactly in the strategic investment budget is a challenge, and current IT budgeting practices typically do not allow for much flexibility. On the one hand, such practices can create a "use it or lose it" mentality; if money is not spent in the fiscal year, it will disappear. "This leads to some creative accruals and aggressive forecasting," said the focus group. On the other hand, IT managers who want to ensure there is enough money for key expenditures create "placeholders" (i.e., approximations of what they think a project will cost) and "coffee cans" (i.e., unofficial slush funds) in their budgets. The artificial timing of the budget process combined with the difficulties of planning and estimation and reporting complexity, can lead to a distortion in the accurate reporting of what is spent.

IT Budgeting Practices That Deliver Value

Although there is general agreement that current budgeting practices are flawed, there are still no widely accepted alternatives. Within IT itself, companies seem to be experimenting with ways to tweak budgeting to make it both easier and more effective. The following five practices have proven to be useful in this regard:

1. *Appoint an IT finance specialist.* Many companies now have a finance expert working in IT or on staff with the CFO working *with* IT. "Getting help with finance has really made the job of budgeting easier," said one manager. "Having a good partnership with finance helps us to leverage their expertise," said another. Financial specialists can help IT managers understand their costs and drivers in new ways. Within operations, they can assist with cost and value analysis of services and infrastructure (Gruman 2006) and also manage the "translation" process between the functional IT budget and the fiscal IT budget. "Finance helps us to understand depreciation and gives us a deeper understanding of our cost components," a focus group member noted. Finance specialists are also being used to build and monitor business cases for new projects, often acting as brokers between IT and the business units. "They've really helped us to better articulate business value. Now they're in charge of ensuring that the business gets the benefits they say they will, not IT." The improving relationship between finance and IT is making it easier to gain acceptance of IT budgets. "Having dedicated IT finance people is great since this is not what IT managers want to do," said a participant.

2. *Use budgeting tools and methodologies.* About half of the members of the focus group felt they had effective budgeting tools for such things as asset tracking, rolling up and breaking down budgets into different levels of granularity, and reporting. "We have a good, integrated suite of tools," said a manager, "and they really help." Because budgets serve so many different stakeholders, tools and methodologies can help "slice and dice" the numbers many ways, dynamically enabling changes in one area to be reflected in all other areas. Those who did not have good or well-integrated tools found that there were gaps in their budgeting processes that were hard to fill. "Our poor tools lead to disconnects all over the place," claimed an IT manager. Good links to the IT planning process are also needed. Ideally, tools should tie budgets directly to corporate strategic planning, resource strategies, and performance metrics, enabling a further translation among the company's accounting categories and hierarchy and its strategic themes and targets (Norton 2006).

3. *Separate operations from innovation.* Most IT managers mentally separate operations from innovation, but in practical terms maintenance and support are often mixed up with new project development. This happens especially when IT organizations are aligned with and funded by the business units.

Once IT funds and resources are allotted to a particular business unit rather than to a strategic deliverable, it is very difficult to reduce these allocations. Agreement appears to be growing that operations (including maintenance) must be fully financially separated from new development in order to ensure that the costs of the first are fully scrutinized and kept under control while focus is kept on increasing the proportion of resources devoted to new project development (Dragoon 2005; Girard 2004; Gruman 2006; Norton 2006). Repeatedly, focus group managers told stories of how their current budget processes discourage accuracy. "There are many disincentives built into our budgeting processes to keep operational costs down," said one manager. Separating operations from innovation in budgets provides a level of visibility in IT spending that has traditionally been absent and that helps business unit leaders better understand the true costs of delivering both new development and ongoing services.

4. *Adopt enterprise funding models.* It is still rare to find organizations that provide corporate funding for enterprisewide strategic IT initiatives, yet there is broad recognition that this is needed (Norton 2006). The conflict between the need for truly integrated initiatives and traditional siloed budgets frequently stymies innovation, frustrates behavior designed for the common good, and discourages accountability for results (Hope and Fraser 2003; Norton 2006; Steele and Albright 2004). It is therefore recommended that more organizations will adopt enterprise funding models for at least some IT initiatives. Similarly, decentralized budgeting for core IT services is declining due to the cost-saving opportunities available from sharing these. Since costs will likely continue to be charged back to the differing business units, the current best practice is for IT operation budgets to be developed at an enterprise level.

5. *Adopt rolling budget cycles.* IT plans and budgets need attention more frequently than once a year. Although not used by many companies, an eighteen-month rolling plan that is reviewed and updated quarterly appears to be a more effective way of budgeting, especially for new project development (Hope and Fraser 2003; Smith et al. 2007). "It is very difficult to plan new projects a year in advance," said one manager. "Often we are asked for our 'best estimates' in our budgets. The problem is that, once they're in the budget, they are then viewed as reality." The artificial timing of budgets and the difficulty of estimating the costs of new projects are key sources of frustration for IT managers. Rolling budget cycles, when combined with integrated budgeting tools, should better address this problem while still providing the financial snapshots needed by the enterprise on an annual basis.

Conclusion

Although IT budget processes have been largely ignored by researchers, they are a critical linchpin between many different organizational stakeholders: finance and IT, business units and IT, corporate strategy and IT, and different internal IT groups. IT budgeting is much more complex and difficult to navigate than it appears. In this chapter we have outlined some of the challenges faced by IT managers trying to juggle the realities of dealing with both IT operations and strategic investments while meeting the differing needs of their budget stakeholders. Surprisingly, very few guidelines are available for IT managers in this area. Each organization appears to have quite different corporate financial policies, which, in turn, drive different IT budgeting practices. Nevertheless, IT managers do face many common challenges in budgeting. Although other IT practices have benefited from focused management attention in recent years (e.g., prioritization, operations rationalization), budgeting has not as yet been targeted in this way. However, as business and IT leaders begin to recognize the key role that budgets play in implementing strategy and controlling costs, they will hopefully make a serious effort to address the budgeting issues faced by IT.

Chapter Discussion Questions

1. Discuss some ways that CFOs and IT leaders might have differing points of view about IT costs.

2. Should organizations see IT as a cost center or not?

References

Buytendijk, F. "New Way to Budget Enhances Corporate Performance Measurement." Gartner Research Report, ID: 423484, January 28, 2004.

Dragoon, A. "Journey to the IT Promised Land." *CIO Magazine*, April 1, 2005.

Girard, K. "What CIOs Need to Know about Money." *CIO Magazine* Special Money Issue, September 22, 2004.

Goldberg, M. "The Final Frontier for CIOs." *CIO Magazine* Special Money Issue, September 22, 2004.

Gruman, G. "Trimming for Dollars." *CIO Magazine*, July 1, 2006.

Hope, J., and R. Fraser. "Who Needs Budgets?" *Harvard Business Review* 81, no. 2 (February 2003): 2–8.

Hu, Q., and J. Quan. "The Institutionalization of IT Budgeting: Empirical Evidence from the Financial Sector." *Information Resources Management Journal* 19, no. 1 (January–March 2006): 84–97.

Jensen, M. "Corporate Budgeting Is Broken—Let's Fix It." *Harvard Business Review* 9, no. 11 (November 2001): 95–101.

Kobelsky, K., V. Richardson, R. Smith, and R. Zmud. "Determinants and Consequences of Firm Information Technology Budgets." Draft paper provided by the authors, May 2006.

Koch, C. "The Metrics Trap ... and How to Avoid It." *CIO Magazine*, April 1, 2006.

Norton, D. "Linking Strategy and Planning to Budgets." *Balanced Scorecard Report*. Cambridge, MA: Harvard Business School Publishing, May–June 2006.

Overby, S. "Tips from the Budget Masters." *CIO Magazine* Special Money Issue, September 22, 2004.

Smith, H. A., and J. D. McKeen. "IT in 2010." *MIS Quarterly Executive* 5, no. 3 (September 2006): 125–36.

Smith, H. A., J. D. McKeen, and S. Singh. "Developing IT Strategy for Business Value." *Journal of Information Technology Management* 18, no. 1 (June 2007): 49–58.

Steele, R., and C. Albright. "Games Managers Play at Budget Time." *MIT Sloan Management Review* 45, no. 3 (Spring 2004): 81–84.

CHAPTER 8

Managing IT-Based Risk[1]

Not so long ago, IT-based risk was a fairly low-key activity focused on whether IT could deliver projects successfully and keep its applications up and running (McKeen and Smith 2003). But with the opening up of the organization's boundaries to external partners and service providers, external electronic communications, and online services, managing IT-based risk has morphed into a "bet the company" proposition. Not only is the scope of the job bigger, but also the stakes are much higher. As companies have become more dependent on IT for everything they do, the costs of service disruption have escalated exponentially. Now when a system goes down, the company effectively stops working and customers cannot be served. Criminals routinely seek ways to wreak havoc with company data, applications, and Web sites. New regulations to protect privacy and increase accountability have also made executives much more sensitive to the consequences of inadequate IT security practices—either internally or from service providers. In addition, the risk of losing or compromising company information has risen steeply. No longer are a company's files locked down and accessible only by company staff. Today, company information can be exposed to the public in literally hundreds of ways. Our increasing mobility, the portability of storage devices, and the growing sophistication of cyber-threats are just a few of the more noteworthy means.

The job of managing IT-based risk has become much broader and more complex, and it is now widely recognized as an integral part of any technology-based work—no matter how minor. As a result, many IT organizations have been given the responsibility of not only managing risk in their own activities (project development, operations, and delivering business strategy, etc.), but also of managing IT-based risk in all company activities (e.g., mobile computing, file sharing, and online access to information and software). Whereas in the past companies have sought to achieve security through physical or technological means such as locked rooms and virus scanners, understanding is now growing that managing IT-based risk must be a

---

[1] Excerpted from "A Holistic Approach to Managing IT-Based Risk," *Communications of the Association for Information Systems* 25, article 41 (December 2009): 519–30 by H. A. Smith and J. D. McKeen. Used with permission from Association for Information Systems, Atlanta, GA: 404-413-7444; www.aisnet.org. All rights reserved.

strategic and holistic activity that is not just the responsibility of a small group of IT specialists but, rather, part of a mind-set that extends from partners and suppliers to employees and customers.

This chapter explores how organizations are addressing and coping with increasing IT-based risk. First we look at the challenges facing IT managers in the arena of risk management and propose a holistic view of risk. Next we examine some of the characteristics and components needed to develop an effective risk management framework and discuss a generic framework for integrating the growing number of elements involved in it. Lastly, we describe some successful practices organizations could use for improving their risk management capabilities.

A Holistic View of IT-Based Risk

With the explosion in the past decade of new IT-based risks, it is increasingly recognized that risk means more than simply "the possibility of a loss or exposure to loss" (Mogul 2004) or even a hazard, uncertainty, or opportunity (McKeen and Smith 2003). Today, *risk* is a multilayered concept that implies much more is at stake.

> IT risk has changed. IT risk incidents harm constituencies within and outside companies. They damage corporate reputations and expose weaknesses in companies' management teams. Most importantly, IT risk dampens an organization's ability to compete. (Hunter and Westerman 2007)

As a result, companies are now focused on "enterprise risk management" as a more comprehensive and integrated approach to dealing with risk (Slywotzky and Drzik 2005). Although not every risk affecting an enterprise will be an IT-based risk, the fact remains that a large number of the risks affecting the enterprise have an IT-based component. For example, one firm's IT risk management policy notes that the goal of risk management is to ensure that technology failures or data integrity do not compromise the company's strategic objectives, the company's reputation and stakeholders, or its success and reputation.

In spite of the increasing number and complexity of IT-based threats facing organizations, it remains difficult to get senior executives to devote their attention (and commit the necessary resources) to effectively manage these risks. A global survey noted, "while the security community recognizes that information security is part of effective business management, managing information security risk is still overwhelmingly seen as an IT responsibility worldwide" (Berinato 2007).[2] Another study of several organizations found that none had a good view of all key risks and 75 percent had major gaps in their approach to IT-based risk management (Coles and

---

[2] This attitude is beginning to change due to numerous high-profile data breaches. For more about how organizations are approaching information security, see "Balancing Information Security with Enablement," www.itmgmtforum.ca.

Moulton 2003). In short, while IT has become increasingly central to business success, many enterprises have not yet adjusted their processes to incorporate IT-based risk management (Hunter and Westerman 2007).

Knowing what's at stake, risk management is perennially in the top ten priorities for CIOs (Hunter et al. 2005), and efforts are being made to put effective capabilities and processes in place in IT organizations. However, only five percent of firms are at a high level of maturity in this area, and most (80 percent) are still in the initial stages of this work (Proctor 2007). Addressing risk in a more professional, accountable, and transparent fashion is an evolution from traditional IT security work. At a Gartner symposium the following was pointed out:

> [T]raditionally, [IT] security has been reactive, ad hoc, and technically-focused.… The shift to risk management requires an acceptance that you can't protect yourself from everything, so you need to measure risk and make good decisions about how far you go in protecting the organization. (Proctor 2007)

Companies in the group largely reflected this transitional state. "Information security is a primary focus of our risk management strategy," said one manager. "It's very, very visible but our business has yet to commit to addressing risk issues." Another stated, "We have a risk management group focused on IT risk, but lots of other groups focus on it too.… As a result, there are many different and overlapping views, and we are missing integration of these views." "We are constantly trying to identify gaps in our risk management practices and to close them," said a third.

There is, however, no hesitation about identifying the sources of risk. Every company in the group had its own checklist of risk items, and the experts have developed several different frameworks and categorizations that aim to be comprehensive (see Appendix A for some of these). What everyone agrees on is that any approach to dealing with IT-based risk must be holistic—even though it is an "onerous" job to package it as a whole. "Every category of risk has a different vocabulary," explained one focus group manager. "Financial, pandemic, software, information security, disaster recovery planning, governance and legal—each view makes sense, but pulling them together is very hard." Risk is often managed in silos in organizations, resulting in uncoordinated approaches to its management and to decision-making incorporating risk. This is why many organizations, including several in the focus group, are attempting to integrate the wide variety of issues involved into one holistic enterprise risk management strategy that uses a common language to communicate.

The connection among all of the different risk perspectives is the enterprise. Any IT problem that occurs—whether with an application, a network, a new system, a vendor, or a hacker (to name just a few)—has the increasing potential to put the enterprise at risk. Thus, a holistic view of IT-based risk must put the enterprise front and center in any framework or policy. A risk to the enterprise includes anything (either internal or external) that affects its:

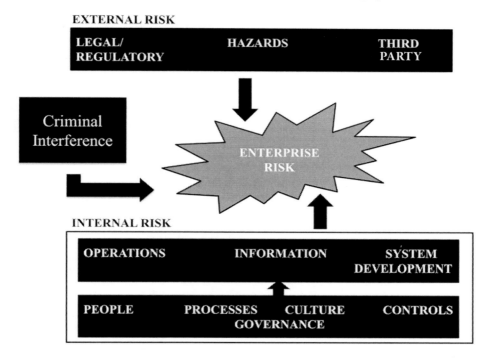

Figure 8.1 A holistic view of IT-based risk

- Brand
- Reputation
- Competitiveness
- Financial value
- End state (i.e., its overall effectiveness, efficiency, and success)

Figure 8.1 offers an integrated, holistic view of risk from an enterprise perspective. A wide variety of both internal and external IT-based risks can affect the enterprise. Externally, risks can come from the following:

- Third parties, such as partners, software vendors, service providers, suppliers, or customers;
- Hazards, such as disasters, pandemics, geopolitical upheavals, or environmental considerations;
- Legal and regulatory issues, such as failure to adhere to the laws and regulations affecting the company, including privacy, financial reporting, environmental reporting, e-discovery, and so on.

Internally, some risks are well known, such as those traditionally associated with IT operations (availability, accessibility) and systems development (not meeting schedules or budgets or delivering value). Others are newer and, although they must be managed from within the organization, they may include both internal and external components. These include the following:

- Information risks, such as those affecting privacy, quality, accuracy, and protection;
- People risks, such as those caused by mistakes or lack of adherence to security protocols;
- Process risks, such as problems caused by poorly designed business processes or by failure to adapt business processes to IT-based changes;
- Cultural risks, such as risk aversion and lack of risk awareness;
- Controls, such as ineffective or inadequate controls to prevent or mitigate risk incidents;
- Governance, such as ineffective or inadequate structure, roles, or accountabilities to make appropriate risk-based decisions.

Finally, there is the risk of criminal interference, either from inside or outside the organization. Unlike other types of risk, which are typically inadvertent, criminal actions are deliberate attacks on the enterprise, its information, or sometimes its employees or customers. Such threats are certainly not new. Everyone is familiar with viruses and hackers. What is new, however, is that many more groups and individuals are targeting organizations and people. These include other national governments, organized crime, industrial spies, and terrorists. "These people are not trying to bring systems down, like in the past," explained a group member. "They are trying to get information."

Holistic Risk Management: A Portrait

Tackling risk in a holistic fashion is challenging, and building an effective framework for its management will not occur overnight. It is therefore important to keep the big picture in mind, or the process could degenerate into overwhelming bureaucracy. It is interesting to note that there is much more agreement from the focus group and other researchers about what effective risk management *looks like* than *how* to do it. This section presents an impressionist portrait of what constitutes holistic risk management in order to show what this big picture should portray. A closer look at the detailed elements composing this picture will also be needed, but first it is essential that all people and functions involved in risk management agree on what image is being created. Otherwise, if one person is trying to create a Picasso while another is painting *Whistler's Mother*, it is unlikely that the resulting portrait will be pleasing to anyone!

With this in mind, we sketch some of the characteristics and components of a portrait of effective, holistic risk management:

1. *Focus on what's important.* "Risks are inevitable," admitted a manager. "The first question we must ask is 'What are we trying to protect?'" said another. "There's no perfect package, and some residual risk must always be taken." A third added "Risks are inevitable, but it's how they're managed—our

response, contingency plans, team readiness, and adaptability—that make the difference." In short, risk is uncertainty that matters, something that can hurt or delay an enterprise from reaching its objectives (Hillson 2008). Although many managers recognize that it's time to take a more strategic view of risk, "[W]e still don't have our hands around what's important and what we should be monitoring and protecting" (Berinato 2007). Risk management is not about anticipating all risks but about attempting to reduce significant risks to a manageable level (Austin and Darby 2003) and knowing how to assess and respond to it (Slywotzky and Drzik 2005). Yet, more than protecting the enterprise, risk management should also enable IT to take more risk in the safest possible way (Caldwell and Mogul 2006). Thus, the focus of effective risk management should not be about saying "no" to a risk, but how to say "yes," thereby building a more agile enterprise (Caldwell and Mogul 2006).

2. ***Expect the image to change over time.*** Few companies have a good grasp of risk management because IT is a discipline that is evolving rapidly (Proctor 2007). As a result, it would be a mistake to codify risk practices and standards too rapidly, according to the focus group. Efforts to do this have typically resulted in "paperwork without context," said one manager. Group members agreed that within a particular risk category, risk management actions should be "continuous, iterative, and structured." In recognition of this reality, most participant organizations have a mandatory risk assessment at key stages in the development process to capture the risk picture involved with a particular project at several points in time. Many also have regular, ongoing reviews of required operational controls on an annual or biannual basis to do the same thing. In addition, when incidents occur, there should always be a process for evaluating what happened, assessing its impact, and determining if controls or other management processes need to be adapted (Coles and Moulton 2003). Finally, organizations should be continually attempting to simplify and stream-line controls wherever possible to minimize their burden. This is a process that is often missed, admitted one manager.

    However, despite the fact that each of these steps is useful in keeping one aspect of the risk picture in mind, it is also essential to stand back from these initiatives and see how the whole image is developing. It is this more strategic and holistic view that is often missing in organizations and that firms often fail to communicate to their staff. One of the greatest risks to organizations comes from employees themselves, not necessarily through their intentional actions, but because they don't recognize the risks involved in their actions (Berinato 2007). Therefore, many believe it is time to recognize that risk can-not be managed solely through controls, procedures, and technology but that all employees must understand the concepts and goals of risk management because the enterprise will always need to rely on their judgment to some extent (Symantec Corporation 2007). In the same vein, many managers also need to better understand this risk picture because they frequently do not comprehend the size and nature of the risks involved and thus resource their management inappropriately (Coles and Moulton 2003). As a result they tend also to delegate many aspects of risk management to lower levels in the organization, thus preventing the development of any longer-term, overall vision (Proctor 2008; Witty 2008).

3. *View risk from multiple levels and perspectives.* Instead of dealing with security "incidents" in a one-at-a-time manner, the group's managers are trying to do a better job of root-cause analysis and understanding risks in a more multifaceted way. To date, risk management has tended to focus largely on the operational and tactical levels, but the managers suggest that risk management should also be viewed in a strategic way. One manager explained, "We need to assess risk trends and develop strategies for dealing with them. Tactics for dealing with future threats will then be more effective and easier to put in place." Another noted, "We must aim for redundancy of protection—that is, multiple layers, to ensure that if one layer fails, others will catch any problems."

Furthermore, risk, security, and compliance are often intermixed in people's minds. Each of these is a valid and unique lens through which to view risk, with the challenge arising when all three are seen as being the same. For example, one expert noted that 70 percent of a typical "security" budget is spent on compliance matters, not on protecting and defending the organization (Society for Information Management 2008), and this imbalance means that overall spending in many firms is skewed. One firm uses the "prudent man" rule to deal with risk, which recommends a diversity of approaches—being proactive, prevention, due diligence, credibility, and promoting awareness—to ensure that it is adequately covered and that all stakeholders are properly protected. Monitoring and adapting to new international standards and laws, completing overall health checks, and analysis of potential risks are other new dimensions of risk that should be incorporated into a firm's overall approach to risk management.

Developing a Risk Management Framework

With the big picture in mind, organizations can begin to develop a framework for filling in the details. The objective of a risk management framework (RMF) is to create a common understanding around risk, to ensure that the right risks are being addressed at the right levels, and to involve the right people in making risk decisions. An RMF also serves to guide the development of risk policies and integrate appropriate risk standards and processes into existing practices. No company in the focus group had yet developed a comprehensive framework for addressing IT-based risk, although many had significant pieces in place or in development. In this section, we attempt to piece these together to sketch out what an RMF might contain.

An RMF should serve as a high-level overview of how risk is to be managed in an enterprise and can also act as a structure for reporting on risk at various levels of detail. Many companies have created risk management policies to guide staff about how IT risk and security are to be treated and all staff are required to read and sign them. Unfortunately, such policies are typically so long and complex as to be overwhelming and ineffective. "Our security policy alone is two hundred pages. How enforceable is it?" complained a manager. Another noted that the language in his company's policy was highly technical, which resulted in considerable noncompliance in following the recommended best practices. A plethora of committees, review boards, councils, and control centers are often designed to deal with one or more aspects of risk management, but they actually contribute to the general complexity of managing IT-based risk in an organization.

It should not be surprising that this situation exists, given the rapidity with which technologies, interfaces, external relationships, and dependencies have developed within the past decade. Organizations have struggled to simply keep up with the waves of legislation, regulation, globalization, standards, and transformation that seem to continually threaten to engulf them. An RMF is thus a starting point for providing an integrated, top-down view of risk, defining it, identifying those responsible for making key decisions about it, and mapping which policies and standards apply to each area. Fortunately, current technology makes it easy to offer multiple views and multiple levels of this information, enabling different groups or individuals to understand their responsibilities and specific policies in detail and see links to specific tools, practices, and templates, while facilitating different types of reporting to different stakeholders at different levels. By mapping existing groups, policies, and guidelines into an RMF, it is easier to see where gaps exist and where complexities in processes should be streamlined.

A basic RMF includes the following:

- **Risk category.** The general area of enterprise risk involved (e.g., criminal, operations, third party, etc.);
- **Policies and standards.** These state, at a high level, the general principles for guiding risk decisions, and they identify any formal corporate, industry, national, or international standards that should apply to each risk category.[3] For example, one company's policy regarding people states the following, in part:

> Protecting the integrity and security of client and corporate information is the responsibility of every employee. Timely and effective reporting of actual and suspected privacy incidents is a key component of meeting this responsibility. Management relies on the collective experience and judgment of its employees.

Another company policy regarding culture states, "We need to embed a risk management focus and awareness into all processes, functions, jobs, and individuals."

---

[3] Some international standards include Committee of Sponsoring Organizations (COSO) of the Treadway Commission, www.coso.org; SAI Global, www.saiglobal.com; and the Office of Government Commerce's Management of Risk, www.ogc.gov.uk/guidance_management_of_risk.asp.

- **Risk type.** Each type of risk associated with each category (e.g., loss of information, failure to comply with specific laws, inability to work due to system outages) needs to be identified. Each type should have a generic name and definition, ideally linked to a business impact. Identifying all risk types will take time and probably require much iteration as "there are an incredible variety of specific risks" (Mogul 2004). However, developing lists and definitions is a good first step (Baccarini et al. 2004; Hillson 2008; McKeen and Smith 2003) and is already a common practice among the focus group companies, at least for certain categories of risk.
- **Risk ownership.** Each type of risk should have an owner, either in IT or in the business. As well, there will likely be several stakeholders who will be affected by risk-based decisions. For example, the principal business sponsor could be the owner of risk decisions associated with the development or purchase of a new IT system, but IT operations and architecture as well as the project manager will clearly be key stakeholders. In addition to specialized IT functions, such as IT security, audit and privacy functions in the business will likely be involved in many IT risk-based decisions. Owners and stakeholders should have clear responsibilities and accountabilities. In the focus group, some major risk types were owned by committees, such as an enterprise risk committee; or the internal audit, social responsibility, and risk governance committee; or the project risk review council on which stakeholder groups were represented.
- **Risk mitigation.** As an RMF is developed, each type of risk should be associated with controls, practices, and tools for addressing it effectively. These fall into one of two categories: compulsory and optional. Group members stressed that overemphasis on mitigation can lead to organizational paralysis or hyper-risk sensitivity. Instead, participants stressed the role of judgment in right sizing mitigation activities wherever possible. "Our technology development framework does not tell you what you have to do, but it does give you things to consider in each phase," said one manager. "We look first at the overall enterprise risk presented by a project," said another, "and develop controls based on our evaluation of the level and types of risk involved." The goal, everyone agreed, is to provide a means by which risks can be managed consistently, effectively, and appropriately.[4]
- **Risk reporting and monitoring.** This was a rather controversial topic in the focus group. Although everyone agreed it is important to make risk and its management more visible in the organization, tracking and reporting on risk have a tendency to make management highly risk averse. One manager said:

> We spent a year trying to quantify risks and developing a roll-up report, but we threw it away because audit didn't understand it and saw only one big risk. This led to endless discussion and no confidence that IT was handling risk well. Now

---

[4] "Risk Management Guide for Information Technology Systems" (csrc.nist.gov/publications/nistpubs/800-30/sp800-30.pdf), the National Institute of Standards and Technology's Special Publication 800-30, provides guidance on specific risk mitigation strategies.

we use a very simple reporting framework presenting risk as high, medium, or low. This is language we all understand.

There are definitely pressures to improve risk measurement (Proctor 2007), but clearly care must be taken in how these metrics are reported. For example, one company uses a variety of self-assessments to ensure that risks have been properly identified and appropriate controls have been put in place. However, as risk management procedures become better understood and more codified, risk reporting can also become more formalized. This is occuring at present with operational process controls and fundamental IT security, such as virus or intrusion detection.

Risk monitoring is an ongoing process because levels and types of risk are changing continually. Thus an RMF should be a dynamic document that changes as new types of risk are identified, business impacts are better understood, and mitigation practices evolve. "We need to continually monitor all categories of risk and ask our executives if the levels of risk are still the same," said a focus group member. It is clear that failure to understand how risks are changing is a significant risk in itself (Proctor 2007). It is therefore especially important to have a process in place to analyze what happened when an unforeseen risk does occur. Unless efforts are made to understand the root causes of a problem, it is unlikely that effective mitigation practices can be put in place (Austin and Darby 2003).

Improving Risk Management Capabilities

Risk management in most areas does not yet have well-documented best practices or standards in place. To that end, the focus group identified several actions that could lead to the development of effective risk management capabilities:

- *Look beyond technical risk.* One of the biggest inhibitors of effective risk management is too tight a focus on technical risk, rather than on business risk (Coles and Moulton 2003). A traditional security approach tends to exclude this, often focusing only on technical threats or specific systems or platforms.
- *Develop a common language of risk.* A clearer understanding of business risk requires all stakeholders—IT, audit, privacy, legal, business managers—to speak the same language and use comparable metrics—at least at the highest levels of analysis where the different types of risk need to be integrated.
- *Simplify the presentation.* Having a common approach to discussing or describing risk is very effective, said several focus group members. While the work that is behind a simple presentation may be complex, presenting too much complexity can be counterproductive. The most effective approaches are simple: a narrative, a dashboard, a "stoplight" report, or another graphic style of report.
- *Match the approach to the level of risk.* Risk management should be appropriate for the level of risk involved. The most effective practices allow for the adaptation of controls while ensuring that the decisions made are visible and the rationale is communicated.

- *Standardize the technology base.* This is one of the most effective ways to reduce risk, according to the research, but it is also one of the most expensive (Hunter et al. 2005).
- *Rehearse.* Many firms now have an emergency response team in place to rapidly deal with key hazards. But it is less common that this team actually rehearses its disaster recovery, business continuity, or other types of risk mitigation plans. One manager noted that live rehearsals are essential to reveal gaps in plans and unexpected risk factors.
- *Clarify roles and responsibilities.* With so many groups in the organization now involved in managing risk in some way, it is critical that roles and responsibilities be documented and communicated. Ideally, this should be in the context of an RMF. However, even if an RMF is not in place, efforts should be made to document which groups in the organization are responsible for which types of enterprise risk.
- *Automate where appropriate.* As risk management practices become standardized and streamlined, automated controls begin to make sense. Some tools can be very effective, noted the focus group, provided they are applied in ways that facilitate risk management, rather than becoming an obstacle to productivity.
- *Educate and communicate.* Each organization has its own culture, and most need to work with staff, business managers, and executives to make them more aware of risk and the need to invest in appropriate management. Some organizations, like one insurance company in the focus group, are so risk-phobic that they need education to enable them to take on more risk. Such companies could benefit from better understanding their "risk portfolio" of projects (Day 2007). Such an approach can often help encourage companies to undertake more risky innovation initiatives with more confidence.

Conclusion

Organizations are more sensitized to risk than ever before. The economy; the regulatory and legal environment; business complexity; the increasing openness of business relationships; and rapidly changing technology have all combined to drive managers to seek a more comprehensive understanding of risk and its management (Rasmussen 2007). Whereas in the past risk was managed in isolated pockets by such functions as IT security, internal audit, and legal, today recognition is growing that these arenas intersect and affect each other. And IT risk is clearly involved in many types of business risk these days. Criminal activity, legal responsibilities, privacy, innovation, and operational productivity, to name just a few, all have IT risk implications. As a result, organizations need a new approach to risk, one that is more holistic in nature and that provides an integrative framework for understanding risk and making decisions associated with it. Accomplishing this is no simple task, so developing such a framework will likely be an ongoing activity, as experts in IT and others begin to grapple with how to approach such a complex and multidimensional activity. In this chapter we have not tried to present a definitive approach to risk management.

There is general agreement that organizations are not ready for this. Instead, we have tried to sketch an impression of how to approach risk management and what an effective risk management program might look like. IT managers and others have been left to fill in the details and complete the portrait in their own organizations.

Chapter Discussion Questions

1. Prioritize the top five risks that Google should focus its risk management efforts on.

2. What are the key risks a company should consider when introducing a new technology?

References

Austin, R., and C. Darby. "The Myth of Secure Computing." *Harvard Business Review*, June 2003.

Baccarini, D., G. Salm, and P. Love. "Management of Risks in Information Technology Projects." *Industrial Management + Data Systems* 104, no. 3–4 (2004).

Berinato, S. "The Fifth Annual Global State of Information Security." *CIO Magazine*, August 28, 2007.

Caldwell, F., and R. Mogul. "Risk Management and Business Performance Are Compatible." Gartner Research Report, ID: G00140802, October 18, 2006.

Coles, R., and R. Moulton. "Operationalizing IT Risk Management." *Computers and Security* 22, no. 6 (2003).

Day, G. "Is It Real? Can We Win? Is It Worth Doing? Managing Risk and Reward in an Innovation Portfolio." *Harvard Business Review*, December 2007.

Hillson, D. "Danger Ahead." *PM Network*, March 2008.

Hunter, R., and G. Westerman. *IT Risk: Turning Business Threats into Competitive Advantage*. Boston: Harvard Business School Press, 2007.

Hunter, R., G. Westerman, and D. Aron. "IT Risk Management: A Little Bit More Is a Whole Lot Better." *Gartner EXPCIO Signature Report*, February 2005.

McKeen, J. D., and H. A. Smith. *Making IT Happen: Critical Issues in IT Management*. Chichester, England: John Wiley & Sons, 2003.

Mogul, R. "Gartner's Simple Enterprise Risk Management Framework." Gartner Research Report, ID: G00125380, December 10, 2004.

Proctor, P. "IT Risk Management for the Inexperienced: A CIO's Travel Guide to IT 'Securistan.'" Presentation to Gartner Symposium ITxpo 2007 Emerging Trends, San Francisco, CA, April 22–26, 2007.

———. "Key Issues for the Risk and Security Roles, 2008." Gartner Research Report, ID: G00155764, March 27, 2008.

Rasmussen, M. "Identifying and Selecting the Right Risk Consultant." Forrester Research Teleconference, July 12, 2007.

Slywotzky, A., and J. Drzik. "Countering the Biggest Risk of All." *Harvard Business Review*, April 2005.

Society for Information Management. "Executive IT security." Private presentation to the SIM Advanced Practices Council, May 2008.

Symantec Corporation. "Trends for July–December 2006." *Symantec Internet Security Threat Report* XI, March 2007.

Witty, R. "Findings: IT Disaster Recovery Can Upsell Business Continuity Management." Gartner Research Report, ID: G00155402, February 19, 2008.

Appendix A
A Selection of Risk Classification Schemes

McKeen and Smith (2003)

- Financial risk
- Technology risk
- Security
- Information and people
- Business process
- Management
- External
- Risk of success

Baccarini, Salm, and Love (2004)

- Commercial risk
- Economic circumstances
- Human behavior
- Political circumstances
- Technology and technical issues
- Management activities and controls
- Individual activities

Jordan and Silcocks (2005)

- Project risk
- IT services
- Information assets
- IT service providers and vendors
- Applications
- Infrastructure
- Strategic
- Emergent

Rasmussen (2007)

- Information security risk
- Policy and compliance
- Information asset management
- Business continuity and disaster recovery
- Incident and threat management
- Physical and environment
- Systems development and operations management

Combined Focus Group Categories

- Project
- Operations
- Strategic
- Enterprise
- Disaster recovery
- Information
- External
- Reputation
- Competitive
- Compliance and regulatory
- Forensic
- Opportunity
- Ethical
- Physical
- Business continuity
- Business process

CHAPTER 9

Building a Strong Relationship with the Business[1]

There is no doubt that a strong business–IT relationship is now critical to the success of an organization's strategic and effective use of IT (Bassellier and Benbasat 2004; Kitzis and Gomolski 2006). With the rapid evolution of IT in business, simply "keeping the lights on" and delivering systems on time and on budget are not enough. Today, IT's ability to deliver value is closely linked with the nature of its relationship with a large number of business stakeholders. Recognizing this, many IT functions have tried to become "partners" with the business at the most senior strategic levels, although with limited success (Gordon and Gordon 2002). It has become clear from these initiatives that business–IT interactions are more complex and more highly resistant to change than first assumed and that building a strong relationship with business is a major challenge for most IT leaders.

We know that the nature and quality of the business–IT relationship are affected by many factors such as the subfunction of IT involved (e.g., operations, application development), the business unit involved, the management levels involved, changing expectations, and general perceptions of IT (McKeen and Smith 2008). However, research suggests that IT managers are still somewhat naïve about how relationships work in business and that interpersonal interaction and clear communication are often missing between the groups. We have also learned that perceptions of the value IT delivers are correlated with how well IT is perceived to understand and identify with the business (Anonymous 2002; Gold 2006; Tallon et al. 2000).

Nevertheless, we still know very little about the elements that contribute to a strong relationship between IT and business, or even about how to characterize such a relationship (Day 2007). In this chapter we first look at the nature of the business–IT

---

[1] Excerpted from "Building a Strong Relationship with the Business," *Communications of the Association for Information Systems* 26, Article 19, April 2010, 429–40 by H. A. Smith and J. D. McKeen. Used with permission from Association for Information Systems, Atlanta, GA: 404-413-7444; http://aisnet.org/?. All rights reserved.

relationship and how an effective relationship could be characterized. Then we examine each of the four foundational elements of a strong, positive relationship, and make suggestions for how IT managers could strengthen them.

The Nature of the Business–IT Relationship

"The IT-business relationship is a set of beliefs that one party holds about the other and how these beliefs are formed from the interactions of … individuals as they engage in tasks associated with an IT service" (Day 2007). The business–IT relationship in organizations tends to span the full range of relationship possibilities. Some members of the focus group felt they had generally healthy and positive relationships, and others labeled them negative or ineffective. Overall, "there's still a general perception that IT is slow, expensive, and gets in the way," said one manager. Even the focus group member with the most positive business–IT relationship admitted it was "not easy," and one set of researchers has described it as typically "arduous" (Pawlowski and Robey 2004).

Although "you can't have a one-sided relationship," as one focus group manager remarked, agreement is almost universal that IT needs to change if it is to improve. Literally dozens of articles have been written about what IT *should* be doing to make it better. For example, IT should better understand the fundamentals of business and aim to satisfy the "right" customers (Kitzis and Gomolski 2006); act as a knowledge broker (Pawlowski and Robey 2004); get involved in the business and be skilled marketers (Schindler 2007); manage expectations (Ross 2006); convince the business that it understands its goals and concerns and communicate in business language (Bassellier and Benbasat 2004); and demonstrate its competencies (Day 2007). In short, "IT has to keep proving itself" to the business to demonstrate its value (Kaarst-Brown 2005). Thus practitioners and researchers both stress that cultivating a strong business–IT relationship is "a continuous effort" (a focus group member); "ongoing" (Luftman and Brier 1999); a "core IT skill" (Feeny and Willcocks 1998); and "emergent" (Day 2007).

On the business side of the relationship, two features stand out. First, business managers are often disengaged from IT work, according to both the focus group and researchers (Ross and Weill 2002). For example, in some cases in the focus group, IT staff have taken on business roles in projects in order to get them done. Second, it is clear that what business wants from this relationship is continually changing. "The business–IT relationship is cyclical," explained one manager. "The business goes back and forth about whether it wants IT to be an order taker or an innovator. Every time the business changes what it wants, the relationship goes sour."

So what *do* we know about the business–IT relationship in organizations? First, we know it is a multifaceted interaction of people and processes. It is unfortunately true that the existence of positive relationships between individual business and IT professionals does not necessarily mean that interactions will be positive on a particular development project, with the IT help desk, with an individual business unit, or between IT and the business as a whole (McKeen and Smith 2008). Because relationships manifest themselves in so many ways—formal and informal, tacit and explicit, procedural and cultural—we must recognize that their complexity means that they don't lend themselves to simplistic solutions (Day 2007; Guillemette et al. 2008; Ross 2006).

Second, we know that difficult, complex relationships often exhibit lack of clarity around expectations and accountabilities and have difficulty with communication (Galford and Drapeau 2003; Pawlowski and Robey 2004). This in turn leads to lack of trust. In the business–IT relationship, "complexity often arises when expectations differ in various parts of an organization, leaving a CIO with the difficult task of reconciling them and elucidating exactly what the IT function's mission and strategic role should be" (Guillemette et al. 2008). Several focus group members complained that different parts of their business expect different things from IT. "In some parts of our business, they want IT to be an order-taker; in others, they want us to be thought leaders and innovators," stated one manager. Another noted, "We live in an age of unmet expectations. There's never enough resources to do everything the business wants us to do."

Third, assumptions by the business about IT tend to cluster into patterns. One researcher has identified five sets of assumptions: 1) IT is a necessary evil, 2) IT is a support, not a partner, 3) IT rules, 4) business can do IT better, and 5) business and IT are equal partners. Business leaders who espouse one of these sets will tend to have similar ideas about who should control IT's direction, how central IT is to business strategy, the value of IT skills and knowledge, how to justify IT investments, and who benefits from IT (Kaarst-Brown 2005). Building on this idea, another study has also shown that business–IT relationships tend to vary along similar patterns. Different organizations tend to adopt one of five IT value profiles and expect IT to behave in accordance with the profile selected (see Appendix A). Problems arise when the assumptions and value profiles espoused by IT conflict with those of the organization or a specific part of the organization. As a result, many disconnects are often present in the relationship. For example, although IT departments and organizations often seek to be a business partner, their participation in this way is not always welcomed by the business (Pawlowski and Robey 2004).

Focus group members defined a strong business–IT relationship in ways that recognize each of these factors. To them, it should include the following:

- Clearly defined expectations, governance models and accountabilities;
- Trust between the two groups;
- Articulation and incorporation of corporate and client values and priorities in all IT work;
- A blurred line between business and IT (i.e., no "us vs. them");
- IT dedicated to business success;
- IT serving as a trusted advisor to the business;
- Mutual recognition of IT value.

In short, a strong business–IT relationship is one where realistic, mutual expectations are clearly articulated and communicated through individual and procedural interactions and where both groups recognize that all facets of this relationship are important to the successful delivery of IT value.

Characteristics of the Business–IT Relationship

- IT has to keep proving itself.
- The business is often disengaged from IT work.
- Business expectations of IT change continually.
- The relationship is affected by the interaction of many people and processes at multiple levels.
- Clarity is often lacking around expectations and accountabilities.
- Business assumptions of IT tend to cluster.
- There are many disconnects between the two groups.

The Foundation of a Strong Business–IT Relationship

Strong relationships do not simply happen. They are built over time, and if they are to deliver value for the organization, they must be built to endure (Day 2007). The focus group told several stories of how the business–IT relationship in their organization had deteriorated when a business or IT leader changed or when a project wasn't delivered on time. Because it can so easily become dysfunctional, constant attention and nurturing are needed at all levels, said the focus group. However, building a strong relationship is not easy to do. Although there is no shortage of prescriptions, the sustained nature of problems in this relationship suggests that some underlying root causes need to be addressed. Appendix B provides one organization's view of what is needed in this relationship.

We have suggested previously that four components must be in place in order to deliver real business value with IT: competence, credibility, interpersonal interaction, and trust. The focus group reviewed these components and agreed that they also form the foundation of a successful and effective business–IT relationship. The focus group saw that developing, sustaining, and growing a strong business–IT relationship in each of these areas is closely intertwined with IT's ability to deliver value with technology. Therefore, a consistent and structured initiative to strengthen the business–IT relationship in these dimensions will also lead to an improved ability to deliver value successfully (see Figure 9.1). In the remainder of this chapter, we look at these four components in turn, discussing in detail how each acts as an important building block of a strong business–IT relationship and suggesting how each could be strengthened.

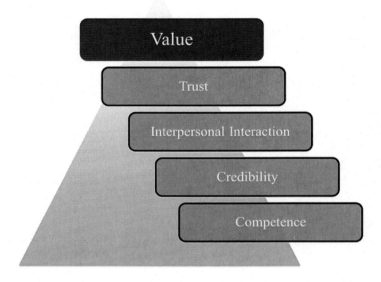

Figure 9.1 Strong relationships are built on a strong foundation.

Building Block #1: Competence

Although a competent IT organization that consistently delivers cost-efficient and reliable services is the bare minimum for an IT function, businesses today expect a great deal more of both their IT organizations and their IT professionals. Many IT organizations have adopted an internal service model in order to "operate IT like a business" and have demonstrated that they can provide services as effectively as external service providers, but these competencies fall short of what business now expects of IT (Kitzis and Gomolski 2006). Researchers and practitioners have identified a number of new competencies that are now required—to a greater or lesser extent—from all IT professionals.

First and foremost, IT staff need *business knowledge*. This goes beyond basic knowledge of a single business unit to include the "big picture" of the whole organization. IT personnel need to understand the business context in which their technologies are deployed, including organizational goals and objectives, capabilities, critical success factors, environment, and constraints. At all levels they need to be able to "think about and understand the development of the business as [any other business] member would and participate in making [it] successful in the same way" (Bassellier and Benbasat 2004). Furthermore, they need to be able to apply their business understanding to help the organization visualize the ways in which "IT can contribute to organizational performance and look for synergies between IT and business activities" (Bassellier and Benbasat 2004). In this regard, an important competence an IT department and its staff can bring to an organization is cross-domain and cross-functional business knowledge (Kitzis and Gomolski 2006; Wailgum 2008a).

Developing business knowledge does not mean that IT staff should become businesspeople but that they should be able to demonstrate they understand the business' goals, concerns, language, and processes and are working to help achieve them (Feeny and Willcocks 1998). One focus group organization surveyed its senior managers about IT and found that these managers felt IT staff had a poor understanding of the business; as a result, they didn't trust IT's ideas.

Other key competencies which IT must cultivate include the following:

- **Expertise.** This includes having up-to-date knowledge, being able to support a technical recommendation, applying expertise to a particular business situation, and offering wise advice on risks, options, and trade-offs, as well as the ability to bring useful new ideas and external information (e.g., about new technologies or what the competition is doing with technology) to the business (Joni 2004; Pawlowski and Robey 2004).
- **Financial awareness.** Awareness of how IT delivers value and the ability to act in accordance with this value is a rare and prized skill (Mahoney and Gerrard 2007). All the focus group members felt pressure to continually demonstrate the business value of IT and recognized a strong need to make all IT staff more aware of such concepts as ROI, total cost of ownership, and how IT affects the bottom line and/ or business strategy.
- **Execution.** It is not enough to understand the business and develop a vision; IT must also operationalize them. Since much of the business–IT relationship is dynamic—that is, continually being re-created—every IT action speaks about its competence. It is well known that the inability to deliver an individual project on time and within budget will undermine the business's view of IT's overall competence. However, it is also the case that the actions of IT operations, the help desk, and other IT subfunctions will also be held up to similar scrutiny. As one focus group manager stated, "Poor delivery of *any* type can break a relationship."

In short, if the IT function is not seen to be competent at executing basic IT services or able to communicate in business terms, it will simply not be given an opportunity to participate in higher-order business activities, such as planning and strategy development (Gerrard 2006).

Strengthening Competence

- **Find ways to develop business knowledge in all IT staff.** Focus group members use "lunch and learn" sessions, job shadowing, and short-term assignments in the business to accomplish this, but they recognize that more needs to be done to develop this competence.
- **Link IT's success criteria to business metrics.** This not only lifts IT's perspective to larger business concerns, but it also introduces all IT staff to the key financial and other measures that drive the rest of the organization.

- *Make business value an explicit criteria in all IT decisions.* Asking why the business should care about a particular IT decision, and how it will affect the business in both the long and short term, changes the focus of IT professionals in a subtle but very effective way, enabling them to communicate even technical decisions in business terms.
- *Ensure effective execution in all IT activities.* This ensures that IT sends a consistent message of competence to all parts and levels of the organization.

Building Block #2: Credibility

Credibility is the belief that others can be counted on to do what they say they will do. It is built in many ways. Keeping agreements and acting with integrity, honesty, and openness are essential behaviors, whereas lack of timely and substantive responses and failure to observe deadlines can undermine it (Greenberg et al. 2007; Feeny et al. 1992). Focus group managers concurred that credibility is very important to the business–IT relationship. Although in earlier days credibility was largely about the ability to deliver systems on time and on budget, now earning and maintaining credibility with the business has become more complex. Today's IT projects often involve many more elements (e.g., multiple platforms, risk management, adherence to laws and standards) and stakeholders than in the past, and the methods and tools of delivery are constantly changing. Furthermore, new research shows that it is typically the "little things" that can be most significant in undermining credibility and that people often make decisions based on IT's attention or inattention to such details (Buchanan 2005). One study concluded that "each and every IT service incident and event must be considered for its long-term influence" (Day 2007).

IT staff often assume that because they are *competent* they will be *credible*, but this is an invalid assumption. A recent survey of CIOs found that they wished their developers "didn't appear so clueless to the rest of the organization" (Wailgum 2008b). It is essential, therefore, that competence be *demonstrated* in order for others to feel someone is credible (Ross 2006). This is especially important in relationships where there is little face-to-face interaction. In these cases in particular, work must be visible and communication constant in order to demonstrate credibility (Hurley 2006).

Strengthening Credibility

- *Communicate frequently and explicitly.* Make progress and accomplishments visible in clear and nontechnical ways. Focus group members found that when difficult decisions are planned together and clearly articulated in advance, much less tension develops in the relationship.
- *Pay attention to the "little things."* Wherever possible, take steps to provide prompt feedback and responses to queries and to ensure consistently high-quality service encounters.

- *Utilize external cues to credibility.* Examples include awards, endorsements from third parties, and the experience and background of IT staff. These specifics can be very useful when starting a new relationship with the business.
- *Assess all business touch points.* All focus group members stressed the need to really listen to what the business says about its expectations and the problems it feels exist in the relationship. Just the effort alone sends a strong and positive message about the importance of this relationship, said a manager. However, he also stressed that undertaking such a review creates expectations that changes will be made, so regular reports back to the business about what is being done to improve things are especially important.

Building Block #3: Interpersonal Interaction

The business–IT relationship is shaped by the development of mutual understanding, interests, and expectations, which are formed and shaped during a wide variety of interpersonal interactions (Gold 2006). Business–IT interactions must be developed and nurtured at many different levels in the business–IT relationship, said focus group managers, and although CEO–CIO interactions can set the tone for the relationship, the connections at multiple touch points contribute to its overall quality (Flint 2004; Prewitt 2005). The following are the four significant dimensions of interpersonal interaction:

- *Professionalism.* This is the unarticulated set of working behaviors, attitudes, and expectations that serves as the glue which keeps teams of diverse individuals working together toward the same goal. These behaviors are not only carefully watched by the business, they are also just as important *within* IT, said the focus group. Members noted that difficult internal IT relationships can lead to problems delivering effective IT services. Five sets of attitudes and behaviors contribute to developing IT professionalism: 1) comportment (i.e., appearance and manners on the job), 2) preparation (i.e., displaying competence and good organization), 3) communication skill (i.e., clarity and etiquette), 4) judgment (i.e., the ability to make right choices for the organization), and 5) attitude (i.e., caring about doing a job well and about doing the right thing for the company) (McKeen and Smith 2008).
- *Nontechnical communication.* Over and over, research has found that the inability to communicate clearly with the business in its own terms can undermine the business–IT relationship (Bassellier and Benbasat 2004; Kitzis and Gomolski 2006). Today, because IT staff work across many organizational boundaries, they must also be effective at translating and interpreting needs—not only from business to technology and vice versa, but also between business units—in order to enable members of different communities to understand each other (Wailgum 2008a). Increasingly, as IT programs and services are delivered collaboratively *by* external partners and *to* external partners, clarity in communication is becoming mission critical.

- **Social skills.** The social dimension of the business–IT relationship is often ignored by both sides, leading to misunderstandings and lack of trust (Day 2007). Social bonds help diverse groups build trust and develop a common language, both of which are essential to a strong relationship. Socialization also helps build mutual understanding, enabling all parties to get comfortable with one another and uncovering hidden assumptions, which may become obstacles to success (Kaarst-Brown 2005). Socialization also develops empathy and facilitates problem solving (Feeny and Willcocks 1998).

  Unfortunately, many IT organizations are structured in ways that create barriers between business and IT. For example, the use of "relationship managers" to act as interfaces between IT and the business is a mixed blessing. Although individually, these managers may be skilled and viewed positively by the business, focus group members noted that their position often leads them to act as gatekeepers to the business. One manager told of being hauled on the carpet to explain his lunch with a business manager (a personal friend), which hadn't been approved by the relationship manager! "We need a broad range of social interactions with the business," said another manager. "We use account managers, but we also encourage interactions through such things as lunches and social events." Ongoing, face-to-face interaction is the ideal, but with today's virtual teams and global organizations, other forms of social interaction, such as networking and collaboration tools, are being introduced to help bridge gaps in this area. In a virtual environment, social bonds can be more important than in a more traditional workplace, but they are harder to develop (Greenberg et al. 2007).

- **Management of politics and conflict.** The business–IT relationship can be turbulent, and IT personnel are not noted for their skills in dealing with the conflicts and challenges involved. Furthermore, conflict and politics tend to be exacerbated by the types of projects most commonly undertaken by IT—that is, those that cross internal and external organizational boundaries (Weiss and Hughes 2005). As a result, IT functions and personnel need ways to effectively address conflict and use it to deliver creative solutions. All too often, conflict is avoided or treated as a "hot potato" to be tossed up the management hierarchy (Weiss and Hughes 2005). Straight talk and the development of a healthy give-and-take attitude are fundamental to dealing with conflict at its source. Experts also recommend the development of transparent processes for managing disagreements and frank discussions of the trade-offs involved in dealing with problems (Pascale et al. 1997). These not only help stop damaging escalation and growing uncertainty but also help to model conflict-resolution skills for the staff involved.

  Failure to understand the role of politics in a particular organization makes IT personnel less effective in their business interactions because they cannot craft "win–win" solutions. Thus, all IT staff need to understand something about politics and how it can affect their work. At more senior levels, it is imperative that IT professionals learn how to act "wisely and shrewdly in a political environment"

(Kitzis and Gomolski 2006). Since politics is part of every business relationship and cannot be avoided, IT personnel must learn how to work with it, said focus group members.

Strengthening Interpersonal Interactions

- *Expect professionalism.* IT managers must not only articulate professional values and behaviors, they must *live* them and measure and reward them in their staff.
- *Promote a wide variety of social interactions at all levels.* Whether face-to-face or virtual, sharing information about each other's background and interests is an important way to bolster working relationships at all levels. Even where formal relationship managers are in place, IT leaders should encourage all IT staff to connect informally with their business colleagues. "Social interaction facilitates quick problem ownership and resolution and helps to develop a common language," said a focus group participant. Although the need for socialization increases as one moves up the organizational hierarchy, even at the lowest levels staff should be expected to spend about 10 percent of their time in this type of interaction (Kitzis and Gomolski 2006).
- *Develop "soft skills" in IT staff.* Although the need for interpersonal skills in IT has never been greater, many companies still give their development short shrift, preferring instead to stress technical competencies. In developing interpersonal skills, formal training should be only one component. It is even more important that IT managers take time to develop such skills in their staff through mentoring and coaching. Many focus group members have implemented "soft" skills development initiatives informally, but they also have admitted that the pressure to be instantly productive often detracts from both business and IT participation in them.

Building Block #4: Trust

Effective interpersonal interactions, a belief that the job at hand will get done and get done right, and demonstrated business and technical competence are all required to facilitate trust that IT can be a successful partner with the business. But *even if* these are in place, proactive measures are still needed to actually *build* trust between the two groups. In many firms, an underlying sense of distrust of IT *as a whole* remains:

> IT's processes are notoriously convoluted and bureaucratic, leaving the business unsure of how to accomplish their business strategies with IT. From strategy alignment to prioritization to budgeting and resourcing to delivering value to managing costs, it must be clear that what IT is doing is for the benefit of the enterprise, not itself. (McKeen and Smith 2008)

The most important way to build trust at this level is through effective governance. The story of how one CIO managed to transform the business–IT relationship at Farm Credit Canada illustrates its importance:

[At FCC, when Paul MacDonald became CIO], IT was considered a necessary evil. Business people were afraid of it and wished it would just go away.... [Transforming this relationship] was a very difficult and complex job—especially for cross-functional processes. Clear responsibilities and accountabilities had to be defined.... "It's all about clarity of roles and responsibilities," MacDonald said. The new IT governance model was validated and refined through sessions with key business stakeholders. "These sessions were important to demonstrate that we weren't just shuffling the boxes around in IT," [MacDonald] said.... MacDonald also made sure that the new model actually worked the way it was supposed to. "There were cases where it didn't ... and with these, we made changes in our processes." He attributes his willingness to make changes where needed to his ability to make the new model actually function the way it was supposed to....

"Today, at FCC user satisfaction is very high and IT is seen as being indispensable...." [MacDonald] stressed that it is important to review and refine the new governance model continually. "There were some things that just didn't work," he said. "We are still constantly learning." (Smith and McKeen 2008)

Effective governance should be designed to build common business goals and establish a good decision-making process (Gerrard 2006). Mature processes in IT and transparency about costs develop trust (Levinson and Pastore 2005; Overby 2005). A focus group manager stated succinctly: "More transparency equals fewer surprises and you get transparency through governance." Aspects of governance that have enhanced trust in focus group organizations include integrated planning, defined accountabilities, a clear picture of mandates and authorities, and clarity around how work gets done.

Another focus group manager explained the importance of governance in this way:

In the past, we couldn't break the trust barrier. Now, [with an effective governance structure] we are more proactive and are fighting fewer fires. Our processes ensure proper escalation and a new focus on value. In short, governance captures the value of a good relationship and good fences make good neighbours.

Trust is essential for both superior performance and for developing the collaborative relationships that lead to success (Greenberg et al. 2007). It is developed through consistency, clear communication, willingness to tackle challenges, and owning up to and learning from mistakes (Upton and Staats 2008). Both inconsistent messages to stakeholders and inconsistent processes and standards can seriously undermine trust (Galford and Drapeau 2003).

Nevertheless, it must be stressed that there is no optimal form of governance (Gordon and Gordon 2002). The key is to develop a model of IT governance that addresses the business's *expectations* of its IT function. Thus, an IT organization can best build trust if it clearly understands the organization's priorities for IT and designs its governance model to match (Guillemette et al. 2008).

Strengthening Trust

- *Design governance for clarity and transparency.* IT leaders should assess how the business views IT processes—from the help desk on up. It is important to recognize that all processes play a very visible role in how IT is viewed in the organization and that clear, effective, and fair processes are needed to break the "trust barrier" between business and IT at all levels.
- *Mandate the relationship.* Although it may seem counterintuitive, companies have had success from strictly enforcing relationship basics such as formal roles and responsibilities, joint scorecards, and the use of common metrics. Such structural measures can ensure that common expectations, language, and goals are developed and met.
- *Design IT for business expectations.* Clearly understanding the *primary* value the business wants IT to deliver can help IT understand how to focus its process and governance models (see Appendix A).

Conclusion

There is clearly no panacea for a strong business–IT relationship. Yet the correlation between a good relationship and the ability to deliver value with IT makes it imperative that leaders do all they can to develop effective interpersonal and interfunctional business–IT relations. It is unfortunately still incumbent on IT leadership to take on the bulk of this task, if only because it will make IT organizations more effective. Business–IT relationships are complex, with interactions of many types, at many levels, and between both individuals and across functional and organizational entities. In this chapter we have not only identified and explored what a strong business–IT relationship should look like in its many dimensions, but we also have described the four major components needed to build it: competence, credibility, interpersonal skills, and trust. Unfortunately, business–IT relationships still leave a lot to be desired in most organizations. Recognizing that what it takes to build a strong business–IT partnership is so closely related to what is needed to deliver IT value may help to focus more attention on these mission-critical activities.

Chapter Discussion Questions

1. Are the four building blocks of relationships necessary in all relationships?
2. What soft skills are most important for IT staff?

References

Anonymous. "Senior IT People Excluded from IT Decision-Making." *Career Development International* 7, no. 6/7 (2002).

Bassellier, G., and I. Benbasat. "Business Competence of Information Technology Professionals: Conceptual Development and Influence on IT-Business Partnerships." *MIS Quarterly* 28, no. 4 (December 2004).

Buchanan, L. "Sweat the Small Stuff." *Harvard Business Review* (April 2005). hbr. org/2005/04/sweat-the-small-stuff/ar/1 (accessed March 10, 2011).

Day, J. "Strangers on the Train: The Relationship of the IT Department with the Rest of the Business." *Information Technology and People* 20, no. 1 (2007).

Feeny, D., B. Edwards, and K. Simpson. "Understanding the CEO/CIO Relationship." *MIS Quarterly* 16, no. 4 (1992).

Feeny, D., and L. Willcocks. "Core IS Capabilities for Exploiting Information Technology." *Sloan Management Review* 39, no. 3 (Spring 1998).

Flint, D. "Senior Executives Don't Always Realize the True Value of IT." Gartner Research Report, ID: COM-22-5499, June 21, 2004.

Galford, R., and A. Drapeau. "The Enemies of Trust." *Harvard Business Review* #R0302G, February 2003.

Gerrard, M. "Three Critical Success Factors in the Business/IT Relationship." Gartner Research Report, ID: G00143352, October 18, 2006.

Gold, R. "Perception *Is* Reality: Why Subjective Measures Matter and How to Maximize Their Impact." *Harvard Business School Publishing Balanced Scorecard Report*, July–August, 2006.

Gordon, S., and J. Gordon. "Organizational Options for Resolving the Tension Between IT Departments and Business Units in the Delivery of IT Services." *Information Technology and People* 15, no. 4 (2002).

Greenberg, P., R. Greenberg, and Y. Antonucci. "Creating and Sustaining Trust in Virtual Teams." *Business Horizons* 50 (2007).

Guillemette, M., G. Paré, and H. Smith. "What's Your IT Value Profile?" *Cahier du GReSI #08-04*. Montréal, Canada: HEC Montréal, November 2008.

Hurley, R. "The Decision to Trust." *Harvard Business Review* #R0609B, September 2006.

Joni, S. "The Geography of Trust." *Harvard Business Review* #R0403F, March 2004.

Kaarst-Brown, M. "Understanding an Organization's View of the CIO: The Role of Assumptions About IT." *MIS Quarterly Executive* 4, no. 2 (June 2005).

Kitzis, E., and B. Gomolski. "IT Leaders Must Think Like Business Leaders." Gartner Research Report, ID: G00143430, October 26, 2006.

Levinson, M., and R. Pastore. "Transparency Helps Align IT with Business." *CIO Magazine*, June 1, 2005.

Luftman, J., and T. Brier. "Achieving and Sustaining Business-IT Alignment." *California Management Review* 41, no. 1 (Fall 1999).

Mahoney, J., and M. Gerrard. "IT Value Performance Tools Link to Business-IT Alignment." Gartner Research Report, ID: G00152551, November 2, 2007.

McKeen, J. D., and H. A. Smith. *IT Strategy in Action.* Upper Saddle River, NJ: Pearson-Prentice Hall, 2008.

Overby, S. "Turning IT Doubters into True Believers: Executive Summary." *CIO Research Reports,* June 1, 2005.

Pascale, R., M. Millemann, and L. Gioja. "Changing the Way We Change." *Harvard Business Review,* November–December 2007.

Pawlowski, S., and D. Robey. "Bridging User Organizations: Knowledge Brokering and the Work of Information Technology Professionals." *MIS Quarterly* 28, no. 4 (2004).

Prewitt, E. "The Communication Gap." *CIO Magazine,* June 1, 2005.

Ross, J. "Trust Makes the Team Go 'Round." *Harvard Management Update* 11, no. 6 (June 2006): 3–6.

Ross, J., and P. Weill. "Six IT Decisions Your IT People Shouldn't Make." *Harvard Business Review* #R0211F, November 2002.

Schindler, E. "What IT Can Learn from the Marketing Department." CIO Web 2.0 Advisor, September 21, 2007. https://www.cio.com/article/2374319/it-organization/what-it-can-learn-from-the-marketing-department.html (accessed March 10, 2011).

Smith, H. A., and J. D. McKeen. "Creating a Process-Centric Organization at FCC: SOA from the Top Down." *MIS Quarterly Executive* 7, no. 2 (June 2008): 71–84.

Tallon, P., K. Kramer, and V. Gurbaxani. "Executives' Perceptions of the Business Value of Information Technology: A Process-Oriented Approach." *Journal of Management Information Systems* 16, no. 4 (Spring 2000).

Upton, D., and B. Staats. "Radically Simple IT." *Harvard Business Review* #R0803, March 2008.

Wailgum, T. "Eight Reasons Why CIOs Think Their Application Developers Are Clueless." *CIO Magazine,* September 3, 2008b.

———. "Why Business Analysts Are So Important for IT and CIOs." *CIO Magazine,* April 16, 2008a.

Weiss, J., and J. Hughes. "Want collaboration? Accept—and Actively Manage—Conflict." *Harvard Business Review* #R0503F, March 2005.

Appendix A
The Five IT Value Profiles

Each of the following profiles provides a unique way for IT to contribute to an organization. One is not "better" than the other, nor is one profile more or less mature than any other. Each represents a different, consistent way of organizing IT to deliver value. Each is different in five ways: main activities, dominant skills and knowledge, the business–IT relationship, governance and decision-making, and accountabilities.

Profile A: Project Coordinator. This type of IT function coordinates IT activities between the business and outsourcers. The primary value it delivers is organizational flexibility through the IT outsourcing strategy it establishes and through promoting informed IT decision-making in the business units. The Project Coordinator function works with the business units, helping them formalize their requirements, and then finds an outsourcer to develop and implement what is needed. The Project Coordinator also manages the relationships between vendors and business units, not only with the organization's current activities but also in planning for the future by developing strategic partnerships.

Profile B: Systems Provider. The primary mission of the Systems Provider is to provide the organization with quality information systems at the lowest possible cost. Strategically, the Systems Provider uses the organization's business plans to set IT's goals, prepare budgets, and determine the resources needed to implement the organization's strategy for the required systems development projects.

Profile C: Architecture Builder. The primary mission of this type of IT function is to link the firm's various business units by integrating computerized systems, data, and technological platforms. The Architecture Builder seeks to design a flexible architecture and infrastructure that will meet the company's needs. The architecture builder typically receives broad strategic direction from the organization and designs an architecture and infrastructure with which the organization can implement its strategy.

Profile D: Partner. The main objective of the Partner IT function is to create IT-enabled business capabilities to support current business strategies. IT and the business collaborate to achieve a two-way strategic alignment that is developed iteratively and reciprocally over time. The Partner is a catalyst for change in business processes and seeks to improve organizational efficiency. As guardian of the organization's business processes, the Partner's mission therefore extends far beyond its technological tools.

Profile E: Technological Leader. The Technological Leader tries above all to use innovation to transform the organization's strategy. IT's main objective is to identify opportunities, find innovative organizational applications for technology that will enable the organization to secure a significant competitive advantage, and then implement such applications.

(*Source:* Guillemette et al. 2008)

Appendix B
Guidelines for Building a Strong Business–IT Relationship
The following excerpt provided by a focus group member is from a company memo on improving the business–IT relationship:

Now more than ever we must truly understand the business transformation agenda. This requires us to potentially interact differently than in the past or in a mode beyond what our executives may be looking for. We must:

- Stop acting as and being viewed as order-takers once IT projects have been identified.
- Develop an understanding of business improvement ideas before they become initiatives or projects.
- Be prepared to offer alternative perspectives on business solutions.
- Be part of the strategic equation and have "feet on the street."
- Engage early before ideas and issues turn into projects.
- Continue to shape the solution during pre-concept and concept phases.

To develop a relationship with the business units where we are viewed as trusted advisors and as adding value, we need to truly be part of their decision-making process and team. We must ask ourselves:

- Are we considered a member of the business' senior leadership team?
- Are we consulted before decisions are made or just asked to execute what has already been decided?
- Are we involved in shaping the content of the strategic agenda not just its schedule?

Creating a consistent forum for one-on-one strategic interaction should allow us to rise above the normal churn of issues, projects, or other regularly scheduled meetings and be positioned to truly start understanding where our help is needed. Potential short-term next steps include the following:

- Get invited to each business unit's leadership team meetings.
- Schedule a monthly 1-1 strategy meeting with no set agenda.

CHAPTER 10

Enabling Collaboration with IT[1]

Our increasing connectedness is driving new ways of working together to deliver business value. Globalizing organizations, outsourcing, mobile work, innovation, interorganizational teams, innovation, and reaching out to suppliers and customers are feeding today's need to improve collaboration within firms. And of course IT is at the center of these trends. A study on what makes widely dispersed virtual teams effective found that, contrary to expectations, technology is a significant factor in facilitating their success (Majchrzak et al. 2004). However, literally hundreds of software packages are being promoted for improving collaboration. These technologies, social networking, content management, and new ways of communicating (e.g., blogs, wikis, instant messages, tweets) appear almost daily and are being adopted and adapted rapidly in the wider society. They are challenging many of the traditional conventions of how work is done and the role of IT functions themselves.

As the menu of available technologies widens and becomes virtually free, and as employees clamor to use them anywhere, anyplace, and anytime, IT managers are asking many questions including these:

- What is the business value of these technologies?
- What is the best way to assess them and make decisions about their use?
- How can these technologies best be managed and adapted for organizational purposes?

Businesses are experimenting with different types of collaboration, such as those listed above, and IT functions are often expected to make collaboration happen through the implementation of technology, even though technologies are only one piece of any collaboration initiative. Certainly IT functions provide the "heavy lifting," such as connectivity and information integrity (without which most collaboration efforts would not be effective), and a well-designed IT architecture is a key enabler

---

[1] Excerpted from "Enabling Collaboration with IT," *Communications of the Association for Information Systems* 28, article 16 (March 2011): 243–54 by H. A. Smith and J. D. McKeen. Used with permission from Association for Information Systems, Atlanta, GA: 404-413-7444; www.aisnet.org. All rights reserved.

of collaboration (Johansen 2007). And at the most basic level IT also protects the privacy and security of information and users. But how new applications are implemented is often as important as the technology itself in delivering business value. As one IT manager stated, "We sometimes jump directly to the tool without thinking through the strategy and tactics involved." As a result, IT managers can sometimes feel that the deployment of collaboration is less than optimal.

In this chapter we explore IT's role in enabling collaboration in organizations, and at the same time what IT's role should not be (i.e., what responsibilities and accountabilities should properly be the function of the business). We identify the principal forms of collaboration used and the primary business drivers involved in them, how business value is measured, and the roles of IT and the business in enabling collaboration. First we look at some of the reasons why collaboration is becoming so important in organizations and the business value it enables. Next we examine some of the different characteristics of collaboration in various organizations. Our focus then switches to the key components of a collaboration program, how these influence its effectiveness, and IT's role in promoting collaboration. We conclude with a series of recommendations for IT managers to use as a guide for how they can best facilitate collaboration in their organizations.

Why Collaborate?

There is no doubt that information and communications technologies are enabling different ways of working—within organizations and between them. Who could imagine corporate life without email? Without Google? Without smart phones? These technologies and others have changed forever how we interact with others both personally and professionally, how we share information, and where work gets done. Thus it should be no surprise that there's strong interest in collaboration among business practitioners and academics alike. A simple Internet search on this topic yields literally thousands of articles. And it is no secret that what we are seeing now is just the tip of the technology iceberg. Whether we do or do not yet actually use the next generation of collaboration/social networking technologies in our work, everyone has heard about them: instant messaging, Skype, Twitter, Facebook, and others. No one is a stranger to speculation about how these technologies are going to continue to change the face of organizations.

Almost any business or IT journal contains speculative "think pieces" or case studies about how essential it will be to collaborate (in various ways) in the future and how failing to do this will result in the organization becoming a dinosaur (Amabile and Khaire 2008; Lynch 2007; Romano et al. 2007). And it is certainly without question that hundreds of new technologies—including hardware, software, applications, and services—are currently being promoted to businesses as enabling collaboration and all of the benefits it will bring. Yet business and IT managers are struggling to cut through the hype to get at the real value collaboration will bring. They have seen this before in both the "Internet bubble" and the knowledge management fad and know from bitter experience with previous generations of groupware, knowledge management, and collaboration investments that achieving positive results is not as easy as plugging in a piece of technology (Iandoli 2009a). Many managers have a long history of deploying collaboration technology and seeing it gather dust (McAfee 2006).

It is therefore no surprise that the focus group reported a great deal of conflicting feelings in their organizations about collaboration, from wildly enthusiastic to highly skeptical. One company has invested substantial amounts of time and money in collaboration technologies and in adapting its organizational culture and behaviors accordingly, and believes that they have become more productive, effective, and successful as a result. On the other hand, another manager reported his company's senior executives were grumbling that no one has yet given them a real business need for collaboration. Some members reported that there's a lack of business push for collaboration in their organization, and others stated that their business units were "coming around in some areas because they feel they need to be where their customers are." Most agreed that virtual interaction is becoming increasingly commonplace and that the percentage of time employees work virtually (and therefore need collaboration technology) is increasing (Drakos et al. 2009; Romano et al. 2007). One study found that spending on collaborative software represents one-fifth of most organizations' technology budgets, but business leaders are still uncertain if these investments are improving either collaboration or the quality of work (Cross et al. 2005). This sentiment was reflected by most of the focus group participants. "We're still experimenting with collaboration," explained one. "We don't have a business project, but we're developing a collaboration strategy."

Because collaboration is evolving so rapidly, it's difficult to definitively articulate the business drivers and benefits involved. However, there appear to be six main categories of potential business value:

1. *Topline value.* A great deal has been written about the importance of collaboration in improving and/or increasing creativity and innovation in organizations. One study found that collaboration technologies play a critical role in improving knowledge, creating and sharing practices, and in developing new processes, products, and services (Fink 2007). Another noted "great ideas can come from anywhere and IT has dramatically reduced the cost of accessing them" (Pisano and Verganti 2008). The expectation is that collaboration both across an organization and with customers, suppliers, and other third parties will strengthen an organization's ability to identify new business opportunities and formulate creative solutions (Fink 2007). The goal is "real time, rich, location independent collaboration" by creative teams that can rapidly process and assimilate knowledge from many different sources and apply it in practical ways (Gordon et al. 2008). This type of value is especially important in highly dynamic and competitive industries where the generation of a large number of new, good ideas is critical to competitive advantage. Within the focus group,

most organizations were just beginning to recognize how technology, collaboration, and innovation could be harnessed to change their business models, products, and services. "We're beginning to see our executives more open to these concepts and how changing how we work together and with our customers can make a difference," said a participant. One firm has included collaboration and innovation in its performance review criteria. Nevertheless, these appear to be the exceptions, and focus group managers mainly commented that their business leaders were not yet really thinking about how technology could help them in this area.

2. *Cost savings.* In a number of focus group companies, collaboration is seen as having real cost-savings potential in ways such as reducing travel costs through virtual meetings, improving communications, and enabling remote access to documents. Participants noted that collaborative technology facilitates the work of global and virtual teams by compressing work flow, reducing development costs, increasing communication, minimizing misunderstandings, improving coordination between groups, and enabling linkages with vendors, suppliers, and customers that speed up the supply chain and other work processes.

3. *Effectiveness.* There is wide recognition that collaboration technology, used properly, can make group work more effective. This is particularly true for virtual teams. For example, one focus group company uses social networking technologies (behind its firewall) to enable team members from around the world to learn about each other, have fun events, and understand each others' customs and culture. "This has been really useful for us in building strong global teams," said the manager involved. Collaboration technology, particularly unified communications, is especially useful in integrating remote and mobile workers seamlessly into team or project activities. It enables them to "touch down" in an office and plug into the applications and information they need, wherever they are in the world. Increasingly, too, for many professionals whose work consists of participation in a number of ad hoc projects, collaboration technology enables them to more effectively juggle a variety of commitments. One firm uses it extensively for its multidisciplinary projects, such as disaster recovery planning. Finally, online education is a big application of this technology, allowing employees to participate from a variety of locations, have virtual and real-time discussions, and incorporate learning into the demands of their workday.

4. *Accessibility of people.* A key feature of collaboration and its associated technology is that it provides a company with access to a much broader range of skills, capabilities, resources, and services than have been traditionally available. Collaboration technology significantly expands the number of potential partners and expertise available to a company (Pisano and Verganti 2008), and in recent years different types of interorganizational alliances—from supply chain integration to design coordination to innovative partnerships—have become commonplace (Attaran 2007). However, it is the ability to

access internal expertise that is currently of most interest to the focus group companies. Only one firm had successfully implemented a comprehensive enterprise directory, including phone book, expertise location anywhere in the organization, reporting structures, and connection with social networking information. Yet even this firm recognized how difficult building such a capability can be. "Over the years, it has been a huge stumbling block for us," one focus group member said. Other members were envious. "We're trying to build this facility," said one, "because right now it's really hard for us to find people in our organization." Ideally, this type of accessibility also enables the development of communities of interest within the organization—either work-focused or built around personal interests. In our virtual, networked world that is rapidly losing the "human touch" and is characterized by "ephemeral relationships," these communities can help build staff morale and create a sense of belonging (Tebbutt 2009; Thomas and Bostrom 2008).

5. *Accessibility of information.* One of the biggest benefits of collaboration and its associated technology is that it makes information much more accessible than in the past. Information repositories such as the intranet enable the management and sharing of digital content on an as-needed basis (Chin et al. 2008). Other technologies, such as wikis, support the creation of new content and its publication. These tools enable information and knowledge-sharing across time and space in ways that were unheard of a few years ago (Fink 2007). Many focus group members believe that portal and content management applications will be the biggest value of collaboration. But they also feel it will take a lot of work to get there. "Our intranet is just a garbage scow of information," sighed one manager. "The same document can exist in literally hundreds of places." Another noted, "While our corporate level content is well managed, it gets messier and messier the lower down in the organization you go. We need much more information management and filtering to make our Intranet really useful." Finally, although everyone agrees that collaboration will only be successful if more information is made more widely available, there is still a great deal of fear that "someone will do something bad with it," which explains why in many organizations the default position is not to share.

6. *Flexibility.* The world is becoming increasingly volatile, uncertain, complex, and ambiguous and this is creating a highly dynamic business environment for many companies (Johansen 2007). Flatter, more networked, and collaborative structures create the right work and leadership environment, facilitating fluid workforces and speedy decision-making and providing transparency of information and capabilities while retaining clarity around the organization's beliefs, values, and responsibilities (Reeves et al. 2008). A networked organization, with situational leadership, less structure, and the ability to create new capabilities through its networks, will be much more able to cope with these challenges. Flexibility will involve space, technology, and protocols for working in networks and will exist at

the intersection of real estate, HR, and IT (Johansen 2007). Flexibility underlies many of the reasons why focus group members are interested in collaboration. Although most are still seeing this as a need within a more traditional, hierarchical organizational structure, some recognize that their structure and governance practices will have to change substantially.

Characteristics of Collaboration

Although there is much talk about the benefits of collaboration and the need for more of it in organizations, clarity is significantly lacking about what collaboration actually is. As one focus group member put it, "If you asked a hundred people to describe collaboration, you would get a hundred different answers. There's a huge disparity in understanding about this topic." There is also significant confusion about the terminology of collaboration. Collaborating is a human activity whereas collaboration technology is the hardware, software, and applications that enable the work of collaboration (Camarinha-Matos et al. 2009). Finally, the group noted that collaboration is often used interchangeably with such terms as networking, social networking, and cooperation. It is therefore important to be clear about the range and scope of collaboration in organizations, including who is involved in collaboration, what type of work is being done, and where it is being done, since these have a direct bearing on how the IT function can best support collaboration with technology (see Figure 10.1).

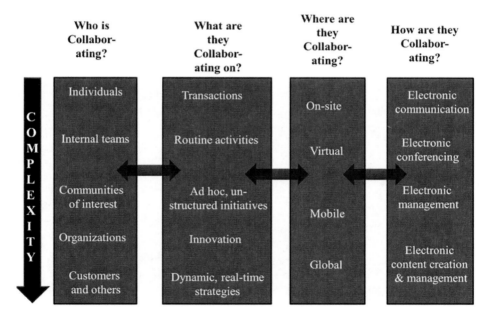

Figure 10.1 The range and scope of collaboration

- **Who is collaborating?** At its simplest, *collaboration* describes work that is done jointly with others (Wikipedia 2011). In modern organizations, this covers a lot of territory. Sometimes collaboration can be as basic as two people working together to achieve a goal, but it also refers to a wide spectrum of different types of collaborative participants. In organizations there can be collaboration within teams (both formal and ad hoc), between business units, and within communities of interest. Collaboration can also occur beyond a firm's boundaries, including between an organization and its customers, between one or more organizations (as in a supply chain or an innovative partnership), and, as we are beginning to see, with the world at large (also known as "mass collaboration"). As organizations have become more comfortable with collaborative work, they are extending it in new ways and to more and more types of participants. Most focus group organizations still focus on internal collaboration, yet there was general agreement that the trend is toward opening up collaboration beyond organizational boundaries. At present, most organizations are fairly "locked down" but have practices in place to enable key suppliers and trusted third parties to access internal company data and work collaboratively with internal participants.

- **What are they collaborating on?** Collaboration can take many forms. The early wins in organizations, according to the focus group, were simple transactions. These included emails, conferencing, extranets with partners, and basic workflow. Next came collaboration around routine activities, such as access to information and its reuse; ease of information creation and publishing; and coordination of experts to solve common problems and to reduce the work involved in mundane tasks such as coordination and planning (Cross et al. 2005; Edmonston 2008; Fedorwicz et al. 2008). Most organizations in the focus group have substantial initiatives in this area, although they believe there's more work to be done, especially in such matters as improving content management and creating enterprise directories. A third type of collaboration is more unstructured in nature and includes the development of communities for various purposes, creating collaborative work environments where innovation can occur, and collaboration for issue and information management. Most focus group members had only just begun to understand how best to leverage this type of collaboration, and their efforts in this area are still mainly experimental. However, one firm has created a new technology adoption environment where any technology innovation can be shared and where others can use and provide feedback about its utility and effectiveness. The most challenging form of collaboration is probably best epitomized by the online gaming community. Here, various participants work together in real time to achieve structured goals under rapidly changing conditions. Dynamic collaboration is characterized by speed of decision-making with incomplete information, the ability to modify decisions in response to changing conditions, trial and error, the continual need to address and deal with risk, hyper-transparency of information, and situational leadership (Reeves et al. 2008). None of the organizations in the focus group had achieved this type of collaboration, but all recognized that this is increasingly the way members of the younger generation expect to work. They also felt that, as business challenges become more complex, organizations will have to find better ways of collaborating in this way.

- *Where are they collaborating?* Increasingly, collaboration needs to take place on an anywhere, anytime basis. Inside organizations, members noted the need for more meeting spaces and meeting rooms as well as "touch down" areas where contractors and outside staff can temporarily set up office. Almost all focus group organizations already support virtual and mobile work, at least to some extent. Several members of the group also routinely utilize international or global teams where collaboration takes place across time zones, national boundaries, cultures, and language groups. Some were also beginning to experiment with different forms of collaboration with individuals and enterprises beyond their organizational boundaries, which requires dealing with different organizational cultures, practices, processes, systems, and data.

- *How are they collaborating?* Collaborative technology comprises the tools that are used to facilitate the work of collaboration. These fall into four main categories: electronic communication (such as email, instant messaging, blogs), electronic conferencing (i.e., video conferencing, meeting software), electronic management (i.e., file sharing, activity assignment, task management), and electronic content creation and management (i.e., publishing tools, enterprise directories). However, newer collaborative technologies, such as social networking applications, tend to fall into multiple categories depending on how they are used (e.g., for communication or information creation). As a result, the boundaries between the categories are blurring with the rapid evolution of this technology.

Components of Successful Collaboration

Understanding what collaboration and its potential benefits are is important to achieving an awareness of how collaboration can be effectively used in an organization, but the high failure of collaboration projects suggests that successful collaboration requires mastering how to implement and manage it (Schuh et al. 2008). The key challenges for managers (both business and IT) are to create a supportive working environment and motivational conditions and to develop the skills and organizational arrangements within which collaboration can flourish (Fedorwicz et al. 2008; Thomas et al. 2007). Four components of collaboration must work together to ensure successful collaboration of any type (MacCormack and Forbath 2008):

1. *People.* Collaborative work requires different skills than more traditional forms of work. In particular, strong communication skills are essential. This is especially true the more work is mediated through technology, is virtual, and operates across organizational and cultural boundaries (Romano et al. 2007). Cultural differences around social expectations; the need for more openness,

flexibility, and interdependence in work assignments; the need to develop trust in an "opaque" environment (i.e., one that lacks many traditional social cues); and differences in organizational practices all add up to a requirement for managers to rethink how people will work together in this new world of work (Evans and Wolf 2005; Fiore et al. 2008). Inexperienced teams, lack of management attention, and different expectations of partners are some of the major reasons why collaboration initiatives can fail (Schuh et al. 2008). Thus when implementing collaboration, managers should be aware that it is not "business as usual" and should pay more attention to the social and behavioral changes that will be necessary (Edmonston 2008; Thomas and Bostrom 2008). One focus group manager noted, "You cannot overemphasize the importance of culture. It will make or break you." Finally, as the complexity of the tasks involving coordination increases, so does the need for management attention to coordination (Schuh et al. 2008). In short, creating the working environment within which collaboration occurs becomes the primary role of the manager, rather than monitoring individual productivity or performance. Signs that these efforts have been successful are engaged, satisfied, and committed staff who fully participate in collaborative processes (Nohria et al. 2008). Conversely, managers who cultivate a fear of failure or who do not protect their staff from what is often a larger, hostile corporate environment are likely to see collaborative initiatives fail (Amabile and Khaire 2008).

2. *Program.* Collaboration needs to be part of a coherent program to create and capture value, not a series of stand-alone efforts (Schuh et al. 2008). It is highly unlikely that collaboration initiatives will achieve an organization's goals unless they are managed holistically (MacCormack and Forbath 2008). Furthermore, it is essential that managers understand the strategic trade-offs involved in collaboration and make conscious decisions about how to structure and govern it. This is especially true when external partners are involved (Pisano and Verganti 2008). Most important, organizations need to understand how to use their knowledge and information assets comprehensively. Focus group members stressed that well-organized, searchable information is the foundation for any type of collaboration, and this resource requires a significant investment to develop and maintain. As a result, many companies are working primarily on content management strategies. In addition, high-level decisions need to be made about how to develop new collaboration capabilities, determine what types of collaboration the organization seeks to engage in, what policies are needed, and how to create an environment where the desired collaboration can thrive. Two key principles of any collaboration program are emergence (i.e., the recognition that we don't always know who will make the greatest contribution to a problem in advance) and planned serendipity (i.e., designing

a working environment where underexplored relationships between people, data, and applications can become visible) (Majchrzak 2009).

3. **_Processes._** Within a strategic and holistic approach to collaboration, it is important to develop processes that support or help manage this type of work. Since collaboration is a moving target in the modern enterprise, managers need ways to rapidly learn what is working and what isn't and to make changes as the work unfolds (Edmonston 2008). Managers also need a process to take advantage of successful innovations and a way of recognizing failures and killing them off quickly (Amabile and Khaire 2008). Effective processes are also required to support collaborative teams and partnerships, to help them know what they know and coordinate their thinking (Johansen 2007). Specific processes that the focus group identified as being supportive of collaboration include administrative practices that recognize the convergence of many different types of communication (the management of which is often separated), content management processes, the ability to identify a "single source of truth" (i.e., the official documents pertaining to any topic), and the creation of parameters to help staff understand how and under what conditions they can collaborate. Conversely, a siloed focus and an emphasis on process efficiency above all else will likely stifle collaboration (Kleinbaum and Tushman 2008).

4. **_Platforms._** These are the tools, technologies, and standards that enable people to share data and to work together seamlessly from a variety of locations. The advent of cheap connectivity has been the driving force behind many new ways of collaborating in recent years (Smith and McKeen 2008), yet efforts to promote collaboration have focused largely on connectivity with little recognition of the other factors that make it effective (Cross et al. 2005). Technology is a key resource in enabling collaboration, but it must be designed to achieve the organization's goals and fit with its culture and practices. As with the other components of collaboration, the objective of a platform is to create an environment within which collaboration can take place, rather than the traditional systems approach of hardwiring specific information and work processes (Iandoli 2009b). An effective technology platform should support plug-and-play communications, provide access to information, and enable the transformation of information into knowledge. It should also provide tools for the rapid creation of communities, teams, and networks; be based on open standards; and be flexible and adaptive (Camarinha-Matos et al. 2009; Iandoli 2009b). However, most focus group organizations are nowhere near creating such a platform. Most are still questioning whether they should invest in collaborative technologies rather than look for ways to coherently manage a set of business tools for collaborative work (Drakos et al. 2009).

The Role of IT in Collaboration

Clearly, the IT function alone cannot make collaboration happen, even if it provides robust collaboration technology. The business plays a critical role in determining its strategy and creating processes and a working environment that make it possible to collaborate for business value. That said, there is still no answer to where an organization's collaboration strategy "belongs." In most organizations IT still owns it and as a result the whole field of collaboration is an opportunity for IT managers to demonstrate real business leadership (Lynch 2007; Mann 2008). CIOs can work with business executives to identify and orchestrate collaborative capabilities, coordinate enterprise services, and educate leaders about opportunities and possibilities.

In addition, IT leaders have some very specific technology responsibilities that must be put in place to enable collaborative work to occur. At present, four major technology areas must be addressed iteratively and concurrently. These are merely the fundamentals, however. Since this field is evolving rapidly, IT leaders must be prepared to continually reassess all aspects of collaboration technology, its governance, and policies and to rebalance these as necessary (Smith et al. 2007).

1. *Communication.* A significant and growing area of collaborative technology is enabling a wide spectrum of communications options, from voicemail to video and everything in between. "Users increasingly see communications and collaboration not as separate activities but as a smooth continuum of modalities where the difference between talking on the phone and posting on a wiki becomes a matter of choice and preference" (Mann and Elliot 2007). As such unified communications become a technological reality, IT leaders will need to develop an architecture that supports them as a single technology spectrum rather than as separate components. Gartner Group predicts that phone directories, email, voicemail, instant messaging, presence awareness, computer telephony, and conferencing technologies will increasingly converge, leading to serious organizational challenges in how these services are managed (Mann and Elliot 2007). Other types of communication and collaboration software, such as voice, call centers, mobile, team workspaces, and social software will not be part of this convergence and will have to be appropriately managed as they too evolve. Ultimately, communications technology will be embedded in all business applications and will need to be ubiquitous, reliable, secure, and integrated (Andriole 2006).

2. *Information access and management.* Developing an improved information-processing capability, including accurate and visible information, manipulability, exchangeability, and ease of information transfer is a primary goal for all IT functions in supporting collaboration. One focus group member explained his mandate as follows: "We want to make it easy for anyone to share information via the intranet, to support collaboration with information, and to link people to documents and vice versa." To accomplish this goal, it is important for organizations to reduce the number of databases and data management platforms

they maintain and to develop their intranets into robust information-sharing platforms. Typically, organizations also need a document-management system with proper versioning and access controls, although these systems are notoriously difficult to integrate with other information-management tools. We're finding it really hard to upload and share documents," said one manager. "It's a big headache for us." Content management, particularly at the business unit and team levels, is also challenging as the use of many separate tools tends to replicate information in a relatively unmanaged fashion. In most companies, attention needs to be paid to integrating fragmented information resources, improving information visibility, filtering and navigation, and establishing principles for information access (Cain 2008; Thomas et al. 2007).

Several focus group companies commented that perception is still widespread in their organizations that if information is made more widely available "bad things will happen." "We instinctively don't want to share," said one manager. Managing the tension between the need for information availability to facilitate collaboration and protecting the organization from the associated risks is an area where IT managers should be working proactively to ensure they deliver the optimal value (Gordon et al. 2008; Smith et al. 2007).

3. *Security and risk.* It is a primary responsibility of the IT function to protect the integrity of its systems and data. This is becoming increasingly more challenging as both internal and external organizational boundaries break down and new forms of collaboration are introduced (Smith et al. 2007). IT managers recognize that removing the traditional layers of separation between departments and enterprises makes the organization more vulnerable and their job more difficult. For this reason, IT departments can often be viewed as obstacles to collaboration (Gordon et al. 2008). There is no easy answer to this dilemma. Companies need safe and secure communications, but it is no longer possible to use "stovepipe" security to ensure this. Instead, IT functions must improve security architectures and infrastructures and continually assess the balance between the openness required by collaboration and the risks involved. Focus group members noted that security must become more granular and principles-based. "We are beginning to develop a policy for how we as a company use social networking tools," said one manager. "The broader the team, the greater the risks involved." Another added, "We need better authentication tools, and we must be clearer about the types of information that can be shared." Others noted that security must be commensurate with the risks involved. "We must use the most appropriate tools for the particular task at hand." Finally, they pointed out that this task is about to get much more difficult as companies begin to open themselves up to collaboration with their end customers. "This is a huge challenge that we have not yet faced up to," said one.

4. *Technology integration.* The more IT can achieve integration of data, applications, hardware, and software, the easier it will be to provide the information and tools needed to facilitate collaboration. Focus group members recommended massive simplification and rationalization of applications, databases, and software as a precursor to any significant collaboration initiative. The drive to collaboration is also behind the increasing interest in industry-neutral and global IT standards of all types (Chituc et al. 2009). "Technology should be a facilitator of collaboration, not an obstacle," said one manager. "Our users want to plug-and-play in this area, and we can only achieve this through standardization." Some organizations in the focus group provide "canned" collaboration tools, such as blogs, personal Web sites, team sites, and wikis that allow the rapid formation of ad hoc teams and ease of social networking. These can then be tailored to particular needs requiring just enough information so they can be effectively managed and decommissioned in the longer term.

In addition, centralized and integrated structures within IT for developing enterprisewide communications and collaboration capabilities can facilitate synergistic interactions between these tools and create useful cross-technology opportunities that might not previously have been obvious (Sanders 2007). Focus group organizations varied widely in this area. Some assigned IT a leading role in delivering collaboration technology, and others are implementing it on a more piecemeal basis. All agreed, however, that without centralized support for this technology, it is unlikely to deliver enterprise-level value.

These four collaborative technology building blocks are the most critical elements to which IT should pay attention at present. Looking ahead, new technologies are already on the horizon, and these will require continual assessment from IT managers as to their usefulness and ease of integration into the existing organizational infrastructure and collaboration architecture. Some of these technologies include dynamic modeling tools, simulation engines, visualization tools, data reduction and summarization applications, and intelligence-gathering tools. In short, IT managers are going to have to remain aware in this very rapidly changing market and be willing to adapt quickly to changing conditions. Paying attention to these four fundamental building blocks now will enable them to do this more easily and effectively in the future.

First Steps for Facilitating Effective Collaboration

Given the multifaceted nature of collaboration and its many potential but as yet unproven benefits, IT managers could understandably adopt a wait-and-see approach. In fact, this is what many members of the focus group are doing: talking about strategy and planning small pilots to test the waters. But amid all the confusion, they also had some practical ideas for ways that organizations could begin to approach this complex and dynamic new way of working with and using technology.

1. ***Develop a coherent vision.*** Effective collaboration requires a multidisciplinary approach and a shared business–IT vision (Lynch 2007). It is essential that such a vision begin with understanding the organization's values, legal requirements, and core intellectual property. From this, a strategic perspective can be developed about what the business wants to accomplish with collaboration and what types of technology would best support it. Focus group members suggested that developing a vision for collaboration must be approached carefully because "the judgment line is shifting rapidly" and our static paradigms of work are rapidly becoming much more dynamic. These factors will change business models and strategies and affect how companies will need to manage the complex business environment of the near future. Ideally, a vision for collaboration should include a unified strategy and business models, tools, and experiments to help the organization gain further insights. The vision's ultimate goal should be to nurture an internal working environment (and in the longer term a broader business ecosystem) that will enable productive collaboration to emerge. At this early stage, both business and IT leaders should play a key role in articulating a collaboration vision and in connecting it to the right people who can make it happen.

2. ***Plan for adaptation.*** If there's one aspect of collaboration about which everyone agrees, it's that collaboration is complex and continually evolving and will require significant and ongoing management attention (Schuh et al. 2008). Organizations, and particularly IT functions, need to develop "flexing skills" to cope with the rapid development of collaboration and its associated technologies (Iandoli 2009b). Focus group members noted that their organizations are already becoming flatter and more complex as collaboration and networks emerge. "Business is speeding up, and we will need new skills for coping and adapting rapidly," said one. It is essential that organizations develop processes for learning what is working with collaboration and what isn't and mechanisms for sharing these lessons. Above all, the management of collaboration needs to be multidisciplinary and responsive to change.

3. ***Start with specific fundamentals.*** Facilitating effective collaboration will take time—both to build a strategy and to get the technology fundamentals in place. Many organizations have specific "pain points" that could be worthwhile places to start putting energy into collaboration. In the focus group, these were clearly around information management and access. "Our Intranet is unmanaged and not relevant," complained one manager. Another noted that it was very hard finding people in his organization. "We'd love to have a 'blue pages' to enable us to start internal social networking," he said, referring to one firm's internal company directory. In addition, several participants noted that their office space doesn't support collaboration. "We need to have many more collaborative workspaces," she noted. A simple assessment of these gaps and some management

attention to them could lead to a great improvement in how people are able to collaborate.

4. ***Establish principles of behavior.*** As noted above, much of the governance of collaboration is based on principles, rather than rules. The most basic principle is transparency, not only of information but also of behavior (Majchrzak 2009). Some focus group companies have already established a code of conduct to govern electronic communication and collaboration, and others are working on one. A big fear is that providing improved communication will enable employees and customers to post negative comments about the organization. One important way of allaying these fears is to eliminate online anonymity. "Anonymity results in bad behavior," said one manager. "With a clear online identity, negativity is quickly found out and is usually self-policed by others in the community." Another noted, "In a business environment where all posts are traceable, abuse is unlikely." As social networking takes hold in our culture, and organizations explore ways they can use it to connect with their customers, they are realizing that establishing rules of etiquette for how to do this is important. "We have a hard and fast rule that if you are using social networking to do business, you must state your company affiliation," said a manager.

Cultural and behavioral practices are changing as a result of collaboration, and agreement is widespread that these will require serious management attention. For example, as staff become empowered to innovate and make real-time decisions, organizations will need to foster increased psychological safety so people don't fear being penalized if they make a mistake (Edmonston 2008). Similarly, work will need to be done to align work management and human resources practices, as well as incentives, if collaboration is to really make a difference (Cross et al. 2005). Finally, as connectivity becomes more pervasive and global, companies will have to develop policies and practices that enable staff to achieve an effective work–life balance. For example, one global firm has developed a small scheduling application to determine the least invasive time to have a meeting across different time zones. Tools can also be used to assist staff with controlling their accessibility and protecting their privacy (Mann 2008).

5. ***Gradually move beyond the firewall.*** None of the focus group companies was comfortable as yet extending collaboration beyond their firewalls, except in very tightly controlled circumstances (e.g., with vendors or third-party service providers). Major concerns about risk, privacy, and corporate liability remain. These issues need to be discussed and managed so that the power of collaboration can be realized. For example, one firm's privacy officer is now involved in determining what information can and cannot be shared. Some initial external target groups will include retirees, clients, and business partners. "We are gradually working through our concerns because of the unbelievable power of these tools," one manager said.

Conclusion

Collaboration is a complex concept with uncertain benefits and requires major organizational change. The drive to adopt collaboration is being accelerated by the possibilities enabled by information technology, which support real-time, global communication and anytime, anywhere access to information. In addition, companies are feeling considerable pressure to adopt collaboration technology because of its increasingly widespread use among individuals, many of whom are becoming their employees. There is no question that collaboration will play a major role in how we work and live in the future. However, as we move into this new era, companies are taking their time to determine how best to take advantage of what collaborative technology has to offer. In this chapter we have identified the major ways companies might want to collaborate and the benefits that are anticipated from each. We have also explored some of the major characteristics and components of collaboration in order to clarify concepts and to distinguish between the work of collaboration—a human activity—and collaboration technology, which facilitates it. Effective collaboration will not result from simply implementing more collaboration software. Instead, it will require a proactive and holistic strategy that integrates business goals and technology potential. All aspects of collaboration and collaboration technology are in their infancy, so it is understandable that many companies are proceeding cautiously into this new world. But both technology and practice are moving so quickly that it is time for managers to put some collaborative fundamentals in place. IT managers have an opportunity to provide business leadership around collaboration if they can clearly articulate its business potential and benefits, rather than focusing on the technology itself.

Chapter Discussion Questions

1. What forms of collaboration have you personally experienced at work or school and what have been their advantages and drawbacks?
2. Consider one of these. How could organizational leaders have made it more effective for you?

References

Amabile, T., and M. Khaire. "Creativity and the Role of the Leader." *Harvard Business Review* 86, no. 10 (October 2008).

Andriole, S. "The Collaborate/Integrate Business Technology Strategy." *Communications of the ACM 49*, no. 5 (May 2006).

Attaran, M. "Collaborative Computing: A New Management Strategy for Increasing Productivity and Building a Better Business." *Business Strategy Series* 8, no. 6 (2007): 387–93.

Cain, M. "Key Issues for Unified Communications and Collaboration, 2008." Gartner Research Report, ID: G0015672, April 10, 2008.

Camarinha-Matos, L., H. Afsarmanesh, N. Galeano, and A. Molina. "Collaborative Networked Organizations—Concepts and Practice in Manufacturing Enterprises." *Computers and Industrial Engineering* 57, no. 1 (2009): 46–60.

Chin, K., D. Gootzit, and J. Mann. "Key Issues for Portals, Content Management and Collaboration Best Practices Projects." Gartner Research Report, ID: G00155820, April 24, 2008.

Chituc, C., A. Azevedo, and C. Toscano. "A Framework Proposal for Seamless Interoperability in a Collaborative Networked Environment." *Computers in Industry* 60, no. 5 (June 2009): 317–38.

Cross, R., J. Liedtka, and L. Weiss. "A Practical Guide to Social Networks." *Harvard Business Review* 83, no. 3 (March 2005).

Drakos, N., C. Rozwell, M. Cain, and J. Mann. "Key Issues for Social Software and Collaboration Initiatives, 2009." Gartner Research Report, ID: G00164866, January 30, 2009.

Edmonston, A. "The Competitive Imperative of Learning." *Harvard Business Review* 86, nos. 7/8 (July/August 2008).

Evans, P., and B. Wolf. "Collaboration Rules." *Harvard Business Review* 83, nos. 7/8 (July/August 2005).

Fedorowicz, J., I. Laso-Ballesteros, and A. Padill-Melendez. "Creativity, Innovation and e-Collaboration." *International Journal of e-Collaboration* 4, no. 4 (2008): 1–10.

Fink, L. "Coordination, Learning and Innovation: The Organizational Roles of e-Collaboration and Their Impacts." *International Journal of e-Collaboration* 3, no. 3 (2007).

Fiore, S., R. McDaniel, and F. Jentsch. "Narrative-Based Collaboration Systems for Distributed Teams: Nine Research Questions for Information Managers." *Information Systems Management* 26, no. 1 (Winter 2009): 28.

Gordon, S., M. Tarafdar, R. Cook, R. Maksimoski, and B. Rogowitz. "Improving the Front End of Innovation with Information Technology." *Research–Technology Management* 51, no. 3 (May/June 2008): 50–58.

Iandoli, L. "JITCAR Special Issue—IT Collaboration in Organizations." *Journal of Information Technology Case and Application Research* 11, no. 1 (2009a).

———. "Leveraging the Power of Collective Intelligence Through IT-Enabled Global Collaboration." *Journal of Global Information Technology Management* 12, no. 3 (2009b).

Johansen, B. *Get There Early: Sensing the Future to Compete in the Present.* San Francisco: Berrett-Koehler, 2007.

Kleinbaum, A., and M. Tushman. "Managing Corporate Social Networks." *Harvard Business Review* 86, nos. 7/8 (July/August 2008).

Lynch, C. "Five Things Wikipedia's Founder Has Learned About Online Collaboration." *CIO Magazine*, June 28, 2007. https://www.cio.com/article/2438588/relationship-building-networking/five-things-wikipedia-s-founder-has-learned-about-online-collaborat.html (accessed March 9, 2011).

MacCormack, A., and T. Forbath. "Learning the Fine Art of Global Collaboration." *Harvard Business Review* 86, no. 1 (January 2008).

Majchrzak, A. "Social Networking and Collaboration." Presentation to the Society for Information Management's Advanced Practices Council, Atlanta, Georgia, January 21–22, 2009.

Majchrzak, A., A. Malhotra, J. Stamps, and J. Lipnack. "Can Absence Make a Team Grow Stronger?" *Harvard Business Review* 82, no. 5 (May 2004): 131–37.

Mann, J. "Q&A: Answers to Practical Questions About Collaboration Tools." Gartner Research Report, ID: G00154888, February 1, 2008.

Mann, J., and B. Elliot. "The New Market for Unified Communications and Collaboration." Gartner Research Report, ID: G00153236, November 23, 2007.

McAfee, A. "Enterprise 2.0: The Dawn of Emergent Collaboration." *MIT Sloan Management Review* 47, no. 3 (Spring 2006): 20–28.

Nohria, N., B. Groysberg, and L. Lee. "Employee Motivation: A Powerful New Model." *Harvard Business Review* 86, nos. 7/8 (July/August 2008).

Pisano, G., and R. Verganti. "Which Kind of Collaboration Is Right for You? *Harvard Business Review* 86, no. 12 (December 2008).

Reeves, B., T. Malone, and T. O'Driscoll. "Leadership's Online Labs." *Harvard Business Review* 86, no. 5 (May 2008).

Romano, N., J. Pick, and N. Roxtocki. "Editorial Introduction to the Special Issue on Collaboration Issues in Cross-Organizational and Cross-Border IS/IT." *Journal of Information Technology Theory and Application* 8, no. 4 (2007).

Sanders, N. "An Empirical Study of the Impact of e-Business Technologies on Organizational Collaboration and Performance." *Information Systems and Operations Management* 25, no. 6 (2007): 1332–347.

Schuh, G., A. Sauer, and S. Doering. "Managing Complexity in Industrial Collaborations." *International Journal of Production Research* 46, no. 9 (May 2008): 2485–498.

Smith, G., K. Watson, W. Baker, and J. Pokorski. "A Critical Balance: Collaboration and Security in the IT-Enabled Supply Chain." *International Journal of Production Research* 45, no. 11 (June 2007).

Smith, H. A., and J. D. McKeen. "Social Computing: How Should It Be Managed?" *Communications of the Association for Information Systems* 23, Article 23 (August 2008).

Tebbutt, D. "The Business Value of Collaboration Software." *CIO Magazine*, February 17, 2009. https://www.cio.com/article/2430675/it-organization/the-business-value-of-collaboration-software.html (accessed March 9, 2011).

Thomas, D., and R. Bostrom. "Building Trust and Cooperation Through Technology Adaptation in Virtual Teams: Empirical Field Evidence." *Information Systems Management* 25, no. 1 (2008): 45–56.

Thomas, D., R. Bostrom, and M. Gouge. "Making Knowledge Work in Virtual Teams." *Communications of the ACM* 50, no. 11 (November 2007).

Wikipedia. "Collaboration." en.wikipedia.org/wiki/Collaboration (accessed March 9, 2011).

Enterprise Architecture at Nationstate Insurance[1]

Jane Denton looked around at her assembled senior IT leadership team who were waiting to hear what she was going to say. Most were leaning forward eagerly, though some appeared more cautious. They were a good team, she knew, and she wanted to lead them well. A seasoned CIO, with a whole career behind her in IT, Jane was the newly appointed global CIO of Nationstate Insurance. This would be her last job before retirement in three years, and she wanted to find a way to make a lasting difference in this company. Nationstate was an excellent company. Jane had done her homework and learned that it was one of the largest in the US, with a worldwide presence in personal and commercial insurance, and had recently been voted one of Forbes' "Best Big Companies." It had good systems, good user-IT relationships, and good people. But the company aspired to be great and Jane wanted to help them by taking IT to the next level. She knew that the world was changing—largely as a result of technology—and she knew that IT and its traditional approach to systems development was also going to have to change. "Our IT function needs to become more cutting edge in adopting emerging technologies," she had told the CEO shortly after she was hired, "and we need to become more flexible and agile in our approach to development work." Now she had this time and this team to accomplish her goals.

It was much easier said than done. Like almost every large organization, Nationstate had a hodgepodge of different systems, data, and processes—most serving just one of its six business units (BU). Nationstate's decentralized structure had served it well in the past by enabling individual BUs to respond quickly to changing market needs, but a couple of years before Jane's arrival, recognizing the need for some enterprise thinking, the CEO had created a federated structure with some centralized functions, including parts of IT. So some of IT was now centralized and shared by all the BUs (e.g., operations) and reported directly to Jane, while the rest (e.g., system development) was

---

[1] H. A. Smith and J. D. McKeen, "Enterprise Architecture at Nationstate Insurance," #1-L11-1-001. Smith School of Business at Queen's University, September 2007. Reproduced by permission of Queen's University, Smith School of Business, Kingston, Ontario, Canada.

decentralized. Each BU had its own CIO and IT staff who reported jointly to the BU's president and to Jane.

This potentially unwieldy structure was made more palatable by the fact that the business unit CIOs had great business knowledge and were well trusted by their presidents. In fact, it was central IT that was often seen as the roadblock by the BUs. She had never led an IT organization like it, she reflected, and in her first few months she had made a considerable effort to understand the strengths and weaknesses of this model and how responsibilities had been divided between centralized enterprise services and the decentralized IT groups (each quite large themselves) in the business units. Now she thought she had a good enough handle on these that she could begin work with her senior leadership team (the BU CIOs) to develop a plan to transform IT into the kind of technology function Nationstate would need in the years to come.

"I know you are both enthusiastic and apprehensive about transformation," she said. "We have a great organization and no one wants to lose that. We need to be responsive to our business needs but we also need to incorporate new development techniques into our work, do a better job with emerging technologies, and begin to rationalize our application and technology portfolios. We have duplicate systems, data, and software all over the place. Our CEO and the BU Presidents want to see us use our technology resources more efficiently, but more than that, they want our leadership in using technology *effectively* for the organization as a whole. We can't do this if we're all working in separate silos."

Heads began nodding around the room as she continued, "At present, every business unit has its own IT architecture and architects and each of you believe you are making the 'right' technology decisions *but* you are all doing it differently." The head nodding stopped and a mood of wariness took over. "No one in our organization has the big picture of what we have and where we need to go. We have to learn what makes sense for us to do at an enterprise level and what's best left in the business units. Architecting our technology, information, business, and applications properly is the key to doing it right."

"What exactly are you proposing?" asked Owen Merton, CIO of the Casualty Division. "I think you're right that we need an enterprise architecture, but I don't want to lose the good work we've done at the BU level."

"Well, I really want to centralize all architecture," said Jane. "I think that's what works best in other organizations and that's going to be the most effective way to make it work here. "BUT," she added, "I'd like to speak with each of you individually and with your senior architects before I do. I'm open to your ideas as long as they address the needs that I've just outlined."

Over the next two weeks, Jane listened carefully to what the divisional CIOs had to say. They all agreed with Owen that the relationships with the BUs were extremely important and centralizing architecture had to be done carefully. All of them had heard horror stories about the "architecture police" in other companies—hard-line techies who set standards and created blueprints and insisted on them being followed in spite of the difficulties their policies caused for the business.

"Architecture can't live in an ivory tower," explained Vic Toregas, CIO of Claims. "It has to be rooted in the reality of our business and it can't be seen to slow things down." Jane agreed. "We must make sure that our architecture function is designed and managed to ensure rapid delivery to the business."

On the other hand, Nick Vargo, CIO of Group Health, was concerned that without a strong enforcement mechanism, standards wouldn't be followed. "What's the point of having standards if we don't enforce them?" he asked.

Jane's head whirled. It wasn't going to be easy to strike the right balance between developing a good, sustainable process that would provide a blueprint for where the company needed to go and enable the company to build the common capabilities it would need for the future, while delivering solutions quickly and flexibly for the BUs. "What we don't need is a 'Winchester Mystery House,'" she reflected, "recalling the famous local house whose owners kept adding to it over many years with no overall plan.

She became more worried when she began to speak with the BU architects, with an eye to appointing one of them as her Chief Enterprise Architect. They seemed to be technically competent but were not what she would call "relationship people" or business strategists. The job, as she envisioned it, would combine strong leadership skills, a good understanding of the business and excellent communication skills to translate *why* the business should care about architecture, with strong technical skills. Her day became a bit brighter when she began her final interview with Seamus O'Malley, the Senior Architecture Manager of the Commercial BU.

As they spoke, Jane was impressed with his vision and pragmatism, as well as his strong communication skills. By the end of the hour she knew she had found her new Chief Enterprise Architect. "I'd like you to take this new job," she told him. "I think you are the right person to ensure we have the standards, tools, and practices in place to develop a common architecture for Nationstate." Seamus thought for a moment before replying. It was a great offer but he had his doubts that Jane's plan would work and this situation had to be carefully handled.

"Thank you for your faith in me," he began diplomatically, "but I would like to suggest a slight modification to your plan. You see, I've been an architect in centralized organizations and there has always been an 'us versus them' mentality between the architecture group and both the rest of IT and the business units." Jane recalled the horror stories of the "architecture police." "So what I'd like to propose is a compromise. I would become Chief Enterprise Architect but I would also remain Senior Architect for Commercial and involve the other BU Senior Architects in creating a strong enterprise architecture that works for us all. That way, no one will see me as just 'the enterprise guy' and whatever standards we set and decisions we make centrally will affect me in Commercial, just like they'll affect all the other BUs. When the other business units see that I'm willing to eat my own dog food, I think they'll be more ready to accept the standards and changes we'll be introducing."

While not sure the compromise would work, Jane agreed to try it for a year, and Seamus set out to build a centralized architecture function from scratch.

With the authority given to him by Jane, all of the BU senior architects now had a dual reporting relationship: to their CIO and to him as the Chief Architect.

At his first weekly meeting with the BU Senior Architects, Seamus outlined his role and agenda. "As you know, each of us has been individually responsible for developing an effective IT architecture for our business units, but we haven't done any coordination between them. That is no longer good enough for our business needs and I, with your help, have been given the job of establishing an *enterprise* architecture that will create an enterprise technology blueprint for Nationstate, which we will all have to follow in the business units. I want to work collaboratively with you so that we come up with a plan and processes that will work for each of us in the business units, as well as for the enterprise as a whole. We will need to build our enterprise architecture slowly but steadily so that people will trust us, and that means having good governance, good processes, and a collaborative approach to this work," he stated. "Our first priority is building strong relationships with both Jane and the other CIOs and our BU Presidents. Enterprise Architecture sits in the middle between these groups, so good relationships are essential." "However," he continued, "we are going to need a way to establish and enforce standards—enterprise ones, not the ones you have now—and this is going to be difficult to explain."

"I'll say," remarked Sarah Jensen, the Senior Architecture Manager from Personal Insurance. "What do we say when the business asks why they can't do something that's important to them because our 'standards' won't let them?"

"That's a good question Sarah," said Seamus, "and it gets right to the heart of why architecture is important. We need to present architecture in ways that are easy for the business to understand, without scaring or threatening them. For example, we need an application reduction strategy designed to eliminate duplication, reduce complexity, and save money. The business already understands the pain of having to jump from system to system and knows that owning two cars is more expensive than one. If we explain it to them in this way, they will understand the advantages of having a single system and a single workflow."

"But isn't good architecture about *more* than cost savings?" asked Michael Lee, Senior Architecture Manager from Claims. "We need to develop a foundation of common information, tools, and processes so that we're not reinventing the wheel going into the future. And someone needs to decide what new technologies we're going to need and where we're going to use them. There are so many new applications and devices coming out every day now, we're going to be in a real mess if we don't do this properly."

"You're exactly right," said Seamus. "These things do have to be managed for the good of the enterprise—both to make it more effective *and* more efficient. But it's *how* we manage them that's important. If we put lots of bureaucracy in place and don't add value, no one is going to support us and they'll find ways to undermine what we are trying to do. We can't take a 'field of dreams' approach to architecture. We need to attach our work to real business value and real projects. Once our leaders understand this, we'll get their support."

"So here's our challenge," Seamus told his assembled team a few minutes later. "We need to design an Enterprise Architecture function that does all these things. It's got to be a process that comes up with the standards and guidelines that each of you can live with and support in the BUs. And, as you know, I myself will have to live with them in Commercial as well.

"Here's what I believe we need to accomplish as soon as possible," he stated, flashing a PowerPoint slide on the screen:

1. An enterprise governance process to set architecture strategy, policies, and standards for technology, applications, and information that reflects the federated structure in the organization;

2. A means of monitoring that all new projects comply with the agreed-upon architecture while ensuring that this process doesn't present an obstacle to getting IT projects completed quickly;

3. A process for allowing "variances" to the current standards, if necessary, and a way to manage them back to the agreed-on standards;

4. A means of identifying important new IT capabilities and services that should be shared by the enterprise;

5. A means of evaluating emerging new technologies and setting standards for them;

6. Identification of roles and responsibilities for the Enterprise Architecture function and the Line of Business Architecture functions;

7. Development of a means of incorporating feedback and continuous improvement into our work.

"I want to blend and weave our work into the architecture teams we already have in the business units as much as possible," Seamus concluded. "This will keep us close to business needs and enable us to get enterprise value from the teams we have in place. And I don't want to add any more process than we need to at an enterprise level. For example, if the Claims group needs a new technology, their architecture group could do the preliminary evaluation and make recommendations for what we should do. *But* we need to ensure that the resulting decision is a good one for the entire enterprise.

"I've got to report back to Jane in a month, so I'd like you to think about what might and might not work for your division and for us as an enterprise. I've scheduled a couple of working sessions for us over the next two weeks so we can hash this out. We have an exciting opportunity to take IT to the next level at Nationstate if we do this right, so let's not mess this up."

Discussion Questions:

1. List and describe all of the potential benefits (and costs) that Nationstate would realize from the establishment of an enterprise-wide architecture as envisioned by Jane Denton.

2. Build a business case for Seamus O'Malley to present to the senior management team at Nationstate in order to get their buy-in. In addition to benefits and costs, the business case must answer the "what's in it for me" question that the BU Presidents all have.

3. Seamus O'Malley is rightfully worried about governance (i.e., making sure that the enterprise architectural standards are adopted by all BUs). Both he and Jane are wary of forced compliance because such measures lead to "architecture police." What governance procedures could they put in place that would win "hearts and minds"; that is, BU architects would comply with the enterprise architecture standards because they believe in them, not because they are forced to comply with them?

Transforming IT at Global Digital Imaging

"We are *your* images!" proclaimed the various posters showing different types of uses for images—from personal to professional photos, x-rays to ultrasound, brain scans to jaw scans—down the long hallway away from the boardroom. As Ray Henderson strode out to the elevator, the tagline evoked many images in his own head—images of the proud company he had joined as a fresh-faced university grad that had ranked high in the Fortune 1000 and whose products and technologies were used and copied all over the world. It also evoked images of the hideous debacle of the last few years as its executives struggled with the downward spiral of its business as competitors and cheaper digital products undermined its traditional revenue sources. "At least I'm getting out while the getting is good," he thought.

In an effort to regroup, both financially and strategically, his company, World Heliographics (WH), had begun to sell off its assets. Unfortunately, Ray's division, medical film, was among the first to go. As the CEO had just informed him, it had been sold to a successful private equity firm that would hold 100 percent of its assets and take an active role in its future activities. It would now become a separate business, Global Digital Imaging (GDI), and Ray would be expected to deliver significant value for its new owner–investor, VE Investments. "They have an experienced management team and a proven ability to build businesses," the CEO told him. "If you can give them the returns they want, they will keep you on as President."

As he stepped onto the elevator, Ray felt both exhilarated and apprehensive about this new opportunity. Mentally, he started an inventory of the new company's assets. With operations in more than 150 companies, revenues of about $3 billion, and 12,000 staff, it was a substantial company in its own right. But operating independently of a much larger parent company created headaches in a number of areas, requiring the development of separate functions in HR, finance, facilities, and IT. The thought of this last issue struck him hard. "What are we going to do with all the systems?" he asked himself. It would be relatively easy to hire good people to manage the other corporate entities, but IT was a different kettle of fish. And the *last* thing he wanted was to worry about IT … not when so much was riding on how well GDI performed as a freestanding company.

There was a lot to do in very little time, and soon GDI was a *legal* entity. On Day 1, Ray called his senior people together. "Our first priority is to run as a company independent from WH as quickly as possible," he said. "We need to think like a young, agile company and not like a large, entrenched bureaucratic organization. Fortunately, we've got the transition team from VE Investments to help us." And indeed, it was only a few months before complete separation was accomplished, that is, everywhere *except* IT.

"Why is this so difficult?" Ray grumbled to the temporary CIO, Fred Gamble. "We have a number of problems," Fred said cautiously, observing the fire in Ray's eyes. "Because legally, GDI didn't officially exist until the actual divestiture took place, no contracts could be signed or service level agreements established until then. As a result, GDI has inherited a 'mini WH' IT function with all its flaws, so we now have a smorgasbord of technology." Fred explained that all applications, data, and infrastructure had been purchased and replicated to create a parallel organizational structure just to keep the business running during divestment. "So this means that not only are our systems not integrated, they are not designed for our type of company," Ray concluded bluntly.

The search for a new CIO began in earnest the next day. "I need an experienced and proven CIO to formulate a vision for a transformed IT function," he told the search firm he hired to help him. "You understand IT much better than I do so find me someone who is able to undertake a challenging transformation on multiple fronts at once."

The winning candidate was Ben Perry, a career IT executive, who joined GDI one year after it was created. "I knew I had a mandate to transform IT," recalled Ben later. "And I knew we had to make some big changes, but I underestimated just how big these changes were going to be. There were a number of things we had to fix. We were still tethered to WH through some technology. The plans to disconnect had slipped four or five times and there was now a major lack of confidence about this separation. Our systems were outdated and not designed for a company dealing with healthcare products for medical practitioners. Our costs were too high and unpredictable. We needed to get our costs under control in order to free up funds for new investments. We had 700 core applications and needed 200–300 at the most. We had multiple financial and email systems, no architecture or standards, and exact copies of every type of infrastructure and application that WH had. It was like the Wild West!"

"Ben walked into a mess," agreed Henderson. "IT was an obstacle to our being able to operate effectively and efficiently. I knew that IT was the key to our future so we needed to both clean up our act and find how to better balance technology and business strategy to move us forward. We needed basic competencies so we could use IT to differentiate our company and get us better information." He left it up to Ben to oversee the transformation and bring GDI's business leaders on board.

"Ben understood both leadership and technology. That combination is hard to find. That's why he got the job. He had my support but, if I had to sell these changes myself, I wouldn't have needed him," explained Ray.

Ben's transformation mandate and the reality of GDI's situation pulled him in two different directions. On the day he arrived, for example, the entire data center crashed. Observing how it was handled made him realize "Our IT organization is a minefield. We have a lot of tactical staff who spend their time firefighting and trying to deal with the different pieces of the organization, but it isn't making anything better."

But that was just the beginning of IT's problem, as he soon discovered. There was no alignment with business on either tactical or strategic goals, and though the entire executive suite complained constantly about IT, there were no processes in place, such as portfolio management and prioritization, that would help educate business leaders about how to make IT investment decisions and confirm the direction they wanted IT to go. There was a considerable lack of role clarity and accountability, and this problem was exacerbated by a matrixed organization structure with dotted lines going everywhere.

Resisting the urge to start fixing immediate problems, Ben spent his first few weeks information gathering and listening to business leaders, trying to understand their pain points. He also implemented a business partner survey, much to the consternation of his own staff. "What is he doing?" they complained to each other. "He's not *doing* anything!" Ben resisted this implied criticism. "Our IT strategy and governance were non-existent," Ben explained to his staff later. "I needed to be sure I understood the business' issues and their root causes before I did anything else."

After a thorough assessment, Ben called his directors together to share his plans for the future. First up was the new mission statement declaring that the IT organization would:

- Provide effective, reliable infrastructure and applications;
- Improve customer satisfaction;
- Become more cost effective;
- Partner effectively with the business;
- Become a great place to work.

Ben explained that, "This is in keeping with what our executives want us to accomplish. Each component links IT activities directly to business concerns. It is important that we hold ourselves accountable to our new mission. But more on this later."

Next up was the new organizational chart. Ben started with the appointment of Teresa Danton as Director of IT Strategy & Planning, the Project Management Office (PMO) and Governance. As Ben explained, her job was to support the new organizational design by bolstering the existing, ineffective PMO and introducing new governance practices that would eventually result in a comprehensive governance framework. "We need execution discipline to deliver business value through our IT programs and portfolios," Ben stated. "We need to develop the standards and best practices to do this and acquire the tools and methodologies to streamline project delivery and enhance quality. In addition, Teresa will be responsible for time tracking and billing, project planning and reporting, and financial planning and tracking. She will also measure everything so we can report on our progress to the business. Governance is a critical success factor for our transformation."

Next, the rest of the IT leadership team was revealed: a Director of Operations, whose goal was to run the key business systems as efficiently as possible by streamlining resources and reducing costs; a Director of Relationship Management, whose job was to move the IT culture from being order-takers to solution-providers and eventually strategic partners; a Director of Enterprise Architecture responsible for developing a technology roadmap and a transition plan to move the organization from its current technology state to its planned future state; a Director of Data Security & Privacy whose job was to organize, safeguard, and ensure the availability of all data assets in a manner that protected the privacy of individuals; and finally a Director of Application Development whose job was to acquire new systems through purchase or development to support the business through automation. Ben kept talent management—critical to IT transformation—for himself. "Spin-offs are dirty work when it comes to people," Ben told his team. You've already seen that not everyone at the senior management level was able to handle the changes involved and this is true for the rest of our staff as well. "Some of our people will need to move to our outsourcers as we realign our contracts, but others simply do not have the right skills.

For the next hour and a half, Ben dealt with questions and invited his leadership team to discuss their issues and concerns with their new assignments. "I want us all in agreement here," he told them, "because my next job is convincing the business that we will be able to accomplish this mission." All heads nodded in unison. Then he dropped the bomb! "And the first way we're going to do this is to cut the cord with WH!" he proclaimed, holding up a mouse with a dangling tail.

"I needed to find a way to bring together our new directors as a team," recalled Ben later. "Our culture was highly risk averse. We had tried and failed to do this separation several times and there was a sense of hopelessness about it. We needed to focus on this first because nothing else could be done until we were able to operate as a separate entity free from the old WH culture. I challenged our directors to rally and work together to achieve this key goal. It took several months but we did it, and we learned that we could push ourselves to accomplish a goal successfully. It was a first step in changing our culture."

While the whole IT organization was engaged in the "cutting the cord" project, Ben started communicating his vision of IT's mission and the new organizational structure to his business partners and to IT staff through a series of town hall meetings. But to really sell the business on the benefits of the IT transformation and obtain their cooperation, Ben needed something more concrete. At the next weekly directors' meeting, he declared, "It is time to start delivering on our mission. We need to develop a plan of action." Not only would the plan have to align with the overall mission, but it would have to address issues at three levels: strategic, tactical, and operational. Calling them "buckets," Ben explained: "Bucket number one is building the basics. We have to stabilize and simplify our systems and operations. Bucket number two is table stakes. That is, we have to make sure we have the right strategic platform that will enable us to do business and match what our competition is doing. Bucket number three is building differentiators and targeting strategic innovation. I know that most of you can't even begin to think about buckets two and three because you're so busy dealing with day-to-day problems, but we need to make time to do *some* work in this area, so we are not just fighting fires."

Ben concluded the meeting by tasking each of his directors to develop an integrated mission and execution plan for the next three years that would be consistent with the overarching vision for IT. "We need to present both a holistic understanding of the transformation involved and a step-by-step roadmap for how to get there. Each year, each of you should have activities in each of the three buckets I've identified," he said. "Clearly, your first year or two will be heavily weighted in building the basics, but I want to see accomplishment in each bucket every year and, as we move into year three, I would expect most of the basics to be addressed and considerably more strategic innovation to be taking place. Furthermore, I expect every goal you identify to be measurable and linked to our mission. We will develop a scorecard for each of the goals of our mission and report quarterly to the business. You have a month. At that time, we will integrate your individual plans and pull everything together into a comprehensive three-year plan. This will keep us all on the same page. And you will each have clearly defined accountabilities." He paused, "Any questions?"

Not surprisingly there were no questions. As everyone filed out of the room, Ben signaled to Teresa. "I wanted to talk with you about your role in this planning exercise. As I see it, governance is *the* critical part. Without effective governance, we have no insurance that the right decisions will be made by the right people in the right time frame in order to deliver the value we want. Before you share anything with the other directors, I'd like to review your governance ideas with you. If you let my assistant know as soon as you have something, we'll book some time. Got to run."

Back at her desk, Teresa fought the urge to panic. "I can't believe that Ben is expecting *me* to be the expert on governance," Teresa thought as she tried to figure out how to begin. Within a few minutes thanks to Google, Teresa learned that:

> IT governance is a framework of processes and structures that specify who makes decisions about and who is accountable for the IT function and its work.... It is not about what specific decisions are made or how groups are organized and led. Effective IT governance is designed to encourage desirable behavior in the use of IT that is consistent with an organization's mission, strategy, and culture. (Weill 2004)

This last statement resonated with Teresa. All she had to do was to create a set of processes that would incentivize the right decision makers to make the right decisions!

In fact, the often-used example of effective governance involved dividing leftover cake between two children. You let one child cut the cake and the other select a piece. And presto, all by itself the process guarantees an effective outcome.

Further investigation showed that a governance framework was somewhat more complex. It covered three levels: board, enterprise, and business unit. She also found that effective enterprise-level governance should address several elements including architecture, security and privacy, operations, strategic projects, IT capabilities, and data.

Realizing that there was no way that she could tackle all the different elements of governance all at once, Teresa decided to focus exclusively on strategic projects for her first meeting with Ben. It was clear that strategic projects presented the most immediate problem in the organization and a governance framework was urgent. New strategic applications development initiatives to enable the fledgling company to survive and compete effectively had to be identified and funded. To accomplish this, the number of existing systems had to be reduced dramatically, possibly by 75 percent. And these decisions had to be made without delay. The key governance questions boiled down to:

1. What overall process should be followed to identify key (existing or new) initiatives?
2. How should they be evaluated?
3. What criteria should be used to prioritize them?
4. Who should make these prioritization decisions?
5. How frequently should the decision makers meet?
6. How will development and implementation progress be measured and reported to the business?

It did not take Teresa long to develop the mission and guiding principles for a proposed governance structure for GDI:

> The IT governance mission is to develop and maintain effective controls for IT's management, execution, and measurement processes, which result in high performance and low risk while ensuring strategic alignment and maximum value for the business.

That was the easy part. Her real challenge was to create a set of well-articulated governance processes and disciplines at the enterprise level to ensure that strategic initiatives would be prioritized, developed, implemented, and aligned with the business' strategic vision. "It's going to be difficult," she thought, "but if we make sure that everything aligns to this mission, people will begin to see why we're doing this." She turned to her keyboard and began to map out a plan.

Discussion Questions

1. Differentiate between "management" and "governance."

2. Create a set of governance processes at the enterprise level to ensure that strategic initiatives at GDI are prioritized, developed, implemented, and aligned with the business' strategic vision.

Delivering Business Value with IT at Hefty Hardware[1]

"IT is a pain in the neck," groused Cheryl O'Shea, VP of retail marketing, as she slipped into a seat at the table in the Hefty Hardware executive dining room, next to her colleagues. "It's all technical mumbo-jumbo when they talk to you and I still don't know if they have any idea about what we're trying to accomplish with our Savvy Store program. I keep explaining that we have to improve the customer experience and that we need IT's help to do this, but they keep talking about infrastructure and bandwidth and technical architecture, which is all their internal stuff and doesn't relate to what we're trying to do at all! They have so many processes and reviews that I'm not sure we'll ever get this project off the ground unless we go outside the company."

"You've got that right," agreed Glen Vogel, the COO. "I really like my IT account manager, Jenny Henderson. She sits in on all our strategy meetings and seems to really understand our business, but that's about as far as it goes. By the time we get a project going, my staff are all complaining that the IT people don't even know some of our basic business functions, like how our warehouses operate. It takes so long to deliver any sort of technology to the field, and when it doesn't work the way we want it to, they just shrug and tell us to add it to the list for the next release! Are we really getting value for all of the millions that we pour into IT?"

"Well, I don't think it's as bad as you both seem to believe," added Michelle Wright, the CFO. "My EA sings the praises of the help desk and the new ERP system we put in last year. We can now close the books at month-end in 24 hours. Before that, it took days. And I've seen the benchmarking reports on our computer operations. We are in the top quartile for reliability and cost-effectiveness for all our hardware and systems. I don't think we could get IT any cheaper outside the company."

---

[1] H. A. Smith and J. D. McKeen, "Delivering Business Value with IT at Hefty Hardware," #1-L10-1-001. Smith School of Business at Queen's University, May 2010. Reproduced by permission of Queen's University, Smith School of Business, Kingston, Ontario, Canada.

"You are talking 'apples and oranges' here," said Glen. "On one hand, you're saying that we're getting good, cheap, reliable computer operations and value for the money we're spending. On the other hand, we don't feel IT is contributing to creating new business value for Hefty. They're really two different things."

"Yes, they are," agreed Cheryl. "I'd even agree with you that they do a pretty good job of keeping our systems functioning and preventing viruses and things. At least we've never lost any data like some of our competitors. But I don't see how they're contributing to executing our business strategy. Surely in this day and age with increased competition, new technologies coming out all over the place, and so many changes in our economy, we should be able to get them to help us be more flexible, not less, and deliver new products and services to our customers quickly!"

The conversation moved on then, but Glen was thoughtful as he walked back to his office after lunch. Truthfully, he only ever thought about IT when it affected him and his area. Like his other colleagues, he found most of his communication with the department, Jenny excepted, to be unintelligible, so he delegated it to his subordinates, unless it absolutely couldn't be avoided. But Cheryl was right. IT was becoming increasingly important to how the company did its business. Although Hefty's success was built on its excellent supply chain logistics and the assortment of products in its stores, IT played a huge role in this. To implement Hefty's new Savvy Store strategy, IT would be critical for ensuring that the products were there when a customer wanted them and that every store associate had the proper information to answer customers' questions.

In Europe, he knew from his travels, IT was front and center in most cutting-edge retail stores. It provided extensive self-service to improve checkout; multichannel access to information inside stores to enable customers to browse an extended product base and better support sales associates assisting customers; and multimedia to engage customers with extended product knowledge. Part of Hefty's new Savvy Store business strategy was to copy some of these initiatives, hoping to become the first retailer in North America to completely integrate multimedia and digital information into each of its 1,000 stores. They'd spent months at the executive committee meetings working out this new strategic thrust—using information and multimedia to improve the customer experience in a variety of ways and to make it consistent in each of their stores. Now they had to figure out exactly how to execute it, and IT was a key player. The question in Glen's mind was how could the business and IT work together to deliver on this vision, when IT was essentially operating in its own technical world, which bore very little relationship to the world of business?

Entering his office, with its panoramic view of the downtown core, Glen had an idea. "Hefty's stores operate in a different world than we do at our head office. Wouldn't it be great to take some of our best IT folks out on the road so they could see what it's really like in the field? What seems like a good idea here at corporate doesn't always work out there, and we need to balance our corporate needs with those of our store operations." He remembered going to one of Hefty's smaller stores in Moose River and seeing how its managers had circumvented the company's stringent security protocols by writing their passwords on Post-it notes stuck to the store's only computer terminal.

On his next trip to the field he decided he would take Jenny, along with Cheryl and the Marketing IT Relationship Manager, Paul Rivera, and maybe even invite the CIO, Farzad Mohammed, and a couple of the IT architects. "It would be good for them to see what's actually happening in the stores," he reasoned. "Maybe once they do, it will help them understand what we're trying to accomplish."

A few days later, Glen's emailed invitation had Farzad in a quandary. "He wants to take me and some of my top people—including you—on the road two weeks from now," he complained to his chief architect, Sergei Grozny. "Maybe I could spare Jenny to go, since she's Glen's main contact, but we're up to our wazoos in alligators trying to put together our strategic IT architecture so we can support their Savvy Stores initiative and half a dozen more 'top priority' projects. We're supposed to present our IT strategy to the steering committee in three weeks!

"I need Paul to work with the architecture team over the next couple of weeks to review our plans and then to work with the master data team to help them outline their information strategy," said Sergei. "If we don't have the infrastructure and integrated information in place, there aren't going to be any Savvy Stores! You can't send Paul and my core architects off on some boondoggle for a whole week! They've all seen a Hefty store. It's not like they're going to see anything different."

"You're right," agreed Farzad. "Glen's just going to have to understand that I can't send five of our top people into the field right now. Maybe in six months after we've finished this planning and budget cycle. We've got too much work to do now. I'll send Jenny and maybe that new intern, Joyce Chan, who we're thinking of hiring. She could use some exposure to the business, and she's not working on anything critical. I'll email Jenny and get her to set it up with Glen. She's so great with these business guys. I don't know how she does it, but she seems to really get them onside."

Three hours later, Jenny Henderson arrived back from a refreshing noontime workout to find Farzad's request in her priority in-box. "Oh #*!#*@!" she swore. She had a more finely nuanced understanding of the politics involved in this situation, and she was standing on a land mine for sure. Her business contacts had all known about the invitation, and she knew it was more than a simple request. However, Farzad, having been with the company for only eighteen months, might not recognize the olive branch that it represented, nor the problems that it would cause if he turned down the trip or if he sent a very junior staff member in his place. "I have to speak with him about this before I do anything," she concluded, reaching for her jacket.

But just as she swiveled around to go see Farzad, Paul Rivera appeared in her doorway, looking furious. "Got a moment?" he asked and, not waiting for her answer, plunked himself down in her visitor's chair. Jenny could almost see the steam coming out of his ears, and his face was beet red. Paul was a great colleague, so mentally putting the "pause" button on her own problems, Jenny replied, "Sure, what's up?"

"Well, I just got back from the new technology meeting between marketing and our R&D guys, and it was just terrible!" he moaned. I've been trying to get Cheryl and her group to consider doing some experimentation with cell phone promotions—you know, using that new Japanese bar coding system. There are a million things you can do with mobile these days. So she asked me to set up a demonstration of the technology and to have the R&D guys explain what it might do. At first, everyone was really excited. They'd read about these things in magazines and wanted to know more. But our guys kept droning on about 3G, 4G, LTE, and HSPA technology and different types of connectivity and security and how the data move around and how we have to model and architect everything so it all fits together. They had the business guys so confused we never actually got talking about how the technology might be used for marketing and whether it was a good business idea. After about half an hour, everyone just tuned out. I tried to bring it back to the applications we could develop if we just invested a little in the mobile connectivity infrastructure, but by then we were dead in the water. They wouldn't fund the project because they couldn't see why customers would want to use mobile in our stores when we had perfectly good cash registers and in-store kiosks!

"I despair!" he said dramatically. "And you know what's going to happen, don't you? In a year or so, when everyone else has got mobile apps, they're going to want us to do something for them yesterday, and we're going to have to throw some sort of stopgap technology in place to deal with it, and everyone's going to be complaining that IT isn't helping the business with what it needs!"

Jenny was sympathetic. "Been there, done that, and got the T-shirt," she laughed wryly. "These tech guys are so brilliant, but they can't ever seem to connect what they know to what the business thinks it needs. Sometimes, they're too farsighted and need to just paint the next couple of steps of what could be done, not the 'flying around in jetpacks vision.' And sometimes I think they truly don't understand why the business can't see how these bits and bytes they're talking about translate into something that it can use to make money." She looked at her watch, and Paul got the hint. He stood up. "Thanks for letting me vent," he said. "You're a good listener."

"I hope Farzad is," she thought grimly, as she headed down the hall. "Or he's going to be out of here by Thanksgiving." It was a sad truth that CIOs seemed to turn over every two years or so at Hefty. It was almost predictable. A new CEO would come in, and the next thing you knew, the CIO would be history. Or the user satisfaction rate would plummet, or there would be a major application crash, or the executives would complain about how much IT cost, or there would be an expensive new system failure. Whatever it was, IT would always get blamed, and the CIO would be gone. "We have some world-class people in IT," she thought, "but everywhere we go in the business, we get a bad rap. And it's not always our fault."

She remembered the recent CIM project to produce a single customer database for all of Hefty's divisions: hardware, clothing, sporting goods, and credit. It had seemed to be a straightforward project with lots of ROI, but the infighting between the client divisions had dragged the project (and the costs) out. No one could agree about whose version of the truth they should use, and the divisions had assigned their most junior people to it and insisted on numerous exceptions, workarounds, and enhancements, all of which had rendered the original business case useless. On top of that, the company had undergone a major restructuring in the middle of it, and a lot of the major players had changed. "It would be a lot easier for us in IT if the business would get its act together about what it wants from IT," she thought. But just as quickly, she recognized that this was probably an unrealistic goal. A more practical one would be to find ways for business and IT to work collaboratively at all levels. "We each hold pieces of the future picture of the business," she mused. "We need to figure out a better way to put them together than simply trying to force them to fit."

Knocking on Farzad's door, she peeked into the window beside it. He seemed lost in thought but smiled when he saw her. "Jenny!" he exclaimed. "I was just thinking about you and the email I sent you. Have you done anything about it yet?" When she shook her head, he gave a sigh of relief. "I was just rethinking my decision about this trip, and I'd like your advice." Jenny gave her own mental sigh and stepped into the office. "I think we have a problem with the business and we need to fix it—fast," she said. "I've got some ideas, and what to do about the trip is just part of them. Can we talk?" Farzad nodded encouragingly and invited her to sit down. "I agree with you, and I'd like to hear what you have to say. We need to do things differently around here, and I think with your help we can. What did you have in mind?"

Discussion Questions

1. Overall, how effective is the partnership between IT and the business at Hefty Hardware? Identify the shortcomings of both IT and the business.

2. Create a plan for how IT and the business can work collaboratively to deliver the Savvy Store program successfully.

SECTION III

IT-Enabled Innovation

Chapter 11: Developing Thought Leaders in IT
Chapter 12: Managing Disruption in IT
Chapter 13: IT's Role in a Culture of Experimentation
Chapter 14: Improving the Customer Experience: An IT Perspective
Chapter 15: Moving Towards an API Economy
Chapter 16: Preparing for Artificial Intelligence

Mini Cases for Section III:

- Enterprise Transformation at Trustworthy Insurance
- Innovation at International Foods
- Consumerization of Technology at IFG

CHAPTER 11

Developing Thought Leaders in IT

There is no question that both business and the IT industry are operating in times of unprecedented change characterized by considerable uncertainty (Mansharmani 2012, Kiron et al. 2015). On one hand, our increasingly connected and global economy and new business models driven by new digital technologies mean that businesses are finding it difficult to navigate the vague and poorly defined conditions in which they find themselves (Mansharmani 2012). On the other, new technologies are emerging all the time that could facilitate new business opportunities or undermine existing revenue streams. In the middle of all of this sits the organization's IT function, which is charged with assessing emerging technologies on behalf of the organization and assisting business leaders with determining where and how they can add value, often in fundamentally different ways than in the past. And on top of this, IT is being asked to radically change how it works to become more agile, effective, and faster, all while ensuring that the current day-to-day business of the organization flows smoothly!

It is within this context of unrelenting change that organizations are looking for thought leaders to guide them. "This is something we talk constantly about because the business wants it and IT wants to partner with the business," said one IT manager. "Business is looking to IT for ideas that will help make it better," said another, noting the value of a really good idea. But what really is a thought leader? And where does he or she fit into an IT organization? Can thought leaders be developed? Or are they born? IT organizations are wrestling with this concept and how it connects into their mandate to be innovative and agile digital strategists.

In this chapter we examine these questions, starting with a discussion of the nature of thought leadership and how it fits with IT's mandate. Following this, we describe some of the characteristics of an effective IT thought leader. Finally, we explore how IT functions can foster thought leadership successfully as well as the ways thought leadership can be inhibited in organizations.

What is a Thought Leader?

There are many different and fuzzy conceptualizations of what makes a true thought leader (Prince and Rogers 2012). As a result, most people have no idea what the term means when it is used (Kim 2014). The focus group noted that thought leadership is not proactively defined in their organizations. "We define leadership and strategy, and we have a small innovation program, but we don't focus specifically on thought leadership," said one manager. Nevertheless, it is talked about so much in organizations that the term has actually been the subject of satirical columns that hold the "thought leader" up as "a new paragon to command our attention." (Brooks 2013).

What is clear is that thought leadership is a highly desirable characteristic both for organizations and for individuals to have at all levels. "We know that there is great power in good ideas," said a manager. "And that even little ideas can have great impact." But what does thought leadership look like in practice? There is no real consensus about this. The following is a short list of how thought leaders are described by the literature and the focus group:

- A thought leader is an authority in a specialized field whose expertise is sought and often rewarded (Wikipedia 2016).
- Thought leaders look for ways to make the organization better … there are no extrinsic rewards (focus group).
- Today's thought leaders can read complex business situations and bring out the best in other people. Thought leaders require personal traits that far exceed expert knowledge (Brendel 2016).
- Executives are increasingly defined by the degree to which they engage internal and external audiences with actions and ideas that are inspiring and selfless, and that extend well beyond the scope of their core mandate (Kim 2014).
- Thought leaders can be anywhere in the organization. Being in a position of power does not make one a thought leader (focus group).
- Thought leaders are strategic thinkers. They nurture relationships and social networks, asking good questions of others, and synthesizing that information into actionable intelligence (Brendel 2016).
- Thought leaders look for inflection points. They educate and create awareness. They give away their ideas to be operationalized (focus group).
- Thought leaders change the way people think and what they do. The best ones are actually trying to address a problem at hand and not just talk about it (Kim 2014).
- Real thought leadership tends to be disruptive and uncomfortable (focus group).
- Thought leaders must be willing to buck the status quo (Brosseau 2016).
- Thought leadership can come from group dynamics and discussion (focus group).
- Thought leadership stems from passion (focus group, Brosseau 2016; Kim 2014).

Connecting all these dots into a coherent picture of a thought leader can be frustrating, but some key themes emerge from these statements. It appears that thought leadership can be exercised in many different contexts in both business and IT. It is also clear that it relates to an idea to make things better or do things differently, and this often challenges the status quo as a result. In addition, it takes more than a good idea to provide thought leadership, though good ideas are where it starts. Thought leaders need to have knowledge, credibility, and persuasiveness to bring their ideas to a point where they'll get traction, even if they don't implement them themselves. In short, "While we really don't know how to get thought leadership, we know it when we see it," concluded a focus group manager.

Thought Leadership and IT

Thought leadership is an important component of IT work at all levels, said the focus group, whether or not it has a formal mandate to do it. "We must accept that the business wants thought leadership from us," said a manager. This can be accomplished in different ways and at different levels, according to the context involved. "A thought leader can be in any role," said one manager. "He or she could be a technology leader, have deep business knowledge, provide horizontal leadership across company silos, or be in a formal position to provide long-term leadership. Thought leadership can also be born at different stages of an initiative." The common theme is the *idea*.

Innovation and thought leadership work hand-in-hand, the group agreed. In another focus group, members explained how IT ideas work in innovation:

Innovation … refers to the process whereby a company creates new things that deliver value … The first stage is ideation—generating innovative ideas. There are many ways of doing this, ranging from focused executive meetings to the modern online version of the suggestion box. Ideation addresses two questions: How do we get people to share their ideas? How do we respond to their ideas? In most cases, the focus group has found that there are lots of ideas out there. Attempts to stimulate innovation led to an initial deluge of new ideas. However, with very little ability to screen and prioritize or act on them, the ideas soon dried up … [because] the biggest reason why people do not share their ideas is that past experience has shown them that management doesn't respond to or act on them.

But thought leadership is also different from innovation. "Thought leaders *spark the innovation cycle*," a manager explained. "They provide the connection, the synthesis, and the intellectual energy to start down a different path."

Thought leadership in IT also has a strong technology connection, although "we can't think about technology too narrowly," said a manager. As we have noted elsewhere:

> A perennial business complaint is that IT is not helping it see and implement the potential of new technologies fast enough. At the same time, there are also many cases where business has rejected IT requests for experimentation with new technology because it feels *there are other things that will bring a higher and more immediate return on investment.* (Smith and McKeen 2013b)

This highlights an important distinction between thought leadership and managing emerging technologies. Thought leaders *"energize their organizations around imagining their possibilities"* (Smith and McKeen 2014). Thought leaders must not only understand technical possibilities, they must "raise the game," "motivate others to see them as well," and "work with groups to change their mindset and collaborate to deliver on the new idea," said the focus group. "It's a change agent role."

Although it is more common for IT leaders to speak of new or emerging technologies, what organizations really want is insights into how best to *apply technology* in the marketplace (Cusumano 2011). "Our business units want to know: What will enable me to execute better, faster, or cheaper?" said one manager. Often, however, the vision for how to use emerging technologies is unclear and unarticulated, leaving both business and IT frustrated and confused (Mangelsdorf 2012; Fitzgerald et al. 2014). In such cases both groups are vulnerable to making inappropriate choices.

This underscores a third important distinguishing element of thought leadership. It is a *leadership* role requiring a number of soft skills that are now essential at all levels of the IT organization, chief of which is communication. Elsewhere, we have noted the importance of developing general leadership skills further down in IT than in other parts of the organization:

> There is no question that individuals within IT have more opportunities to affect an organization, both positively and negatively, than others at similar levels in the business. This fact alone makes it extremely important that IT staff have much stronger organizational perspectives, decision-making skills, entrepreneurialism, and risk assessment capabilities at lower levels. Today, because even small decisions in IT can have a major impact on an organization, it is essential that a CIO be confident that his/her most junior staff have the judgment and skills to take appropriate actions. (McKeen and Smith 2012)

The focus group stressed that although formal IT leaders are not necessarily thought leaders, leadership is implied in the concept of thought leadership. These distinguishing features of thought leadership work together to deliver *business impact* (see box on next page). One manager described an initiative in his organization that brought each of these dimensions of thought leadership into it (identified in brackets):

> We implemented an application design change [sparks new idea] through relocation of mainframe processes [applies technology to make new things possible]. This was enabled by a group of architects who had a wider vision of systems and

Distinguishing Features of an IT Thought Leader

- Sparks innovation with new ideas;
- Energizes others around new possibilities;
- Applies technology for value;
- Leads in context;
- Delivers business impact.

architecture [energizes others] and motivated by their desire to deliver on their mandate [leadership in context]. This resulted in one million fewer batch jobs each year [delivers business impact].

Finally, the group stressed that it is important for organizations not to rely on external providers for thought leadership. "Most external providers don't know the dots to connect," said one manager. "They compare us with organizations that look like us. This can lead to a self-affirming ecosystem that believes 'we're good.'" Internal thought leaders pay attention to what's happening in much wider contexts outside their organizations, such as academia, research organizations, and other sources beyond their industry. They also scan the market for new ideas and emerging technologies that will enable them to lead cross-organization and internal ideation and innovation teams to leverage their business model (Burton et al. 2016).

In summary, thought leadership in IT is a central part of the innovation process both within IT and in the business. It challenges current ways of thinking and working in an organization by seeking out new ideas, new technologies, and new ways of putting processes and products together and then *leading* the appropriate groups to help them see the real possibilities for value in this new approach. Figure 11.1 summarizes the place of thought leadership within the organization. It shows that thought leadership sits squarely at the center of current business and technical practices and new business and technical opportunities, and serves as the starting point for innovation, nurturing new ideas until they gain support in the organization. This is a challenging, often thankless task, but one that gets at the very heart of the role business wants IT to play in today's complex and uncertain world.

Characteristics of an IT Thought Leader

Although the group had difficulty defining thought leadership in general terms, it was very clear about the characteristics of a good IT thought leader. "We may not know exactly what a thought leader is," said a focus group participant, "but we know one when we see one." Although the ideas a thought leader comes up with are important, the skills that he or she uses to sell them and the ability to synthesize his/her ideas with those of others are essential for a successful thought leader, said the group. Some of the key characteristics of a thought leader in IT are:

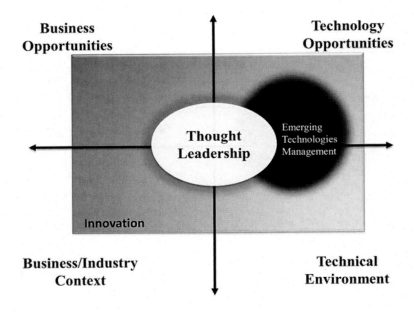

Business
Opportunities

Technology
Opportunities

**Thought
Leadership**

Emerging
Technologies
Management

Innovation

Business/Industry
Context

Technical
Environment

Figure 11.1 Thought leadership is central to IT's innovation responsibilities.

- *Idea-generator.* A thought leader is forward thinking and adaptive, offering intellectually attractive ideas. He/she thinks outside the box and sees things in ways that others don't.
- *Visionary.* A thought leader is more than just an idea creator and more than a subject matter expert. She has a natural curiosity and insight into a situation and takes an idea to the next level, working it through, and seeing patterns. Because of this, a thought leader sees a path forward when others can't.
- *Consultant.* A thought leader helps others think through ideas and looks for ways to add value. He recognizes the importance of *selling* the idea to others, not pulling control levers.
- *Synthesizer.* A thought leader connects the dots between their idea and other people's ideas to provide a more compelling vision.
- *Collaborator.* A thought leader listens to others and adjusts her ideas based on their input, rather than clinging to an original idea. She recognizes that thought leadership is a process of leading the refinement of an idea and that teamwork can make good ideas better. A thought leader is therefore happy to share the credit for a successful idea.
- *Courageous.* A thought leader believes in his idea and challenges others or disrupts established ways if necessary. "He is sometimes a lightning rod for change," said a manager. "He questions how things work and puts forth ideas that do not align with the views held by others."

- **Persistent.** A thought leader understands that unconventional ideas are rarely, if ever, accepted immediately. She recognizes that influencing others to follow a new path is invariably a process of communication with many people over an extended period of time.
- **Communicator.** Thought leaders recognize that selling their ideas is a must. "This involves tuning into the zeitgeist of the situation," said a manager. They package ideas effectively and simplify complex situations, articulating ideas in ways that resonate with others, making them want to move ahead. In this regard, storytelling is a very useful skill.
- **Credible.** A thought leader has credibility with the subject area involved, either in the business or in the technical function. As a result of this credibility, people follow thought leaders because they believe in what they're selling.
- **Action-oriented.** While not necessarily a formally appointed leader, a thought leader drives action related to an idea and leads others to deliver a useful outcome. As a result, thought leaders need some implementation skills to understand and assist the delivery process.
- **Self-motivated.** A thought leader works for intrinsic value and the opportunity to make a bigger difference.

See box for how these characteristics come together in a real thought leadership example.

Thought Leadership in an IT Function

"One of our enterprise architects became convinced [self-motivated] that DevOps would be valuable in her organization [idea generator, visionary]. She read widely [credible], wrote papers about it [synthesizer] that she passed around to key IT managers [courageous, communicator]. Slowly [persistent], she encouraged people to discuss what might be involved [collaborator, consultant], and quietly supported pilot efforts to explore its value [action-oriented]." (Focus group member)

Fostering Thought Leaders in IT

Improving thought leadership in IT involves not only accessing and utilizing people's ideas but also creating an environment in which thought leadership is nurtured. Clear communication about the company's strategy and end goals from its leaders is a broad prerequisite or else thought leaders might develop disruptive ideas that don't add value (Fenn and Messaglio 2016). Thought leaders come in three types: natural thought leaders who don't have to be nurtured; one-hit wonders who may have a single good idea; and thought leaders who can be developed and taught over time. Each of these can benefit from a number of proactive steps IT leaders can take to foster leadership skills in their departments.

The first step is to harvest the ideas that people have, concluded the focus group. Many companies have already introduced some activities to collect and assess ideas from a broad spectrum of employees and others. IBM's "Innovation Jams" in which employees and ultimately vendors, partners, and spouses were invited to contribute ideas were among the first to formalize this process.[1] Other firms have introduced innovation contests (Smith and McKeen 2013a) or hackathons, where individuals or groups are invited to submit ideas, which are refined by the crowd, and some selected for a proposal to business leaders and prototyping. These are designed to surface unrecognized opportunities. Other ways of doing this are through workshops to help envision a future state or business model and by introducing an internal venture capital model (Applegate and Meyer 2016; Fenn and Mesaglio 2016). Effective processes collect, refine, and connect good ideas to raise the game for the organization. One of the least effective ways to do this, said the participants, is to create an elite innovation group, because this tends to discourage contributions from non-group members. However a company chooses to collect new ideas, it is imperative that they be seen to utilize them. "Organizations not only need great ideas, they need to deliver on them," said one manager. Failure to do so is the single biggest reason why people do not participate in idea-generating activities, said the focus group. "You must take these ideas seriously," said another manager. "There must be evidence from senior management that something is happening with them."

Some companies have also changed their hiring and staff evaluation procedures to reflect their desire for more thought leadership skills. "Innovation is now one of our nine staff competencies," said one manager. "We are hiring for thought leadership aptitude," said another. "We have implemented an annual achievers innovation award," said a third. The key skills they are looking for, in addition to those mentioned above, include intellectual curiosity, empathy, broad experience with deep skills in one or more areas; and the ability to synthesize and apply different perspectives in a variety of business contexts (Morelli and Holub 2008). These people may be currently working as or aspiring to be enterprise architects or relationship managers whose roles naturally cross internal and external boundaries (Mok and Berry 2016).

Thought leadership can also be fostered both at an individual and a group level. Some focus group companies have formal technology leadership programs for new talent with high potential. These provide several rotations in different parts of the organization to give them cross training and a broader perspective before settling them in a particular area. Others provide coaching for high potential talent. "We provide opportunities for our best people to work on prominent projects," said a manager. "This empowers them to stand out." Another company encourages IT staff to visit the business to find out how users really use the technology currently provided. "If you think you understand how they're actually using it, you're wrong. These visits are always enlightening," said another. Use of multidisciplinary teams creates

---

[1] https://www.collaborationjam.com/.

opportunities to build relationships and stimulate ideas. These blend individuals with creative skills, user experience, engineering background, and functional knowledge to foster, evaluate, and implement new ideas. They also help build cross-functional relationships that can be useful in the future.

In addition, companies need to create a positive environment where thoughts and leadership can flourish at all levels. This is probably the biggest challenge for IT management (McKeen and Smith 2012). Unfortunately, organizations often take creative people and put them in soul- and idea-crushing environments (Fenn and Messaglio 2016). "We need to have a general culture where people feel free to express their ideas," said a manager. "This involves good, open leadership at all levels." Companies and leaders also need to be able to listen for and act on new ideas. "We train our leaders how to dialogue with their direct reports to promote a positive environment," said another.

A big challenge is to guard against "big egos" in an organization—those who dismiss or appropriate others' ideas. And some groups can be threatened by disruptive ideas—particularly if they are not part of that group—and fail to follow up on them. "Some parts of our company don't want thought leadership," said a manager. "We need to find a good fit for our thought leaders or they will be frustrated."

Finally, companies must ensure that staff have the *time* at all levels to work as thought leaders. Work stress, information overload, and multitasking can all inhibit the processes used for reasoning and forward thinking (Webb 2016). "Organizations must give people permission to spend time on these activities," said a manager. "Too often we're too busy and swamped with everyday work to do this." Leaders must promote taking breaks and going offline for important thinking to foster thought leadership. They should also encourage staff development in non-traditional subjects and foster connectivity and education (Bannister et al. 2015; Webb 2016).

Conclusion

Thought leadership is what business wants from IT. That said, it can often be a struggle to deliver. Traditional, hierarchical, siloed organizations tend to inhibit the type of creative, cross-functional thinking needed in thought leadership. Failure to make thought leadership a management priority can mean that organizations lack the processes and culture needed to foster it at all levels. Task-oriented management and pressure to deliver on a day-to-day basis can squelch innovative ideas. IT is moving into a brave new world where creativity, innovation, and new ways to deliver value are the norm. It is therefore imperative that IT adopt new ways to foster this type of thinking by creating opportunities to generate and harvest new ideas, promoting ways to develop and encourage thought leaders, and ensuring an encouraging culture that provides positive feedback, opportunities to develop cross-functional relationships and knowledge, and the time to engage in forward thinking and idea synthesis.

Chapter Discussion Questions

1. Differentiate thought leadership and emerging technology management in terms of necessary skills.

2. Describe what would happen in an organization that was successful at managing emerging technology but lacking in thought leadership.

References

Applegate, L., and A. Meyer. "Launching 1871: An Entrepreneurial Ecosystem Hub." *Harvard Business School Case N1-816-090*, April 20, 2016.

Bannister, C., J. Pennington, and J. Stefanchik. "IT Worker of the Future." *Deloitte Tech Trends 2015*.

Brendel, D. "It's Time to Revisit the Concept of Thought Leadership." *Huffington Post*, May 16, 2016. http://www.huffingtonpost.com/david-brendel/its-time-to-revisit-the-c_b_9979600.html.

Brooks, D. "The Thought Leader." *New York Times*, December 16, 2013.

Brosseau, D. "What is a thought leader? FAQ." *Thought Leadership Lab*. http://www.thoughtleadershiplab.com/Resources/WhatIsaThoughtLeader (accessed August 2, 2016).

Burton, B., M. Blosch, J. Dixon, and C. Howard. "Define Your Future Role as a CTO in the Digital Age." Gartner Research Report, ID: G00312950, July 20, 2016.

Cusumano, M. "How to Innovate When Platforms Won't Stop Moving." *MIT Sloan Management Review* 52, no. 4 (Summer 2011).

Fenn, J., and M. Messaglio. "Drive a Creative Culture Through Activities, Education and Attitude." Gartner Research Report, ID: G00304117, June 10, 2016.

Fitzgerald, M., N. Kruschwitz, D. Bonnet, and M. Welch. "Embracing Digital Technology: A New Strategic Imperative." *MIT Sloan Management Review* 55, vol. 2 (Winter 2014).

Kane, G., D. Palmer, A. N. Phillips, and D. Kiron. "Is Your Business Really Ready for a Digital Future?" *MIT Sloan Management Review*, July 2015.

Kim, C. "Think You're a Thought Leader?" *Financial Post*, March 7, 2014.

Mangelsdorf, M. "What it Takes to be a Serial Innovator." *MIT Sloan Management Review* 53, no. 4 (Summer 2012).

Mansharamani, V. "All Hail the Generalist." *Harvard Business Review*, June 4, 2012.

McKeen, J. D., and H. A. Smith. *IT Strategy: Issues and Practices (2nd ed.)*. Upper Saddle River, NJ: Pearson Prentice-Hall Education, 2012.

McKeen, J. D., and H. A. Smith. *IT Strategy: Issues and Practices (3rd ed.)*. Upper Saddle River, NJ: Pearson Prentice-Hall Education, 2015.

Mok, L., and D. Berry. "Ten Absolute Truths about Talent Management in Digital Business." Gartner Research Report, ID: G00303502, July 11, 2016.

Morelli, D., and E. Holub. "Inside the Concept of Versatilists: What are They and How do CIOs Develop Them?" Gartner Research Report, ID: G00159537, September 9, 2008.

Prince, R., and B. Rogers. "What is a Thought Leader?" *Forbes*, March 16, 2012.

Smith, H. A., and J. D. McKeen (a). "Organic Innovation at EMC." https://www.ciobrief.ca, 2013.

Smith, H. A., and J. D. McKeen (b). "Innovation with Technology." https://www.itmgmtforum.ca, 2013.

Smith, H. A., and J. D. McKeen (c). "Managing Emerging Technologies." https://www.itmgmtforum.ca, 2013.

Webb, C. "How Small Shifts in Leadership Can Transform Your Team Dynamic." *McKinsey Quarterly*, February 2016.

Wikipedia. "Thought Leader." https://en.wikipedia.org/wiki/thought_leader (accessed August 2, 2016).

CHAPTER 12

Managing Disruption in IT

"Disruption" is undoubtedly a hot topic. It describes a number of different but related challenges facing both business and IT leaders. First, industries and companies are dealing with new threats from non-traditional competitors using new technologies in new ways to scoop up their most profitable revenue streams. As a result, "disruption has moved from an infrequent inconvenience to a consistent stream of change that is redefining markets and entire industries" (Plummer et al. 2016b). One survey of board of directors' members found that 32 percent believe their company's revenue will be under threat in the next five years and 60 percent want to spend more to directly address these potential disruptions (Weill and Woerner 2015). That means more work for IT, which must play catch-up. Second, new technologies are being continually developed and brought to market. Business leaders know that in order to stay relevant they must constantly survey these technologies to determine which they should adopt to deliver new forms of value and stay ahead of the curve (Weldon and Rowsell-Jones 2015). This means that IT is expected to participate or even lead these evaluations and analyses and develop proofs of concept. Third, with all these new technologies and new applications comes the threat of new disruptions—either malicious or accidental—to an organization's existing infrastructure and legacy environment (Sheffi 2015). Since IT is also charged with ensuring business continuity and information security, this has become no small task now that online devices are everywhere. Finally, IT is faced with disruption in its own delivery models from cloud computing, global outsourcing and managed services, the need for continually changing new skills, and ongoing pressure from business to deliver faster, better, and cheaper.

"The good news is that because of all this disruption, our organizations now understand the new value of IT," said a senior IT manager. "They have much bigger appetites for new technology than a few years ago." "But the bad news is that disruption can be a noun, a verb, or a profanity depending on the situation and what you are talking about," explained another. The focus group noted that although disruption is challenging many fundamental assumptions, it is also an opportunity that can be managed. "The key is ensuring that we are proactive wherever possible, not reactive," said a third manager. "Change is a choice that can be planned; disruption is not a choice and is therefore chaos."

IT organizations are stepping up to these challenges in a number of ways, including implementing new methodologies such as agile and DevOps, developing new capabilities such as thought leadership and analytics, and examining new ways of understanding the value of IT, such as through experimentation. However, there is still a sense that this is not enough and that IT is struggling to keep up. In this chapter we explore the concept of disruption in IT and how to effectively deal with it. In the first section we look at the nature and sources of disruption in organizations and how these affect IT work. Next we look at how IT is responding to these and to disruptions in IT work itself and evolving to become a new type of technology organization. Then we examine what the IT of the not-so-distant future might look like as a result of today's disruptive forces. In the final two sections we discuss best practices in managing disruption and some steps managers might take to help turn the chaos of disruption into the opportunity of change.

Disruption in Organizations

The term "disruption" usually means a change or disturbance to a current or settled way of doing something (Yokelson et al. 2016). Although technology is not always *the* cause of disruption, it is generally involved in some way. Often disruption is the result of a combination of the new capabilities offered by a technology, complementary products and services that build on that technology, and changes in the expectations of and behaviors in a culture, market, or process as a result (Yokelson et al. 2016). The telephone, for example, was a new technology that was not disruptive of current ways of working or living until it was made widely available to businesses and members of the public and until phone companies provided the network of wires, operators, and service people that made it possible for people to connect with each other in an entirely new way. It may be many years before the full impact of a new technology is apparent, as new ways to incorporate it or to adapt behaviors and structures evolve. These secondary ripple effects can be even more disruptive (Plummer et al. 2016a). Thus with the addition of mobility and online connectivity the telephone is still a disruptive influence, albeit one that was never anticipated by its inventors or early users.

Today disruption is a more serious concern for organizations than it has been in the past because of the vast number of possible changes enabled by a literal explosion of new technologies and new forms of connectivity. These changes are so rapid that it is almost impossible to keep up with them, let alone determine which ones might be useful or lead to fundamental alterations in the processes of creating, producing, and delivering an organization's products and services (Plummer et al. 2016a). Current business environments are fraught with hype and noise about disruption and new technologies, making it extremely difficult for organizations to see the truly disruptive threats and opportunities (Smith et al. 2016). Because of this, organizations have become fearful that they are vulnerable to competition from unexpected sources (Gans 2016) or risks from unanticipated events (Sheffi 2015). Many are aware of

Christensen's classic study of disruptive innovation, which found that successful businesses can fail in the face of technological change because they tend to ignore innovations in favor of following the paths that have made them successful. Essentially, they don't move forward until it is too late (Gans 2016). And all leaders are aware of companies that have not anticipated some of the risks and vulnerabilities associated with their technology and whose businesses have subsequently been damaged.

In short, companies are concerned that new technologies or new uses of existing technologies can be utilized by a non-traditional competitor to develop innovative capabilities, products, or services that will undermine their traditional markets and sources of value, thereby making their current business models and assumptions obsolete (Plummer et al. 2016a, Berman and Marshall 2014). These disruptive forces create new connections, linking institutions and individuals in new ways, breaking down established boundaries, and making it possible to orchestrate complex value chains through ecosystems of organizations (Berman and Marshall 2014, Grossman 2016). Often, it is difficult for an existing organization to catch up because of its embedded culture, processes, and systems that are designed for its current structure and activities.[1] Figure 12.1 summarizes these new disruptive sources.

Because technology is at the root of most disruption, it is natural for business leaders to look to IT for guidance, insights, leadership, and protection. Ideally, the focus group agreed, it is IT's role to bring new technology opportunities to the business, help its leaders distinguish between hype and true disruption, and protect the organization from information security risks. "Our business is increasingly exposed to disruption from new technology," said a manager. "Our customers' increased appetite for digital

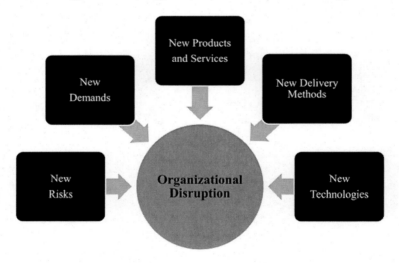

Figure 12.1 Sources of organizational disruption

---

[1] "Conway's Law" holds that any organization that designs a system will produce a design whose structure is a copy of the organization's current communication structure.

capabilities is causing a lot of disruption for us," added another. Unfortunately, "our company faces hundreds of industry pushes and pulls," said a third. "We in IT simply cannot make these changes overnight."

Speed of response is central to dealing with disruption and can spell the difference between planned change and survival (Sheffi 2015). The focus group and others agree that disruption can be managed if it can be anticipated and responded to quickly and efficiently (Gans 2016). In fact, disruptors themselves may not be in the best position to take advantage of their ideas. If established organizations can recognize the indicators of a disruption early, they can bring their resources and complementary assets to bear and shift advantage to themselves (Plummer et al. 2016a). How to do this effectively is the real challenge for organizations.

Disruption and IT

IT is called upon to assess new technologies, develop new products and services in response to customer and business demands, support new delivery channels, and manage the risks involved. Yet while it is supporting the business in dealing with disruptive forces, IT is also in the midst of being disrupted itself. The same types of forces affecting the business also affect IT functions independently of the business. Many operations groups are being disintermediated by cheaper cloud-based infrastructure-as-a-service or outsourcing arrangements. Similarly, development functions are being displaced by ready-made software-as-a-service or outsourcing. Business demands for faster, better, and cheaper delivery are driving new development and operations methodologies. And demands to address disruption in the marketplace are driving increased innovation and experimentation with a variety of new vendors and other partners. In short, IT is facing a "double-whammy" of disruption—in the business it is part of and in the IT industry itself. Managing this dual disruption "is a bit like playing whack-a-mole," said one IT manager. "You just get one issue under control and two or three more pop their heads up!"

Disruption in IT is not a new problem, said the focus group, noting that new technologies and modes of delivery have long been part of the ongoing evolution of their functions. However, they did agree that moving to new modes of infrastructure and service delivery is likely to have dramatic impacts on the structure and function of the IT organization of the future. As in the business, disruption in IT is about more than new technology (Kushida et al. 2015). In both areas, successful disruption solves problems, some of which are obvious and others that customers didn't know they had until they were presented with an alternative (Adams 2016). The most obvious pain point between IT and the business has long been cost. Cloud computing and outsourcing both reduce the cost of technology by enabling it to be shared. While this is not a new idea, the combination of vastly improved connectivity and new operational software has given cloud computing "legs." As a result, "IT now has a mandate to choose software-as-a-service wherever possible," said a manager.

Another problem these disruptions address is responsiveness. The focus group admitted that their organizations were not only seen as expensive but "mind-numbingly slow" to process business requests. "It takes our organization many meetings to answer a question posed by the business when all they want is an opinion," said a manager. Many IT processes are both slow and cumbersome and not designed to function in a business environment requiring both speed and flexibility. "There is much frustration both in IT and in the business with the time IT takes when we need to be nimble," said another manager. "Our IT is currently structured for efficiency, not effectiveness," said a third. "We need to change how we work and this may cost more."

IT processes are such a significant obstacle to change that some organizations may just give up the effort. In one case, IT's unwillingness to change led to the wholesale outsourcing of its operations function. "This demonstrates that if we get hidebound in IT, disruption will be wrought upon us," said a manager. Changing internal processes is a challenge, given IT's inclination for making things stable and structured. Often senior IT management is either not aware of the problems caused or is unwilling to make the effort to oversee true and extensive process change. "In many cases, we could fix the process but it's easier to outsource it and let them solve the problems," admitted a manager.

The focus group was adamant that disruption in IT should be seen as an opportunity and healthy change rather than a threat to its existence. "Much disruption is coming from our business' increased appetites for digital capabilities," said a manager. "They are now willing to pay for us to develop or acquire these capabilities in the best way we can." "Disruption can be a problem if it's just you," said another. "But if you work with partners, you can bring in the best ideas." This positive attitude and can-do spirit does not underestimate the scope of the changes that will be needed to proactively and successfully manage the significant disruptions that are currently underway, to a greater or lesser degree, in all IT functions.

Disruption and the Future of IT

"Cloud is forcing everyone to rethink IT," said a manager. In business, less than a decade ago a new company would have to invest substantial funds and time in developing IT systems so it could compete. Today these are available on a pay-as-you-go basis from anywhere in the world at a much lower cost (Griffin 2015). The good and bad news is that cloud lowers the bar for accessing both commodity IT services and innovative ones (Kushida et al. 2015). From an IT point of view, cloud makes it easier to deploy standardized applications (e.g., for HR, CRM) quickly and across organizational silos. It also enables rapid experimentation and prototyping at a relatively low cost. And it dramatically changes the "how" of computing, "driving a fundamental paradigm shift from the computing of scarcity to the computing of abundance" (Kushida et al. 2015). IT organizations are trying to adapt accordingly by using cloud services wherever possible and saving scarce internal resources for mission-critical IT activities.

More complex services and larger outsourcing relationships are also evolving to address disruption. However, instead of rigid contracts based on uptime and break/fix, companies are looking for more flexible and shorter-term contracts based on a business solution purchase that are more fluid in pricing, structure, and terms (IDG 2016). Since it is rare that a single provider will offer all the components an organization needs, the job of IT will increasingly involve integrating several agreements and determining the optimal combination of providers and skills (IDG 2016).

The focus group agreed with these predictions. "IT will eventually become a portfolio of services provided by arm's length providers," said a manager. As a result, tight central control and delivery of technology will diminish and IT applications will increasingly become a business-managed concern. Already, the business is becoming directly involved in developing applications through agile methodologies, and digital demands are outpacing foundational IT work. "IT will increasingly focus less on the digital layer in-house and seek to achieve speed through developing partnerships," said another.

The focus group believes that IT will therefore become more of a planning and integration function in the future, dealing with the many new variables, risks, and uncertainties introduced by the organization's new partnerships and delivery mechanisms (Weldon and Rowsell-Jones 2015). Key differentiating activities will be kept in-house, while commoditized services, such as much of operations, will be outsourced. "But we can't outsource risk management," explained a manager, "so this will still be an important IT function."

There are still a number of roadblocks to achieving this ideal future state. These fall into three major categories:

1. **Processes and structures.** IT's existing processes can inhibit what is possible to do and how people think about these possibilities. The group identified funding processes and governance as being significant potential roadblocks, as well as line-of-business thinking. "We need to shift to enterprise and design thinking and focus more on the overall ease of doing business with our company," said one member. This has been shown to be a major contributor to the success of a company (Adams 2016). More emphasis should also be placed on organizing IT to support value chains rather than on achieving efficiency. "We must stress IT services, not salaries; and business value, not cost. Our business now ranks agility and capabilities higher than cost," said a manager.

2. **People.** A new type of IT function will call for new IT capabilities and skills. "Many of our people can't change with a process and don't have the skills to undertake new IT roles," said one manager. Nevertheless, the focus group was optimistic. "I'm always surprised at how positive the outcomes of a change are," another said. "People see change as an opportunity and want to learn." Clearly efforts need to be made to retrain existing staff, while also bringing in new people to catalyze change. Many companies are also successfully using innovation

hubs to expose their staff to new ways of thinking and working (Smith and McKeen 2016).

3. *Technology.* Almost all existing companies are encumbered with existing legacy systems. These are often based on brittle infrastructure and inhibit changes in the ways that information is processed, stored, and used (Kushida et al. 2016). It is a reality that these systems cannot always be replaced by software-as-a-service as yet and so must be supported and operated. "We've had a directive to use software-as-a-service wherever possible for the past five years, but we sometimes need to build our own applications," said a manager. "And we still have over 1,000 applications to support, compared with about 150 cloud applications."

Managing the evolution toward the IT organization of the future involves addressing each of these areas as well as understanding and coordinating the interplay between new technology use, disruption, and innovation, and individuals, stable processes, emerging processes, and, more broadly, organizational structure, strategy, and performance (Yeo and Marquardt 2015).

Managing Disruption in IT

Despite fears that disruptive influences are lurking just around the corner, there is widespread agreement that disruption can be managed. "Innovation and disruption are linked but are not the same," explained a manager. "Innovation is a *proactive* response to disruption. Our job is to continually look for new opportunities." Most organizations today are seeking ways to proactively incorporate disruption *before* it is forced upon them and there several ways to do this effectively (Sheffi 2015; Gans 2016; Adams 2016). These general approaches to managing disruption must then be adapted to reflect specific contexts and functions.

The first goal of managing disruption is to *stay relevant.* And the first step towards this is changing attitudes and behaviors, processes, and structures to make them more flexible and positive towards change. This requires ensuring that an organization's sense of purpose is embedded in its culture and its common outcomes and that this purpose is both compelling for customers and engaging for employees (Yeo and Marquardt 2015). Often those affected by a change tend to focus on the problems involved rather than on the bigger picture. They may focus on how new technology could affect their work rather than its impact on service delivery. These negative views can constrain change, but engaging entire groups to look at their work from a customer's point of view or as a learning opportunity can enable the needed changes (Yeo and Marquardt 2015). Leaders in both IT and the business must provide this overall context so the people involved can work together to make shared decisions and take a positive stance toward change.

To facilitate this goal, senior leaders must be clear about their strategy and values (Beer et al. 2016). If they are not committed to a new direction or do not adopt changes in their own behavior, this will prevent honest conversation about problems that arise, such as poor coordination due to organizational design, talent issues, and barriers to effectiveness in processes. "These barriers almost always appear together and block the systemic changes needed," notes one study (Beer et al. 2016). Effectively managing disruption means being open to redesigning organizational roles, responsibilities, and relationships to overcome barriers, undertaking process consultations, coaching to help people become more effective in a new design, adjusting organizational and individual performance metrics to incorporate new expectations, and providing training where needed. In short, it is essential to recognize that the *primary target* for managing disruption is the *organization*, followed by training and education for individuals (Beer et al. 2016).

The key to being able to manage *specific* disruptions is to be able to detect them quickly and respond appropriately. There is no perfect way to do this and not all disruptions will be detectable (Sheffi 2015). Nevertheless, business and IT leaders must be vigilant together in scanning for both immediate disruptions and potential future ones. Ideally, they should create joint capabilities to explore and examine which disruptive elements are most critical to the organization (Yokelson et al. 2016). This means being able to track disruptions, prioritize their importance, and create practical approaches to dealing with them. Doing this effectively requires incorporating both business and technical contexts (Yeo and Marquardt 2015). It also means taking out *learning options* through experiments and proofs of concept that explore how to make sense of new technologies and ways of working, said the focus group. "Our senior leaders must carve out time to learn and understand the potential of new technologies," said a focus group member. "We don't want disruption for disruption's sake. We want change to be planned and to have an expected outcome."

Finally, organizations must re-evaluate how they approach and manage risk. Traditionally, IT's approach to technology has been risk-averse (Welson and Rowsell-Jones 2015). Now it is being asked to become more agile, experimental, and open to risk in order to deal with disruptive influences. "Our business leaders must recognize that more risk comes with these new approaches," said a focus group manager. "They must also understand that many of our experiments will be designed to learn one thing and fail fast and are not slated for implementation. As well, we will need staff and time to convert successful proofs of concept into a stable reality." Organizations still need reliable, secure, and cost-effective technologies to run their ongoing business. New and traditional approaches to IT work require different processes of funding and governance and different success metrics. Ultimately, however, both must integrate into an operating environment. Recognizing that bimodal (or two-speed) IT is essential to managing disruption, organizations will also need capabilities to bridge the gaps between the two modes of working (Plummer et al. 2016b).

First Steps for IT Managers

With these general principles of managing disruption in mind, the focus group had several IT-specific recommendations for IT managers:

- *Embrace disruption.* "Disruption is here to stay," said a manager. "No organization or industry is immune. There are only different flavors of disruption." The focus group agreed that the worst thing an IT leader can do is ignore disruption. "If you identify a disruption and don't do something about it, it just becomes bigger and bigger," said another. They stressed that planning for disruption is essential. "We thought we had it covered with a new innovation group and methods but we didn't think through our business model and user experience," admitted a manager. "We now understand that we need to think things through differently."

  Having a big vision is important, they noted, but it is equally essential to pay attention to the little things as well. "Disruptive change is easy to do badly," said a manager. The focus group described several situations where people were laid off due to new forms of delivery, and significant knowledge was lost. "When displacing people, the goal should be minimal impact. It's important to slice finely," said a manager. When changes are made, leaders should be open to hearing from people about their pain points. "Making sure that little things are working can make all the difference," a manager noted.

  The group underscored the value of looking outside the organization for new ideas and of challenging assumptions. "Ideally, we should be bringing people together from many different backgrounds and industries, including customers, vendors, suppliers, and start-up firms, as well as other companies, to undertake experiments and build ecosystems," said a manager. "It's important for IT leaders to ask people outside of IT what it can do differently," said another.

- *Make innovation a priority.* Because innovation is the proactive response to disruption, IT leaders should give careful thought to how to enable it in their organizations. Facilitating innovation requires working at the intersection of what is possible with technology, desirable for customers, and viable in the marketplace. Thus successful innovation involves a number of components both inside and outside the organization and close collaboration between them. It is also important to recognize that innovative concepts need to be comprehensively deployed. This means that both IT and business must commit not only to the additional resources needed to develop and integrate experimental designs and technologies with the organization's production technical environment, but also to the time and resources needed to make the process and structural changes required for their success. This commitment goes far beyond that required to develop a proof of concept but it's fundamental to successful transformation.

- *Redesign enterprise architecture.* The focus group agreed that the enterprise architecture group in IT is the right function to drive efforts to identify and manage disruption. "They can see things the business can't because of their role," said a manager. However, this also means the group must change its role and look at architecture's job differently. "Enterprise Architecture needs to aim to get ahead of the curve and become more evangelical and consultative," added another. Unfortunately, many architects still live in an ivory tower, they said, and don't want to change.

A redesigned architecture function must be able to scan and prioritize new technologies and work with business and IT leaders to explore new modes of delivery, new applications, and new ways of working that combine both business and technical knowledge. It will also advise on the related policy and governance issues of initiatives such as cloud services or new forms of outsourcing. Most importantly, the architects involved must be open to change. As one expert noted, "They must hold strong opinions weakly. The worst mistake is to overly rely on one piece of strong information or an assumption, [but] the second worst mistake is to not form an opinion at all" (Yokelson et al. 2016). Finally, they must always be scanning to determine how much change is too much, keeping an eye on its impact on organizational stability, risk levels, and people, and advising the leaders accordingly.

- **Insist on business participation.** It is wrong to leave managing disruption to the CIO alone, said the focus group. "The best opportunities come from adding the right context to them," said a manager. As many organizations have found when adopting new agile methodologies, insisting on active business participation results in much better outcomes. This is not a new concept, but it gains further urgency when it comes to disruption. "IT can see things that the business cannot see because it is focused too narrowly," said a manager. "But the business adds knowledge of the customer and context. Working together clarifies our vision and helps us establish options for the future." "We can ask the business different questions and help them look in different directions," added another. "This helps them think more broadly about the future."

- **Develop new capabilities.** It goes without saying that IT organizations will need new capabilities to successfully manage disruption. The focus group suggested that IT needs new external competencies that will help them better understand their end customers and how to build and leverage ecosystems. This is consistent with new research about innovation that has found that the most successful innovations are those that help customers get a job done well (Adams 2016). Internally, more attention needs to be paid to process assessment and redesign since many IT processes, such as technology lifecycle management, risk management, and incident management, may not work with new business models or new forms of technology or ways of working.

Conclusion

Disruption in the global economy driven by new technologies is a fundamental shift in production paradigms that will have far broader impacts than how it affects individual IT functions or organizations (Kushida et al. 2015). Nevertheless, it is incumbent on IT leaders to take steps to lead their organizations into this uncertain future not only by demonstrating *what* must be done but also *how* it should be done. Managing disruption in IT is complex. It requires IT to develop or improve its skills in many areas, most especially in its partnership with business. It also involves all levels of the organization, from the top down. In this chapter we have pointed to the need for IT to transform itself in order to be successful in managing disruption. This can best be done by first improving the *IT function* and how it facilitates change. It is also time to take a closer look at the organizational processes, structures, and lines of communication both within IT and between IT and the business that inhibit innovation and speed of change. "You can't say this isn't your job anymore," concluded an IT manager. "This simply must be done."

Chapter Discussion Questions

1. The prediction is that "IT will eventually become a portfolio of services provided by arm's length providers." If this happens, explain how it would be effective at countering the five major disruptive forces described in Figure 12.1.
2. Three main obstacles to change are processes/structure, people, and technology. Argue for why people will always constitute the greatest barrier.

References

Adams, S. "Clayton Christensen on What He Got Wrong about Disruptive Innovation." *Forbes.com*, October 3, 2016.

Beer, M., M. Finnstrom, and D. Schrader. "Why Leadership Training Fails." *Harvard Business Review* 94, no. 10 (October 2016).

Berman, S., and A. Marshall. "Reinventing the Rules of Engagement: Three Strategies for Winning the Information Technology Race." *Strategy and Leadership* 42, no. 4 (2014): 32–22.

Gans, J. "Keep Calm and Manage Disruption." *MIT Sloan Management Review* 57, no. 3 (Spring 2016): 83–90.

Griffin, M. "CIOs Need to Plan and Prepare for Disruption." *CIO*, June 2, 2015.

Grossman, R. "The Industries that are Being Disrupted the Most by Digital." *Harvard Business Review* digital article, March 21, 2016.

IDG Contributing Editor. "Like Everything Else, IT Service Contracts Ripe for Disruption." *CIO*, September 1, 2016.

Kushida, K., J. Muarray, and J. Zysman. "Cloud Computing: From Scarcity to Abundance." *Journal of Industry, Competition and Trade* 15, no. 1 (March 2015).

Plummer, D., D. Smith, and D. Yockelson (a). "Disruptions and Disruptors are Reshaping the Digital Landscape." Gartner Research Report, ID: G00308591, August 17, 2016.

Plummer, D. et al. (b). "Top Strategic Predictions for 2017 and Beyond: Surviving the Storm Winds of Digital Disruption." Gartner Research Report, ID: G00315910, October 14, 2016.

Sheffi, Y. "Preparing for Disruptions Through Early Detection." *MIT Sloan Management Review* 57, no. 1 (Fall 2015): 31–42.

Smith, D., D. Plummer, and D. Yokelson. "Disruptions and Disruptors: Use Digital Business Lenses to Uncover Secondary Disruptions." Gartner Research Report, ID: G00316474, October 5, 2016.

Smith, H. A., and J. D. McKeen. *IT Strategy: Issues and Practices 3rd. Ed.* Upper Saddle River, NJ: Pearson, 2015.

Smith, H. A., and J. D. McKeen. "Leveraging Your Business Ecosystem." *The CIO Brief* 22, no. 3 (2016).

Weill, P., and S. Woerner. "Thriving in an Increasingly Digital Ecosystem." *MIT Sloan Management Review* 56, no. 4 (Summer 2015): 27–34.

Weldon, L., and A. Rowsell-Jones. "Three Steps to Help CIOs Anticipate and Respond to Digital Disruption." Gartner Research Report, ID: G0020156, April 21, 2015.

Yeo, R., and M. Marquardt. "Think Before You Act: Organizing Structures of Action in Technology-induced Change." *Journal of Organizational Change Management* 28, no. 4 (2015): 511–28.

Yokelson, D., D. Smith, and D. Plummer. "Disruption and Disruptors: Differentiating Disruption from Features." Gartner Research Report, ID: G00316473, October 31, 2016.

CHAPTER 13

IT's Role in a Culture of Experimentation

One of the newest buzzwords in the world of IT is "experimentation." According to many, the *old* ways of working in IT are not sustainable given the changing face of business and technology complete with new competitive forces, new business models, digital strategies, big data, and emerging technologies. These are all converging to pressure companies, and by extension, IT, to work faster, smarter, and more effectively (Kane 2016, Blosch et al. 2016). In recent years a majority of IT functions have begun to use agile methods to become more flexible and responsive to business needs, and when this has not proven fast enough, to introduce DevOps as well. But with the growing need for companies to become more digital, while keeping up with, and even anticipating, evolving customer demands, the concept of experimentation has been promoted as a way to test potential responses to market changes without making large risky investments (Schulte and Potter 2014).

As with so many other new trends in IT, adopting experimentation requires a host of other changes to be effective. At present, "many companies lack the capabilities for rapid change management and experimentation ... and this inability will exacerbate dramatically." IT leaders are therefore struggling to better understand where, how, and whether experimentation can be used in their functions (Schulte and Potter 2014). Culture plays a huge role in this area. "Experimentation is toxic to our conservative organization," said one manager. "IT usually focuses on THE solution so changing is tough," said another. "We've never really defined the difference between innovation and experimentation, so this is a confusing concept," said a third.

These comments highlight several issues related to experimentation and IT. First, experimentation is not being introduced in a vacuum. It is part of a whole host of new ways of working that are being introduced or recommended in IT, including: agile methods, DevOps, innovation, digital strategy, thought leadership, management of emerging technologies, and data strategy. These are designed to address a number of industry, business, and technology changes, such as mobility, improving the customer experience, the Internet of Things, big data, cloud services, and new sources of value. Experimentation can thus be an appropriate response to some changes and not to others. Second, experimentation involves risk-taking, which is exactly the opposite of how IT staff have been trained to work. Third, experimentation is not a panacea but a tool to be used wisely. And fourth, adopting experimentation means dramatically changing how people in IT think and work, and this means adapting many IT processes and, indeed, the whole organization's culture to facilitate it.

In this chapter we begin by discussing what is meant by experimentation and why an organization would choose to experiment. Next we explore a variety of ways that experimentation fits into the IT organization. Then we look at the experimentation life cycle and how it connects with more traditional IT delivery mechanisms. Finally, we make some recommendations for how IT managers can get started with experimentation in their own organizations.

What is Experimentation?

Experimentation in business is a strategy to reduce uncertainty and deal with disruption (Berman and Marshall 2014). Or as one focus group manager stated, "It's a tool to explore the art of the possible." There are a variety of definitions of this term. Some are more scientific, such as:

> A process conducted under controlled conditions to … prove a cause-and-effect relationship [and] support the validity of a hypothesis, theory, principle, supposition, procedure, business case or … something previously untried with technology." (Schulte and Potter 2014)

Others are more generic:

> Experimentation in a business context is the systematic approach to gaining fundamental insight into the underlying issues of a business opportunity or challenge. Its goal is to reduce the amount of uncertainty associated with a complex, multi-variable problem. The outcome is insight into what might work … and what might not. (Potter et al. 2016)

Although some experiments are straightforward, such as online A/B testing, where one variable in a web site is changed and the response gauged, the vast majority of business problems are much more complex (Thomke and Manzi 2014). This is particularly true when a business is a mix of online and bricks-and-mortar.

Experimentation is also a tool for innovation in IT and is often a prerequisite for introducing a disruptive product, service, or business model (Blosch et al. 2016). As such, it must be used appropriately. There are several reasons for undertaking an experiment, including: testing hypotheses, validating assumptions, and reducing uncertainty. The key is to be clear about what is being tested and what the organization wants to learn and to design experiments accordingly (Thomke and Manzi 2014). Experiments must also be carefully designed to prevent systemic bias, sampling errors, and the Hawthorne effect.[1] These issues highlight the fact that new skills are required for successful experimentation.

Even with these preconditions in place, only about one-third of experiments successfully validate their hypotheses (Schrage 2015). The focus group stressed that "success" in an experiment is not always achieving the results expected. "We shouldn't always expect success," said a manager. If an experiment is well designed and carried out, there is much to be learned from failure (Thomke and Manzi 2014). It is therefore important to ensure that failed experiments enter a feedback loop where what was learned leads to new experiments (Schulte and Potter 2014). "We don't always leverage our experiments in this way," said a manager. "An experiment should be just the beginning. The true value comes from analyzing and exploiting the data collected" (Thomke and Manzi 2014). Smaller and more focused experiments can make it easier to learn from and build on the results involved and also to combine results with other forms of customer data (Bingham et al. 2014; Schrage 2015).

In addition to learning, there are other less tangible benefits from experimentation, said the focus group. "Having business and IT work together for the same outcome, being able to acknowledge discomfort, pushing the boundaries little by little, and reframing questions all open organizations up to new ways of thinking and working," said a manager. They also help organizations better understand where value is for their customers and which ideas are the most promising. Experiments also help organizations to "fail fast," which reduces the higher costs and risks of other types of innovation. Finally, experimentation helps organizations relax more about change. "IT always says 'it will take 18 months and cost one million dollars,'" said a member. "With experimentation I can overcome the natural 'no' from IT and plant seeds of change in our business organization." "I keep saying, 'don't worry, we're just experimenting' to everyone and keep exploring new ideas," said another.

Within the category of experimentation, the focus group identified several different types of experiments:

- *Opportunistic experiments.* These explore individual ideas or responses to competitors' innovations. They are designed to answer the following questions: Can we do it? Should we do it? Can we do it in ways that add more value?
- *Strategic experiments.* These are designed to explore future visions of a business model or new products and services. They can also be focused on testing key assumptions of a new strategy (Sund et al. 2016).
- *Data experiments.* These explore ways of collecting, analyzing, and displaying existing and new forms of data (e.g., from sensors) to provide new insights (Thomke and Manzi 2014).
- *Customer experiments.* These seek to find out what innovations will work best for customers to improve their experience and influence retention or to increase sales (Browning and Rammashesh 2015).

---

[1] Where participants perform better because they are aware they are being monitored.

- *Business model experiments.* These explore new modes of delivering an organization's products and services with digital technologies. Typically, they involve digitizing one or more aspects of a company's offering.
- *Intra-company experiments.* These are designed to explore how two or more companies in an ecosystem can work together to deliver value. Typically, they involve companies of different types and sizes, and experiments seek to balance costs and benefits appropriately.
- *Behavior change experiments.* These experiments aim to change internal behaviors by enhancing buy-in to new ideas. "The trick is to let others take the credit for new ideas," said a manager. "For example, we have staff make their own training videos so that they are front and center in a change."

Experimentation and IT

If experimentation is a useful tool for exploring what an organization doesn't know, how does it fit into IT and its work? The focus group identified five areas in IT that should incorporate experimentation into its activities:

1. *Strategy.* Experimentation is often believed to be the antithesis of strategy, as if it were a series of one-off opportunistic events. But studies show that it is experimentation within strategy that yields the most valuable results (Bingham et al. 2014; Posner 2015). This does not mean that strategy should be inflexible, but that it should provide overall direction and alignment for experiments. Strategy serves as a screen for new ideas and a yardstick with which to measure experimental success (Collis 2016). By being more focused in the opportunities selected for experimentation and more disciplined about which opportunities to approach first, organizations can pursue the most advantageous opportunities in a sequence so that each experiment builds on the learning from the previous ones (Sund et al. 2016; Bingham et al. 2014). Using a strategic vision as a filter ensures that the right questions are asked and empowers local experimentation to refine them over time. Thus experimentation becomes emergent strategy as it identifies current mismatches, gaps, or opportunities to improve an organization's fit in the marketplace (Collis 2016).

   The focus group agreed that visionary leadership asking the right questions is essential to effective experimentation. "Leaders can also help us evaluate the results of an experiment and decide whether to end, continue, or amend it," said a manager. "In our most recent experiment, as soon as they saw the results, they were eager to fund more work." The results of carefully structured, sequenced experiments can lead either to radical changes in products or business models or walking away from what initially appeared to be an attractive opportunity (Bingham et al. 2014). "Ideas come from everywhere but strategies are about going somewhere in particular, never about going everywhere." Experimentation within the context of strategy enables a disciplined approach to understanding the nature of opportunities and the linkages among them and helps an organization move in a sequenced fashion from their current state to a desired end state (Hunter et al. 2014).

2. *Architecture.* Architecture has an important role to play in experimentation, said the group. Like strategy, architecture forms a context within which experiments should take place. "We provide a predefined set of tools and open-source software for experimentation," said a manager. "And we still need to govern what happens in experiments." Another added, "Architecture used to just say 'No' in the past when people wanted to do new things. Now we ask why and work with experimenters." Architects can also play a broker/facilitator role for those with good ideas, identifying people who might wish to support experiments and ensuring that all points of view are heard in an experiment. "We set the culture by identifying a go-to person," said a manager. "We also ensure openness to failure and mentor experimenters to ensure they define success carefully and promote their work publicly." Finally, it is often architects who capture lessons learned so that they can be built upon in the future.

3. *Development.* Experimentation should be a precursor to other, more permanent forms of development, so there needs to be a clear understanding of what will constitute success and this will likely not be the same metrics as with other types of development. It is self-evident that experimentation calls for a flexible and iterative approach to development—one that incorporates rapid learning, adjustments, and a cross-functional team (Bingham et al. 2014; Conforto et al. 2016). "Agile and DevOps methodologies have helped us change our culture positively to accept this type of development," said one participant. Yet experiments also need discipline in project management and the design of performance metrics.

Experiments can be threatening to others, both in development and in the business, and communication about their purpose and longer-term benefits to the company is essential as these initiatives take shape (Sund et al. 2016). One manager noted that his company is experimenting with a new digital platform for its products, but there is considerable confusion about its purpose and its development practices. "We know we need a digital platform but we aren't selling much with this experimental one and it is using non-standard tools that won't work in the future, yet there seems to be no plan to change it or turn it off."

This situation underscores two key problems with executing experiments: when to stop them and when to move them into the full development process. By definition, experiments should be short term but the reality is, when business people see something they like, they don't want to turn it off and wait for the 18 month/$1 million solution. "This is our nightmare scenario," said a manager. Yet it is an extremely common one, which emphasizes the importance of developing experiments within an architectural framework and governed by clear success criteria and a formal evaluative process to which all stakeholders agree in advance. Failure to do so means supporting "lame duck" experiments much longer than desirable and eating up resources that could be more effectively used elsewhere (Ballé et al. 2016).

4. ***Structure.*** Organization structure is not the first thing that comes to mind with experimentation, but it is an important consideration, said the focus group. Many companies are organizationally rigid and find it difficult to fit new experimental units into existing structures, particularly when experimenting with new business models. This is one reason why experiments can fail (Sund et al. 2016). Tension and power struggles for funding and other resources are also common since experimentation typically doesn't fit with existing prioritization, business case, and resourcing practices. There is no obvious answer to these challenges but they must be dealt with if experimentation is to be successful.

Many companies have consigned experimentation to a lab or an offsite location in the belief that, if freed of organizational constraints, it will flourish (Kane 2016; Applegate et al. 2016). This approach views innovation centers as places where all LOBs (lines of business) can come together to address common problems. According to proponents, the key benefit of this approach is its ability to foster synergies across the business anchored in the belief that innovation is best nurtured away from the mainstream business (McKeen and Smith 2012). Others have created separate but not offsite IT and business units to drive experimentation. Here the goal is to place innovation centers internally, either within IT or within specific LOBs in order to more closely tie IT experiments to "real" problems/opportunities and encourage business buy-in (McKeen and Smith 2012).

Neither solution has been totally successful. Separating out experimentation can solve some immediate resourcing issues and tensions, but in the longer term, organizations still need to contend with the fact that their core business is what sustains them. As John Hegel explains, in most companies there's an unstated agreement that experimental units can do what they want in their sandboxes but if they come back to the core business, they will be crushed (Kane 2016).

Ideally, establishing an organizational structure suitable for experimentation should be an experiment itself. Organizations shouldn't settle too quickly on a structure because this is an aspect of the business that needs to be fully explored and experimented with before learning what works best (Sund et al. 2014). A critical element of any new organization structure is that it supports learning, not just in the experimental group but also in the broader organization. For example, reviews should be used as cross-functional learning events to make sure various stakeholder groups are on the same page (Ballé et al. 2016). After all, the primary goal of experimentation is not to undertake a successful experiment but to support business transformation, challenge entrenched assumptions, and evolve dynamically (Ballé et al. 2016; Kane 2016; Schrage 2016).

5. *Capabilities.* Experimentation is an art, not a science, said the focus group. While organizations must facilitate it, much of the success of experimentation devolves to the people involved. New capabilities are needed in both IT and business, and these will be different from those traditionally needed in the core business (Sund et al. 2016). From a management perspective, senior leaders need to have visionary skills to set the right context for experimentation and process design skills to create a work environment that supports and accelerates learning (Ballé et al. 2016). Leaders must signal clearly that failure is acceptable and expected since one of the biggest issues holding organizations back from exploring is fear of failure and the belief that failure gets punished (Kane 2016).

Within IT, staff need skills for framing problems, working with data, testing prototypes, and collaboration, in addition to agile methods (Ballé et al. 2016; Conforto et al. 2016). They must market their ideas in new and more accessible ways, such as through graphics and stories, said the focus group. And they must also be able to deliver and learn continuously (Ballé et al. 2016). "Many of our existing IT staff won't successfully transition into this new environment," said a manager. "So we will need to bring in staff with new capabilities and insights from outside the firm."

Teams also must be designed differently to balance a much wider selection of skills including data science, statistics, business analytics, financial modeling, industrial design, innovation management, psychology, and social sciences (Blosch et al. 2016). They need broader stakeholder representation and commitment to more frequent and detailed reviews. The goal should be developing teams that know how to learn—teams that can translate disruptive ideas into experimental questions and hypotheses, grapple with real issues, work within standards, and solve problems creatively, all with the idea of improving an organization's products and services and their fit to markets, production, and its industry (Ballé et al. 2016; Blosch et al. 2016).

Although the focus group strongly believed that IT has a mandate to experiment, it recognized that change is tough for their organizations and the types of change involved in making experimentation a reality are hard to articulate and even more difficult to execute. As with experiments themselves, the best way to become an IT organization that fosters experimentation is to experiment with the IT components involved.

The Experimentation Life Cycle

"One of the things we struggle most with is finding a way to formalize experimentation," said a focus group manager. "We need to understand where experimentation fits into our traditional development and production life cycles." Although there is no clear experimentation life cycle, the consensus is that experimentation is part of the innovation process, falling after ideation—where ideas are collected and evaluated—and before the formal development process (even if it's agile) begins (Browning and Ramashesh 2015). The focus group identified several stages of experimentation that are roughly sequential, even though they may iterate several times (see Figure 13.1):

- **Set the culture.** As mentioned above, having a culture that supports experimentation and its high probability of negative outcomes is an essential prerequisite to undertaking experimentation (Browning and Ramashesh 2015). This needs to come from the organization's senior leadership, which will provide the resources, directives, and structure for experimentation. Ideally, one business person and one IT person will be responsible for experimental initiatives. These people should understand the organization's vision for the future, be strong communicators, and have the skills to design and evaluate experiments.
- **Find sponsor(s).** Experiments should not be undertaken in a vacuum, said the focus group, but should be consistent with where the company or a business unit wants to move. Finding a sponsor is the acid test of whether an idea has "legs" and will be worth the experimentation. Without one, it is likely that even successful experiments will fail to find traction in the organization. One focus group member found this out the hard way. "We didn't involve the business in our dashboard experiment

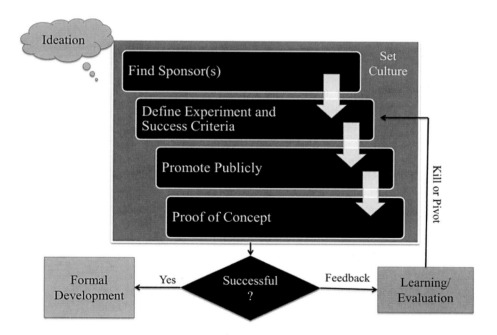

Figure 13.1 The experimentation life cycle

and when we presented the results to them, they didn't want anything to do with it because they felt threatened and hadn't been involved," she said. Although business sponsorship is the ideal, many participant organizations also had some experiments underway with only IT sponsorship. These were of two types: to test out a new technology or to develop an idea that appears to have promise but which the business doesn't yet "get." Clearly, neither of these can go forward very far without business sponsorship, but occasionally it is worth undertaking a small internal IT experiment so that business leaders can see something that will capture their imagination. "When our leaders saw what we could do with our data, they immediately began asking for more," said another manager.

- **Define experiment and success criteria.** This is a critical step. Experiments need to be focused and have clear success criteria. A design should articulate a hypothesis to test and what result is expected. Early-stage experiments should be simply designed to get very quick feedback, possibly initially from internal users or customer focus groups. Success criteria should also be focused on what the experiment is testing, such as understanding which market demographics would be interested in a new offering. These criteria should be clearly agreed on in advance by all stakeholders as they will form the basis of the learning and evaluation stage.

- **Proof of concept.** The goal of this stage is not to build *the* solution but a minimal viable product to test an idea and see if it makes sense. Iterative development is essential for experiments, although very early stages might not be technology based but could be mock-ups or storyboards. As with agile development, speed is of the essence, but iterations will likely be even more rapid with experiments, since there is much less certainty.

- **Learning and evaluation.** This stage is the focus of the experimentation process for several reasons. First, it is critical to assess the results of the experiment. What happened? What do the data say? Often, it will be important to dig down into the results to determine what can be learned from an experiment. Common pitfalls include: looking only at overall outcomes, not at specific market segments; canceling the experiment too early when uptake is slow and not understanding the underlying reasons for this; and dragging the experiment on too long when initial results are not borne out over a longer time period. A second reason to carefully assess results is to determine if there were design or planning issues that undermined them. Often human error and systemic bias can lead to less-than-clear results. Such situations can feed back into the experimental design stage.

Third, what is learned will help direct future experiments. "Pivoting" is a key component of experiments as leaders increasingly understand more clearly how to develop an idea. Some key types of pivots include: zooming in on a particular feature; refocusing on a particular customer segment; reframing the business model proposition; changing the mix of channels involved; and changing the technology involved (Blosch et al. 2016).

Fourth, experimental results should be assessed with regard to the overall process of strategic transformation. Success could lead to the development of new products or services but all results will feed back into the strategy development process and dynamically help guide business strategy and transformation. Success could also lead to a series of related experiments to test improvements to existing products and services and/or features or new products and services. The goal is to conduct an ongoing number of experiments within a particular strategic context, rolling out the successful ones and re-evaluating the not-so-successful ones. Finally, learning should lead to an assessment of the skills, capabilities, and resources needed. Is more business participation needed? Is funding adequate? What new capabilities should be added to the team? Are there cultural or procedural roadblocks? Each of these questions should be addressed as part of this stage and the results fed back to sponsors and the leaders responsible for experimentation.

Getting Started with Experimentation

As with all new ways of working, experimentation will take time to become engrained in an organization's culture. The focus group had several recommendations for IT leaders who wish to get this change started:

- *Provide space and time for experimentation.* Experimental thinking uses a different type of brain power that requires a disengagement from current tasks and activities (Posner 2015). Nurturing it requires people to gain a psychological distance from more performance-oriented work. Companies that wish to promote a culture of experimentation need to provide places and spaces for it—both physical and virtual—where people can take time away from their day-to-day activities to think, interact, cross-pollinate ideas, and design experiments related to different topics (Berman and Marshall 2014). This does not require a separate location and dedicated resources, at least initially, but it does mean recognizing and respecting that a certain percentage of everyone's time should be devoted to this type of work. One focus group organization has dedicated Friday afternoon as "thinking time" to be used for learning. "I don't care what my people do with it as long as they bring back something they've learned," said a manager.
- *Use cross-functional teams.* "I've learned the hard way that you have to involve business in experimentation or whatever you come up with is likely to fail," said a manager. The best way to do this, said the focus group, is to start a relationship with colleagues in the business. "Use food and drink," said a manager. "Spend some time cultivating them. Be humble and ask for their ideas and opinions. Be a little fuzzy if you've got an experiment underway so they can help." Many focus group companies now participate in offsite innovation labs, which involve a combination of technology and business partners. Others prefer to create internal cross-functional experimental teams that can seed changes back to the broader organizational culture, helping it learn from failure and become more comfortable with uncertainty

(Blosch et al. 2016). Some experiments will also involve customer participants through focus groups.

- **Establish new ways to fund and govern experiments.** It is clear that experimentation cannot and should not compete with other types of IT projects, and that organizations need to develop quick and effective ways to engage in, fund, and disengage from experiments (Blosch et al. 2016). One focus group company has created a combined innovation council. "We've recognized that we can't do things in silos so we've brought the business and IT together to experiment with how to manage experiments more effectively," said a manager. Another organization uses a "dragon's den" approach to experiments, where their proponents pitch their ideas to business leaders to obtain preliminary funding. "This emphasizes that experiments must be tied to a business problem," said the manager involved. All agreed that investment should be tied to individual iterations. "That way, we always ensure that we are going in the right direction for our company," explained a focus group member.

- **Reduce known unknowns.** Experiments actually comprise two sets of unknowns: things we don't know we don't know (unknown unknowns) and things we know we don't know (known unknowns). The key to an effective experiment is to reduce the knowable unknowns by focusing attention on things that can be made more certain, such as results, processes, communication, goals, vision, and requirements (Kane et al. 2015). "Many of our experiments fail because of human factors, such as poor planning, rushing design, and other things," said a manager. The remaining known unknowns are driven by complexity. Reduced complexity can be achieved through experiment decomposition and thorough planning, as well as scenario analysis and frequent communication. Experts also recommend using long interviews with users to pick up weak signals, using data mining to better understand the phenomenon to be studied, and incorporating a balance of local autonomy and central control into an experiment's design (Kane et al. 2015).

- **Rethink the role of failure in the enterprise.** Celebrating failure and what has been learned is central to developing a culture of experimentation, agreed the focus group, but it can be hard to sell this concept to the organization. Many leaders consider an experiment a failure if it does not bear out its hypothesis. Changing the culture means getting comfortable with failure and accepting some risks. Often the pressure to claim success keeps many experiments going on too long (Blosch et al. 2016). "The worst thing is when you can't wind down an experiment and there are organizational politics associated with it," said a manager. Senior leaders therefore need to openly talk about failures and then deploy what has been learned in future experiments. This is the best way to keep more ideas and innovations flowing, agreed the focus group.

- **Build on what you learn.** "We had an experiment that wasn't a business success but when we looked at the results we realized we could use the technology involved as a platform for other products and services," said a manager. "That learning was really key and, of course, we learned that this particular business opportunity should not be pursued as well." Focus group managers recommended experimenting first with IT staff as customers and then with internal staff as it gives them firsthand experience before taking a bigger risk with customers. "We experimented with mobile business intelligence tools with carefully selected participants," said another. "But others caught wind of it and it became a movement. Then the Board heard of it and wanted it too so we were able to experiment further. It was perfect!" Although not all experiments are successful in proving their hypotheses, they should all inform strategy. The key is learning from the results and then pivoting. The focus group stressed that experiments should be seen as a journey, not a road map. "Miracles come in small steps." said a manager. "You learn and then you adjust."

Conclusion

Few individuals or organizations are comfortable with experimentation but most recognize that it is necessary for survival in the brave new world of the future, when we will be bombarded with increasing amounts of change from all fronts. There are lots of ideas in organizations, but until recently there has been little support for following up on them and few ways to do so. In this chapter we have shown that introducing experimentation into an organization must be done holistically. Culture, capabilities, strategy, processes, governance, funding, HR practices, and functions must all be on board to do it successfully. Learning from failures is essential. As a result, experimentation is not for the faint of heart. But the fact remains that organizations *are* experimenting and obtaining results, and this increases pressure on others to do the same. Developing a culture where experimentation is accepted and even expected is the first step. Learning to experiment effectively will take longer and may require some process and structural experiments as well. However, the payoff will be the ability to navigate much more confidently in a world of continuous and dynamic change.

Chapter Discussion Questions

1. Argue that there is no such thing as a failed experiment if properly designed.
2. Should someone from the business always lead experiments or are there situations where someone from IT should lead?

References

Applegate, L., and A. Meyer. "Launching 1871: An Entrepreneurial Ecosystem Hub." *Harvard Business School Case N1-816-090*, April 20, 2016.

Balle, M., J. Morgan, and D. Sobek. "Why Learning is so Central to Sustained Innovation." *MIT Sloan Management Review* 57, no. 3 (Spring 2016).

Berman, S., and A. Marshall. "Reinventing the Rules of Engagement: Three Strategies for Winning the Information Technology Race." *Strategy and Leadership* 42, no. 4 (2014).

Bingham, C., N. Furr, and K. Eisenhardt. "The Opportunity Paradox." *MIT Sloan Management Review* 56, no. 1 (Fall 2014).

Binns, A., B. Harreld, C. O'Reilly, and M. Tushman. "The Art of Strategic Renewal." *MIT Sloan Management Review* 55, no. 2 (Winter 2014).

Blosch, M., N. Osmond, and D. Norton. "Enterprise Architects Combine Design Thinking, Lean Startup and Agile to Drive Digital Innovation." Gartner Research Report, ID: G00295415, February 4, 2016.

Browning, T., and R. Ramashesh. "Reducing Unwelcome Surprises in Project Management." *MIT Sloan Management Review* 56, no. 3 (Spring 2015).

Collis, D. "Lean Strategy." *Harvard Business Review*, March 2016.

Conforto, E., E. Rebentisch, and D. Amaral. "Learning the Art of Business Improvisation." *MIT Sloan Management Review* 57, no. 3 (Spring 2016).

Hunter, R., M. Mesaglio, and O. Chen. "Experimentation is Key to Strategy in the Era of Digital Business." Gartner Research Report, ID: G00260164, September 17, 2014.

Kane, G. "The Dark Side of the Digital Revolution." *MIT Sloan Management Review Digital*, 2016.

Kane, G., D. Palmer, A. Phillips, and D. Kiron. "Is Your Business Ready for a Digital Future?" *MIT Sloan Management Review* 56, no. 4 (Summer 2015).

McKeen, J. D., and H. A. Smith. *IT Strategy: Issues and Practices (2nd ed.)*. Upper Saddle River, NJ: Pearson Education, 2012.

McKeen, J. D., and H. A. Smith. *IT Strategy: Issues and Practices (3rd ed.)*. Upper Saddle River, NJ: Pearson Education, 2015.

Posner, B. "Why You Decide the Way you Do." *MIT Sloan Management Review* 56, no. 2 (Winter 2015).

Potter, K., M. Smith, and S. Buchanan. "Definitions Required to Guide Business Unit IT Strategies." Gartner Research Report, ID: G00299635, April 21, 2016.

Schrage, M. "Embrace your Ignorance." *MIT Sloan Management Review* 56, no. 2 (Winter 2015).

Schulte, A., and K. Potter. "CIOs Must Drive Rapid Change and Experimentation in the Enterprise for Greater Innovation and Competitive Advantage." Gartner Research Report, ID: G00260204, November 5, 2014.

Smith, H. A., and J. D. McKeen. "Developing a Digital Strategy." http://www.itmgmtforum.ca, 2015.

Sund, K., M. Bogers, J. Villarroel, and N. Foss. "Managing Tensions Between New and Existing Business Models." *MIT Sloan Management Review*, Summer 2016.

Thomke, S., and J. Manzi. "The Discipline of Business Experimentation." *Harvard Business Review*, December 2014.

CHAPTER 14

Improving the Customer Experience: An IT Perspective

It used to be so simple. Customers "experienced" a company through its products or services. Brand managers handled the products and customer service handled any problems with services. Products were bought in only one or two ways and services were developed accordingly. Thus a store was the sole channel for retail products, while the agent was the sole channel for insurance products and so on. Today, of course, we live in a very different world of multi-channel access, thanks to a plethora of new web-based computing devices. Now we can find products and services anywhere in the world, undertake transactions 24/7 from almost anywhere with our mobile devices, and compare and contrast our perceptions, feelings, and the quality of interactions with others through social media. As a result, an increasing number of businesses are looking to differentiate themselves not just on products or services but also on a superior customer experience (Thompson 2011).

Recognizing the need and delivering an outstanding customer experience are two different matters. While all organizations give their customers an "experience"—either positive or negative, few as yet have committed the time and resources to analyze, manage, and improve it on an ongoing and holistic basis (Davies and Thompson 2009). So where does IT fit into this mix? As with so much else, information technology is essential to the solution but not the whole answer. There are many stakeholders, technologies, and even strategies involved and no one "silver bullet" (Thompson 2011). And yet "it is clear now that technology will be playing an increasingly important role in delivering positive customer experiences and, when implemented poorly, can destroy them" (Thompson 2011). A key challenge is delivering a consistent experience across all channels, but technology is also important for improving both front office and online knowledge management, and listening and responding to customers after interactions are completed. As well, in order to address these matters, there is considerable foundational work that needs to be undertaken by IT, such as integrating all information about a customer, analyzing the different processes involved in dealing with customers, and even coming up with a clear definition of what the customer experience *is* (Thompson and Herschel 2009).[1]

In order to better understand the IT function's role in creating and improving an organization's customer experiences, the focus group was asked to consider a number of questions such as their organization's definition of "customer experience," who key stakeholders are, and the strategic importance of improving the customer experience and the role of IT in doing so. They were also asked to describe the key IT foundational elements involved, the specific activities their IT organization is undertaking to improve their customers' experience, and any new skills and capabilities IT will need to do this. In this chapter we integrate the practical wisdom of these managers with other research. We first examine the nature of customer experience—both its business value and its many dimensions. Then we describe the role technology plays in creating experiences for customers and helping companies understand their customers' experiences. Finally, we look at the foundational elements an IT organization must put in place in order to be able to support and deliver enterprise customer experience initiatives, and we describe some of the advice focus group managers had for others trying to improve their customers' experience with IT.

Customer Experience and Business value

Improving their customers' experience was the top strategic priority for many members of the focus group and an extremely high priority for all the others. A global study of CEOs found that 88 percent of all CEOs selected "getting closer to the customer" as the most important dimension of realizing their business strategy. It noted:

> Customers encountering new products, services and experiences … are growing less loyal to their brands…. Reputations can be built and burned by opinions shared online, texted or tweeted by friends, bloggers and advocacy groups. CEOs told us they need to re-ignite customer interest and loyalty or risk losing ground to competitors. (Berman and Korsten 2010)

There are many good business reasons for this strong interest in creating a positive customer experience. First and foremost, studies show that a consistent and excellent customer experience positively impacts an organization's bottom line. One found strong returns on investment of up to 50 percent are related to initiatives designed to improve customer experience (Dardan et al. 2007). Profit and growth are primarily stimulated by customer loyalty, which in turn is stimulated by customer satisfaction, which is driven by positive customer experiences with an organization and its brands and services (Thompson and Herschel 2009).

---

[1] Voice of the Customer, Customer Relationship Management, Master Data Management, Customer Experience Management and multi-channel distribution are all interrelated aspects of this concept.

Conversely, today's customers are more willing to complain, switch brands, and tell others about it (Thompson and Davies 2011). "In our competitive world, customer acquisition is expensive, so we want to retain them once we get them," said a manager. For example, 59 percent of customers will stop doing business with a brand after just one bad experience in just one channel (Gagnon et al. 2005). On the other hand, 82 percent of consumers will recommend a brand to friends and family if they have a satisfying experience with it (Kioa and Zapf 2002).

Second, customer experience can also be a strong company differentiator—both positive and negative—thereby directly affecting sales. For example, Apple's consistent ability to delight its customers and make their experience with its products enjoyable, illustrates that *how* a product or service is provided is as important as *what* is provided (Meyer and Schwager 2007). In fact, an excellent customer experience is one of the most sustainable forms of business differentiation (Thompson 2011). In contrast, poor-quality experiences can humiliate an organization and damage its credibility and stock prices, and lead to customer determination to do business elsewhere (Thompson 2011; Meyer and Schwager 2007).

Efforts to improve customers' experience can also result in a number of other less well-known benefits to an organization, such as improved customer data quality, reduced operations and service costs, more effective brand launches, and better segmentation and marketing (Sarner and Davies 2011). While customer experience projects typically look at customer-facing applications, there are other less obvious impacts on customers from back-end processes, such as billing and logistics (Thompson and Davies 2011). One manager found that her company's invoicing practices not only had the largest impact on customer experience, but also a very strong potential to dissatisfy. Poor customer service at the end of the sales cycle in particular can have a strong negative impact on customer experience, as anyone who has been trapped in "voicemail hell" or stuck on hold can attest (Alcock and Millard 2007). And good customer service that enables customers to solve their problems with a minimum amount of time and interaction can both save the company money and dramatically improve customer satisfaction (Jacobs 2011; Hopkins 2010).

In short, today's customers have growing expectations of the organizations they deal with. They don't want to waste time, they want better options, and they want their relationship with an organization to be recognized and respected (Hopkins 2010). The gap between their expectations and their experience spells the difference between an organization's ability to delight them or to repel them and will directly affect a firm's competitive advantage. Unfortunately, this gap is only too apparent in most modern organizations. While 8 percent of customers described their experiences with organizations as superior, 80 percent of companies believe that they provide superior service (Meyer and Schwager 2007). Focus group members agreed that their companies had not focused on creating a good customer experience in the past. "We are gradually changing our behaviour to ask what we can do to become more customer-centric," said one manager. "We are recognizing that while our vision for the *type* of customer relationships we want is strong, we need to do a much better job in *delivering* on projects that will build them," said another.

The Many Dimensions of Customer Experience

"Customer experience" is a multidimensional concept that is often misunderstood or poorly defined by organizations (Thompson and Herschel 2009). For example, many organizations do not distinguish between surveys that measure satisfaction with a particular experience or at a point in time and customer experience, which is a more comprehensive, holistic, and continuous accumulation of a variety of experiences with all aspects of an organization (Meyer and Schwager 2007). As a focus group manager explained, "We are beginning to recognize that we must understand *all* our customers' needs and experiences across *many* dimensions such as price, personal interaction, promotions, products, processes, and place."

Customer experience is thus not just customer service or customer relationship management, although these are key components of it. Nor is it derived from a single interaction or channel. It also varies according to the type of customer involved because experiences are both rational and emotional (Davies and Thompson 2009). Altogether, it encompasses customer touch points from every part of an organization, across multiple channels and departments, and the full sales cycle from marketing to order processing to billing to post-sales service.

As well, it incorporates *both* positive and negative experiences. One focus group company assesses its touch points along two dimensions: their potential to delight or dissatisfy, and the size of the impact if they succeed or fail. "All our departments must recognize that they have a role to play in creating a positive (or negative) customer experience," said its manager. "We need to better understand customer perceptions of our entire organization," said another "and to recognize that different customers may have different experiences." Customer experience is also influenced by whether or not a company is perceived to be actively working to address its problems (Markey et al. 2009). In short, customer experience is an enterprise challenge that reaches across all parts of an organization, touch points, and channels (Doughterty and Murthy 2009).

Some additional dimensions of customer experience include:

• **Consistency and reliability.** Customer experience is shaped by expectations and these, in turn, are positively influenced by products and services that deliver consistently across channels, over time, and as promised (Thompson 2011).

• **Knowledge and data.** The ability of an organization to assist, support, and educate its customers is based on how well knowledge about products, services, and customer preferences is either built into its customer-facing applications or made available to its staff (Jacobs 2011). In addition, organizations need to know *about* its customer experiences in order to better understand and act to improve them (Dougherty and Murthy 2009).

- *Timeliness.* Clearly, the best time to positively influence a customer's experience is while the customer is interacting with the organization. The longer it takes to accomplish an interaction, the less likely a customer will be satisfied. This is particularly true if an experience is mediated by technology. Members cited studies that showed that 65 percent of customers abandon online shopping carts if frustrated (Kioa and Zapf 2002). They also stated that their firms lose millions of dollars if their Web sites are down even for a few minutes.
- *Innovation.* Since it is now a strategic differentiator for organizations, innovation is an increasingly important dimension of the customer experience. While many think first about innovative usability, some suggest there are whole new layers of customer experience that can be improved through the innovative use of technology (Berman and Korsten 2010; Martin 2011). For example, one company that manufactures medical scanning equipment used IT to create a personalized environment with pictures and sound that helps reduce anxiety in patients—something that had never previously been thought of as a role for technology (Verganti 2011).

Finally, the focus group managers and researchers both stressed that it is important for companies to hear what their customers are saying about their experiences and take action to improve problems. "We are now undertaking a wide variety of feedback initiatives," said a manager, "because we need a more nuanced understanding of how

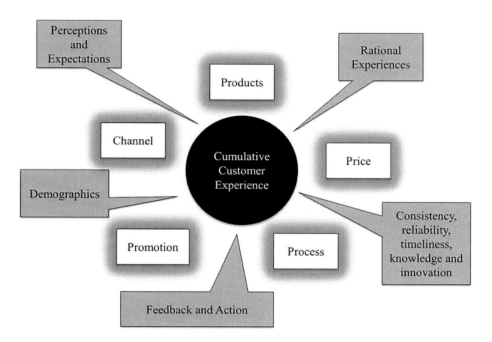

Figure 14.1 A customer's experience has many dimensions.

customers are experiencing our company." Unfortunately, too many organizations fear what data will reveal about their organizations and don't stress this dimension (Meyer and Schwager 2007). Getting real-time customer feedback is especially important so that problems can be quickly identified. In today's connected world, rapid action to correct problems is the best way to deal with specific issues that arise. "We are implementing technology to get near real-time feedback so we can take corrective actions at once," said one manager.

Figure 14.1 combines all these dimensions into one holistic view of customer experience.

The Role of Technology in Customer Experience

Organizations rely on technology for nearly every facet of customer interaction, making IT a significant component of the customer experience (Violino 2005). Studies show that companies are investing considerably in technologies that will affect customer experiences. Ninety-one percent have automated some aspects of the customer experience and 61 percent say they are investing in IT in order to improve it (Violino 2005). There are literally hundreds of vendors selling many different technologies to "help" (Davies et al. 2011). A focus group manager described the scope of IT's influence in her organization as follows: "Technology and IT play a big role in a variety of customer experiences. We're using in-store kiosks for self-service; providing better information for our staff; better analyzing our customer data; improving our web site; training our staff better; simplifying our returns process, integrating products and services across all our lines of business and offering the same consumer campaigns across all channels."

There are several broad categories of technology that are typically thought of in relation to customer experience management. These include technologies that are customer-facing, such as customer relationship management (CRM), interactive voice recognition (IVR), and online and mobile self-service applications. However, as we have noted, there are many other customer touch points in organizations where IT is used, such as billing, complaints and dispute resolution, and incorporating technology into innovative products and services, that will also affect the customer experience. Finally, there are the underpinning technologies, such as master data management, knowledge management, infrastructure management, and metrics and analytics that will in the longer term make a huge difference in how a customer experiences an organization.

The use of technology, however, by no means guarantees a positive customer experience. All too often technology is substituted for people in an effort to slash costs, resulting in a *less* satisfying or negative experience, rather than using it to create more meaningful and positive experiences (Verganti 2011; Davies et al. 2011). Members of the focus group agreed with this assessment. "We've used IT for cost reduction, seeing our customer service as a factory model," said a manager. Bad technology unfortunately leads to a bad or mediocre customer experience. For example, one study found that some companies hide behind their web sites so that customers have no way to communicate with a human being (Weill 2008).

Effective architecture underpins a consistent and holistic approach to addressing an organization's customer experience needs. "We have typically proceeded to implement customer-oriented technology without the end architecture in mind and this has been a mistake," said a manager. "As a result, we've made assumptions in key decisions based on superficial analysis." Architecture is essential for delivering a consistent, cross-channel customer experience and for ensuring that all touch points are well integrated, explained another manager.

There is broad agreement that the most positive (and cost-effective) customer experiences come from the right combination of investments in improved processes and knowledgeable and empowered employees (Davies and Thompson 2009; Jacobs 2011; Verganti 2011). Ideally, the channel used to interact with a company should be the choice of the customer. Customers will then self-select an appropriate channel depending on the nature of the transaction, customer perceptions, time of day, and concerns about privacy and security (Alcock and Millard 2007). Thus an effective use of technology doesn't degrade one channel (e.g., the telephone) in order to promote another (e.g., a web site). Often this approach is not deemed to be cost-effective. However, although enforced self-service can result in substantial cost savings for an organization, it can also translate into no service and become a brand destroyer (Alcock and Millard 2007). In contrast, where technology that takes direct customer input into consideration is adopted, experiences tend to be viewed more positively (Sarner and Davies 2011).

Customer Experience Essentials for IT

There is no shortage of advice about what IT needs to do in order to facilitate a positive customer experience. The group agreed that there are five essential capabilities that IT needs to develop, which will serve as foundational elements for whatever customer initiatives a company decides to focus on:

1. *Visioning.* The ability to creatively envision how to create a more positive experience for customers came up over and over in the group. "We need to stop seeing IT as a back office function," said one manager, "and develop better skills in researching emerging technologies and doing experiments." Another added, "We need to work more closely with the business and ask the right questions so we can do creative problem solving." Research stresses that innovation is critical to delighting customers and that organizations can boost their capacity for innovation by making more of an effort to understand them (Martin 2011). As Apple's success has shown, "We must stop thinking that copying others will yield uniquely attractive results" (Martin 2011). Instead, IT needs to envision what technology can make possible and broaden its horizons about what can

be done to make services more meaningful (Verganti 2011). Many of these will only be discovered through experimentation and trying out new ideas in the field, said the focus group. Still others will come from "thinking like a customer" and leveraging current capabilities. From these dreams, business and IT then need to develop the strategies and capabilities that will deliver differentiated interactions with customers (Feig 2007).

2. **Customer focus.** Group members concurred that improving customers' experience involves their companies and IT functions becoming more customer-centric and that doing this properly will involve redefining large parts of business processes and systems. "The first thing we are doing is identifying specific touch points where customers come into contact with our organization and analyzing their journeys through the processes involved," said one manager. Many experts in the field also stress the need to analyze actual customer experience, rather than the generic experience (Alcock and Millard 2007). In order to become more customer-focused, IT staff must understand and internalize the customers' point of view. Finding ways to make the customer experience real for IT staff will build customer empathy and improve IT's ability to design appropriate technology. This can be done by sharing customer stories and letters, and by engaging front-line staff to share their experiences with customers. In addition, having selected IT staff meet with customers has been shown to have a demonstrable impact on the quality of a design from a user's point of view and to be a significant source of inspiration for innovation (Grant 2011; Heller 2011).

3. **Designing for utilization.** Since it must be assumed that all IT projects will have an impact on customer experience, designing for a positive experience is now a key IT capability (Thompson and Davies 2011; Shih 2012). There are several components of effective design from a user point of view. First, it must be useful. Second, it must be useable. Third, it must be used. The real test of a good design is therefore not its features but its utility (Alcock and Millard 2007). One focus group manager cited a study that showed that 65 percent of customers abandon online shopping carts due to usability barriers, at a potential loss of $25 billion (Kioa and Zapf 2002). "We should not be rewarding [IT] for 'bloatware,'" said one researcher, "but for stuff that people use and are happy to use and are willing to pay to use…. It's customer use that really matters now" (Hopkins 2009).

Other important elements of customer-centered design include the ability for a customer to personalize how he/she interacts with a company by having a choice of different channels and combinations of human and technical interaction (Alcock and Millard 2007). For example, it's not good design to force customers to use a Web site or IVR when they have complex needs or prefer to speak with a human being. Properly designed technology will encourage customer use of technology but incorporate options for them. Similarly, business processes should also be designed to prevent customers from being handed off or made to wait (Feig 2007). The goal of good customer experience design is to make it easy for people to interact with a company and to minimize frustration across all touch points (Hopkins 2010). Finally, focus group managers emphasized that an outstanding customer experience extends to the design of the full range of customer interactions. "We should be designing an end-to-end experience that addresses both upstream and downstream needs, as well as purchases," said one.

4. ***Data management.*** The delivery of complete, current, and accurate data is central to the ability to provide high-quality customer service with technology (Feig 2007; Jacobs 2011). This is one reason why many of the focus group's companies are undertaking master data management initiatives (Davies 2011). Good information is not only important for customer service representatives who interact with customers, it is also essential for the managers and executives who are working to understand how best to address customer needs (Davies 2011). Focus group members pointed out that data should enable managers to understand the customer experience from a variety of perspectives across an organization, help resolve problems at first contact (a well-known satisfier), and identify problems that should be addressed.

   Going forward, even more data and better data classification systems will be needed in order to personalize company services and offerings to its customers (Davenport et al. 2011). "We want to create personalized, memorable experiences," said one manager and that means having good data for customers and about them so that we can measure and fine tune the customer experience." The growing availability of social, mobile, and location data is creating new data sets that can be mined to better serve and delight customers. However, since this is a huge field, it is also important to be selective about the data that will be used to meet corporate strategies (Hopkins 2010).

5. ***Delivery.*** Execution is where it all comes together. Well-designed customer experiences can easily fall apart if they are not executed well, and this is too often the case, according to the group. The number one order of business, they said, is to deliver existing products and services reliably and consistently across channels and products. Several members acknowledged that their companies had different customer service experiences for different products or different locations. They also spoke about having multiple customer experience initiatives in different business units, which didn't integrate or weren't consistent. "Ideally, the customer experience should be seamless across all channels," said a manager. Others underlined the importance of having both good technology and knowledgeable and caring staff who are themselves supported and empowered by good technology. The key to effective execution of a customer experience therefore is to deliver technology that enables the right balance of

human "touch" and technical convenience for a particular customer in a particular situation (Alcock and Millard 2007).

First Steps to Improving Customer Experience

"Improving customer experience is a journey, not a project," said a manager. Addressing it will take multiple small improvements that together add up to create an overall positive impact (Thompson 2011). Members of the focus group had some advice and recommendations for those beginning this journey.

First, it's important to take a holistic approach to it and doing this requires central management. "We want to have 'one company and one customer,'" said a manager. "In the past, each business unit had their own unique approaches to improving customer experiences. Now, we want to make it part of everything we do, so we've created an EVP of Customer Experience." Another company has also created a senior vice president position to address all dimensions of customer experience. "This is giving us a single, shared view of the customer across the entire value chain," said the manager. Studies show that 75 percent of companies still have fragmented customer processes that are disconnected or disorganized. Appointing a single senior executive with responsibility to improve customer experience thus provides the executive sponsorship that many enterprise-wide initiatives often lack (Thompson 2011).

Second, companies need to think clearly about the kind of value they want to create with their customer experience strategy (Hopkins 2010). Unfortunately, this critical discussion is often ignored as companies leap directly to what technology can do for them. However, if value is not addressed, it is doubtful that IT will be able to deliver what is expected (McKeen and Smith 2012). Thus a company should first ask, "What kind of world am I trying to create?" before determining what technology they need to deliver it (Hopkins 2010). Focus group managers agreed strongly. "In the past, we've traded off customer ease of use for cost containment and we've lost customers," said one. "We've realized that acquiring new customers is expensive and retaining them is important." Another cited research showing that having a clear customer relationship management strategy and value proposition is a strong contributor to profitable growth (Berman and Korsten 2010).

Third, it follows that an *integrated* business and IT strategy is needed to develop a roadmap for improving the customer experience and to design the initiatives that will operationalize it. A manager explained, "We believe that establishing a cross-functional team, mapping key journeys from a customer point of view, and assessing gaps in our corporate capabilities are critical to developing an effective strategy to improve customer experience." Another stated: "We have decided to have one view of the customer and one common set of business rules. This is giving us common ground for cohesive business–IT strategy development because we are all hearing the same message."

Fourth, IT needs to identify and develop new capabilities to deal with customers, not just business users. "We want people who keep the big picture in mind and who can connect the dots," said a manager. Another added, "We need people with a blend of business and IT skills—who can think like a customer, communicate in business language, and ask 'so what?' questions." Skills in designing experiments, learning about new and emerging technologies, usability design and testing, and working with customers are all currently in short supply. "We must meet our customers on their own turf," said a manager. "While not all IT people can speak with customers, we must be able to collaborate with our business colleagues and particularly with front-line staff to test new ideas." One company is doing this by creating and engaging its various customer "communities" to learn about how to improve its customer experiences with different demographic groups.

Finally, the focus group stressed that IT must keep working away at the basics—common data, integration across applications and channels, and reliability. "We need to develop a single source of truth," said a manager. "This is the best way to ensure that we all have the same understanding and are working towards the same ends." Customers want and value simplicity, and common data and integration ensures that interactions are easy and convenient (Hopkins 2010). These three basics are essential to delivering a *consistent* experience that will develop a positive perception of a company and its products, which in turn will lead to customer satisfaction, loyalty, and ultimately profitability (Thompson and Herschel 2009).

Conclusion

Until relatively recently customers' experience with a company was simply a by-product of whatever business strategy an organization selected. Outsourcing, IVR, online "self-service," and complex processes that seemed to be designed to confound the customer while saving the company money were the order of the day. Consequently, when a company did appear to care about its customers' experience, it was a breath of fresh air. Apple's huge success is based largely on its "obsess[ion] about [customers'] experience and being dedicated to creating unique improvements to delight them ... cobbled together in the most magical ways with the [customer] rather than the scientist at the center of the picture" (Martin 2011).

Today, customer experience is recognized by most organizations as being essential to their current and future success, and as a result it has become a top priority for most executives. IT plays an integral part in almost all customer experience initiatives, and this fact is putting new pressures on the IT function to become more customer-centric and to think differently about how technology is delivered to the organization. As the members of this focus group made clear, everything a company does—and especially its technology—must now be designed with the customer in mind. This is a significant shift of mindset for IT staff in particular, but it is an essential one if technology is going to be able to deliver on its potential to delight and differentiate. For companies the stakes are high: change to meet rising customer expectations or lose out against the competition and risk losing customer loyalty and corporate reputation.

Chapter Discussion Questions

1. Why do most organizations force their customers to experience a menu-based IVR system?

2. Cite a personal example of how you were "delighted with technology" when making a purchase?

References

Alcock, T., and N. Millard. "Self-service – but is it good to talk?" *BT Technology Journal* 25, nos. 3/4 (July/October 2007): 313–20.

Berman, S., and P. Korsten. *Capitalizing on Complexity: Insights from the Global Chief Executive Officer Study*. IBM Institute for Business Value, 2010. http://public. dhe.ibm.com/common/ssi/ecm/en/gbe03297usen/GBE03297USEN.PDF.

Dardan, S., R. Kumar, and A. Stylianou. "The Impact of Customer-related IT Investments on Customer Satisfaction and Shareholder Returns. *The Journal of Computer Information Systems* 47, no. 2 (Winter 2007): 100–112.

Davenport, T., L. Mule, and J. Lucker. "Know What Your Customers Want before They do." *Harvard Business Review* 89, no. 12 (December 2011): 84–92.

Davies, J., and E. Thompson. "Manage the Customer Experience to Improve Business Performance." Gartner Research Report, ID: G00169030, June 30, 2009.

Davies, J., J. Jacobs, and M. Maoz. "Balance Customer Experience with Customer Service Productivity in Customer Service Automation Initiatives." Gartner Research Report, ID: G00216492, September 13, 2011.

Dougherty D., and A. Murthy. "What Service Customers Really Want." *Harvard Business Review* 87, no. 9, Reprint Number: 00178012 (2009).

Feig, N. "BPM: Beyond Workflow – Banks are Using Business Process Management to Improve the Customer Experience." *Bank Systems and Technology* 44, no. 7 (July 2007): 32–37.

Gagnon, J., H. Kleinberger, and G. Morrison. *The Customer-Centric Store: Delivering the Total Experience*. IBM Institute for Business Value, 2005. http://www-935. ibm.com/services/us/imc/pdf/g510-4027-the-customer-centric-store.pdf.

Grant, A. "How Customers Can Rally Your Troops." *Harvard Business Review* 89, no. 6 (June 2011).

Heller, M. "The Customer Will See You Now; CIOs and their Teams Must Spend More Quality Time with End Customers." *CIO* 24, no. 7 (February 1, 2011).

Hopkins, M. "Value Creation, Experiments and Why IT Does Matter." *MIT Sloan Management Review* 51, no. 3 (Spring 2010): 57–61.

Jacobs, J. "Case Study: Exploiting Agent Knowledge to Enhance Customer Experience." Gartner Research Report, ID: G00213917, July 6, 2011.

Kioa, K., and M. Zapf. *ISM/Forrester Research Report on e-Business*, October 2002. http://www.ism.ws/ISMReport/content.cfm?ItemNumber=14177.

Markey, R., F. Reichheld, and A. Dullweber. "Closing the Customer Feedback Loop." *Harvard Business Review* 87, no. 12 (December 2009).

Martin, R. "Canada, Like Steve Jobs, Should Zero In on Innovation." *The Globe and Mail*, November 21, 2011, B3.

McKeen, J. D., and H. A. Smith. *IT Strategy: Issues and Practices*. Upper Saddle River, NJ: Pearson Education, 2011.

Meyer C., and A. Schwager. "Understanding Customer Experience." *Harvard Business Review* 85, no. 2 (February 2007).

Sarner, A., and J. Davies. "Balance Customer Experience with Marketing Productivity in Marketing Automation Initiatives." Gartner Research Report, ID: G00216115, September 2, 2011.

Shih, G. "In Silicon Valley Designers Emerge as Rock Stars." Reuters, April 16, 2012. http://uk.reuters.com/article/2012/04/16/oukin-uk-designers-startup-id UKBRE83F1BD20120416.

Thompson, E. "Key Issues for Customer Experience Management 2011." Gartner Research Report, ID: G00213321, June 8, 2011.

Thompson, E., and G. Herschel. "The Definition of Customer Experience Management." Gartner Research Report, ID: G00169354, August 7, 2009.

Thompson E., and J. Davies. "Ranking Technology Projects by Improved Customer Experience." Gartner Research Report, ID: G00227323, November 9, 2011.

Verganti, R. "Designing Breakthrough Products." *Harvard Business Review* 89, no. 10 (October 2011): 114–20.

Violino, B. "Focus on Customer Experience." *Information Week*, no. 1054 (September 5, 2005): 59.

Weill, N. "Five Things I've learned; Actors Know a Thing or Two about Serving the Customer." *CIO* 21, no. 9 (February 15, 2008).

Moving Towards an API Economy

With the advent of mobile technologies, we have all realized how connected we are. But we don't often realize how this connectivity takes place or where it is leading us as individuals, organizations, or economies. With the addition of the Internet of Things (IoT), there will soon be literally billions of devices in our homes, businesses, and elsewhere all wanting to interact with each other and with a variety of software, and generating zettabytes of data (Susain 2016).

This connectivity is increasingly being enabled by application programming interfaces (APIs). The basic idea of an API is that the owner of one application creates a set of access methods that can be called by another application. The API is documented and, if used correctly, it creates a level of abstraction between the two applications. Through this means changes can be made to either application without affecting the way they interact.

This is not a new concept in IT. Programmers have used something similar for several decades to standardize communication between a system's modules, thereby isolating chunks of functionality and reducing errors (Clark 2016). However, APIs have gained new attention in recent years because technology start-ups (unburdened by legacy systems) have used them to achieve faster time-to-market and create new functionality by accessing data and chunks of functionality (e.g., Geolocation) *externally* as well as internally. As a result, larger organizations are now increasingly relying on external APIs to help them do the same (O'Neill 2016).

But APIs are more than basic tools for application developers and data scientists. By enabling the rapid reuse and recombination of disparate data and functionality, they also facilitate the development of completely new products and services, and they allow companies to participate in ecosystems of organizations without the traditional need for extensive negotiation and customization of information systems. In addition, they are now enabling companies of all sizes to tap into specialized services such as cognitive computing and IoT networks that are too difficult, expensive, or time-consuming to reproduce in-house (Narain et al. 2016).

These new capabilities enabled by APIs mean that APIs are now not just a technical element of IT, but they have become a strategic business priority that will change the nature of organizations and business models as well (Collins and Sisk 2015; Narain et al. 2016). And as the commercial exchange of business functions and capabilities using APIs expands, it is predicted that an API economy will also evolve to utilize them more effectively. But today, understanding how and where to use APIs remains a challenge for both business and IT leaders, and despite the hype there still is much to learn about the effective utilization of APIs to deliver business value.

In this chapter we explore how organizations are approaching the opportunities and challenges of using APIs. We begin by better defining what an API is, where it fits in with other IT work, and how APIs are expected to deliver value. Then we examine how the use of APIs is anticipated to lead to economic transformation. Following this, we present a framework for thinking about API usage in organizations and offer some practical advice for how leaders can get started with APIs.

What is an API?

APIs are multipurpose tools that provide simple external interfaces for a variety of purposes (Clark 2016). The focus group explained that an API is an arm's length, shareable interface that acts as a common communication channel providing access to data and capabilities. "In the past, business logic and presentation were combined in a single system," said a manager. "Now, we keep channels separate from logic." An API is therefore a standardized software component acting independently of its host application and enabling bridges to be built between applications (whether inside or outside the organization) to bring together disparate functionality to create new forms of value (Malinverno 2016).

The term "API" is often used interchangeably with "SOA" and "microservices." Although some have attempted to distinguish between these, the fact is that "it is impossible to gain agreement on how they relate to each other." The tools are merging and combining in our thinking (Clark 2016). One focus group manager noted that "microservices are a way of building fine-grain composable functionality and APIs are the interface to it. Microservices talk through APIs." Others simply state, "APIs expose assets like data, algorithms, and transactions [and] make it easier to integrate and connect people, places, systems, data, things, algorithms, to create new products/services and business models" (Collins and Sisk 2015).

It is more helpful to distinguish APIs based on the functionality they enable:

- *System APIs* provide a means of communicating and interacting with legacy systems. For example, a company may need to call a balance transaction from legacy system to use in its mobile app. System APIs remove the need to know specific protocols and/or business logic unique to the underlying legacy systems.

- *Business APIs* are composable services that include logic, such as "customer lookup," or "provide account summary," or "present a consolidated view." They offer hybrids or combinations of services and could be internally or externally focused.
- *Experience APIs* shape services for a user interface (UI), such as for a mobile app. "These emphasize how we engage with customers," said a manager. "They're not about core business logic but about shaping data to a UI and speed of response.
- *Algorithm APIs* provide access to a particular piece of computational logic.

Until recently, APIs have been built on a one-off basis by individual project teams (Collins and Sisk 2015), and it has often been assumed that APIs are easy to consume by others (O'Neill 2016). The reality, however, is that APIs add new layers of complexity to IT services, and companies are now looking for more formal ways to manage them. Organizations are also concerned about the risks involved of becoming more connected online in myriad ways (Longbottom 2015). Thus there is a need for API management tools (Columbus 2017; Golluscio et al. 2017).

Three types of tools simplify the consumption and use of APIs:

1. *API portal.* A portal gives developers the ability to discover APIs and experiment with them (Clark 2016). If APIs are exposed to external developers, they also provide a means for developers to register to use APIs and pay them if they develop a useful product/service using organizational data/functionality. In addition a portal provides protocols and policies for allowable interactions.

2. *API mediation.* This manages the authorization and security between the calling and responding functions of APIs, as well as managing audit and information transformations (Longbottom 2015; Malinverno et al. 2017). It supports all API interactions (i.e., between developer and external APIs and between IT systems and devices). API mediation also ensures security (including authentication, authorization, and protection), traffic management, and orchestration so that APIs can be customized for different constituencies and usage monitoring (Golluscio et al. 2017).

3. *API portfolio.* Since APIs are not transient, they must be managed over their life cycle (i.e., establishing a clear definition of value, a defined audience, and measurement of effectiveness) (Collins and Sisk 2015).

Because they enable an organization's core assets to be reused, shared, and monetized and thus extend the reach of existing services and possibly create new revenue streams, APIs are now considered a business model driver worthy of boardroom consideration (Collins and Sisk 2016). And by creating a platform for digital commerce, APIs are the foundation for every digital strategy (Malinverno et al. 2017). However, APIs and API management are still in their earliest stages and companies have much to learn about how to use them effectively and how to fit them into their broader business strategies (Columbus 2017).

The Value of APIs

An important factor in being successful with APIs is an understanding of their potential value and how and where they should be used. Although there is a great deal of hype in business about using APIs to sell corporate data and generate more revenue, the reality is that "few companies have mastered these capabilities and they take years to develop. Many companies *want* to do this but the problem is that it's very difficult to do" (Wixom 2016).

Much of the confusion about APIs stems from complexity about the different ways they can be used to deliver value. There are four primary ways that value can be derived from APIs:

- **APIs for improvement.** Due to their enhanced ability to integrate applications, APIs can streamline development processes and dramatically reduce an organization's time-to-market with new products (Columbus 2017). These advantages help organizations improve customer experience, comply faster with new regulations, and rapidly expose their products and services to the broadest possible audience (Collins and Sisk 2015).

- **APIs for leveraged products and services.** A second way of using APIs is to differentiate a product or service by enhancing it with data, new forms of presentation, or new functionality (Wixom 2016). This is done by providing access to some of an organization's APIs to carefully vetted external developers. These help companies offer an improved customer experience, add new digital products, and open new business channels to the market (Narain et al. 2016; Malinvero et al. 2017). They also enable the orchestration of a number of different APIs to facilitate new business processes while providing real-time integration. For example, software vendors now provide organizations with a number of common insurance functions through APIs, such as VIN lookup, address verification, and real-time verification of insurance. A key component of delivering value in this way is having a clear understanding of customer needs because these must be reflected in the APIs and the apps that are subsequently created (Columbus 2017).

- **APIs for interorganizational innovation.** Organizations may also seek "frictionless" transactions with trusted partners to leverage each other's data and services in order to reduce costs and time (Narain et al. 2016). To do this, a company offers a subset of APIs to its business partners. The more business-sensitive the API, the more tightly these partners are vetted and managed (Malinverno 2016). The value in sharing APIs may come from selling data, attracting new customers, or retaining existing ones through competitive differentiation.

- **APIs for continuous platform innovation.** The most visionary form of API value derives from opening up company data and services to a much broader and more open ecosystem of developers and organizations to enable them to create radically new products, services, and business models. Predictions are that APIs will be "the new conduits through which future innovation can and will be realized globally and drive the next level of differentiation" (Narain et al. 2016). In this scenario, a company creates a platform of APIs that supports the creation of an external ecosystem with connections to new marketplaces and communities. These APIs open new business channels, bring in more clients, maximize client retention, and enable the development of apps a company either doesn't have the time, ideas, or the resources to develop (Malinverno et al. 2017). Here APIs may be saleable products that generate revenue every time they are "called" (Clark 2015). An example of this type of API use is Salesforce, which uses APIs to jump-start new solutions and offerings from other developers.

Each of these approaches to API value requires different capabilities and organizational commitments to strategy, design, and execution (Wixom 2016). To better understand these, leaders should ask the following questions about any API initiative:

• How is value created with this API?
• How is value measured?
• Who owns the value generation?
• Whose problem is solved?
• What are the key risks?

The API Economy

The API economy is a catchphrase suggesting that APIs are a rapidly expanding economic force (Longbottom 2015). It is characterized by a "marketplace driven by data that uses APIs to reach customers" (Narain et al. 2016). In this economy, APIs act as the digital conduit linking services, applications, and systems. They enable organizations to share data and applications using easily accessible standards and platforms. These, in turn, allow businesses to make the most of their data to create compelling customer experiences and open new revenue channels. In short, the API economy is the commercial exchange of business functions and capabilities using APIs. It has captured the attention not only of software developers, but also of strategists and business leaders seeking to move to the next level of marketplace differentiation (Narain et al 2016).

What this means is that organizations won't act as lone entities anymore. In the API economy, companies will work together to create more value than either of them could independently (Anuff 2016). Moving forward, APIs will redefine the nature of partnerships, allowing companies to collaborate without the traditional need for extensive negotiation and customization of systems (Narain et al. 2016). APIs are also the enablers that turn individual businesses into platforms (Pettey 2016). As one researcher states, "It's not enough for a business to serve its customers and make money, it has to be a platform and you can't be a platform without APIs" (Anuff 2016). And it's not an option. Focus group participants noted that APIs are being forced on them in a variety of ways. "Our regulators are now requiring us to provide APIs," said one member. Another stated, "In banking, if you want to participate in foreign exchange, you must use them." "APIs have already externally changed the game we're in," said a third.

In our present economy, products and services from a supplier are pushed to customers either directly or through intermediaries (Isckia and Lescop 2015). In the future, APIs will evolve from enabling simple connectedness to supporting remote interactions across a network, to platforms where APIs facilitate and accelerate new service development, to ultimately becoming the actual product or service a company delivers (Collins and Sisk 2015). As such they will become the fuel that keeps companies competitive and drives a significant economic shift. In an API economy, the products are APIs and the market is global (Malinverno 2016).

The API economy can thus be viewed as a set of business models and channels that provide secure access to functionality and data (Malinverno 2016). These create a platform that attracts partners who will develop and market its products (Isckia and Lescop 2015). Together, all entities affiliated with a platform act as a business ecosystem that builds on the strengths of others, takes advantage of shared affiliations, and draws in new participants.

By connecting people, businesses, and things into digital platforms through APIs, the API economy will be driven by a different economic logic. Platforms will serve as mediating entities that create value by facilitating interactions between agents that operate on different sides of a digital market (Hoelsch and Ballon 2015). And the pace of change will constantly accelerate through recombinations of resources and knowledge. A platform's success will depend not only on the platform's owner but also on its members' ability to innovate. When a platform has attained a critical mass of participants, entry barriers will be high. Competition will be about who has the best platform strategy and the best ecosystem to back it up (Isckia and Lescop 2015). Differentiation will come from the APIs available and how motivated developers are to create applications using them (Malinverno et al. 2016).

A Framework for Thinking about APIs

Focus group companies were in the earliest stages of thinking about API strategy. "At present, we are driven by demand," said a manager. "If there's a market we want to participate in, we must use APIs." Others noted that much of their API use is motivated by internal productivity. "We've justified API use by reusability and simplicity," said a member. "Our business leaders believe that APIs mean reuse which means go fast." Another added, "Large companies also have internal customers and they have the same types of problems as our external customers. Sharing data internally can deliver real value. We're gaining tons internally."

They admitted they were struggling to articulate a comprehensive API strategy. "We need to figure out what data we're going to expose both internally and externally and how we are going to manage both levels," said a manager. "It's a struggle about where to focus because of the different layers involved," added another. In addition to the strategic complexity involved, organizational leaders are debating the risks of using APIs in external marketplaces. "Our executives are scared of external exposure," stated a member.

There is broad recognition that companies must begin to think about external APIs, and the focus group had numerous ideas on how to do this. Some want to create their own marketplaces that attract others to their platform. This model is particularly appealing to industries with a few large players and lots of peripheral development, as in banking, where there are lots of small Fintech companies experimenting and innovating with particular banking functions. Others are looking at externally sourced data to determine how they can incorporate it into their own apps and systems to make them richer and more contextual. Some are exploring how they might best monetize their own data for external consumption. Companies are also exploring partnering as an alternative to fully open markets. "We're using APIs primarily as a means of integrating with software-as-a-service," said a manager. Still others are focusing on making themselves easy to work with through APIs. "It's all about selling more stuff. Competition is easier if you are easy to integrate with," said a manager. One manager concluded, "We have no major external drivers. APIs feel more like a survival strategy to us."

Most large companies are approaching APIs cautiously while recognizing that APIs and their management must be tackled. If the four types of API value are configured according to whether they enable broad use of an organization's APIs or a more limited set, and whether they use a closed (or tightly managed) API market or an open one, an *evolutionary* framework emerges. This traces API use from limited, closed, internal approaches to more controlled external uses to more wide-open strategic uses (see Figure 15.1). Companies can then consider how best to incorporate each component of this framework into their overall API strategy.

- *Closed API market; limited API use.* This stage uses APIs to help organizations improve internally. Improving APIs internally requires thinking about improving data quality and standards and decomposing legacy systems into pieces of functionality for ease of access. Thus this work helps build data and service management skills and acts as a foundational piece for other API work (Wixom 2016). Due to their substantial legacy environments, most large companies tend to start at this point.
- *Open API market; limited API use.* As companies gain experience and confidence with APIs, they could decide to become a modular producer of plug-and-play products or services. Providing access to a limited set of APIs enables external developers to add value to an organization's products and services. This stage helps a company enhance its customer experiences in a variety of ways and creates new channels, enhanced products, and broader markets (Weill and Woerner 2015).

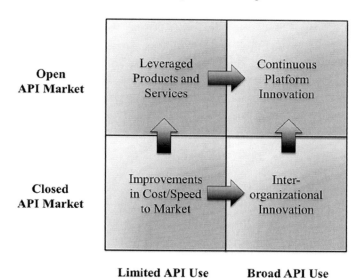

Figure 15.1 An API usage framework

- *Closed API market; broad API use.* This stage uses APIs to enable a limited number of partners to more broadly share data and functionality (Anuff 2016). Here organizations attempt to offer real-time integration and build a limited ecosystem of trusted companies with complementary skills to add value and help them differentiate their products and services.
- *Open API market; broad API use.* This stage supports continuous innovation in an ecosystem (Isckia and Lescop 2015). It provides a branded platform and uses APIs to generate sales through both partners and third parties (Weill and Woerner 2015). It supports the continuous implementation of new configurations of products, market approaches, processes, technologies, competencies, and management systems. It also represents a new way of solving problems and discovering new business opportunities, leaving them to the external marketplace to solve. It also delivers new revenue streams through monetizing API use and new sources of value by delivering new groups of customers. Focus group members noted that this approach is more frequently used by "tech companies" such as Google or Netflix. "These are not representative of our business models," said a member.

This stage is the most challenging to implement and carries the most risk. However, it is also the most rewarding (Narain et al. 2015). It is very important to get the value proposition right and to remember that the ecosystem must provide sustainable incentives and rewards to API providers, developers, and users (Anuff 2016) (see box).

> ### Doing Business with APIs
>
> Of the top 50 most downloaded apps in Apple's app store, only a handful are fully functional with Siri .... What happened? Many developers chose not to sign onto the [APIs] ... to integrate the assistant ... because Apple only let Siri be used in six categories ... and that knocked just about everyone out.... It was just too restrictive....
>
> Slow uptake [of APIs] from app developers risks further denting Siri's credibility, already bruised by the growth of Alexa [and] Google Assistant .... Siri is struggling as other assistants get smarter.... Apple's rivals have gotten developers on board where Apple hasn't. Alexa ... just passed 15,000 available "skills" ... [while] ... Apple lists fewer than 100 ways to use Siri.
>
> (Adapted from Graham, 2017)

Regardless of the starting point, there are a number of common questions that companies will need to address when beginning to work with APIs, although these may have different answers depending on the approach(es) used. These include:

- Which of our platforms need APIs? How can we improve our understanding of the different approaches involved?
- How should we establish *options* for our future?
- If we are building external APIs, which internal APIs might they depend on?
- How can we motivate and manage both internal and external developers using our APIs?
- How can we attract and build partnerships to enhance our API strategy?
- How can we best integrate complementary products?
- What monetization strategy should we use: free; pay per use; tiered access; revenue sharing; subscription; or premium access?
- How will our architecture need to change with our API strategy?
- How should we assess the quality and value of an API?
- How will we manage an API's life cycle over time?

Getting Started with APIs

It's clear that APIs will require a lot of change not only in business strategy, but also with the more practical aspects of how APIs are conceived, developed, managed, and governed. Managers therefore need some practical ways to think about how to get started using APIs. The focus group had the following advice for other business and IT leaders:

1. ***Identify potential sources of API value.*** First and foremost, organizations should seek to solve their customers' problems. This step transitions an organization from 'know your customer' to 'know how your customer needs to change'; from making products easy to use to understanding customers' behavioral needs;

from monitoring usage to monitoring value created; and from identifying unrecognized needs to converting unrecognized needs to 'must haves' (Wixom 2016). Having a strong focus on the customer and creating customer-centric APIs are essential to the success of any API initiative (Columbus 2017). This means taking an outside-in perspective rather than focusing on internal complexities or organizational siloes (Collins and Sisk 2015).

Sharing with APIs can meet strong institutional resistance. Ultimately, the focus group stated, it is the business that must decide whether this sharing will help or hurt, but leaders should ensure that their organizations take a longer-term view of their customers and understand what is and is not differentiating about their business.

2. **Develop API governance.** As a new element of an organization's business and technology strategy, APIs have mostly been adopted on an as-needed basis by whomever wishes. As a result, the focus group noted that there has been a proliferation of APIs without much coordination and oversight. API governance serves many functions. First, it ensures that new APIs are aligned with business strategy (Maliverno et al. 2017). Second, it establishes management, coordination, and control over API use by putting registration, cataloging, and monitoring practices in place. Without these, there is a risk of sharing private or mission-critical data unwittingly (O'Neill 2016). Third, it makes common investments in the organization's platform to balance the tensions involved— between control and creativity, standardization and variety, and individual and collective needs. In short, it acts as the regulator of the organization's platform (Isckia and Lescop 2015).

A key debate in many focus group organizations is about API ownership. Members agreed that the business owns APIs but felt that recognition of the overarching issues and interdependencies involved was generally missing in business. They advised being pragmatic about how much control to exert, at least at these early stages. "The best thing to do at first is to monitor how APIs are developed and used and to spend governance dollars on remediation," said one member. "Plan big and start small." Initially, a governance group should seek to identify the APIs currently in use, and understand their usage and what agreements are in place (O'Neill et al. 2017). From here, it can work to reduce redundancies, rationalize providers, optimize traffic, and reduce costs (O'Neill 2016). By treating APIs as corporate assets that need management throughout their life cycle, governance emphasizes their importance to the organization (Maliverno 2016).

3. **Change how you think.** "The most important change we in IT need to make is in our minds," said a manager. "Traditional systems development is like the soviet economic model—we will decide what you use; APIs on the other hand are more capitalistic because there's a marketplace." This mindset shift must extend to both strategists and developers. With APIs and microservices,

software becomes the creative composition of pieces of functionality and data that can be pulled together quickly rather than a monolithic application (Narain et al. 2016).

4. *Adopt new tools and capabilities.* Although not every project will require the use of APIs, those aimed at delivering value or new capabilities, or at innovation and exploration, will need to use new methods of development such as agile techniques and DevOps, as well as new API-oriented standards and methods (Gilpin and Marshall 2017). Initially at least, IT will need to become bimodal—operating in both new and traditional ways (Maliverno et al. 2017).

There are two approaches to building API capabilities: building them on a product-by-product basis, or building an internal API practice that creates APIs strategically (Gilpin and Marshall 2017). At present the companies in the group are focused on learning how to build and use APIs on a one-off basis, but members recognized that more effort should be taken in the future to design and coordinate APIs, ensuring that they expose the right data and functionality. "We have started with a vocabulary about APIs," said a manager, "and established standards and component names." This includes a common understanding of the data involved (e.g., a credit card number), and published definitions of what an API needs. Focus group managers suggested that organizations also need standards and protocols, methods about how to build a good interface, documentation guidelines, and clarity around service level agreements in order to develop and use APIs effectively. And if an organization is using external developers, it must have a means of registering and controlling their access to company APIs. "We need guidelines and documentation," said a manager, "or we're going to have a literal forest of APIs. Ideally, this should be done at the enterprise level, no matter where APIs are developed or consumed."

API tools are evolving rapidly, and with third parties each having their own API interfaces, managing the API environment is still fraught with complexities and standards are difficult to establish and maintain (Longbottom 2015). IT leaders must therefore continue to monitor this marketplace and be prepared to evolve their tools and platforms as the API economy develops (Collins and Sisk 2015).

5. *Build APIs first.* "It is best practice to build the API before coding," said a member. The group agreed that APIs must be "rock solid" in design and connect to the common needs of the organization. Although the services underneath them may evolve, an API defines the nature of the company's connection with its consumers and this shouldn't be taken lightly. Involving a broad spectrum of stakeholders and designing APIs based on future ecosystem requirements, rather than on existing infrastructure and data models, is also perceived as best practice (Malinervo et al. 2017).

6. ***Ensure control.*** Secure access to APIs is the foundation of the API economy. Without authentication and authorization, organizations are vulnerable in many ways. "We need to prove to our regulators that no one can see or manipulate our data," said a manager. "We need visibility about who is accessing it, how often, and where." Connections must therefore be certified and control has to be part of every change. With external APIs in particular, organizations need to develop secure ways to communicate and share. "There's much more rigor around this when APIs are involved," said a manager.

7. ***Connect APIs to business metrics.*** One of the most appealing features of APIs, according to the focus group, is the ability to track their usage. "This helps us to know what works," said a manager. "It also makes it much easier to measure business value." Once usage patterns are clear, it is then possible to develop meaningful business measures of an API's value, such as number of users signing up for additional services, or capabilities accessed in new ways (O'Neill et al. 2017). "Linking APIs to business metrics helps us to focus on what APIs to develop and where to invest," said a member. "We should expect a business payback. If an API is not used, it's ineffective."

8. ***Expose and address risks.*** APIs create new levels and types of risk and business leaders are highly sensitive to these. "We must get these risks on our agendas. There are many and we are not adequately addressing them," said a manager. Some risks relate to bad data or poor decisions about data. Others relate to poor choices made by partners or about partners. And most important is reputational damage to core company products (Wixom 2016). Cyber-risks that can be exploited by hackers can be exposed when APIs are introduced (Collins and Sisk 2015). Finally, the effort involved to connect external APIs to existing systems is often underestimated (O'Neill 2016).

   While these are the risks of which companies are most aware, there are other less-obvious ones to address as well. The focus group noted that there is always a danger when an API is retired or a vendor goes out of business. If a company or its consumers depend on it, they may not be able to conduct their business. In some cases, these situations have led to lawsuits (Collins and Sisk 2015). API commercial agreements are often complex and poorly understood, again leading to potential legal liabilities. API pricing is a risk too. Subscriptions for APIs may start small and grow fast, leaving unprepared companies with sticker shock (O'Neill 2016).

Conclusion

Companies are increasingly seeking to connect with external third parties, whether software-as-a-service providers, partners, or app developers. At present, they are being very cautious about doing this through APIs because of the significant risks involved.

However, as with other types of change, the focus group predicted that the risks will be addressed over time and disruption to existing business models will accelerate. "While it's an internal marketplace right now for us," said a manager, "we'll be out there in five years." In this chapter we have described how and why APIs are beginning to change IT and business, and ultimately our economy. We discussed the value APIs are expected to drive and presented a framework for developing API strategies. No one really knows how the API economy will shape up but "one thing we know is that we will look different ten years from now," the group concluded.

Chapter Discussion Questions

1. The API usage framework has all arrows leading to increased usage of APIs. Is there a strategic argument to be made for "closed APIs in limited markets"?
2. Given that most of your favorite apps are based on APIs, are we already in the "API economy"?

References

Anuff, E. "Almost Everyone is Doing the API Economy Wrong." *TechCrunch.com*, 2016. https://techcrunch.com/2016/02/21.

Clark, K. "Microservices, SOA, and APIs: Friends or Enemies?" *developerWorks*, IBM Corporation, January 21, 2016. https://www.ibm.com/developerWorks/.

Collins, G., and D. Sisk. "API Economy: From Systems to Business Services." *TechTrends 2015*, Deloitte Consulting.

Columbus, L. "2017 is Quickly Becoming the Year of the API Economy." *Forbes*, January 29, 2017. https://www.forbes.com.

Gilpin, M., and R. Marshall. "Reinventing Applications as Products for the Digital World." Gartner Research Report, ID: G003277399, May 2017.

Golluscio, E., A. Gupta, and M. O'Neill. "Design API Mediation Layer to Underpin your Digital Business Technology Platform." Gartner Research Report, ID: G00323828, May 5, 2017.

Graham, J. "Why Siri Won't Cooperate with Apps." *Toronto Star*, July 15, 2017, B14.

Hoelch, K., and P. Ballon. "Competitive Dynamics in the ICT Sector: Strategic Decisions in Platform Ecosystems." *Communications & Strategies* 99, Third Quarter, 2015, 51–70.

Isckia, T., and D. Lescop. "Strategizing in Platform-based Ecosystems: Leveraging Core Processes for Continuous Innovation." *Communications & Strategies* 99, Third Quarter, 2015, 91–111, 187, 189.

Longbottom, C. "The API Economy or the API Tower of Babel?" *ComputerWeekly.com*, August 12, 2015. http://www.computer-weekly.com/feature.

Malinverno, P. "The API Economy: Turning Your Business into a Platform (or your Platform into a Business." Gartner Research Report, ID: G00280448, February 19, 2016.

Malinverno, P., K. Moyer, M. O'Neill, and M. Gilpin. "Top 10 Things CIOs Need to Know about APIs and the API Economy." Gartner Research Report, ID: G0031885925, January 2017.

Narain, R., A. Merrill, and E. Lesser. "Evolution of the API Economy." IBM Corporation, 2016.

O'Neill, M. "Establish Governance of External APIs to Avoid Unpleasant Surprises." Gartner Research Report, ID: G00308763, July 22, 2016.

O'Neill, M., P. Malinverno, J. Herschmann, E. Golluscio, and D. Wan. "Create the Role of API Product Manager Part of Treating APIs as Products." Gartner Research Report, ID: G00320767, January 24, 2017.

Pettey, C. "Welcome to the API Economy." June 9, 2016. http://blogs.gartner.com/smarterwithgartner/author/cpettey/ (downloaded July 17, 2017).

Weill, P., and S. Woerner. "Thriving in an Increasingly Digital Ecosystem." *MIT Sloan Management Review* 56, no. 4 (Summer 2015).

Wixom, B. "Generating Business Value from Data." *Society for Information Management Advanced Practices Council*, presentation, May 3–4, 2016.

CHAPTER 16

Preparing for Artificial Intelligence

Despite its long scientific history, artificial intelligence (AI) has only recently become a hot topic for most organizations (Austin 2017; Austin et al. 2016; Andrews et al. 2016). Although AI has been *theoretically* possible for some years, it is due to the convergence of three conditions that it is now making it *practically* possible for its commercial use. First, powerful hardware is now accessible through cloud computing and super computers such as Watson (Austin 2017). Second, the huge amounts of data that drive AI are now available through apps, sensors, and other devices (Rometty 2016). Third, new software such as powerful algorithms, natural language, and machine learning have matured to a point where they can do certain jobs as well as or better than humans (Austin 2017; Rometty 2016).

Excitement about AI is growing in the business world (Andrews et al. 2016) and it is also beginning to creep into our daily lives. Whether it is autonomous driving, medical diagnoses, or stock picking, it is clear that AI is inexorably moving from the realm of science fiction to reality. But, as with any new technology, AI raises some important questions for how it is to be used in today's organizations. "We're really at the very early stages of this technology," said a manager. "But we know it's going to be incredibly transformational. We're just not sure exactly how."

It is widely agreed that AI will be disruptive in a number of ways. First, it is a platform shift—away from the traditional structured ways of doing business towards a more "natural" interaction that adapts to context and conditions (Austin et al. 2016). Second, it requires new ways of managing technology. It "learns" and is "trained"; it isn't programmed. It finds things we didn't know were there and arrives at outcomes we don't anticipate. It will need to be controlled, managed, and monitored in ways we aren't ready for at present (Andrews et al. 2016). Third, it replaces a considerable component of many knowledge workers' jobs and this will have repercussions for both organizations and society (Klotz 2016). And finally, when organizations cede some or all decision-making in an area to AI, they are going to have to address a number of legal and ethical issues related to privacy, accountability, governance, responsibility, and decision-making transparency, as well as a host of social policy considerations (Bernstein 2016).

In this chapter we explore some of these challenges and IT's role in selecting, designing, implementing, and managing AI. We start by reviewing our current understanding of AI, its strengths and weaknesses, and where it fits with other types of technology in use in organizations. Next we look at how organizations are using AI and where they see it will be valuable to them. Following this, we examine a number of dimensions of AI management that will be important during its introductory phase in organizations. Finally, we outline several recommendations for managers who seek to "get AI right."

What is AI?

AI is the broad term that refers to many types of "smart" machines that enable organizations to tackle more complex problems than traditional, structured systems currently allow. It encompasses a number of subtypes, including:

- *Robotics*—where machines do physical work, which can range from manufacturing, to supply delivery in a building, to complex laboratory processing such as blood tests.
- *Machine learning*—where algorithms that improve automatically through experience are used for processing and decision-making (Quora 2017).
- *Neural networks*—inspired by biological neural networks and which aim to mimic brain connections. Machine-based neural networks have developed strong pattern identification skills and can also be a type of machine learning—discovering rules, developing new rules, and tolerating noise and variability in data.
- *Natural language processing*—which includes a variety of technologies that facilitate conversational interfaces between humans and a machine. The most well known is IBM's Watson that used these processes to win *Jeopardy* in 2010. Natural language processing is being introduced to the public through digital "assistants" like Siri and Cortana, and a variety of chatbots.

AI works differently from other forms of technology primarily because it doesn't function in the binary fashion ("if-then-else") used by modern computer programs and doesn't require fixed commands (Andrews et al. 2016; Austin et al. 2016). As a result, it can be used to *augment* human intelligence to make better decisions, analyze massive amounts of data, identify anomalies, and proactively predict events (Moore 2016; Rometty 2016; Hoffman 2016).

Data is the fuel of AI and one of AI's key values is helping us deal with the massive amounts of data currently being created—both structured and unstructured. "In many ways we live in an era of cognitive overload characterized by an exponential increase in the complexity of decision-making" writes one expert. "It's impossible to create protocols, algorithms, or software code to successfully anticipate all potential permutations, trajectories, and interactions" (Rometty 2016). The focus group agreed.

"The driver in IT for AI is our data lakes and how we use them to provide value," said a manager. "As we improve with our big data and analytics initiatives, it is exposing more and more opportunities for how to use AI."

Although AI makes machines "smarter," the focus group stressed that today's AI applications are narrowly focused on a single function, such as image recognition, pattern identification, or a particular task. While they can be spectacularly good at these types of tasks, they still lack general executive functions and, because they are trained by humans, can incorporate human biases into their actions (Austin 2017). For example, Facebook's nudity recognition engine ran into problems when it banned pictures of breastfeeding moms and Michelangelo's statue of David.

As one expert points out,

> Things that are so hard for people, like playing championship-level Go and poker, have turned out to be relatively easy for the machines.... Yet at the same time, the things that are easiest for a person—like making sense of what they see in front of them, speaking in their mother tongue, the machines really struggle with .... General intelligence is what people do ... we don't have a computer that can function with the capabilities of a six year old or even a three year old, and so we're very far from general intelligence. (Higginbotham 2015)

However, AI is evolving rapidly, the focus group noted. "It's all about the human-machine interface really," said one manager. "This line is moving. Twenty years ago, cheque recognition was cutting-edge AI. Today, we just take it for granted." The group also noted that the line between AI and other forms of technology is unclear. "At what point do we say it's AI?," one asked. He noted that self-driving cars use a variety of "AI-like" technology, such as image recognition to identify specific patterns (e.g., a stop sign), a rules engine for things that rarely change (e.g., what to do at a four-way stop sign), and machine learning that uses probabilities and judgment to determine if you should stop at the sign, and for how long, in order to avoid an accident. "Right now, if it's stuff we can't do, we call it AI," another concluded.

What Are Organizations Doing About AI?

Although of high interest to many organizations, AI has not yet made the leap into organizational practice, except in very experimental ways. Many members of the focus group were tinkering or testing AI applications, such as chat bots, but as one noted, "we haven't put them in charge of anything yet." "Right now, it's all fuzzy and experimental," said another. "We're testing right now so that we can learn and make sure it works," said a third.

Focus group members see AI as being part of a continuum that begins with big data, predictive analytics, and business intelligence and expands from there. "As we improve with these, AI will be part of a natural progression," said a manager. "But we believe existing data technologies can still improve our business before we need AI." Another noted, "We're still struggling with how to connect AI to our business." Nevertheless, exploration and experimentation are important to help both business and IT find the right role for AI and the right approach to investing in it. "One of the challenges is that AI is both a technology and a solution," said a manager. "And it flips between the two. We have to learn how to manage it effectively."

Another challenge for organizations is that "most valuable AI platforms are built on narrow, proprietary platforms, while most broad, general-purpose AI platforms lack ready-made valuable AI applications and require buyers in every enterprise to fund the redevelopment of new applications" (Austin et al. 2016). For this reason, most enterprises are not yet exploiting AI. "[They] want and need lower cost, lower risk, faster to deploy and easier to manage solutions that are built on a common technical infrastructure" (Austin et al. 2016). As a result, "The zeal of the possible is tempered by the practical," said a member. The focus group agreed that AI is still so expensive most organizations can't tackle it on their own. Therefore, they are relying on partners and cloud applications to acquire the solutions they are experimenting with.

Members also pointed out that, in these early days of AI, it is difficult to see the full shape of how it might be applied in the future. "Our implementations will be very different ten years from now," said a manager. "At this stage we're just using it to help us build faster processes," said another, "much like the car was initially envisioned to be a faster horse." As a result, many of the common applications of AI at present are in areas where massive amounts of data are required, such as with legal or medical information. In the focus group, two companies are using AI in this way to monitor their security logs for abnormalities. However, "if it recognizes a pattern that doesn't fit, it calls a grown-up (i.e., a human)," said a manager.

Another company is experimenting with using AI for basic underwriting using simple rule sets. "We're just taking baby steps right now," said a manager. "We need to get our data in shape, develop use cases, train the system up, and then reinforce it with more data." And one firm is exploring natural language voice response in its call center but again: "We need more data before it's successful." The focus group stressed that AI still works on the garbage-in, garbage-out rule so improving data and monitoring outcomes are paramount in their AI work. "We need to make sure it works because how would you know it's broken?" explained a manager.

Another organization is taking a different approach, working with IBM's Watson computer to see if it can identify data that might be relevant to its products and services and how it would apply. "We hope to use it to predict new products," the manager said. "We want to use it to differentiate insights from noise." Companies are also learning how *not* to use AI. "We have been looking at robo-investing," said a manager. "But we've learned so far that people don't really want robots making their decisions. We're therefore re-vectoring this technology to stress that it provides *advice* which someone can take or not."

Although companies are experimenting widely with AI for a variety of reasons, members believe that the primary driver is business cost reduction—involving people and processes. "In the long run, we can expect to see a decay of jobs over time as AI is used to replace not only factory workers but also knowledge workers," said a manager. And the cadence of change is speeding up, they said. As they look into the not-so-distant future, they see a world where low-level knowledge workers will be largely replaced by AI, where decisions of all types are made and/or supported by AI, and where data and data scientists will be kings.

Dimensions of AI Management

The focus group identified a number of areas related to AI management that their companies are beginning to explore. Members stressed that AI is not a project but represents a fundamental change in how work is done. As a result, the issues outlined below are merely some of the initial challenges that IT and business management should consider when preparing for AI. As these are addressed and as AI evolves, new dimensions of AI will undoubtedly arise.

- *Digital transformation.* Most of the focus group companies are well down this path, which involves embracing new and different technologies in ways that challenge operational and value assumptions and integrate them with existing technologies to deliver new products, services, business models, revenue streams and/or customer/stakeholder experiences. What many may not have grasped yet is that "digital is not the destination. Rather it is laying the foundations for a much more profound transformation to come. Within five years … all major business decisions will be enhanced by cognitive technologies" (Rometty 2016).
- *Data management.* There is no question that AI requires more and better data to make it effective.

> Data is the lifeblood of AI. To train computers to learn … you have to feed them tens of thousands of examples of something. The computers try to understand what elements of those examples define what makes a cat a cat in an image or what gives meaning to a certain word. The algorithm then gives a statistical weight to each guess that helps the computer "learn" what the right answer is. The computer scientist helps train the algorithm by giving feedback and more examples along the way. (Higginbotham 2015)

"AI is forcing better data management," said a manager. One writer suggests: "Data [is] the world's great new resource. What steam power, electricity, and fossil fuels did for earlier eras, data promises to do for the 21st century—if we can mine, refine and apply it" (Rometty 2016). However to do this, companies need to build strong data functions and address the perennial problems of data ownership, privacy, security, and data classification, as well as the newer areas of big data and its management.

- **Business value.** As with other new types of technology, organizations want to understand how to use AI to deliver value. This value could come from replacing or augmenting human labor or from new products and services that have yet to be conceived. At present, organizations are mostly exploring how other firms are using AI in applications or in specific industries and identifying areas in their own firms that could benefit from AI use (Andrews et al. 2017). Supporting human decision-making is a primary area of interest (Andrews et al. 2016). The focus group added that working with big data and business rules exposes potential opportunities for AI. "We should attack these opportunities as they arise but also allow for synergies to develop and serendipitous sources of value to surface," said a manager. Others pointed out that to truly deliver business value, business practices will likely have to evolve as well. Although it will be IT that will make AI happen, the members agreed, AI implementation must be an enterprise-wide initiative with CEO sponsorship and funding. "AI is going to happen quickly and everyone must be together on this," said a member.

- **Skills development.** There is general agreement that we really don't know much about the specific skills that will be required to work with AI (Austin et al. 2016; Bernstein 2016). What we do know is that they are scarce. The focus group believes that data, analytics, data mapping, quality control, and quantitative measurement will be key emergent skills. "We will also need algorithm and modeling skills," added a manager. Methods for working with AI do not yet exist and this inhibits organizations' understanding of what skills to look for (Austin et al. 2016). At present, the best advice is to seek broad problem-solving skills and the ability to work on fluid teams (Bernstein 2016). In the shorter term, Gartner predicts that by 2019 more than 10 percent of IT hires in customer service will be writing bot scripts (Andrews et al. 2016). The focus group was optimistic about their organizations' abilities to acquire AI skills. "We have some staff already who have AI training and who are eager to use it," said a member. "And if we ask, our people will want to learn new skills." Members stressed the importance of having both business and data expertise in the future, as well as technical skills. "Our skill sets will change and entry level skills will be replaced with automation, but we will train at a more senior level so humans will still have 'skin in the game,'" one concluded.

- **IT's role.** IT's role in the organization will change because it is likely that responsibility for AI will be split between different parts of the enterprise (Andrews et al. 2016). The focus group agreed that IT's role will be primarily that of creating the right conditions for enabling AI and integrating it with existing systems. That said, IT will play a part in many dimensions of AI work including: helping to identify opportunities, clarifying the purpose of an AI implementation, cleansing and identifying data, managing and maintaining the AI environment, helping to select and implement appropriate algorithms and maintaining them, ensuring quality outcomes, building bridges between applications, and coordinating with privacy, legal, and security groups. In addition, it is clear that current IT practices will need to evolve with the advent of AI, particularly enterprise architecture, vendor selection, software development, and business intelligence (Andrews et al. 2017). AI implementation is best suited to iterative development, noted the focus group, so it is important to develop a competence in this area. Finally, it will be essential to create a governance structure that will enable decisions about AI to be made effectively and to ensure accountability for these decisions. The focus group anticipates that, at minimum, an AI implementation will need several sets of approvals from business, IT, legal, HR, and advisory groups.

- *Testing and audit.* Testing is especially critical when working with AI because AI can detect unique and unanticipated patterns in data (Austin 2017). Therefore, traditional methods of testing all code paths aren't sufficient. AI outcomes must be monitored over much iteration with multiple data sets. Sometimes, with the best of intentions, AI simply yields a wrong result. It is therefore the responsibility of testing to ensure that no wayward results occur. Experts caution against the assumption that, once deployed, smart machines will need no further attention (Austin 2017). This is a fallacy that needs to be corrected. AI, for all its strengths, will need to be retrained and retested as new data are collected. Failing to consider "the challenges of continuously maintaining and monitoring an implementation will lead to failure in many enterprises" (Austin 2017). The focus group also noted that many industries require a clear audit trail that will justify decisions made and that can be used to root out discrimination. "Whether or not we participate in decision-making, we are still responsible for those decisions," said a member. "Therefore, where a decision is important, it's essential to have an audit trail built into all AI algorithms."

- *Cognitive ergonomics.* The focus group noted that any AI implementation must fit into an organization's social fabric as well as address specific business opportunities. One of the biggest emerging issues in AI is therefore how this technology will interact with humans. In a world where machines and humans will collaborate on problem solving, decision making, and customer services, organizations need to find the right way to blend humans and machines successfully (Andrews et al. 2016). Cognitive ergonomics is a new field that considers the why and how of AI implementation, taking human and social factors and design principles into account.

Recommendations for Managers

One of the most challenging aspects of AI is that it is leading managers and society at large to consider some of the broader impacts of technology adoption. "There are real social impacts to this technology," said a manager, "and we need to adopt it in a way that is mindful of them." The focus group identified five big issues that need to be tackled when adopting AI:

1. *Ask the bigger questions.* "AI raises many questions that still need to be resolved," said a manager. Within organizations, the focus group easily listed a number of issues that are being discussed by IT leaders, including:

- Should a bot self-identify as a robot?
- Should AI be transparent about how it makes decisions? Is informed consent needed to use AI?
- Who accepts decision responsibility and accountability? The organization? The algorithm supplier? The data scientist?
- Should waivers be required in some cases? Are they ethical?
- What are some of the "back door" implications of AI (e.g., smart TVs that leak data)?

"We don't understand what norms for using AI will be acceptable," said a manager, "and these will likely vary around the world. They are likely to evolve more slowly than the technology itself."

There are even bigger questions that must also be addressed. AI and robotics are beginning to affect labor markets (Bernstein 2016), and most predictions point to increasing levels of job losses over the next ten years (Hoffman 2016). One writer notes, "The disconnect with past work models is happening a lot faster than in the past .... We'll soon see enormous waves of workers put out of work and ill prepared to take on very different jobs" (Bernstein 2016). The focus group was very aware of the potential societal dangers involved in such massive economic displacement and the fact that our institutions are ill-equipped to deal with these changes. "Our welfare, unemployment, retirement systems and our universities all need to adapt," said a manager. Another added, "We need to work to maximize 'friendly' AI to extend human intelligence and open new fields of employment." "There are real social impacts to AI and we all need to work together to identify the questions that need to be asked, establish norms for its use, and reform our social and educational institutions," a third manager concluded.

2. *Beware of anthropomorphism.* "Anthropomorphism is the attribution of human traits, emotions, and intentions to non-human entities and is considered to be an innate tendency of human psychology" (Wikipedia 2017). As computers become more and more human-like in their ability to interact conversationally, it is natural to ascribe human characteristics to them. AI developers try to leverage anthropomorphism to make computers easier to use. While not necessarily unwise, experts warn that the inappropriate use of anthropomorphic metaphors creates false beliefs about the behavior of computers such as overestimating their "flexibility" (Wikipedia 2017). For example, a customer service call center with "chat bots" could lead to disaster if it is unable to address complex human needs. This is a real danger, said the focus group, when companies are under constant pressure to reduce costs.

3. *Work to develop trust.* It is critical that people and organizations be able to trust what technology is able to do (Austin et al. 2016). At these initial stages of AI, this trust must be constantly tested. Organizations can expect vendors to oversell their capabilities as well, leaving people skeptical of what AI can

really do (Andrews et al. 2017). Furthermore, trust will vary by context. One manager noted, "The level of trust required depends on the types of decisions AI is making—less is needed when determining the best route to work—much more when there are safety implications." In addition, trust can be misplaced or abused and this should never be forgotten. "We had total confidence in our automated airplane tracking system until Malaysia Airlines Flight 370 completely disappeared. Such occurrences reveal inappropriate assumptions that are temporarily threatening and require a complete reassessment of how we are using technology," stated a manager.

4. *Build multiple work models.* As the world changes in response to new work practices resulting from adoption of AI, organizations will have to integrate their legacy systems and practices into this fast-paced, rapidly changing environment (Bernstein 2016). No one knows what models will be effective in this new world, so the best advice is to experiment with multiple ones (e.g., crowdsourcing, distant manufacturing or transaction processing, and contract work). Experience with different work models will help develop flexibility and agility and start to modify organizational cultures (Bernstein 2016). Having an adaptive culture will give organizations much more than a one-time advantage. It could be key to their very survival. One manager quoted Charles Darwin: "It is not the strongest of the species that survives, nor the most intelligent, but the one most responsive to change."

5. *Consider open AI.* Open AI is a non-profit artificial intelligence research company, supported by Tesla's Elon Musk, which aims to carefully promote and develop friendly AI in order to benefit, rather than harm, humanity as a whole. It is also an open-source project aimed at creating specifications for AI and associated programs and tools. Its short-term goals are to build tools and algorithms that will be shared publicly and longer term, to develop better hardware that can perform more like a human. An open-source model is a cheaper way to address AI problems, and if it works it could help advance AI for everyone (Wikipedia 2017; Higginbotham 2015).

Conclusion

AI has now moved beyond the realm of science fiction and is just about ready for prime time. It is appropriate to ask ourselves important questions about how it could be used wisely or unwisely in organizations, and what needs to be done to mitigate the larger social impacts it is likely to cause. Preparing for AI is a daunting task. Thoughtful business and IT leaders must not only consider its potential value, but also its broader costs. Anticipating that economic pressure will eventually force AI adoption, organizations should seize the opportunity now to educate themselves about the different ways they can deploy it, and develop principles for its use that will take the larger social context into account. In addition, it is incumbent upon all organizations to work collaboratively with governments and researchers to ensure that the negative impacts of AI are addressed and remediated.

Chapter Discussion Questions

1. Describe a white-collar job that could never be performed by AI. Explain why.
2. Think of a typical process (e.g., paying an invoice) and demonstrate how it could be handled completely by AI.

References

Andrews, W., F. Karamouzis, K. Brant, M. Revang, M. Reynolds, J. Hare, and D. Berman. "Predicts 2017: Artificial Intelligence." Gartner Research Report, ID: G00317025, November 23, 2016.

Andrews, W., D. Berman, A. Linden, and T. Austin. "Artificial Intelligence Primer for 2017." Gartner Research Report, ID: G00318582, February 3, 2017.

Austin, T. "Smart Machines see Major Breakthroughs after Decades of Failure." Gartner Research Report, ID: G00291251, January 4, 2017.

Austin, T., M. Hung, and M. Revang. "Conversational AI to Shake up your Technical and Business Worlds." Gartner Research Report, ID: G00315689, September 30, 2016.

Bernstein, A. "Globalization, Robots, and the Future of Work: An Interview with Jaffrey Joerres." *Harvard Business Review*, October 2016, 74–79.

Higginbotham, S. "Here's Why Elon Musk and Everyone Else is Betting on AI." *Fortune*, December 16, 2015.

Hoffman, R. "Using Artificial Intelligence to Set Information Free." *MIT Sloan Management Review* 58, no. 1 (Fall 2016).

Klotz, F. "Are You Ready for Robot Colleagues?" *MIT Sloan Management Review Digital*, July 6, 2016. http://sloanreview.mit.edu/article/are-you-ready-for-robot-colleagues/.

Moore, A. "Predicting a Future Where the Future is Routinely Predicted." *MIT Sloan Management Review* 58, no. 1 (Fall 2016).

Quora 2017. "Machine Learning." https://www.quora.com/topic/Machine-Learning (accessed March 29, 2017).

Rometty, G. "Digital Today, Cognitive Tomorrow." *MIT Sloan Management Review* 58, no. 1 (Fall 2016).

Smith, H. A., and J. D. McKeen. "Developing a Digital Strategy." Smith School of Business, Queens University, IT Management Forum, 2015. https://smith.queensu.ca/it-forum/index.php.

Wikipedia, 2017. https://en.wikipedia.org/wiki/Anthropomorphism.

Enterprise Transformation at Trustworthy Insurance

CIO Sheila Lee had every reason to be pleased with herself on this crisp winter day. She smiled at her image in the ladies room mirror as she checked her suit jacket. A petite Asian who dressed with flair, she had recently been recognized as one of the country's top 100 most powerful women. A newcomer to Trustworthy Insurance's executive leadership team, she had successfully delivered a huge new enterprise initiative that was central to her company's transformation strategy—on time and on budget.

Concerto Insurance was North America's first fully online direct insurance business—and a new brand of its parent company, Trustworthy Insurance. For the first time, customers could obtain a fully binding quote for their car or home insurance directly online and purchase it without the need to go through a customer service representative or insurance broker to finalize the deal. Although it was entirely IT-based, Concerto had been a significant undertaking for the entire company, Sheila reflected, as she walked down the hall to the boardroom. She couldn't have done it without the CEO's support and that of the entire business leadership team.

When Sheila joined Trustworthy Insurance two years ago it was a midsized multichannel insurance company founded in 1871 with premiums of more than $2 billion annually and $6 billion in assets. Over the years it had experienced considerable growth and change through the acquisition of a number of different brands, including a pet insurance division and a commercial insurance division. Until Concerto, however, its business model had essentially remained the same. It relied on its network of independent brokers who worked in agencies across the country to recommend Trustworthy products. But as CEO Kelly Mason noted in a shareholders' meeting three years' ago, the insurance industry was changing rapidly and companies that didn't keep pace would be left behind.

"We have a vision of becoming a top property and casualty insurer," she had said. "Our executive leadership team is committed to growing our business and we want to deliver the best possible products and service to our customers. We can't do this simply by doing business in the same old way. We have a great broker network and we're fully supportive of it, but our research shows that there are many customers we are not reaching. These are the millennials and more mature individuals who find insurance products needlessly complicated and not designed with their needs in mind. We have found that there are many customers who prefer online transactions rather than working through a broker. These customers are generally younger and have simpler insurance needs and don't need or want to speak with someone to make a purchase. We are going after this demographic with our new Concerto project."

Sheila pushed open the door to the boardroom and nodded at her executive leadership team colleagues. There were smiles all around. Concerto had launched a year ago, first with home insurance and then with car insurance. The early signs were all good—personal line premiums were increasing, and Concerto had already made a splash within the industry by winning numerous innovation awards.

"It really makes a difference when the whole team works together," she thought as she took her seat. Together with the chief underwriter, Jim Jenkins, and the chief marketing officer, Kristen Stewart, she had been part of a transformation leadership team that had set out to redesign the insurance customer experience by combining best-in-class digital standards with deep industry expertise.

The CEO cleared her throat and tapped her pen on the elegant boardroom table calling the meeting to order. "Good morning. As you know I called this meeting to review our enterprise transformation strategy—what we've accomplished and how we'll go forward. We have made considerable progress and I'm proud of our success. But we're in a very competitive business and we cannot afford to rest on our laurels. It's important that we continually assess our business strategy because what we're doing has never been done before. I'd like to give each of you the opportunity to speak to the strengths and challenges of what we've done with Concerto and where you think we need to go as an enterprise. Please be frank as our future depends on your insights and ideas. I've asked Ron to start us off with a financial perspective."

Ron Shostak, Trustworthy's CFO, smiled at the small group of his peers. "I'm going to make this short and informal," he said. "I've just got a few slides." Everyone in the room groaned inwardly knowing his propensity for making long-winded presentations with detailed slides. Nevertheless, the numbers were worth knowing.

"As you know, we have seen strong premium growth from Concerto," he said, showing a dense, multicolored line chart. "Premiums grew 18.8 percent in this past quarter due to our new direct channel. Over the past year, we have continued to make significant investments in Concerto and also in replacing our personal lines' policy administration systems in the back office to support it. However, this cost is reflected in our increased annual combined ratio of 114.4 percent.[1] Even excluding the impact of our investment in Concerto, our adjusted combined ratio is still 104.6 percent, which is too high. And we expect our strategic investments will continue to increase operating expenses over the next few years. However, we hope these investments will

---

[1] Combined ratio reflects claims and adjustment expenses, commissions, operating expenses, and taxes during a defined period as a percentage of net earned premiums for the same period.

begin to improve our operational efficiency over the next few quarters and expect to see profitable growth in the longer term as a result. A key challenge in addressing these numbers has been our underwriting performance that has been poorer than expected. As you know, our goal with Concerto was to rewrite underwriting to make it fully automated for our customers. We will need to continue to tweak this component in order to make it more cost beneficial. And finally, while the market has given us a bit of a break this past year, we can expect it to be tougher on us going forward."

With that, Ron sat down and Kelly nodded at Jim Jenkins. Jim, who looked every bit of the actuary he was, in a pinstripe suit and horn-rimmed glasses, glanced around the room somewhat nervously. "Well," he said, "I guess that puts us in Underwriting on the hot seat. As you all know, automating underwriting has been a significant component of Concerto. We invested heavily in big data so we could access both structured and unstructured data about an individual's home and car without them having to answer numerous questions. This required developing real-time access to a variety of third-party data providers through external interfaces. We can now get comprehensive information about properties in a particular postal area from a variety of service providers and details about an individual's claims and driving history from the insurance bureau and Ministry of Transportation information simply by asking a customer a few key questions. We had to put a lot of work into these questions to get this right. We then developed advanced analytics so we could prepare a binding quote for an online buyer in real time. We wanted to keep things simple and straightforward but to know enough to be able to offer a customer a unique product tailored to their needs. This has been an instrumental component in providing our customers a unique insurance experience."

Jim gazed at the ceiling as if seeking inspiration to continue. After a long pause he said, "As you all know, Concerto suggests three levels of coverage for each customer request: economy, recommended, and premium. However, as you have seen from the financials, there is still work to be done in our underwriting processes. We are constantly working to improve our ability to gather and use information, and tweaking our underwriting algorithms is our number one priority. Our use of big data and real-time analytics has captured global attention in the insurance industry and already sets us apart. Our full attention in Underwriting will now be on making the necessary adjustments to remain price competitive while reducing our combined ratios."

Kristen Stewart then took the floor. Although much younger than everyone else in the room, she had won their respect through her social media acumen and intuitive grasp of customer needs. "Marketing's research played a significant role in the development of the Concerto strategy," she said. "You all know that a key value of our company is our commitment to an exceptional customer experience. That is why we value our brokers so highly and why we invested significantly in customer research before making the decision to develop an online channel. We believe these investments have helped us create a highly customer-centric product with Concerto. We, in Marketing, began this process several years ago with an initiative to explore shifting customer expectations and identify unmet customer needs."

"We found that almost one-half of all personal insurance policies were sold online, and that number was growing annually. But most players in the industry tap into rational marketing drivers such as price. We felt there was also some white space there around an emotional connection. In fact, our research revealed that when it comes to buying insurance 56 percent of purchasing drivers are actually emotional. Combining this with the needs of potential millennial customers, we realized that we could win the hearts and minds of these customers by changing *everything* about their experience with buying insurance, not just putting a traditional insurance experience online. Our goal was to be known as 'not your typical insurance company.' In short, Concerto has been designed to be a parallel digital experience. It doesn't take away from our brokerage offerings but expands our market significantly."

Warming to her topic, Kristen held up three fingers. "When we began work on Concerto, we based it on three pillars: make it simple; make it available at their fingertips; and offer a customized product that best meets customer needs. To this end the Concerto team first mapped the end-to-end customer journey through the discovery, quoting, purchasing, servicing, and claims processes and then ensured these three pillars were addressed at every touch point. Concerto products are also written in everyday language—like we speak—and clean modern design is used in both our print and online materials to help customers easily understand complex topics. They provide an engaging experience for customers that informs and creates connections for them."

"This new approach at Concerto was complemented by a broader shift to an even more customer-centric focus at Trustworthy that positions us as a forward-looking partner in the industry as well as a trusted one. We've simplified our overall image to create a more modern look that better reflects our ambitions as a company. We have refreshed our brand and redesigned our web site to more accurately tell our company story. Our biggest challenge now is to bring what we've learned with Concerto to our broker community to help them offer a best-in-class experience combining advice and digital support. But we aren't sure what this will look like yet."

"Thank you Kristen," said Kelly. "I think we all agree that our new look-and-feel is impressive. I'll now ask Sheila to summarize IT's perspective on Concerto and our ongoing transformation needs."

"Thanks Kelly," said Sheila, walking to the front of the room. "As the newest member of our leadership team, who missed participating in the strategy development process, I deeply appreciate all the support you've given me since I joined Trustworthy. Although Concerto looks like an IT product, what we've just heard reinforces the fact that it's a business strategy and its success required full business participation. From a technology point of view, this was an ideal project. Not only did we have a fully committed business team, we also had Kelly's support at every single steering committee meeting." Gesturing to the room, she bowed briefly to each of them. "It is thanks to each of you that we've come so far so fast."

Smiling broadly, she continued. "When I joined Trustworthy as its CIO, frankly, I was uncertain we could pull this off, but I was very impressed with the discipline I found at all levels. In addition to full business support, I believe a critical success factor for this project was the fact that we were supported in taking a green field approach. By creating a separate office and team, we were freed from having to deal with a lot of legacy technology baggage. Although there was some back-end systems integration to contend with, we got knowledgeable people moved over to the Concerto office to help us. Creating a separate Concerto team enabled us to adopt a collaborative working model that facilitated problem solving."

Sheila's enthusiasm was infectious although the group had only a limited understanding of the technological details she was speaking about. "The Concerto project adopted agile and DevOps practices from the start," she said. "We divided our staff into small multidisciplinary teams so that each could work to continuously develop, integrate, and implement new functionality. We also developed a hybrid model of cloud and on-premise technology that has enabled an agile environment and which now helps us respond to new demands and opportunities extremely quickly. In addition, as Jim mentioned, we incorporated data analytics and accessed big data through application programming interfaces to help us develop a sophisticated technological infrastructure to deliver our products. We are not an entirely standalone entity however. Concerto uses Trustworthy's shared services such as IT, marketing, and HR for many of its functions.

"Turning to the future, we have developed sophisticated management analytics to help us understand site traffic, such as those customers who buy on their first visit, those who decide to seek their quotes on-site and buy later, and those who abandon the site midway through the purchasing process. We are using these metrics to continually assess the success and effectiveness of our online channel and make changes.

"In short, I am delighted with our progress to date," Sheila concluded, as she returned to her chair. "In fact, the main challenge I am dealing with right now is handling our other IT staff who want to know why the Concerto team is having so much fun! And we need to figure out how to bring what we've learned at Concerto back to our parent Trustworthy IT and business organizations."

"Thank you Sheila," said Kelly warmly, as she stood up and began a round of applause. "I think I speak for all of us when I say *we* couldn't have done it without *you*! A business strategy is only as good as its execution and Concerto in my opinion has been superbly executed. Well done!

"Concerto has helped bring our growth strategy to life," Kelly continued. "It started us on a journey of digital transformation but it's just a start. Our next step will be to leverage our Concerto platform and experience for the rest of our business, especially our broker channel. From the beginning, we've been careful in how we managed our broker relationships, but now we have to redesign the rest of the insurance experience by combining digital transformation with deep industry expertise. As I said earlier, we cannot afford to stand still. We either have to disrupt or be disrupted.

Therefore, our challenges are twofold: to continue to improve the Concerto brand, and to apply what we've learned to our other Trustworthy brands and processes.

"I see this as part of our multichannel evolution. It will involve further research, new ways of using data, new delivery mechanisms, new digital services, education, and cultural change. Our focus must continue to be on providing a superb customer experience regardless of the process or channel used. You have all been an important part of our transformation to date. I believe we as a company are unique in that we have taken a multifaceted approach to change. Our competitors have tended to focus only on technology. Fundamentally, the key to our competitiveness has been the successful business–IT collaboration at multiple levels. For this reason, I have decided to create a new position on our executive team here at Trustworthy. Please congratulate Sheila Lee as our new Chief Transformation Officer. She will be working with each of you and our new CIO to lead our company-wide digital transformation forward."

She paused, allowing Sheila to accept the congratulations of her peers. Then turning to Sheila she said, "The ball is in your court Sheila. What's our next move?"

"Thanks, Kelly," Sheila said, standing up and smoothing her skirt. She had known about her new role for two days and had been thinking exclusively about the "next move." She began cautiously. "Each of you has touched on *part* of the challenge we have with Concerto. We need to find ways to manage our costs down. It's not just new business we're after but *profitable* business and business efficiency. We must focus on how to use data to manage the risks of the business—such as exposure to different markets and products, dependence on third-party data, and changing demographics —as well as simply improving underwriting. And we are re-positioning ourselves in the marketplace with our three-pronged approach to customer experience.

"But our bigger challenge *as an organization* is how do we leverage what we have learned with Concerto? First, we have to consider our traditional business, which has been our bread-and-butter. Kelly has just underlined the strategic importance of our agents to the future success of the company. Our agents have been asking lots of questions about their role in our new business strategy and we have many customers who still need their expert advice. Second, we have gained first-mover advantage with Concerto but we already know our competition is creating similar offerings so we have to keep moving ahead with innovative offerings and excellent service. Third, we need to look much more broadly at the competitive forces affecting our industry. My worst nightmare is becoming disintermediated by a non-traditional company, in the same way Amazon cut out booksellers and Uber is undermining the taxi business."

Seeing the faces in the room suddenly looking grim and distressed, it occurred to Sheila that she might have gone too far by sharing her nightmare with the members of the executive team. With Kelly's eyes locked on her, she waved her hands in front of her and said, "But let's not get too far ahead of ourselves. We have problems but they are all good problems and I look forward to working closely with each of you to take us to the next level."

Discussion Questions

1. Flesh out Sheila's nightmare. Describe a scenario where Concerto becomes "disintermediated by a non-traditional company." What impacts would this have on Trustworthy Insurance?

2. Why would this be important to consider before designing any future transformation initiatives?

3. Outline the next steps of a business strategy for Trustworthy Insurance that would extend transformation further into the organization.

Innovation at International Foods[1]

Josh Novak gazed up at the gleaming glass-and-chrome skyscraper as he stepped out of the cab. "Wow!" he thought to himself. "I've hit the big time now." The International Foods Group (IFG) Tower was a Chicago landmark as well as part of the company's logo, which appeared on the packages of almost every type of food one could imagine—breakfast cereals, soft drinks, frozen pizza, cheese, and snack foods, to name just a few. Walking into the tower's marble lobby, Josh could see displays of the company's packaging from its earliest days, when its dairy products were delivered by horse and wagon, right up to the modern global entity it had become.

After signing in with security, Josh was whisked away to the 37th floor by an efficient attendant who walked him down a long hall of cubicles to a corner office overlooking Lake Michigan. On the way, Josh passed display photos of the company's founder, old Jonas Wilton, looking patriarchal, along with several of the family scions who had grown the company into a major national brand before the IPO in the 1980s had made IFG a public company. Josh, having "Googled" the company's history last night in response to this summons, knew that IFG was now the largest purveyor of food products in the world. While many decried the globalization of the food business, IFG kept right on growing, gobbling up dozens of companies each year—some because IFG wanted to stomp on its competition and others because it wanted their good ideas.

Josh's own small company, Glow-Foods, a relative newcomer in the business, was fortunately one of the latter, but Josh was a little puzzled about this command performance. After all, he himself wasn't anyone important. The owners of the company all received multiple millions and were sticking around—as per contract—during the transition. The next level, including Josh's boss, had mostly jumped ship as soon as the "merger" was announced. "This isn't my thing," drawled Nate Greenly over beer one night at the local pub. "Corporate America isn't going to let us stay as we are,

[1] H. A. Smith and J. D. McKeen, "Innovation at International Foods," #1-L09-1-002. Smith School of Business at Queen's University, December 2009. Reproduced by permission of Queen's University, Smith School of Business, Kingston, Ontario, Canada.

no matter what they say. Get out while you can," he advised. But Josh, with a freshly minted MBA in his pocket, thought differently. And so here he was, walking into the CIO's office hundreds of miles away from the cramped loft in Toronto where Glow-Foods was headquartered.

As the office door swung open, two people dressed in "power suits" turned to meet him. "Uh oh, I'm not in Kansas anymore," thought Josh, as he mentally reviewed his outfit of neatly pressed khakis and golf shirt, which was a big step up from his usual attire of jeans and a T-shirt. A tall man with silver hair stepped forward with his hand held out. "You must be Josh," he boomed. "Welcome. I'm John Ahern, and this is my associate, Tonya James, manager of IT marketing. Thanks for coming today. Please, have a seat." Josh complied, slinging his backpack over the corner of the leather chair while taking in the rich furnishings of the office and the panoramic view. After a bit of chitchat about the weather and the prospects of their respective baseball teams, John pulled out a black leather folder.

"Well, we won't keep you in suspense anymore, Josh. As you know, when we took over Glow-Foods we decided to completely align our processes, including IT. It doesn't make any economic sense to run separate data centers and applications, so we already have a team in place to transfer all your hardware and software to our centralized corporate systems over the next month. We'll be replacing your Macs with PCs, and everyone will get training on our ERP system. We're going to keep a small team to deal with the specifically Canadian issues, but other than that we see no need for an IT function in Toronto anymore. Josh nodded, thinking about his friends who would be losing their jobs and all the fun they'd had during those all-nighters brainstorming new ways to help Glow-Foods products go "viral." "Nate was right," he thought glumly. "They don't really get us at all."

"That said," John continued. "We are very impressed with the work you and your team have done in using social networking, mashups, and multimedia to support your marketing strategy. Your ability to reach the under-thirty demographic with technology is impressive." He turned to Tonya, who added. "Here at IFG, we have traditionally marketed our products to women with children. We have a functional Web site—a place where customers can find out about our products and where to buy them. More recently, we've added their nutritional content, some recipes, and a place where customers can contact us directly with questions, but it's really unidirectional and pretty dry."

Josh nodded in agreement with this assessment. The difference in the two companies' approaches was like night and day. Although not everything they had tried at Glow-Foods had worked, enough of it had succeeded that demand for the company's products had skyrocketed. Young adults and teens had responded en masse to the opportunity to post pictures of themselves on the Glow-Foods Web site drinking their Green Tea Shakes in unusual places, and to send a coupon for their favorite Glow-Foods product to a friend. Serialized company mini-dramas popped up on YouTube and viewers were asked to go online to help shape what happened to the characters—all of them using Glow-Foods products extensively. Contests, mass collaboration in package design, and a huge network of young part-time sales reps linked through Facebook all contributed to making the brand hip and exciting, and drove sales through the roof.

John adjusted his French cuffs. "We want to tap into the youth and young adult market with IT, and we think you're the one who can help us do this. We're going to give you a team and whatever resources you need right here in Chicago. With our global reach and much larger budgets, you could do great things for our company." John went on to outline a job offer to Josh that sent tingles down his spine. "I really have hit the big time," he thought as he signed the documents making him a team manager at IFG at a salary that was almost double what he was earning now. He couldn't wait to get started.

Six weeks later he was being walked down the same hall by Tonya, now his immediate boss, and into her office, a smaller version of his with a window looking onto another high-rise. "What's next?" he asked. "I've booked a meeting room for you to meet your new team at 10:30," Tonya explained. "But before that, I want to go over a few things with you first. As the manager of IT Marketing, I am personally thrilled that we're going to be experimenting with new technologies and, as your coach and mentor at IFG, I'm going to make it my job to see that you have the resources and support you need. However, you may find that not everyone else at this company will be as encouraging. We're going to have some serious obstacles to overcome, both within IT and with the larger company. It will be my responsibility to help you deal with them over the next few months as you put your ideas together. But you need to know that IFG may have different expectations of you than Glow-Foods. And you may find you will get a better reception to your ideas if you look a bit more professional." Josh winced and nodded. He'd already ramped up the wardrobe for his first day with a sports jacket, but clearly he needed to do more. "Finally, I'd like you to come up here every Friday afternoon at four o'clock to go over your progress and your plans. My schedule is usually fully booked, but if you have any questions you can always send me an e-mail. I'm pretty good at getting back to people within twenty-four hours. Now let's go meet your team. I think you'll be happy with them."

An hour later Josh and his new team were busy taking notes as Tonya outlined their mandate. "You have a dual role here," she explained. "First, I want you to work with Ben here to develop some exciting new ideas for online marketing. We're looking for whatever creative ideas you have." Ben Nokony was the team's marketing liaison. Any ideas would be vetted through him, and all proposals to the individual product teams would be arranged by him. "Second, I need you to keep your eyes open and your ears to the ground for any innovative technologies you think might work here at IFG. These are our future, and you're our vanguard." Josh glanced around at his team, an eclectic group. They seemed eager and enthusiastic, and he knew they were talented, having had a say in choosing them. With the exception of Ben, all were new to IFG, experienced in using a variety of new media, and under thirty years old. They were going to do great things together, he could see.

The next couple of weeks were taken up with orientation. Ben introduced each of the major product divisions to the team, and everybody had come back from each meeting full of new possibilities. Tonya had also arranged for the team to meet with the chief technology officer, Rick Visser, who was in charge of architecture, privacy and security, risk management, and the technology roadmap. Rick had been pleasant but cool. "Please remember that we have a process for incorporating new technology into our architecture," he explained, as he handed over a thick manual of procedures. "In a company our size we can't operate without formal processes. Anything else would be chaos." The team had returned from that meeting full of gloom that their ideas would all be shot down before they were even tried. Finally, they had met with the IT finance officer. "I'm your liaison with corporate finance," Sheema Singh stated. "You need to work with me to develop your business cases. Nothing gets funded unless it has a business case and is approved through our office."

Finally, having dragged some chairs into Josh's eighteenth-floor and marginally larger cubicle, the team got down to work. "This is ridiculous," fumed Mandy Sawh, shuffling her papers on her lap. "I can't believe you need to book a conference room two weeks in advance around here. Who knows when you need to get together?" "Okay, team, let's settle down and take a look at what you've got," said Josh. One by one, they outlined their preliminary ideas—some workable and some not—and together they identified three strong possibilities for their first initiatives and two new technologies they wanted to explore. "Great work, team," said Josh. "We're on our way."

The problems began to surface slowly. First, it was a polite e-mail from Rick Visser reminding them that access to instant messaging and Facebook required prior approval from his group. "They want to know why we need it," groused Veejay Mitra. "They don't seem to understand that this is how people work these days." Then Ben got a bit snippy about talking directly to the product teams. "You're supposed to go through me," he told Josh's team. "I'm the contact person, and I am supposed to be present at all meetings." "But these weren't 'meetings,'" Candis Chung objected. "We just wanted to bounce some ideas around with them." Next, it was a request from Sheema to outline their proposed work, with costs and benefits, for the next fiscal year—beginning six months from now. "Can't we just make up a bunch of numbers?" asked Tom Webster. "We don't know how this stuff is going to play out. It could be great and we'll need lots of resources to scale up, or it could bomb and we won't need anything." Everywhere the team went, they seemed to run into issues with the larger corporate environment. Tonya was helpful when Josh complained about it at their Friday afternoon meetings, smoothing things over with Rick, helping Josh to navigate corporate procedures, and even dropping by to tell the team they were doing a great job.

Nevertheless, Josh could sense his own and everyone else's frustration as they prepared for their first big project review presentation. "They want us to be innovative, but they keep putting us in a straight-jacket with their 'procedures' and their 'proper way to go about things,'" he sighed to himself. Thank goodness the presentation was coming together nicely. Although it was only to the more junior executives and, of course, John and Rick, he had high hopes for the vision his team was developing to get IFG out and interacting with its customers.

Later that day …

"In conclusion, we believe that we can use technology to help IFG reach its customers in three new ways," Josh summarized after all of his team members had presented their ideas. "First, we want the company to connect directly with customers about new product development ideas through an interactive Web site with real-time response from internal staff. Second, we want to reach out to different communities and gain insights into their needs and interests, which in turn will guide our future marketing plans. And third, we want to implement these and other ideas on the 'cloud,' which will enable us to scale up or down rapidly as we need to while linking with company databases. Any questions?"

There was a moment of silence and then the barrage began. "What's the business value of these initiatives?" asked Sheema. "I can't take them upstairs to our finance committee meeting without a clear commitment on what the benefits are going to be." Ben looked nonplussed. "We don't really know," he said. "We've never really done this before, but we like the ideas." "I'm concerned that we don't bite off more than we can chew," said John thoughtfully. "What if these customers don't like the company or its products and say bad things about us? Do we have any procedures for handling these types of situations?" "There's definitely a serious risk to our reputation here," said Rick, "but I'm more concerned about this 'cloud' thing. We haven't even got cloud in our architecture yet, and this plan could make company intellectual property available to everyone in cyberspace!" Sheema spoke again, "I hate to mention this, but didn't we do something like this community project about ten years ago? We called it knowledge management, and it flopped. No one knew what to do with it or how to handle the information it generated." On and on they went, picking holes in every part of every idea as the team slumped lower in their seats.

Finally, Tonya stood up. "I'd like to thank you all for raising some legitimate and important concerns," she said. "And I'd like to thank Josh and his team for some fine work and some excellent ideas. Marketing was looking for creativity, and we have delivered on that part of our mandate. But now we have a more important job. And that is innovation. Innovation is about more than good ideas; it's about delivering the best ones to the marketplace. We're in a new world of technology, and IT can't be saying 'no' all the time to the business. Yes, we need to protect ourselves, and we don't want to throw money at every half-baked idea, but we've got to find a way to be open to new ideas at the same time. We know there's value in these new ideas—we saw it work at Glow-Foods. That's why Josh is here. He has a proven track record. We just have to find a way to identify it without taking too much risk."

The room sat in silence as Tonya looked from one to the other. At last, John cleared his throat. "You're right, Tonya. We want creativity and innovation, and we need a better way to get it than we have now. I think what we need is a process for creativity and innovation that will help us overcome some of the roadblocks we put in place." As Josh mentally rolled his eyes at the thought of yet another process, Tonya replied. "I think you're partially right, John. Processes do have their place, but we also need some space to play with new ideas before we cast them in concrete. What I'd like to do over the next two weeks is speak with Josh and his team and each of you and then develop a plan as to how we can, as an IT department, better support innovation at IFG."

Discussion Questions

1. In discussion with Josh, Tonya foreshadows "some serious obstacles to overcome." Describe these obstacles in detail.

2. How can Josh win support for his team's three-point plan to use technology to help IFG reach its customers?

Consumerization of Technology at IFG[1]

"There's good news and bad news," Josh Novak reported to the assembled IT management team at their monthly status meeting. "The good news is that our social media traffic is up 3000 percent in the past two years. Our new interactive Web site, Facebook presence, and our YouTube and couponing promotions have been highly successful in driving awareness of our Nature's Glow brand and are very popular with our target demographic—the under-thirties. Unfortunately, the bad news is that our competitors at GPL are eating our lunch with the new mobile apps they've developed."

Everyone frowned at the mention of Grocers' Products Limited, their fiercest competitor, which had the largest chain of integrated food and retail stores in the country and whose Premier Choice products were showcased on their shelves, making it increasingly harder for IFG to get prime space for their top brands.

"Our web and social media presence has helped us begin to develop a relationship with our customers," Josh continued, "but our marketing folks are very worried that we're going to be falling behind, isn't that so, Tonya?"

Tonya James, manager of IT Marketing, nodded her head. As the IT person working directly with marketing, it had been under her watch that IFG had transformed its dowdy online presence into something that was hip and trendy. Together, she and Josh, now manager of IT Innovation, had begun experimenting with new media, creating an innovation process that took a large number of new technologies and ideas for products and services and created a protected "sand box" that enabled trial implementations for employees only. Feedback and experience at this level then helped Josh and his business colleagues select the best ones for development in full "heavy-duty" production mode for the public, complete with privacy and security protection and following all architectural standards. Only then would the Chief Technology Officer, Rick Visser, who was charged with protecting

[1] H. A. Smith and J. D. McKeen, "Consumerization of Technology at IFG," #1-L11-1-002. Smith School of Business at Queen's University, December 2009. Reproduced by permission of Queen's University, Smith School of Business, Kingston, Ontario, Canada.

company data and systems, allow new technologies to be fully integrated into IFG's internal technical environment.

Mark Szabo, the newly appointed head of IFG's Business Intelligence (BI) team, reported next. "As you all know, our executives are screaming for more and more information to help them, but it's not going to be easy. What we have here at IFG is a data mess and it's only going to get worse from what I can see." The picture wasn't pretty, he warned. IFG had thousands of traditional systems, all of which produced data and reports. The problem was that each used somewhat different definitions of important company concepts, like "in stock."

"If our goal is to improve the stocks of our products on the shelves, we'll have to go back to rewrite many of these systems. Some of them believe that a product is "in stock" when it's on the shelves; others when it's in our back room waiting to be put on the shelves; still others when we have received the order from the supplier or when it's arrived at our regional distribution centers." He went on to describe similar problems with varying understandings of such core company data as "customer," "supplier," "employee," and others. "It's hard to tell our executives how 'sales' are going when we don't have a single definition of what 'sales' are!" he said with frustration. "Right now, I've got two people working full time on spreadsheets trying to reconcile data to answer the questions we continually get from the 37th floor," he concluded, referring to the executive suite. "We can't tell them we don't have the information but we need a better way to get it, that's for sure."

The meeting droned on with the CIO, John Ahern, calling on all his managers one at a time. As far as most of them were concerned it was "business as usual" in IT. Josh didn't say anything else in the meeting but he cornered Mark as it broke up. "Have you got time for a coffee? I think we need to talk."

"Sure, what's up?" Mark asked as they headed toward the company cafeteria.

"I liked what you had to say in the meeting about BI," said Josh. "You seem to be one of the few managers here who understands that what we do in IT is going to have to change dramatically over the next few years. And that a lot of our work is going to focus on information—getting it, analyzing it, and delivering it in packages that people can use for their work. I believe that there's a data tsunami rapidly heading our way and we haven't got a clue how to deal with it."

Mark grimaced as he filled his cup with what the cafeteria called "coffee." "I know, I know," he agreed. "I've only been in BI a couple of months but all those articles and books out there about competing on analytics and analyzing unstructured data, like e-mails and tweets and blogs, are making my head spin. If we can't agree on what a 'customer' is, how are we *ever* going to manage the rest?"

Josh made a sympathetic face. "You've got that right, but I'm afraid it's even worse than you think." Over the next thirty minutes he described what he was seeing out in the field as he looked for innovative new technologies and applications that could help IFG.

"You think we have problems with our existing systems, but there are guys out there in our business units buying full-scale applications from the cloud with company credit cards!" He went on to tell Mark about the pressure he was getting from the sales guys to buy everyone iPads so they could write up orders on the road. "We've already been forced by our C-team to buy them and the board iPads, and so far we've kept them locked down tightly, but that's going to change very soon."

Users were also creating local "data marts," which included copies of core company data as well as external data feeds, and then building complex spreadsheets with information derived from these.

"Our business units don't use the centralized company reports anymore," he stated. "They create their own. We've got the 'wild west' out there!"

Mark looked shocked. "What about our company data warehouse? Isn't that what they're supposed to use?" He had spent a few years building the warehouse a while back and the team had put a lot of thought into making it the best they could.

Josh was aware of this but plowed on. He and Mark needed to be on the same page about this if these issues were ever going to be resolved. "The world has changed," he said gently. "Our business guys are online all the time now; software vendors are targeting them directly, and because of the low costs involved they can afford to make an end run around IT. There are literally thousands of free data sets out there, and computing power and storage costs aren't an issue anymore with the cloud. Our data warehouse is seen as a dinosaur. It's inflexible because we insist on reviewing all the data that goes in there for quality and provenance and it takes forever, i.e., 30 seconds, to get a response."

Mark looked down at the table and sighed. "So what you're saying is that all my work in BI is too little, too late?"

Josh thought for a moment before replying. "That's not exactly what I've been saying, Mark. What I meant to point out is that we in IT are caught in the middle between two opposing trends. The first is the trend to analytics and business intelligence that you're working on. That's important. The execs want to get at more information to run the company and it has to be based on good, trustworthy data. There are whole businesses out there that are winning because they've found a way to do this.

"But the other, opposite trend is what I'm seeing. And it's important too. Everyone working in our business is also a consumer of technology, and when the devices and applications they can use in their personal lives are more powerful and flexible than those in their business lives, they naturally want to work around the clunky technology we provide them with and use their own. Since we're now trying to build relationships with our customers, we are going to have to start thinking and working like they do."

"In some ways, this is just like the 'old days' in IT," Mark smiled. "I'm a lot older than you and I remember when those new-fangled PCs came in and everyone in IT was worrying about how we were going to handle people working on their own computers at home. And then when the web first hit business, we had people running around saying 'the sky is falling' and developing their own personal and localized Web sites. We don't handle new stuff well around here, do we?"

Josh grinned. He was notoriously frustrated with the IT "powers that be" who always wanted to lock everything down and wrap it in layers of privacy and security before allowing it out there. "Well, let's just say that I believe we've got some way to go before we can be as innovative as I'd like us to be. We've got to be aware of these trends and how they're going to hit us or our business model could change and we'll be out in the cold. Where are all the bookstores, video stores, and music stores these days? What happened to those companies?"

"You're right of course," said Mark "but we have to get more people involved in figuring out what we need to do here. This is a HUGE issue and we can't 'boil the ocean'! Somehow we need to get our arms around the most important things to do so we can make some sort of progress. Otherwise, we're spinning our wheels and the situation's just going to grow more and more out of control."

"I'll tell you what," said Josh. "Let me speak with Tonya. She's terrific at stick-handling these situations. I'll get back to you with a plan." And with that, they began to talk about the upcoming company softball game as they cleared the table and headed back to their respective cubicles.

Josh laid out the situation for Tonya at the first opportunity he could find in her busy schedule. "So you see," he concluded, "we need the discipline and rigor of BI and all of the good things we in IT can do for our executives and employees if we get them better and more trustworthy information. But we also need to keep moving ahead in the mobile and social space for consumers without putting handcuffs on us. And we need to recognize that the business is likely already doing their own thing on the cloud without IT and using their own personal devices because it's so cheap and easy to do and we don't help them! If we don't somehow figure out how all this stuff fits together—especially the data—we'll never be able to use what we know either operationally or strategically."

"You've done a good job articulating the challenges we're facing," Tonya said. "I know that the Marketing people are putting lots of pressure on me to help them with better information and tools. In my experience, when business is in turmoil they want everything right away and they'll do whatever it takes to get it *now*. What would you say our biggest need is right now?"

Josh fiddled with his pen for a moment. He had hoped Tonya would tell *him*. "Well ...," he said slowly. "We need to be seen to be doing *more* in this space. It's okay to work on the big systems and core data. In fact, that's our main job. But we also need to help the business help itself. With my tiny innovation team, I can't possibly deal with all of the ideas and technologies that are out there. And the business guys are seeing many more opportunities than I can deal with. It's really hard to tell what's going to work and what isn't until they play with things. I can provide some of this in my 'innovation sandbox,' but I don't think that's going to be enough. And ...," he said as another idea popped into his head, "we don't have the right people to do some of this work. We need information analysts, mobile developers, visualization specialists, and lots of business people to work with us and teach us about the business. I don't have all the answers here but we can't stick our heads in the sand and let the world change around us. Are we going to be reactionary or visionary?"

Tonya smiled. "There's never a dull moment around here is there? You've got an important point of view here but I think Rick Visser does too. Just in IT alone, we've got a number of groups that need to have some input on this, in addition to my area. We have to get ahead of this 'tsunami' of yours and be proactive in a way we've never been before. This doesn't mean that we throw all our tried-and-true practices out the window, but it does mean that we should do *some* things differently around here and that means John has to be involved. We need a plan to manage all these new trends and he's in the best position to help us because there are going to be a lot of cultural, organizational, and structural changes involved, not just for IT but for the whole business. But we can't dump this in his lap. We need to do our homework first. I'll talk with him and tell him what we're doing and try to identify the stakeholders involved. Can you come up with some key issues and preliminary recommendations about what you think we should be doing and how we should do it? Sit down with Mark and get his ideas too. Then we'll see if we can get everyone in a room together to 'talk turkey' and hammer out a more proactive IT strategy for handling this mess."

Discussion Questions

1. Describe the problem at IFG as succinctly as you can. Use this description to identify the main stakeholders.

2. IFG can't afford the resources to identify, define, cleanse, and validate all of its data. On the other hand, building yet another data mart to address a specific problem worsens the data situation. Propose a solution that will enable IFG to leverage a key business problem/opportunity using their BI tools that does not aggravate their existing data predicament.

SECTION IV

IT Portfolio Development and Management

Chapter 17: Managing Emerging Technologies
Chapter 18: Enhancing Development Productivity
Chapter 19: Transforming to DevOps
Chapter 20: Managing IT Demand
Chapter 21: Application Portfolio Management

Mini Cases for Section IV:
- Project Management at MM
- Working Smarter at Continental Furniture International
- Introducing Agile Development at American Attire

CHAPTER 17

Managing Emerging Technologies

It seems like IT can never get it right with emerging technologies (ETs). A perennial business complaint is that IT is not helping the business see and implement the potential of new technologies fast enough. At the same time, there are also many situations where business has rejected IT requests for experimentation with new technology because it feels there are other things that will bring a higher and more immediate return on investment.

ETs are a big gamble for business. Investing in them can frequently mean failure—to deliver value, to be adopted, to be strategically significant. However *not* investing in them can mean falling behind, failing to be relevant to customers, losing market share, and having to continually play catch up in IT investment. Finding the sweet spot between these two poles and determining where and how to place bets on emerging technologies is an art, not a science. And it is frequently done poorly, both in business and in IT. As new technologies enter the marketplace at an ever-greater velocity, organizations more than ever need new ways to identify and assess emerging technologies, and to energize their organizations around imagining their possibilities.

There are at least four major components to effectively managing ETs (Weiss and Smith 2007; Fenn 2010). First, they must be identified. Second, they must be assessed for their business and technical potential. Third, potential technologies must be connected with real business needs and opportunities. And fourth, practices and skills must be in place to ensure that the right ETs are implemented at the right time.

Emerging Technologies in Business Today

The challenge of managing ETs is multi-dimensional and not limited to IT itself. Although it is common to speak of new or emerging technologies, what organizations really want is insights into how best to use technology in the marketplace (Cusumano 2011). A significant majority of business executives now believe that technology can transform their businesses but they continue to be frustrated by the slow pace of change and how difficult it is to get great results (Fitzgerald 2014). Although this is not a new phenomenon (McKeen and Smith 1996), the pace of change for organizations has ramped up considerably in recent years. Today, companies in many industries are feeling increased pressure to find and develop innovative technology solutions that outpace those provided by their competition. Thus they are having to move faster and faster just to stay in the same place (Tiwana 2013).

Unfortunately, there is no "one size fits all" approach to addressing this challenge, said the focus group. The need for change and the pace of change depend on a number of factors, such as the market aggressiveness of the firm, the industry involved, risk and regulatory issues, and corporate philosophy (Sarner and Fouts 2013). Therefore, the group concluded that one of the most important questions for companies to ask themselves *before* determining how they want to manage ETs is: *Where do we want to be in the marketplace?* Some firms decide to be leading edge; others prefer to be fast followers; still others want to be in the middle of the pack. Within an organization itself, the appetite for incorporating ETs can also vary by function and between business and IT. "Our business units want to know: What will enable me to execute better, faster, or cheaper?" said one manager. "Our IT organization wants to know: What is the impact of new technologies on our governance, security, and data?"

Once this broad business context of firm readiness to integrate ETs is understood, it is important for an organization to establish an approach to making good decisions about ETs and how they will be used. ETs can be used to transform a business and gain and sustain competitive advantage but only if the strategic priorities of the organization are clear (Weiss and Smith 2007). Often, however, the vision for how to use ETs is unclear and unarticulated, leaving both business and IT frustrated and confused (Mangelsdorf 2012; Fitzgerald et al 2014). In such cases, both groups are vulnerable to making inappropriate choices about ETs. The focus group noted that vendors may try to do an "end run" around IT principles and guidelines and attempt to exploit the business' frustration and ignorance, leaving an organization open to unexpected risks. On the other hand, IT can easily get caught up in new technology "hype" and overlook the business value such technologies should be achieving.

The focus group also pointed out the lack of clarity about what exactly an ET actually *is*. In some definitions, an ET is a technology that is not yet mature in the market; in others, it's any technology an organization isn't yet using. The group noted that their companies also distinguish between emerging *consumer* technologies and new *infrastructure* technologies. "We are much more flexible about adopting ETs on the periphery of our business," said one manager, "but we recognize that we need stability and a different approach to ETs with our core technologies." Overall, managing ETs is a bit like riding a tornado, the group concluded. Nevertheless, they recognized that their organizations need to better address ET management and develop some practices and principles for making good business and technical decisions about ETs.

Identifying Emerging Technologies

There is broad recognition in the technology community that it is not always easy to "know what you don't know." Thus the first step in better managing emerging technologies is to ensure that an organization has effective mechanisms to identify what technologies are available and how they might be used in their organization. For this reason most organizations use a variety of techniques to identify new and potentially useful technologies. These include:

- Vendor and industry conferences, events, and forums;
- White papers;
- Research and analysis boards such as Forrester and Gartner Group;
- Vendor and consultants' reports on future trends;
- Business partners;
- Research by central architecture groups.

The variety of these sources within individual organizations suggests that scanning for new technologies involves creating and tapping into an ecosystem of information offered by a broad variety of sources on an ongoing basis (Weiss and Smith 2007).

In addition, focus group members noted three other ways of identifying emerging technologies:

1. *Observing push technologies*—those that vendors are pushing or selling to create demand—and watching what is being used in the market, talking with peers in their industry or different industries, and addressing technology currency.

2. *Responding to pull technologies*—those that business functions or application development request to meet their specific needs.

3. *Screening for decentralized technologies*—those acquired by the business for their own specific purposes without reference to formal IT processes.

Altogether, this is a daunting task that is made even more difficult by the fact that each of the above types of information may be acquired by more than one IT group or individual. The focus group members noted that one of the biggest problems they had was a lack of communication between people doing this and other aspects of emerging technology work. Although most have a formal enterprise architecture group charged with developing a technology roadmap, the participants noted that such groups are often more removed from business needs than other parts of IT and have a mandate that includes broader infrastructure issues, such as incorporating legacy and upgrading existing technologies. Thus it is important to make managing ETs *someone's* job in the organization, although many may participate in the ET identification process.

Assessing Emerging Technologies

Although it is important to know what ETs are available, organizations have only a limited capacity to absorb them. Therefore it is critical to select only those few that will have the largest business impact. The focus group stressed that it is essential to thoroughly understand the business needs of the organization in order to make this selection. "This is something we need to do better," said one manager. "Our relationship managers are often too focused on more immediate matters and don't always take the time to explore future needs."

Assessment is all the more important because ETs are characterized by a low "signal:noise ratio," which tends to confuse both business and technology people about the potential of a new technology. "Signal" refers to indicators of value to a firm's core business, and "noise" refers to factoids, assertions, and beliefs about a technology that are *not* meaningful signals. "At the earlier stages of the life cycle of an emerging technology, the signal is faint and the noise is overwhelming.... A low signal:noise ratio means that information surrounding an ET is difficult to interpret, leads observers down multiple blind alleys, and requires ... effort and expense to discern meaningful insights" (Tiwana 2013).

Amplifying signals involves working closely with the business to better understand where and how value *could* be delivered with a new technology. One company's ET staff meet regularly with business leaders to ferret out opportunities by asking, "What do you wish you could do in your business if technology could be found to enable it?" (Weiss and Smith 2007). Several companies routinely hold internal briefings or events where selected ETs and their potential can be presented to executives. ET staff need a deep understanding not only of the business and its needs, goals, and strategies, but also of how the industry is developing because ETs can often provide firms with the opportunity to move into adjacent markets or develop products and services that are complementary to those that are already provided in an industry. Finally, business and ET staff can work together to amplify signals by applying different frameworks that challenge existing preconceptions and spot non-obvious applications. For example, each of a company's products and services could be assessed to determine if how they are purchased or delivered could be shifted from physical to digital. (For a more in-depth discussion of these frameworks see Tiwana 2013.) The goal of a preliminary assessment is to understand how an ET might affect the organization's products and services, work, new forms of external engagement, or business models.

Assessing an ET's technical potential involves a different set of lenses and is generally a more straightforward process. All focus group organizations have technology roadmaps that provide a baseline for determining many of the factors that could be critical to this assessment. These include: technical maturity levels; implications for integration, data, security, and operations; and complexity. The focus group also cautioned about reducing "noise," noting that much ET work is simply following the crowd, as opposed to true assessment.

Overall, assessment of any ET involves determining both relevance for the business and technical readiness. It requires having both a deep knowledge of the organization's business and a broad appreciation of technology. The focus group concluded that technology is meaningless unless it is understood in a business context, and they agreed that it is only through strong partnerships with the business that ETs can have the type of impact a business is looking for. "There are two places you can start to assess an ET," explained one manager. "You can look for an interesting technology that has a potential business benefit or you can find an interesting business opportunity and determine how technology can help you do business differently. Typically, you iterate between these two perspectives when assessing an ET, but you do it differently in every case."

Addressing Uncertainty

Once an ET has been deemed both relevant and technologically ready, there is an important further layer of evaluation that must be done, again most likely in several iterative steps. This is addressing the critical question of: *Should we be doing this?* ETs, more than other forms of IT work, by definition involve working with uncertainty. There are at least three types of uncertainty that need to be addressed before making a decision to move forward with an ET:

1. *Market uncertainty.* This is ambiguity about how the market will respond to an innovative new technology or application. One of the key aspects of determining this is assessing what complementary technologies are available that will make a particular innovation an attractive proposition (Tiwana 2013). Today, successful new technologies are unlikely to be stand-alone devices or applications that will single-handedly transform an organization or an industry. Instead, they tend to function with platforms, which act as the foundational technologies/products around which a broad ecosystem of other products and services are built by other companies (Cusumano 2011). When these are tied together, they create complementarities or combinatorial innovations that create new opportunities for business value (Tiwana 2013). Without such complementary products and services, an innovation often fails. Unfortunately, the technology landscape is littered with such technologies that were innovative but ahead of their time because complements were not available. Without these, an organization can be too early to market with a particular technology. Furthermore, bundles of functionality are usually perceived as better value by users. Therefore, a crucial aspect of reducing market uncertainty is to identify the complements that will make an ET viable as an attractive proposition for consumers (Tiwana 2013). Market uncertainty can best be addressed by monitoring the ET ecosystem for the emergence of such complements (Fenn 2010).

2. *Technological uncertainty.* This is ambiguity about the maturity, complexity, or interoperability of any new technology. Many focus group organizations had sophisticated assessment processes for reducing this type of uncertainty. Tools can include: scorecards, radar screens, and watch lists. Enterprise architects have often driven the development of practices in this area. However, the focus

group cautioned that because these groups tend to focus on core infrastructure and have more of a control mindset, there continue to be doubts about whether their organizations are investing in the right technologies for the capabilities they will need. "We need more of a formal incubation process," one manager said. Prototypes and "dabbling" with new technologies are key ways to deal with technical uncertainty because they help develop a deeper understanding of an ET's strengths and weaknesses.

3. **_Economic uncertainty._** Many focus group companies require a business case to proceed with the implementation of an ET, but setting too high a hurdle rate for these innovations will not mitigate uncertainty and will only result in a loss of innovation. Focus group members have found that a lower level of initial rigor is therefore required to prevent this. Also key is getting business sponsorship. "Unless someone wants it enough in the organization to act as a business sponsor, we don't go ahead with it," said a manager. "We go with the energy. We don't fight battles." Pilots can help address gaps in knowledge, determine how best to apply an ET in a live operational environment, and provide valuable information for a more complete business case. In one organization, after assessment has filtered out many ETs, pilots are undertaken with those remaining ones that have found sponsors. Of these, only about 10 to 20 percent actually move on to broader adoption (Weiss and Smith 2007). The key is to fail fast, said the focus group. From assessment to pilot to a decision about broader adoption should only take about three months. Developing mechanisms to achieve this is the best way to ensure that an organization can quickly adapt to changing market conditions (Cusumano 2011).

There is no way to eliminate all uncertainty with ETs, the group concluded, but the more items and people in the ET tornado, the greater the likelihood of getting the right technology in the right place at the right time. As with the assessment step, there is no structured process for addressing uncertainty so evaluating a new technology will typically iterate between each of the above items. Working through these activities will likely eliminate a larger number of technologies that are inappropriate for business, technical, or economic reasons, and provide a milieu that will enable better ideas to become clear.

Managing Emerging Technologies

Although none of the focus group members had a dedicated ET group, there was broad recognition of the need for more attention to ET management. "Most game changing organizations have an ET function," said one manager. Another added, "We need more resourcing for, engagement in, and processes for managing ETs more effectively. It may not be governance _per se_ but we need to do a better job of facilitating it and coordinating knowledge." Many experts agree. An emerging technology process helps organizations become more selectively aggressive so they can counter the hype cycle and make strategic decisions (Fenn 2010). Organizations therefore need to build the skills, structure, and practices to determine which ETs will change the fundamentals of their business or industry and which can be ignored (Sarner and Fouts 2014).

Yet the focus group also pointed out that establishing effective ET management is a challenge. "We've tried three times to create an ET process and no one was motivated to participate," commented one manager. "We don't have any formal mechanisms to track or share information about ETs within IT," said another, "and we need this type of information sharing." The need for speed, the continuous hype and market pressures associated with ETs, existing work with a better business case, lack of sponsorship from business, and poor understanding of exactly *how* this rapidly evolving milieu might be managed successfully, all mitigate against developing a single set of processes for all ETs.

The group suggested that managing ETs for an organization's core infrastructure might need to be different from managing ETs for interaction with customers or specific communities. "We need a formal technology blueprint for our infrastructure," said a manager, "but we can be less formal with the periphery." This is a distinction that has been successfully used in a number of organizations. It suggests that governance for infrastructure is best centralized to enable synergies and scale economies, while decentralization is a better way to spot good business opportunities (Tiwana 2013). "We need the right engagement at the right time," explained a manager, "but it is less than governance and more like facilitation, leveraging knowledge, and coordination."

Organizations also need to develop new skills and capabilities for dealing with ETs because these are not the same as those needed in traditional IT. Focus group participants suggested that the following capabilities are needed:

- Strong business knowledge and ability to speak business language;
- Research skills;
- Visioning skills;
- Ability to partner with the business;
- An open mind, flexibility of approach, and comfort with uncertainty;
- Ability to explore alternatives and take advantage of serendipity;
- Relationship management skills ("but with teeth," said a manager) to work with different parts of the business and different vendors.

The group also stressed that any ET initiative should be designed to "fail fast" and respond rapidly to new information. ET projects are explorations to better understand business, technical, or economic questions. Therefore, the traditional Systems Development Lifecycle (SDLC) approach to IT work is inappropriate for ETs. "These projects are ideal for prototyping and agile methodologies," said a manager. However, once a decision has been made to implement an ET, there should be a formal technology transfer process that ensures an initiative is not adopted without a full business case and proper controls, and without addressing operational considerations.

Finally, the focus group stated that partners or vendors can play an important role in ET work. Typically, this relationship is most effective when helping companies identify new technologies and opportunities and in supporting the technology transfer process. Because of the significant business knowledge required in ET work, this is not an activity that can or should be outsourced (Fenn 2010). Furthermore, partitioning of ET work across more than one organization has been shown to decrease the likelihood of a successful outcome and increase the risk involved (Tiwana 2013). Therefore, companies seeking to develop effective ET management practices should be careful in how they involve vendors in this work.

Recommendations for Getting Started in ET Management

As noted above, there is no single recommended process for managing ETs, and individual companies will approach it differently according to the needs of their business and industry conditions. Nevertheless, there are several general recommendations that can be made to organizations seeking to become more effective in their ET management:

1. *Make ET management someone's job.* Companies that are innovative with ETs have made it a priority and assigned resources to it. These *may* be in IT but may also be in a different organization that works closely with IT. In smaller companies, it may be just one person. However, it is important to note that the job is to coordinate, facilitate, and leverage ET knowledge, *not* to actually do all this work. Identifying, assessing, and evaluating ETs is a joint business–IT responsibility that should involve a number of people throughout the process.

2. *Always tie ET adoption to business value.* All too often, business or IT staff can fall prey to the hype of a spiffy new technology. ET management activities should be designed to help change mindsets in the organization about the possibilities a new technology enables, while never losing sight of the fact that it is the value a technology could provide that is the goal of any initiative.

3. *Educate others.* Many people need education to see the possibilities of a new technology. Prototypes, vendor visits, special events with thought leaders, and multidisciplinary innovation sessions are all helpful ways to encourage others to keep open and thoughtful minds.

4. *Go with the energy.* If a new technology doesn't attract a business sponsor, it should generally be shelved. In some cases, IT may have a budget for developing a few key projects further in order to demonstrate potential value but in short order someone in the business must be convinced enough of an ET's value to put some resources into it.

5. *Be brutal and quick.* With the market moving so quickly, an ET evaluation process must be designed to make rapid decisions. The goal of ET management

should be to identify a wide range of potential technologies and then to rapidly filter them for business relevance, technical readiness, and economic viability and to focus on the very few that are going to deliver the most value to the organization. Short, speedy evaluation cycles will help to ensure the process doesn't get bogged down and that the organization is seen to be effective at evaluating and delivering on new technical capabilities.

6. **Don't downplay uncertainty.** Many companies downplay uncertainty either by setting a high hurdle rate for a new technology to be approved or by assuming that rigorous execution will mitigate it. The first approach can prevent promising new technologies from being adopted while the second can lead to the implementation of technologies that will not deliver the desired value. The key is to better understand whether uncertainty comes from the market or the technology itself and to address it appropriately.

Conclusion

"Riding the ET tornado" is not for the faint of heart. It is both an art and a science to facilitate the right engagement of the right people at the right time. Effective ET management requires both deep business and broad technology skills to identify and evaluate the best technologies for the organization. The skills involved—ideation, agility, open-mindedness, and exploration—are not those in which IT is traditionally strong. Therefore, to further develop an ET capability, it will be important to seek out and encourage those with these skill sets. Although discovering ET opportunities may be "everyone's job," not everyone in IT will have the ability to assess them properly. This is likely why, in most organizations, IT has a poor track record when it comes to adopting new technologies. Therefore, even in the smallest of firms, if there is any desire to explore new technologies and the potential they hold for a business, someone with these types of skills must be given the mandate to facilitate and encourage these activities.

Chapter Discussion Questions

1. There are two options: start with technology and look for a business application or start with a business problem and look for a solution. Which is best?
2. Why not simply adopt a copycat strategy with emerging technologies?

References

Cusumano, M. "How to Innovate when Platforms Won't Stop Moving." *MIT Sloan Management Review* 52 (4), Summer 2011.

Fenn, J. "Driving the STREET Process for Emerging Technology and Innovation Adoption." Gartner Research Report, ID: G0014060, March 30, 2010.

Fitzgerald, M., N. Kruschwitz, D. Bonnet, and M. Welch. "Embracing Digital Technology: A New Strategic Imperative." *MIT Sloan Management Review* 55 (2), Winter 2014.

Mangelsdorf, M. "What it Takes to be a Serial Innovator." *MIT Sloan Management Review* 53 (4), Summer 2012.

McKeen, J. D., and H. A. Smith. *Management Challenges in IS: Successful Strategies and Appropriate Action.* Chichester, England: John Wiley & Sons, 1996.

Sarner, A., and R. Fouts. "Agenda Overview for Emerging Marketing Technology and Trends 2014." Gartner Research Report, ID: G00255386, November 21, 2013.

Tiwana, A. "Separating Signal from Noise: Evaluating Emerging Technologies." *SIM Advanced Practices Council*, July 15, 2013.

Weiss, M., and H. Smith. "APC Forum: Leveraging Emerging Digital Technology at BP." *MIS Quarterly Executive* 6 (2) (2007).

CHAPTER 18

Enhancing Development Productivity[1]

Poor development productivity has been a perennial problem for IT (Brooks 1975; Oman and Ayers 1988; McKeen and Smith 2003). "IT takes too long to deliver" is a common complaint amongst business leaders (Overby 2005). Over the past three decades (or more), a considerable number of panaceas have been proposed for helping organizations get the systems and IT functionality they need better, faster, and cheaper. Structured approaches to programming and design and the introduction of systems development life cycle methodologies were first. Then came automated systems development tools, attempts to measure productivity (e.g., function points), and new development approaches such as RAD (rapid application development). More recently, organizations have sought to buy off-the-shelf software, use middleware to integrate it, or introduce enterprise resource planning systems (ERPs) in order to deliver more functionality at a lower cost. Companies have also realized that the processes *around* systems development, such as system prioritization and enterprise architecture, can have a significant impact on development timelines, and most companies now have procedures in place to manage these activities. Finally, many organizations have turned to contract or outsourced staff—often in other countries—to help them with extra resources during high demand periods or to provide a large group of qualified development personnel at a lower overall cost (Lacity and Willcocks 2001; McKeen and Smith 2009).

Nevertheless, during the past decade the situation has gotten worse in many ways. Changes in technology, connectivity and collaboration, and the introduction of open standards have meant that the IT function is "sitting at the intersection of two powerful and rapidly changing forces—technological innovation and globalization," and IT has become absolutely critical to effective business strategy (McKeen and Smith 2009). Development teams are becoming increasingly complex to manage as they incorporate people and partners from different companies and locations.

---

[1] This chapter is based on the authors' previously published article: H. A. Smith, J. D. McKeen, and W. A. Cram, "Enhancing Development Productivity," *Journal of Information Technology Management* 23, no. 3, September 2012. Reproduced by permission of the Association of Management.

Furthermore, development activities are more challenging, involving "many regulatory, architectural, business, financial, HR, security, and risk management hoops that have … little to do with the traditional design and coding of the past but that need to be orchestrated to deliver a coherent, viable service" (McKeen and Smith 2009). Unfortunately, new systems development techniques have not always kept pace with these changes. Many that have promise, such as service-oriented architecture (SOA), software-as-a-service, and agile development, still have not displaced traditional approaches. At the same time, the new technical and managerial practices needed to support them have not been fully introduced. In short, improved development productivity is still long on promises and short on delivery.

In this chapter we first examine the problem of IT development productivity and how system development practices are changing. We then explore the key obstacles involved in improving development productivity and outline practices that are proven to work. We conclude with recommendations for managers about how to create an improved environment for systems development productivity.

The Problem with System Development

In the past, focus group members explained that "system development" largely meant creating customized software applications for an individual organization. Today, it still means custom building but development also includes selecting, implementing, and integrating packaged software solutions, and, increasingly, integrating smaller, reusable software components with existing legacy applications across a variety of platforms with a variety of development tools. However, although systems development has changed over time, many of the problems associated with it have not changed; that is, there are still very high failure rates with development projects and they are still perceived to take too long, cost too much, and deliver limited business value (Korzaan 2009).

Research has not been particularly helpful in providing ways to improve on any of these fronts. There have been few empirical studies of actual development practices to determine what works and under what circumstances, and there is thus very little on which to base guidelines for different types and sizes of development (Dyba and Dingsoyr 2009). In short, "We need to know more about what we know and don't know about software development" (Adams 2009). One study noted that improvement in software development models and best practices has been a "long slog" since the 1980s and using the traditional "waterfall" model of systems development[2] has "continued to fail in delivering acceptable measures of software development performance" (Royce 2009). The Standish Group's ongoing study of software development success rates shows that in 2009 only 32 percent were considered successful (that is, on time, on budget, and with the required features and functions), while 24 percent

---

[2] By this we mean a system development lifecycle (SDLC) approach in which all requirements are first defined, and then an application is designed, developed, tested, and implemented with few changes.

were considered failures (i.e., they were cancelled or never used). The remaining 44 percent either finished late, were over budget, or had fewer than required features or functions (Levinson 2009). While these measures have improved somewhat since 1994, progress has been agonizingly slow.

Although IT practitioners and consultants have worked hard to define a strict set of rules to guide and govern software development, and have seen some modest gains from such factors as improved governance, project management offices, and better methodologies, many believe that "rules don't work and haven't since 1967" (Berinato 2001). These ongoing problems have meant that system development has long "suffered from way too many management fads and silver bullets *du jour* … and [left managers prey to] consultants and sellers of 'software oil'" (Adams 2009).

Finally, system development continues to be plagued by the difficulty of measuring "productivity." What exactly is a successful systems development project? Many companies define it as meeting schedules and budgets and by the functionality delivered (Levinson 2008). Yet these common metrics typically "do more harm than good" (Cardin et al. 2008). While they are easy for business people to understand, they perpetuate a "myth" that these are the only three factors that make a project successful. Furthermore, they take no account of some major elements that are often responsible for project failure, such as changes in requirements or scope, unreasonable deadlines, project dependencies, and lack of business accountability (Levinson 2008). "We still have no formal productivity metrics," said one IT manager, "and it's not a priority for us." Nevertheless, said another, summarizing the challenge faced by everyone in the focus group, "we are still expected to deliver business value with increasing speed and efficiency."

Trends in System Development

For many years system development has been conceptually seen as a functional engineering project, similar in nature to building a bridge (Chatterjee et al. 2009). Unfortunately, efforts to develop methodologies that embody software engineering principles designed to lead to consistent performance outcomes, while resulting in some improvements, have not been as successful as predicted (Chatterjee et al. 2009; Royce 2009). Therefore, in the past two decades numerous efforts have been made to address system development productivity shortcomings in other ways, including:

1. *Adopting new development approaches.* There are a significant number of new development approaches that their proponents believe address some or all of the problems with the traditional waterfall development method. While a comprehensive assessment of these approaches is beyond the scope of this paper, they can be classified into three major types:
   - *Agile.* Introduced in the 1990s, this approach encompasses a variety of "anti-waterfall" methods of system development, such as spiral, incremental, evolutionary, iterative, and rapid application design (RAD). They stress

the need to incorporate flexibility into system development by breaking up a large project into smaller pieces that can be developed in overlapping, concurrent phases to rapidly deliver business value in a series of short increments. Speed and agility are achieved by collapsing or compressing one or more phases of the waterfall method and by incorporating staged delivery or incremental implementation (Jain and Chandrasekaran 2009).

- *Composition.* This approach models and develops generic components comprising data, processes, and services that can be reused in different development efforts (Plummer and Hill 2009). Based on detailed analysis and architecture, components (e.g., acquire customer name and address) can be plugged into any system without being re-programmed. Initially called "object oriented programming" in the 1990s (McKeen and Smith 1996), and "service oriented architecture" (SOA) more recently, composition has been difficult to achieve because of the intensive modeling and architecting required and the IT organizational changes necessary to adapt to them (Blechar and Norton 2009; Plummer and Hill 2009). With this approach, system development becomes process orchestration, combining various software components into an "application container" (Blechar 2010).

- *Integration.* The 1990s also saw the widespread introduction of packaged software to the marketplace that could be purchased and implemented rather than developed in-house. As a result, many companies, including most of those in the focus group, adopted a "buy don't build wherever possible" philosophy for their generic applications, such as accounting and human resources or customer relationship management. More recently, this marketplace has begun to evolve so that companies can purchase software-as-a-service from the cloud, rather than implementing it within their own organizations. Although preprogrammed, such services or packages still require various amounts of effort to select and then integrate them into an organization's existing processes, platforms, and data (Mahoney and Kitzis 2009; Plummer and Hill 2009).

For most companies, however, adopting new development approaches still involves using them only selectively, and change has been agonizingly slow as a result.

2. *Enhancing the waterfall methodology.* Although new development approaches are gaining ground in organizations, the waterfall remains the predominant system development process for large-scale, industrial-strength projects (Royce 2009; Schindler 2008). The waterfall method is still considered most practical for large system development projects because the engineering principles implicit in it involve formal coordination strategies, centralized decision making, formal communication, and prescribed controls, which help to offset the challenges caused by the increased complexity and interdependencies and reduced communications opportunities on large projects (Xu 2009). The focus

group's presentations concurred with this assessment. "While we are trying to introduce new and more flexible approaches to development, our senior management is not committed to them and [is] resisting them," said one manager. "We're doing lots of experimentation with different development approaches but these are done within our standard methodology," said another. Improving the waterfall development process is therefore still a high priority for most companies. In recent years, organizations have attempted to improve the "maturity" of their traditional software development processes using Capability Maturity Model Integration (CMMI) to move them from ad hoc activities to more managed, better defined, quantifiable processes so they yield standardized, replicable results (Chatterjee et al. 2009; Hanford 2008). For example, one focus group company has created an enhanced delivery framework complete with a process map, detailed activities, templates, inputs, outputs, entry and exit criteria, artifacts, roles, and links to standards. Another manager stated, "We have well-defined SDLC methodologies and standards and procedures are enforced.... [But] we are always looking for applications development best practices to improve them."

3. **_Improved governance._** It has also been accepted that there are a number of factors other than the development process itself that will affect the quality and effectiveness of systems development. Today, in spite of a persistent engineering mindset that permeates system development practices, there is also growing acceptance that building systems can be more of an art than a science. "Systems are a unique and complex web of intellectual property bounded only by vision and human creativity.... They are more similar to movie production [than bridge-building] where no laws of physics or materials apply ... most quality is subjective [and] anything can change" (Royce 2009). To deal with these conditions, some organizations are beginning to adopt governance mechanisms based on economic disciplines that accept the uncertainties involved in systems development—especially at the beginning—and adapt and steer projects through the risks, variances, and moving targets involved (Royce 2009). Thus many focus group companies have adopted different governance practices for different stages of the development life cycle, such as: staged estimates of cost and time, "gating reviews," and quality assessments at different life cycle phases. Other governance mechanisms, such as those used in Sweden, also consider the social and cultural implications involved (Chatterjee et al. 2009). Still others govern by a set of software outcomes, including: flexibility, responsiveness, operational efficiency, quality of interaction, learning, product performance, and benefits achieved (Liu et al. 2009; Smith and McKeen 2010). In the focus group, most managers stressed that compliance with all legislation and regulations has become a further significant governance issue for all their systems initiatives. Some also stressed the need for better governance of the processes that "touch" and impact systems development activities, such as

quality assurance, architecture, security, and testing. In short, governance at a variety of levels is becoming more important to ensure productivity in systems development (Plummer and Hill 2009).

4. *Changing resourcing strategies.* One trend in systems development that is very clear is the widespread use of contractors and outsourced developers to supplement in-house development staff (McKeen and Smith 2009). A major driver behind improved governance, methodologies, standards, and componentization of software is the desire to use cheaper development labor, often located in other countries. This globally dispersed development, however, increases the need for new internal business and technical skills. New resourcing strategies increase the need for better business, technical, and data architecture; improved business analysis; IT strategy that is more closely linked to business; and project managers who can coordinate and leverage the efforts of a diverse group of internal and external IT and business staff to deliver consistent and effective IT products (Plummer and Hill 2009; Blechar 2010). At present, only 28 percent of CIOs believe that they have the right skills in their IT organizations to support these changes (Mahoney and Kitzis 2009). The group agreed that development skills are changing. "Our focus is on improving project management, business analysis, and quality assurance staff," said one manager. "We're stressing the development of relationship management, analysis, and consulting skills," said another. "Improved resource allocation is also essential," said a third, "because there are only so many staff with the necessary skills. In the past, each business unit had dedicated resources; now they all work for the enterprise."

Obstacles to Improving System Development Productivity

It is clear from the above trends that systems development *is* changing and *has* changed to address complaints of poor productivity. However, it is also clear that these changes are still not adequately addressing the problem. There are several reasons why improvements in development productivity have been difficult to achieve. While many of them may not be surprising to long-time IT managers, they bear repeating since they pose significant barriers to success in this area.

First, there is still a need for a more holistic understanding of system development, both within IT and within the business. As noted above, development is a much more complex and uncertain process than was first understood. Too often, our mental models of development appear to be dated—locked into a time in the past when the problem being addressed was straightforward and the programming effort significant. Today, the programming is straightforward, while the problems are highly complex, typically involving many parts of the business and many IT functions and requiring significant business knowledge, technical skill, relationship and communications abilities, and conceptual understanding (Chakraborty et al. 2010). In an earlier look at this subject we noted that *all* activities impacting system development should be considered when trying to improve productivity. "There is a need to ensure that everything works together to further the overall goal. It makes no sense to improve one part of the process if it doesn't accomplish this" (McKeen and Smith 1996). Members of the focus group identified three primary areas where there are currently significant bottlenecks in the development process:

- *Business involvement.* This can be an obstacle to development success at several levels. At the highest level, it is well known that business sponsorship is essential to ensure that the right projects are developed (Hanford 2009). While many organizations have addressed this problem through their governance processes, the focus group stressed that many business leaders still pay only lip service to their responsibilities. This impacts the system development process in several ways. "Our business users take forever to complete their parts, such as agreeing to a proposed solution or signing off on key phases of a project," said a manager. "They don't see how this affects our work, which can't proceed without it." The focus group felt strongly that business users needed more education about their roles in—and impact on—every level of the system development process, including governance, analysis, testing, and change management, in order to make development more productive.
- *Analysis.* "We were very surprised to find that analysis takes about 30 percent of the elapsed time of development," said one manager. "Business analysis is not at the same level of maturity as other parts of development," said another. Analysis can be an obstacle to productivity and effectiveness in many ways, in addition to the time it takes. Significant problems can be caused by failing to clearly define the scope of a project, to understand the dependencies between projects, to identify the changes that will need to be made to business processes when a system is implemented, or to recognize and incorporate the needs of multiple stakeholders in system requirements (Levinson 2008; Lemmergaard 2008).
- *Testing.* Several companies are focusing on testing, which they have found takes between 20 and 40 percent of development effort and resources. "We are spending increasing amounts of money on testing; it's a growing job," said one manager. "It's extremely complex and expensive to set up and maintain test environments," said another. In system development, testing is typically done by three groups: the development team itself, quality assurance, and business users. Delays often occur with the last two groups, who focus on their own needs and optimizing their own processes with little regard for their impact on the progress of an individual project or the business as a whole.

Second, the systems development process itself continues to be problematic. Today many organizations try to force fit all projects to a single development approach, often with disastrous results (Norton and Hotle 2010). If there's one thing that practitioners and managers agree on, it's that whatever development approach is used, it should be appropriate for the project being undertaken. Typically, small projects suffer from too much process when a full-scale, CMMI-style methodology is used, while large projects cannot coordinate all their variables using an agile development approach (Adams 2009). Agile approaches are useful when requirements are not fully known or in rapidly changing business conditions. Yet "for most organizations, [agile development] should be known by the acronym DBSF (delivering bad software fast)" (Norton and Hotle 2010). Conversely, too much process makes a project inflexible and adds layers of red tape that causes a project to bog down (Levinson 2009). Not using a methodology is not the answer because this can increase the risk that important tasks will fall through the cracks or that a project won't be completed on time (Levinson 2008). Members of the focus group were finding resistance to an overabundance of methodology from within IT as well as from the business. Thus the ongoing challenge for IT managers is to find the right balance between structure and consistency, and speed and flexibility.

Third, poor communication on the part of both IT and business tends to create misunderstandings and conflict that can inhibit projects. One of the major goals of a good development methodology is to mediate between all stakeholders to prevent the changes in requirements and scope that result from problematic communication. But communications issues cannot be fully dealt with by a methodology (Liu et al. 2009). "Most of the project management mistakes IT departments make boil down to either a lack of adequate planning or breakdowns in communication, either among the project team or between the project team and the project sponsors. These mistakes can be fatal" (Levinson 2008). While much of the blame for ineffective communication tends to be placed on IT (Smith and McKeen 2010), there is considerable evidence that business people do not take the time or make the effort to understand what is being said to them (Liu et al. 2009). "Our business doesn't want to hear about what we must do," said a focus group manager. Too often, executives rely on simplistic metrics, such as progress against schedule and budget, because they are easy to understand. These in turn perpetuate the perception of poor development productivity (Royce 2009). "Project sponsors latch on to initial estimates ... and because [they] don't understand project complexity and other factors influencing cost and timelines ... they may see a project as a failure ... even if changes resulted in improved value ..." (Levinson August 2008). Improved communication about changes in requirements, cost estimates, and schedules is therefore critical to improving perceptions of development productivity and success (Cardin 2008).

Improving System Development Productivity: What We Know that Works

There is still a lot that we don't know about improving system development productivity, and members of the focus group were actively experimenting with a wide variety of initiatives in this regard, which may or may not be successful. However, they identified five sets of practices that they believe clearly make a significant difference:

1. ***Optimize the bigger picture.*** System development should be seen as only one part of an overall business and technical effort to deliver value to the enterprise. This starts at the top with a clearer understanding of the IT value proposition: delivering strategic insight and leadership; understanding business needs and designing solutions; and sourcing solutions implementation (Mahoney and Kitzis 2009). This bigger picture has a number of implications for both business and IT. First, IT and business strategy must be closely aligned to ensure IT is working on the right things and in the right order, said the focus group. Business and technology architecture functions, combined strategic governance, roadmaps, and improved business and IT relationships should all be designed to deliver *enterprise* value, not IT or business unit value. Second, all aspects of the earlier stages of development need to be reassessed and streamlined, including: governance activities around project approvals, prioritization, and funding; managing demand; educating business people in their roles and responsibilities in system development and holding them accountable; improving business casing; information and solutions architecture; use of proofs-of-concept, prototypes, and use cases; and developing strong project managers with excellent communications skills. Finally, resource management and sourcing strategies must be developed to ensure that staff with the right skills are available when needed; applications development best practices need to be monitored and implemented; and testing and quality assurance should be centralized to eliminate duplication of effort.

   However, while each of these activities is important, none should be optimized at the expense of delivering overall value. All too often, individual functions seek to do the best job possible but forget how their work affects the overall goal. It is therefore important for senior IT leaders to ensure that this goal is kept in mind by all groups involved in delivering solutions to the enterprise. One company has had significant success—reducing cycle time by 30 percent—through such holistic process improvements. Another noted, "Becoming more outcome-focused, optimizing the whole development process and developing a shared business–IT agenda has led to substantial productivity improvements for us."

2. ***Adopt more flexible processes.*** While not all companies are willing to give up on the waterfall development methodology, they all recognize that "just enough" process should be the goal (Hotle 2009). Ideally, a development approach should be matched with the deliverables involved and the level of compliance required (Hotle 2009). Focus group companies were actively exploring ways to accomplish this goal. One company has developed a methodology tailoring tool that helps determine the levels of oversight and control that are needed by outside groups (i.e., security, architecture, operations) according to the level of risk involved. Another company ranks its development projects into three tiers. "Tier 1 is very visible and requires a higher level of formality and governance;

Tier 3 projects are encouraged to adopt more agile approaches," said the manager. A third company is encouraging "smarter execution choices" from a full range of development approaches by enabling teams to choose from a variety of methodologies, depending on business needs. Finally, one manager noted that his organization uses a little bit of everything when it comes to its efforts to improve productivity. "We have adopted a 'buy vs. build' approach and have packaged ERP systems in several divisions; we use composition services for data capture, transformation, and delivery between systems to take the burden away from the system developers; and we use a combination of agile and water-fall methods for new development."

3. *Reduce complexity.* It is widely accepted that complexity is a major cause of slow system development (Chakraborty et al. 2010). Standardization wherever possible therefore reduces complexity and makes development more straight-forward (Royce 2009). While aiming for flexibility, the focus group was also trying to reduce complexity in a number of ways. One organization has cut back on the reporting it requires; for example, limiting the paperwork for its Project Management Office to just a few short questions. "This has helped us a lot," said the manager involved. Using standards is a key way most companies are limiting technological complexity. "Multiple technologies, platforms, languages, and tools mean more complex software engineering," said a manager. Finally, several companies are trying to increase reuse of software components. "We're actually tracking the amount of reuse in each system; doing this has led to a 50 percent increase in reuse and a corresponding 20 percent reduction in defects," said a manager, noting that making reuse a performance metric for systems has been an important factor in its success.

4. *Enhance success metrics.* Success is a multi-dimensional concept that depends as much on perceptions as on objective reality (McKeen and Smith 2009). As noted above, while metrics of progress against schedule and budget are too simplistic for the current development environment, it is also true that IT can overdo the metrics it provides (Levinson 2008). Metrics for system develop-ment should be designed to accomplish four goals and used selectively for different audiences:

   • *Increase buy-in.* System development is a team activity, with business and other parts of IT playing key roles on the team. It is therefore essential that all team members be committed to achieving the same goals. In fact, the more people are committed to a goal, the more likely they are to contribute towards its outcomes (Korzaan 2009). Thus metrics that clearly link a project and its component parts (e.g., architecture, testing, change management) with delivering well-articulated strategic business value are most likely to ensure a coherent and consistent effort to deliver. Such metrics are usually developed in a business case but may also be part of an overall business or technical roadmap and should be kept front and center throughout system development (Smith and McKeen 2010).

- *Promote desired behavior.* Measuring something is an important way to promote behavioral change (Kaplan and Norton 1996). Members of the focus group had therefore developed scorecards to track desirable new development behaviors, such as reuse, quality, and collaboration. These metrics are often designed to change perceptions within IT regarding what management values in systems development.

- *Educate perceptions.* Perceptions can be "educated, trained, and controlled" (Gladwell 2005), and business perceptions of system development productivity need management, transparency, and clear communication. Metrics therefore need to be interpreted for them by IT in light of business conditions and individual situations (Levinson 2008; McKeen and Smith 2009).

- *Monitor performance.* System development performance should be tracked to determine the actual results delivered rather than the progress of the various activities of the software development process (Royce 2009). "We need to become more outcome-oriented so that we don't get bogged down in process," agreed a focus group manager. "This is a fundamental change in IT's mindset." Such a new mindset also supports the shift to newer development approaches such as agile, package implementation, reuse, and delivery of software-as-a-service.

5. *Create a smarter development environment.* Getting "smarter" about development involves improving collaboration, knowledge sharing, and capabilities, and finding new opportunities for leveraging the work that is done. With the boundaries between business and IT becoming increasingly blurred and larger numbers of stakeholders involved in the process (both within IT and in business), development has become both a much more social and multidisciplinary process, while at the same time teams are becoming increasingly dispersed geographically (Chakraborty et al. 2010; Mahoney and Kitzis 2009). Collaboration and knowledge-sharing initiatives can enhance traditional forms of communication, facilitate relationship building, and ensure that there is a single version of the "truth" available to everyone on a project team (McKeen and Smith 2009; Smith and McKeen 2011). Several companies in the group have implemented collaboration and document sharing tools with considerable success. "Our top priority is promoting collaboration with the business," said one manager. Another is implementing knowledge repositories and document-sharing software to enable better access to work that has already been done. Improved search capabilities are also a top priority for companies seeking to improve reuse. Another focus group company is stressing improving its capabilities by creating communities of practice around its four main technology disciplines—project management, business analysis, development, and quality assurance—to create thought leadership that is "more than the sum of its parts" and drive

change throughout the IT organization. One has identified the key gaps in capabilities for its major functional areas and is developing learning paths to close them. Finally, companies are becoming smarter about how they handle requests for compliance projects, such as gathering all compliance requirements together in planning to ensure that they are dealt with "once for all."

Next Steps to Improving System Development Productivity

Although these five general trends in systems development are working well in the focus group companies, their breadth and the integration and behavior change required is daunting. While keeping these "big picture" initiatives in mind, the managers in the group identified five "quicker fixes" that are likely to have an immediate impact on productivity, while furthering these larger goals:

- *Look for and address bottlenecks.* Assessing the entire system development process for bottlenecks in an organization can yield surprising results. One company had no idea how long it took business sponsors to complete sign-offs; another found cumbersome governance processes took inordinate amounts of time to resolve simple conflicts. With time pressures extreme these days, it makes sense to identify and speed up such bottlenecks first, rather than increasing pressure on the core members of the development team.

- *Focus on outcomes.* As noted above, IT metrics have typically measured elements of the process, such as consumption of resources, rather than value delivered. With the development world changing rapidly due to the advent of software services and application assembly, it is essential to refocus both business and IT on *what* functionality is being delivered, not *how* it is delivered. Making the shift to a more dynamic, innovative, and effective IT organization means changing what is measured. One firm now undertakes a quarterly assessment across its entire IT organization of the seven key capabilities it wants to develop: community participation, collaboration, transparency, innovation, agility (i.e., time to value), component-based development, and asset management and reuse. It believes encouraging these behaviors will promote faster time to market for all its development initiatives.

- *Clarify roles and responsibilities.* Several firms have seen commitment to development projects increase, both from internal IT groups and from business sponsors and users, when their roles and responsibilities were clarified. For example, one company clearly explained where IT architecture is accountable in system development, when it should be consulted, and when it should merely be informed. Another provides clarity about who is responsible for resolving development problems. "This has helped us to stop churning and increase motivation," said the manager. Another manager who had overseen a transition from a traditional waterfall IT development organization to an SOA function stated, "Making change is *all* about clarity of roles and responsibilities."

- **Simplify the development environment.** All companies in the focus group had some initiatives to decommission or replace end-of-life or duplicate technologies and applications. Some are attacking this type of complexity more vigorously than others. One firm had slashed its legacy applications by one-third over the past three years. The benefits of a simpler environment are numerous: speed of implementation, flexibility, more investment dollars, and easier new technology deployment. In particular, one firm that had mandated a single desktop and common infrastructure found it dramatically reduced its time to market for new development initiatives.

- **Simplify testing.** Testing has long been seen as a system development bottleneck (McKeen and Smith 1996), and with the addition of more complex technological environments and more stringent compliance regulations requiring separate groups to perform different types of testing, the situation has become much worse in recent years, said the focus group. Therefore, they have each put much effort into streamlining and automating this activity. Many companies have created a centralized test environment with automated scripts and standard tests that dramatically increase throughput. "With these you are not starting from scratch each time," said a manager. Testing tools and methods, including automated regression testing, risk assessments, and analysis of defects, have helped to both speed up the process and provide the necessary documentation of results.

Conclusion

Much has improved in the practice of system development over the past two decades, and if the development environment had stayed static, it is likely that we would perceive productivity to have improved dramatically as well. Instead, systems have become increasingly complex at every level so process improvements have barely made a dent in the dilemma of development productivity. In this chapter we have addressed the ongoing nature of the productivity problems facing IT managers in systems development and how the field is changing. We have examined some of the serious systemic barriers to fundamental change in how systems are developed and documented best practices for dealing with them. There is, unfortunately, no silver bullet when it comes to improving system development productivity, in spite of much effort to find one. While a few organizations are "pushing the envelope" in an attempt to radically change how systems are delivered, for most the improvements are more likely to come as a result of persistent and iterative analysis of what works and what doesn't in their particular organizational context.

Chapter Discussion Questions

1. If a system fails to meet its deadline, how would you know if the system was actually "late" or whether the developers simply failed to estimate the work accurately?
2. Why does the answer to Question 1 matter?

References

Adams, W. "An Agile Cure for All Ills?" *IEEE Software* 26, no. 6 (Nov./Dec. 2009): 8.

Berinato, S. "The Secret to Software Success." *CIO Magazine*, July 1, 2001.

Blechar, M., and D. Norton. "Trends in Model-driven Development, 4Q09-3Q10." Gartner Research Report, ID: G00169442, August 27, 2009.

Blechar, M. "Why You Should Coordinate your SODA, MDM and Business Process Improvement Initiatives." Gartner Research Report, ID: G00175167, March 24, 2010.

Brooks, F. *The Mythical Manmonth: Essays on Software Engineering*. Reading, MA: Addison-Wesley Publishing, 1975.

Cardin, L., A. Cullen, and T. DeGennaro. "Debunking IT Project Failure Myths." Cambridge, MA: Forrester Research, July 28, 2008.

Chakraborty, S., Saonee Sarker, and Suprateek Sarker. "An Exploration into the Process of Requirements Elicitation: A Grounded Approach." *Journal of the Association for Information Systems* 11, no. 4 (April 2010): 212–49.

Chatterjee, S., Suprateek Sarker, and M. Fuller. "Ethical Information System Development: A Baumanian Postmodernist Perspective." *Journal of the Association for Information Systems* 10, no. 11 (November 2009): 787–815.

Dyba, T., and T. Dingoyr. "What Do We Know about Agile Software Development?" *IEEE Software* 26, no. 5 (Sept./Oct. 2009): 6–9.

Gladwell, M. *Blink: The Power of Thinking without Thinking*, New York: Little Brown and Company, 2005.

Hanford, M. "The CMMI for Development Value Proposition for the PMO." Gartner Research Report, ID: G00158078, May 21, 2008.

Hotle, M. "'Just Enough Process' is Built on Deliverables." Gartner Research Report, ID: G00168230, September 22, 2009.

Jain, R., and A. Chandrasekaran. "Rapid System Development (RSD) Methodologies: Proposing a Selection Framework." *Engineering Management Journal* 21, no. 4 (December 2009): 30–35.

Kaplan, R., and D. Norton. *The Balanced Scorecard*. Boston, MA: Harvard University Press, 1996.

Korzaan, M. "The Influence of Commitment to Project Objectives in Information Technology (IT) Projects." *Review of Business Information Systems* 13, no. 4, (Fourth quarter 2009): 89–97.

Lacity, M., and L. Willcocks. *Global Information Technology Outsourcing: In Search of Business Advantage.* Chichester, England: John Wiley and Sons, 2001.

Lemmergaard, J. "Roles in the ISD Process: A Collaborative Approach." *Journal of Enterprise Information Management* 21, no. 5 (2008): 543–56.

Levinson, M. "Common Project Management Metrics Doom IT Departments to Failure." *CIO Magazine,* August 1, 2008.

Levinson, M. "Recession Causes Rising IT Project Failure Rates." *CIO Magazine,* June 18, 2009.

Liu, J., G. Klein, J. Chen, and J. Jiang. "The Negative Impact of Conflict on the Information System Development Process, Product and Project." *Journal of Computer Information Systems* 49, no. 4 (Summer 2009): 98–104.

Mahoney, J., and E. Kitzis. "Integrating the Transformation of Business and IT." Gartner Research Report, ID: G00167927, May 15, 2009.

McKeen, J. D., and H. A. Smith. *Management Challenges in IS: Successful Strategies and Appropriate Action.* Chichester, England: John Wiley and Sons, 1996.

McKeen, J. D., and H. A. Smith. *Making IT Happen: Critical Issues in IT Management.* Chichester, England: John Wiley and Sons, 2003.

McKeen, J. D., and H. A. Smith. *IT Strategy in Action.* Upper Saddle River, NJ: Prentice-Hall, 2009.

Norton, D., and M. Hotle. "Best Development Methods: A Scenario View." Gartner Research Report, ID: G00171772, March 18, 2010.

Oman, R., and T. Ayers. "Productivity and Benefit-cost Analysis for Information Technology Decisions." *Information Management Review* 3, no. 3 (Winter 1988): 31–41.

Overby, S. "Turning IT Doubters into True Believers: IT Value." *CIO Magazine,* June 1, 2005.

Plummer, D., and J. Hill. "Composition and BPM will Change the Game for Business System Design." Gartner Research Report, ID: G00173105, December 21, 2009.

Royce, W. "Improving Software Economics: Top 10 Principles of Achieving Agility of Scale." *IBM White paper,* May 2009.

Schindler, E. "Getting Clueful: 7 Things CIOs Should Know about Agile Development." *CIO Magazine,* February 6, 2008.

Smith, H. A., and J. D. McKeen. "Enabling Collaboration with IT." *Communications of the Association for Information Systems* 28, no. 16 (March 2011): 243–54.

Smith, H. A., J. D. McKeen, C. Cranston, and M. Benson. "Investment Spend Optimization: A New Approach to IT Investment at BMO Financial Group." *MIS Quarterly Executive* 9, no. 2 (2010): 65–81.

Smith, H. A., and J. D. McKeen. "How to Talk so Business Will Listen … And Listen so Business Can Talk." *Communications of the Association of Information Systems* 27, Article 13 (August 2010): 207–16.

Xu, P. "Coordination in Large Agile Projects." *Review of Business Information Systems* 13, no. 4 (Fourth quarter 2009): 29–43.

CHAPTER 19

Transforming to DevOps

DevOps, a concatenation of the terms "development" and "operations," is a relatively new development method that some organizations are adopting to speed up the time between an application's preliminary approval and its eventual implementation (Wikipedia 2017). Faster delivery of applications is as challenging for both infrastructure and operations as it is for development and delivery, if not more so. DevOps is the result of the recognition that neither group can go it alone to achieve this but must work together with a common set of processes and tools (Forrester 2015). It is widely agreed that the overall goal of DevOps is to promote collaboration between Development and Operations staff to improve software application release management by standardizing development environments and maximizing the predictability, efficiency, security, and maintainability of operations processes by making them more programmable and dynamic. However, the detailed definition of what DevOps *is*, is still unclear (Barros et al. 2015; Mueller 2015), and implementing it remains controversial because it challenges conventional IT thinking (Colville 2014). Practitioners point out that a successful DevOps requires a fundamental transformation of how the IT function works, and this involves considerable effort since, as one manager explained, "IT is a big ship to turn around."

Although DevOps adoption is growing in companies, one study found that only 16 percent of firms are currently using it for production projects. By far the largest number of organizations surveyed are still watching its development (40 percent) or planning to implement it in the next two years (31 percent) (Head and Spafford 2015). Those using DevOps claim that it improves deployment frequency, which can lead to faster time to market, lower failure rate of new releases, shortened lead time between fixes, and faster mean time to recovery in the event of a new release crashing. However, many remain skeptical, calling DevOps the latest IT "shiny new object" (Colville 2014). Gartner Group predicts that by 2018, at least 50 percent of organizations using DevOps principles will not be delivering the benefits stated in their original business cases (Head et al. 2015).

Transforming IT to incorporate DevOps involves first developing a better understanding of what problems this approach is attempting to solve, and then exploring what exactly DevOps *is* and the value it can deliver. Following this, managers should be aware of the obstacles they could face when attempting to introduce DevOps, and then begin to develop a multi-level plan to implement it successfully.

What Problem is DevOps Solving?

In recent years, agile methodologies have become increasingly accepted in IT as a way to speed up the creation of new applications. These emphasize collaboration and communication between the analysis, design, and development functions in IT and business users, and are now widely utilized for applications using new technologies (e.g., mobile, social) that are designed to interface with customers.[1] Although these agile methodologies encourage collaboration in *development*, there is rarely integration of these activities with IT *operations*, and this gap causes significant delays in the delivery of new functionality into actual production where it can be used.

With increasing pressure from business to deliver more applications faster without compromising quality, many companies are now recognizing that operations is a bottleneck. "What's the point of agile development if the output of an iteration makes it only as far as a 'test' or 'staging' environment?" said a focus group manager. "People [have begun] to realize that a 'throw it over the wall' mentality from development to operations is just as much of a challenge as [IT] used to have with throwing [business] requirements over the wall and waiting for code to come back" (Greene 2015). "Traditionally, provisioning has been a lengthy process in operations," said a manager. "Moving into production requires many steps: bundling the code, packaging the product, provisioning the environment, and coordinating with the operations staff. It has not been common to release code into production regularly. But we can't wait 16 weeks for this to be done anymore."

Focus group members added that there is also a fundamental difference of mind-sets between the development and operations functions, which causes problems in communication and goals. "Development strives for change," said a manager. "With agile especially, there are new change sets that need to be rolled out to production frequently. But operations strives for stability to make sure all environments run smoothly and without costly service disruptions." This disconnect between development and operations has created a "wall of confusion" between these two areas, that is further exacerbated by IT management structures that often have the two areas reporting separately all the way up to the CIO. As a result, it is not uncommon for the groups to blame each other for unplanned outages and system failures (Edmead 2015).

Finally, there is also recognition that operations itself hasn't changed to keep up with new technological advances. Twenty-first-century operations will increasingly be more virtual than physical, and existing operations principles, processes, and practices have not kept pace with what's needed for success (Wooten 2015). "Resources may

---

[1] More traditional waterfall methods still tend to hang on in many organizations for larger and more back-end systems.

be physical or they may just be software—a network port, a disk drive, or a CPU that has nothing to do with a physical entity" (Loukides 2012). With applications running on multiple virtual machines, they need to be configured identically and managed for resilience. Companies can no longer afford system outages due to failures or downtime for upgrades. Instead, operations specialists must learn to design and work with infrastructure that is monitored, managed, and reconfigured all in real time without interrupting service, in the same way a few large, cloud-based service providers have learned to do.

Making operations more effective, reliable, and flexible therefore has several components:

- Breaking down organizational and communications silos both within operations and between operations and development to facilitate improved productivity;
- Reengineering operations procedures to streamline them and reduce waiting time;
- Designing operational procedures to be more reproducible and programmable and reduce human error;
- Enabling more frequent production releases of code;
- Working with all parts of IT to deliver business outcomes, rather than technical metrics.

This is where the principles and practices of DevOps come in.

What is DevOps?

To a large extent DevOps is an extension of agile principles beyond the boundaries of development to the entire delivery pipeline, since "software isn't done until it's successfully delivered to a user and meets expectations around availability, performance, and pace of change" (Mueller 2015). Extending these principles to operations means that this function must begin to think in terms of delivering an end-to-end service focused on a business outcome, rather than sub-optimizing on their own particular task or, as is often the case, sub-tasks. This has significant implications for the people, processes, and tools involved in both development and operations.

Defining DevOps is challenging because there is no common set of practices, descriptions, or even shared meaning about this concept (Haight 2015b). Instead, there's such a variety of hype, marketing, and commercialized tools promoting it that practitioners can easily perceive DevOps to be an intimidating transformation of Herculean proportions (Greene 2015). In fact, to some, DevOps is about extending agile principles to *all* IT functions, such as quality assurance, security, architecture, and testing, in addition to operations (Wooten 2015). While this is probably desirable at some point in the future, focusing more specifically on how to bring operations and development together should be the primary initial focus for any organization exploring DevOps, said the focus group.

DevOps can be defined as:

A set of practices, tools, and policies based on agile principles which aim to bring infrastructure setup and awareness earlier into the development cycle and to establish consistent, reliable, and repeatable automated deployments. (Adapted from Greene 2015)

It is based on five key principles (Haight 2015a):

1. *Iterative.* DevOps is similar to agile methodologies in that it facilitates projects with high degrees of uncertainty and does not require comprehensive plans.

2. *Continuous.* The ultimate goal of DevOps is continuous delivery of projects into staging and then deployment. It supports rapid change and is never "done."

3. *Collaborative.* All stakeholders share common objectives, trust each other, work together to solve problems, and agree on the mission and metrics of the project.

4. *Systemic.* DevOps applies agile principles to operations and seeks to remove as many constraints to delivery as possible in this function.

5. *Automated.* Wherever practical, automated tools are adopted to link the different steps of the DevOps process—from development and testing, to integration and deployment—to deliver fast, safe, and cost effective solutions, optimizing the entire value chain.

"The goal is 'No Surprises' on delivery," said a focus group manager. At present, many defects and errors appear only when an application moves from the development environment to the testing or production environments, which are often configured somewhat differently. In DevOps, developers and operations specialists work together to specify configuration standards in the development environment, and these continue to be used in the production environment, thereby removing a significant source of error and eliminating considerable elapsed time. Similarly, developers and operations staff work with common toolsets and a common language to achieve common metrics (Forrester 2015). This prevents miscommunication and creates a culture of collaboration, cooperation, and trust that has a wide range of benefits including:

- *Higher-quality software delivered faster and with better compliance.* DevOps tries to prevent issues during development, rather than resolving them during operations. Removal of "friction" between software delivery steps also improves timelines (Forrester 2015).

- *Rapid resolution of problems* with development and operations working together in cross-functional teams in a "no-blame" environment to fix errors and move fixes quickly into production.

- *Reduced risk.* Having the full range of development and operations skills on a project reduces the need for risky handovers to other groups (Wooten 2015). Continuous implementation means that any new release contains fewer changes, making them easier to identify and fix, or roll out as necessary (Greene 2015).

- *Improved efficiency.* Using DevOps tools to automate the development–operations "conveyor belt" speeds up time to market and removes obstacles to implementation so that teams can iteratively implement new functionality reliably and predictably (Wooten 2015). "We've seen a near doubling of output per developer through automating repeatable tasks, freeing them up to focus on higher value tasks," said one focus group manager.
- *More resilient systems and operations.* Resilient systems are those that can adjust their functions before, during, and after an unexpected event (Webb 2011). Operations people are specialists in resilience and can build monitoring techniques into applications that enable more resilient applications. At the same time, automated operations tools make it easier to roll changes back if problems occur and to deploy new ones (Loukides 2012).
- *Improved customer experience and satisfaction.* In contrast to existing process design approaches (e.g., ITIL, Lean, TQM) that look at an initiative from the organization's perspective, DevOps explicitly incorporates recognition of the customer and customer experience into its initiatives by focusing on issues that really matter to them (e.g., utility, convenience, value, delight) (Haight et al. 2015). It focuses on the work that needs to be done to deliver something that is actually usable by a customer (Denning 2015). Internal customers like the continuous delivery of new functionality to the marketplace and the fact that IT is delivering strong stable functions (Loukides 2012).

Focus group members recognized the *potential* for DevOps to deliver these types of benefits, although none had DevOps fully implemented. "We've coordinated all our provisioning processes and seen infrastructure configurations go from taking six months to 30 seconds," said one manager. "We're working on hardware and software standardization so we can create a release path for applications," said another. "Standards are the key but they're tough to implement because there are so many tools involved." "We are having the right conversations and the ideas are percolating through our organization," said a third. "We're more aware of the possibilities and would like to increase the speed of automation between development and operations," stated a fourth.

At present it is clear that DevOps remains more a concept than a reality in most companies. However, as agile principles take root and with continuous pressure to deliver more, better, and faster from business, IT leaders are now taking very serious looks at how DevOps can help them achieve improved business outcomes faster and more effectively. There was a general recognition in the focus group that some or all DevOps concepts are the right way to move forward to improve IT delivery and resiliency. Some have begun pilots within their "new technology" areas to experiment with these ideas and tools. It is just going to be very challenging to make these changes. "Getting DevOps started in Development was relatively easy but integrating it into Operations is a much larger challenge," concluded a focus group manager.

DevOps Challenges

The vagueness of the DevOps definition and the lack of shared understanding about its practices have prevented many organizations from implementing it or implementing it well (Colville 2014; Wooten 2015; Haight 2015B). The focus group managers recognized that there are many other challenges to be addressed by IT in order to ensure the successful implementation of DevOps, including:

- *Current organizational structures.* DevOps requires the development of cross-functional teams with "full stack" understanding of code, systems administration, and infrastructure that are not the norm today (Wooten 2015). Many IT organization structures inhibit collaboration due to their siloed design, and this is one of the most important obstacles for IT managers to consider when thinking about implementing DevOps. "If you want DevOps, you must change how people are aligned," explained a focus group manager. Operations is still seen as a separate function with its own skills and mindset. Deploying DevOps therefore requires breaking down the organizational and cultural walls that have been built between the groups. Even within operations, there are often specialized sub-groups that focus on specific areas of the infrastructure, such as storage or networks.

- *Lack of management support.* As with agile development, business wants the benefits of DevOps but doesn't always support it (Head et al. 2015). IT leaders struggle both with understanding it themselves and also with explaining it to the business. "Transforming to DevOps requires a complete reorganization for end-to-end service," explained a manager. "To make DevOps work we need management to support this with vision, clear expectations, proper tools and software, integration with existing processes and the legacy environment, mindset changes, and general awareness and communication of what is involved," said another. "Our bureaucracy is very slow to change."

- *Organizational constraints.* Other IT groups can also place limitations on how DevOps is implemented in an organization. Architecture, compliance, security, quality assurance, and current legacy environments can each inhibit what can be done and must be considered when adopting this method (Head et al. 2015). In particular, security functions can be concerned about the fact that production code is in a constant state of change and that vulnerabilities could be introduced at any time. Architecture can play an important role in DevOps if it chooses, said the focus group. It can help the organization develop standards for data, integration, and infrastructure, which can facilitate its adoption, as well as recognize repeatable patterns that can be automated and identify appropriate tools for these processes. In operations, ITIL and change management practices developed over many years can be in direct contradiction with DevOps principles, which makes some organizations queasy. "There are reasons for some of these walls that have to do with segregation of duty," said a manager. "We need to be careful about how we break them down."

- ***Lack of budgets.*** A transformation to DevOps requires funding to train existing staff and hire experienced outside staff. Tight budgets and lack of time for training can leave people lacking skills and even understanding of the goals of DevOps (Forrester 2015). "In a project-driven environment, the question is always, 'Who pays?'" said one manager. "We need some elasticity in our budgets to make these changes." Pressures to keep staff lean are particularly strong in operations and mean that it is difficult to get staff from this group to participate in DevOps projects, said the focus group. "Operations is usually too busy for DevOps," commented one manager. "They can't focus on helping developers."

- ***Resistance to change.*** "Culture is a huge factor in changing to DevOps," said a manager. "There is real tension between the old and new ways of working," said another. "People end up gaming the system." A number of individual factors contribute to resistance to DevOps. First, it can be intimidating, requiring IT professionals to understand and use a wide variety of new tools and processes that are difficult to understand (Greene 2015). Second, DevOps changes project methods, operational practices, culture, and tools (Head and Spafford 2015). In particular, new tools automate parts of operations workflow and need operations staff to develop skills working with code-like languages, with which they are not comfortable or familiar. This can lead to fear of loss of control or even loss of their jobs, said focus group members. "We must be very sensitive about this and communicate clearly about these changes," a manager said. Third, neither individuals nor organizations are accustomed to the pace of change involved in DevOps (Head et al. 2015). For operations, the concept of constant releases into production, rather than staged periodic releases, as has been traditional, requires a total change of mindset, and this generates both questions and resistance (Wooten 2015).

  Thus there is widespread recognition that culture plays a significant role in both enabling and inhibiting DevOps success. This perspective was widely recognized in the focus group discussion. "There must be proactive education about how to take on the risks involved in DevOps," said a manager. Another manager noted, "We know we have to get our act together or we will be 'clouded.'"

- ***Tools.*** Automating configuration and the transitions involved in moving from development to testing to production environments is a completely new way of working—both for development teams and for operations specialists—and involves several sets of new tools. DevOps experts speak about "tool chains" where teams create, build, test, version, and deploy a program with outputs from one or more tools acting as inputs into other tools in a pipeline fashion (Haight 2011). Naturally, there has been a literal explosion of new tools to work in this space (Mueller 2015) and many technologists gravitate towards these when deploying DevOps (Wooten 2015). However, DevOps writers stress that DevOps is not about tools but about culture (Loukides 2012), and the focus group agreed. The group also noted that tool vendors are putting increasing pressure on IT to change by continuing to approach business leaders with their new DevOps tools. "It's a constant struggle to stay ahead of the business in this area," said one manager. "We need to find the appropriate tools for us."

- **Collaboration difficulties.** As noted above, operations and development have different mindsets, speak in different languages, and use different tools and metrics. This can result in miscommunication, misunderstanding, and errors. Also, the groups have competing agendas. Development wants to release and test more often and spend less time waiting for someone to configure applications and infrastructure. Operations wants stability and efficiency. As a result, a survey of companies using DevOps found that collaboration difficulties between operations and development and lack of common skills were their top two challenges (Forrester 2015).

- **The need to integrate service providers.** Most organizations deal with an ecosystem of different service providers for a variety of services. Where providers deliver some parts of IT functionality, the DevOps challenge becomes even trickier. Organizations wishing to adopt DevOps must first verify that their service providers are able to implement them (Barros et al. 2015). At present very few service agreements (10 percent) require DevOps delivery (Overby 2015), so IT organizations working with service providers will need to address how to adapt their agreements and expectations with them in order to benefit from this new trend.

- **Lack of skills.** Transforming to DevOps requires the development of skills and capabilities in IT that involve new ways of working, new common languages, new processes, and the ability to work with new tools. Operations specialists on teams are now expected to write the code that will maintain the organization's infrastructure and ensure application resilience (Loukides 2012). New skills in this area include: automation engineering, process ownership, and product management (Eliott 2015). Often these skills are not available in-house and must be hired from outside. Poor process disciplines can also undermine DevOps, especially when more traditional methods are still the dominant portion of IT work (Questex 2015). One study found that both development and operations are skeptical about whether the *other* group has the time or motivation to learn new skills (Forrester 2015). Another study found that lack of investment in developing DevOps skills is a key warning sign of the potential failure of this implementation (Head et al. 2015). Finally, IT leadership must also develop new skills to overlay the right amount of governance and decision making on DevOps teams (Cana 2015).

- **Inadequate fundamentals available.** Such a dramatic transformation in IT requires more than just skills and tools, said the focus group. There are a number of fundamentals that must be put in place for DevOps to be successful. Chief among these are standards, including configuration standards, data standards, and integration standards. Complexity in each of these areas works against what can be done with DevOps, they said, and inhibits the pace of automation. The proliferation of tools also makes standardization tough since they don't always work in a "plug 'n play" fashion, the group said.

Clearly, although desirable in the longer term, DevOps is a huge transformative challenge for IT organizations. "Times are changing and we have to change with them," said a manager, "but people are not always willing to adapt to the new way of doing things. We have to expect some tension along the way."

Getting Started with DevOps

The focus group stressed that there is no single recipe for implementing DevOps. "This is a problem we're trying to solve," said a manager. "For a while it will be an evolution, with many different models of application development running across the full spectrum of services," said another. Many companies are still struggling to adopt agile principles and methods, so the extension of these into DevOps can appear overwhelming. Since the IT industry is still at the early stages of understanding what DevOps *is*, taking the next step of implementing it can be especially difficult. Nevertheless, DevOps is the next obvious step following agile development and the value proposition is compelling. Therefore, it is important for IT managers to at least begin to explore how they might implement DevOps in their own organizations. The focus group had several recommendations about how to do this:

- *Communicate and educate.* The first step to a successful implementation of DevOps, said the focus group, is to define what it means for your organization. Once this has been clarified, the vision, goals, and plan must be communicated to every area of IT from the top down. "Everyone needs to understand the benefit and why processes and structures need to change," said a manager. As the ideas begin to percolate throughout IT, leaders can then begin to establish new expectations around how work gets done.

- *Consult.* Both Dev and Ops staffs should be involved in designing any changes. "Ideally, they should help build the roadmap for achieving full DevOps," said a manager. This process can also identify early the existing obstacles or constraints that will need to be removed. "The goal is to ensure that the right way is the easy way," said a manager.

- *Take incremental steps.* Full DevOps implementation may be some time away for many organizations but there are several ways to "move the ball forward" towards this vision. For example, one focus group organization has now incorporated an operations sign-off for solution approval. Another has started with pilot projects led by experienced staff. "Then, we replace the leads, rinse, and repeat," said the manager, who hopes this strategy will spread DevOps awareness and capabilities throughout IT. Pilots also help demonstrate the value of this approach. Wherever possible, managers should select staff who are the right cultural fit for DevOps and who are open to change. And even though DevOps may be intrinsically more aligned with agile development methods, it is also possible to use some DevOps principles in more traditional development projects to help them improve their consistency and reduce cost (Head and Spafford 2015).

- **Develop cross-functional teams.** A first step in this area is to break down functional silos within operations. "We are creating service streams that focus on the different value components of operations, such as operational readiness, asset management, and performance management, instead of individual technological elements," said a manager. Eliminating operations "towers" and centralizing them promotes more cohesion within operations and is a step toward enabling an operations specialist to represent all operations functions on a DevOps team. Following this, IT teams can be reorganized to deliver end-to-end service with Dev and Ops staff co-located and dedicated to a set of deliverables. "Co-location is key to developing shared goals, common language, and improved communications," said a manager. It also helps to create more resilient systems, ensuring that developers are not divorced from the consequences of their work and that they work together with operations to resolve problems (Loukides 2012).

- **Establish foundational elements.** Tools to automate parts of the DevOps delivery process are important but it is also essential to choose ones that work for a particular organization and that work well together, said the group. The full tool chain doesn't need to be implemented at once. Instead, the group recommended focusing on using automation to fill gaps and address pain points that constrain delivery. Standards are especially important foundational elements because they can help an IT organization change in a safe way, eliminate complexity, and help technologies and skills converge successfully. Standard environments can also be introduced for legacy systems. Finally, an important element of ensuring that both Dev and Ops staff are aligned for delivery is to measure them in the same way. Management can therefore promote greater collaboration by adapting current metrics to measure joint Dev and Ops success in achieving business enablement, improving agility, and correcting problems.

- **Allocate time and money.** This type of fundamental transformative change takes time and costs money, cautioned the group. If necessary, hire some experienced staff or bring in consultants to lead the first few projects and transfer their knowledge to others. However, wherever possible, the focus group felt that existing staff should be trained to develop DevOps competencies.

- **Coach.** Promoting such a significant transformation requires management to facilitate learning, accept more risk, and stimulate communication and collaboration for improved delivery. This necessitates a different style of IT management that is more focused on coaching and removing obstacles and less on command and control, thereby freeing up DevOps teams to do whatever it takes to deliver quality products for the business.

- **Don't get carried away.** DevOps will take hold at varied rates, said an experienced manager. Expect to see different levels of maturity as these new concepts are introduced. Similarly, not all service providers will be ready to implement them so it's important to assess their readiness for this concept. In addition, there may be some components of DevOps for which an organization may not be ready or areas in which it is not required. "DevOps is a capability that must be used where appropriate, not implemented comprehensively," concluded the focus group.

Conclusion

Implementing DevOps successfully is not for the faint of heart. It involves tackling some fundamental assumptions about how IT is supposed to function—breaking down the structural, procedural, and cultural walls that have traditionally divided the development and operations groups. If done well, it will result in faster time to deliver business value and more reliable systems. However, as the long list of challenges in this chapter illustrates, achieving these benefits will be neither easy nor cheap. Organizations will have to decide for themselves the best time to introduce DevOps. Although it is very tempting to wait until the concept, methods, and tools are better defined, the risk of doing nothing is high. With IT functionality and services changing at an exponential rate, managers will have to balance the challenges of change with the risk of getting blindsided and disintermediated by new cloud-based service providers that can deliver faster, better, and cheaper than IT functions can do with their traditional methods.

Chapter Discussion Questions

1. Debate the following statement: Bringing operations into consideration during development (i.e., DevOps) likely helps the eventual transition to operations but also likely slows down development.

2. In this chapter we described a number of challenges to the adoption of DevOps. We also described a number of DevOps strategies (under the heading "Getting Started in DevOps"). Align these strategies with the challenges that they address.

References

Barros, D., J. Longwood, and G. van der Heiden. "DevOps Applied in Outsourced Environment Delivers Business Agility." Gartner Research Report, ID: G00272680, April 29, 2015.

Cana, M., and N. Osmond. "How to Get Started and Deploy Bimodal Capabilities in CSPs." Gartner Research Report, ID: G00275202, July 16, 2015.

Colville, R. "Seven Steps to Start your DevOps Initiative." Gartner Research Report, ID: G00270249, September 16, 2014.

Denning, S. "Agile: It's Time to Put it to Use to Manage Business Complexity." *Strategy and Leadership* 43, no. 5 (2015): 10–14.

Edmead, M. "Lean IT and DevOps: The New Kids on the Block." *CIO*, July 21, 2015.

Elliot, S. "What Makes a DevOps Unicorn?" *CIO*, September 9, 2015.

Forrester Research. "Infrastructure as Code: Fueling the Fire for Faster Application Delivery." Forrester Research Inc. https://go.forrester.com/, March 2015.

Greene, D. "What is DevOps?" Crunch Network. http://techcrunch.com/2015/05/15/what-is-devops/#.d3ik6im:5XYN, May 15, 2015.

Haight, C. "Principles and Practices of DevOps." Gartner Research Report, ID: G00272990, March 12, 2015a.

Haight, C. "How to Scale DevOps Beyond the Pilot Stage." Gartner Research Report, ID: G00272992, March 11, 2015b.

Head, C., G. Spafford, and T. Bandopadhyay. "Avoid DevOps Disappointment by Setting Expectations and Taking a Product Approach." Gartner Research Report, ID: G00280974, October 6, 2015.

Head, I., and G. Spafford. "Step 1 in Delivering an Agile I&O Culture is to Know your Target State." Gartner Research Report, ID: G00272648, March 31, 2015.

Loukides, M. "What is DevOps?" *O'Reilly Radar*. http://radar.oreilly.com/print?print_bc=48235, June 7, 2015.

Mueller, E. "What is DevOps?" The Agile Admin, https://theagileadmin.com/what-is-devops/, November 10, 2015.

Overby, S. "IT Customers Slow to Embrace Outsourced DevOps." *CIO*, August 7, 2015.

Questex Media. "DevOps Will Evolve from a Niche to a Mainstream Strategy, says Gartner." *Networks Asia*, Questex Media Group, March 12, 2015.

Webb, J. "How Resilience Engineering Applies to the Web World." *O'Reilly Radar*. http://radar.oreilly.com/print?print_bc=46361, May 13, 2011.

Wikipedia. "Devops." https://en.wikipedia.org/wiki/DevOps, accessed October 30, 2017.

Wooten, B. "What is DevOps Not?" http://www.infoq.com/articles/devops-in-banking, November 23, 2015.

CHAPTER 20

Managing IT Demand[1]

The need for demand management is well established in business. Gentile (2007) explains: "In order to manage planning, production, and delivery, any properly run business has to be able to balance orders for its products and services (i.e., demand) with its ability to produce them in terms of resource and scheduling constraints (i.e., supply). Otherwise it might produce too little of what is required, too much of what is not required, or deliver late, or have problems with product quality or customer satisfaction." Based on this, one might assume that IT organizations, being in the business of fulfilling organizational demand for their services, would have developed mature practices for managing IT demand. Nothing could be further from the truth. In fact, IT demand management has only recently been ranked as one of the top four priorities by IT leaders (Potter 2010).

This lack of attention is explained by the fact that IT managers have been preoccupied with the *supply* side; that is, delivering products and services faster, better, and cheaper. Concentrating on the supply side makes perfect sense for two reasons: first, it allows IT organizations to concentrate on the things that they can actually control; and second, most IT organizations interpret any role in manipulating IT demand as a political minefield to be conscientiously avoided. As a result, demand management practices have been underutilized. A study by the Hackett Group as reported by Betts (2009) concurs:

> IT has traditionally been more focused on how to meet ever-growing demand than on implementing processes to curb that demand and ensure that the highest value work gets done. As a result, demand management techniques are less mature than other cost control techniques.

What best explains the current interest is that IT demand management offers the means for IT organizations to work more effectively with their business partners. In fact, some see demand management as the next frontier in IT cost efficiency

---

[1] This chapter is based on the authors' previously published article: J. D. McKeen, H. A. Smith, and P. Gonzalez, "Managing IT Demand," *Journal of Information Technology Management* 23, article 2 (2012): 17. Reproduced by permission of the Association of Management.

(newScale 2010). They argue that focusing exclusively on the supply side of the equation without visibility into demand leaves IT organizations unable to perform effective capacity planning. The reality is that better demand management enables better supply management. In order to make good capacity plans, IT must understand the future needs of the business. According to newScale (2010),

> Demand management not only helps IT organizations to shape demand, it also helps them plan for demand and respond to changes in demand to meet business needs while controlling their IT budgets. This increased visibility into demand can help ensure more accurate and business-driven capacity planning.

So after years of squeezing incremental costs out of the supply side of IT only to see those gains disappear into the vortex of mushrooming demands, perhaps it is time to turn attention to the demand side and tackle some key questions such as: How critical is the need for demand management? If there is interest/pressure for demand management, where is this pressure coming from? What are the key drivers behind the demand for IT services? How does demand management impact the existing business–IT relationship? What are the key steps towards managing IT demand?

In this chapter we examine the root causes of demand for IT services, the economics of demand management, and the importance of this issue. We then review a set of standard tools recommended for managing demand and conclude with identifying five key enablers vital for effective demand management.

Understanding IT Demand

In order to better understand demand management, the focus group first discussed the root causes of IT demand. One manager suggested that IT demand is driven by two forces in her organization: "IT initiatives that deliver new capability to the business in support of the broader corporate strategy, and IT initiatives that are required from within to sustain IT's ability to deliver future work or new capabilities." She explained, "Although these drivers mostly represent market and investor pressures, IT is also driving change with its own renewal goals after years of underfunding." Another organization identified "historical autonomy, proliferation, lack of structured architecture, and weak standards" as the key drivers of much of her organization's current demand for IT services. This particular organization was deluged with duplicate and in some cases redundant applications that collectively produced a "black hole" for IT resources.

Clearly IT demand needs to be considered from a development as well as an operational point of view. From an *operational* perspective, organizations need to "run" the business and this translates into baseline demand for IT. Organizations also need to "maintain" their IT assets and this too represents significant demand for IT resources. From a *development* perspective, IT is called upon to deliver new capability to enable the business to remain competitive in the marketplace. So whether it is a "keep the lights on" or a "new channel to market" initiative, both place demands on (and compete for) available IT resources. One organization simply classifies IT demand as discretionary (i.e., strategic), maintenance (i.e., keep the lights on), or regulatory, which his organization lightheartedly refers to as "I want," "I need," and "I must," respectively.

IT demand management is best understood within an organizational context. First, the need to automate business processes and operations is unrelenting and, once automated, automated processes must be supported on an ongoing basis. Hence the workload grows proportionally with the demand and increases year over year. Second, at any point in time the level of IT capacity is relatively fixed, which limits IT's ability to satisfy demand (i.e., the supply side). Third, one way to increase capacity (again the supply side) is to offload certain tasks to third party suppliers (e.g., outsourcing network management). Most organizations exercise this option regularly in order to satisfy increased demand. Finally, the only way for organizations to get ahead of this dilemma is by proactively managing the demand for IT services. Ultimately this will do a better job of satisfying business needs for IT.

According to a Gartner survey (Potter 2010), 84 percent of IT organizations simply do not have the resources to meet enterprise expectations. This leaves only two possible responses. IT organizations can either "do more with less," which focuses on supply side activities (e.g., virtualization, data center consolidation, benchmarking, contract renegotiation), or they can "do less with less" which focuses on demand side activities (e.g., demand management, IT performance management, IT portfolio management, running IT like a business).[2] The first approach (doing more with less) is the quest for increased productivity and the reality is that IT organizations continually pursue enhanced productivity to remove costs from the business.

The second approach (doing less with less) differs dramatically from the pursuit of productivity and thus introduces a different set of challenges for IT organizations. Implicit within a strategy of doing less with less is the notion that perhaps not all of the requests for IT services are vital and that the organization might benefit by rationalizing these demands for IT services. So where the goal of productivity is "doing things right" (i.e., internal efficiency), the goal of demand management is "doing the right things" (i.e., business effectiveness).

This helps to explain why IT organizations have preferred to address the supply side of the demand–supply gap. Certainly it is much easier for IT organizations to exercise control over the supply side, and in fact it is their prerogative to do so. But is IT in a position to shape the demand for IT services? According to Potter (2010), this "conjures up uncomfortable feelings among many IT leaders regarding the political process involved with chargeback and the behaviors created by approving or disapproving emotionally charged IT projects." So perhaps the reason for the failure

---

[2] Gartner (Potter, 2010) actually suggests four possible options. In addition to "doing more with less" and "doing less with less," IT organizations can "do more with more" and/or "do less with more." These two latter strategies, however, are only available within expanding economies or growing markets, respectively.

to address the demand side of the equation is due to a reluctance to say "no" to the business. The question is, after years of effort to support the business and to be seen as being accommodating, how does an IT organization tackle demand management where the goal is to question and ultimately rationalize the demand for IT services? As Cramm (2004) asks, "What right does IT have to tell the business what they can and cannot have?"

The Economics of Demand Management

The field of economics has used the concept of demand management for years. In its most elemental form, demand management is the "art or science of controlling economic demand to avoid a recession" (Wikipedia 2011). The notion of demand management has also been focused to control consumer demand for environmentally sensitive goods. The economic notions of demand management that are most applicable for IT organizations, however, are those that apply to the "management of the distribution of, and access to, goods and services on the basis of needs" (Wikipedia 2010). Here the tools are *policies* that allocate existing resources according to a hierarchy of neediness and the underlying idea is for "the government to use tools like interest rates, taxation, and public expenditure to change key economic decisions like consumption, investment, the balance of trade, and public sector borrowing resulting in an 'evening out' of the business cycle" (Wikipedia 2010).

This latter view suggests how to approach demand management. Instead of asking IT organizations to act as "traffic cops" and/or imposing sanctions on capital spending to artificially curtail demand, the economics approach is to create a system of policies and procedures coupled with adequate governance to ensure that the allocation of scarce IT services goes to the highest-value opportunities (Cramm 2004). The goal is to capture and prioritize demand, assign resources based on business objectives, and engage in projects that deliver business benefits. But as is frequently the case, what appears simple conceptually presents in reality a formidable set of challenges. To address these challenges, the focus group discussed three commonly used tools for demand management and identified what they considered to be five key organizational enablers for the effective management of IT demand.

Three Tools for Demand Management

Most experts (e.g. Betts 2009) advocate the use of tools for managing the organizational demand for IT resources, including project portfolio management, service catalogs, and chargeback. These are described briefly with an accompanying explanation of how they work to shape demand.

- *Project portfolio management (PPM).* These are processes designed to rationalize and prioritize IT investment decisions based on objective criteria. PPM allows an organization to understand and quantify business needs and the investments needed to deliver software to achieve those benefits (Hotle et al. 2010). With effective PPM, demands for IT resources are vetted in accordance with governance procedures that result in a justified list of IT investments that satisfy the needs of business leaders. IT demand is limited and shaped to the extent that only those projects that succeed in passing through the PPM process are funded. According to Cram (2004), PPM results in a "multi-year forecast of IT spending that constrains overall demand and results in increased project scrutiny."

- **Service catalog.** Here discrete IT service offerings are associated with a price per unit. As an example, hardware services might include costs for a standard desktop/laptop/tablet configuration and a standard smart phone configuration; application services might include costs for developing a business case, designing a solution, building a solution, and/or implementing a solution. According to Young (2011), a service catalog is a "service order- and demand-channeling mechanism intended to make it easier for end consumers to request and buy things from IT." Knowing what is available and what it costs allows business managers to make informed demands for IT services and, to the degree that these services are standardized, shapes this demand appropriately. According to one manager, this clarification of IT services affects demand by "allowing managers to order from a menu rather than saying I'm hungry."
- **Chargeback.** This is a financial management technique that charges consumers according to the volume of IT services consumed (i.e., operations) or work done on their behalf (i.e., new development). Thus IT demand is controlled through direct price-based allocation to business consumers as motivation to act rationally and to discourage unnecessary demands. This approach to demand management results in a set of IT investments that are justifiable and affordable by business managers.

The adoption of these strategies appears to be widespread. As a case in point, the organizations in the focus group have long deployed chargeback and PPM and most are in the process of building service catalogs. The benefits of these three strategies, according to newScale (2010), accrue independently and collectively:

> Best practices for demand management start with defining standardized services, exposing those services to customers via an IT service catalog, controlling and shaping demand through guided self-service, and providing cost transparency through showback or chargeback. The results: great adoption of cost-effective service options, consumption choices that result in lower IT costs, and effective planning to meet business needs and minimize over-capacity.

Although acknowledging the usefulness of these three tools, the focus group characterized them as "necessary but insufficient." They argued that the benefits derived from these tools are often more IT-related than business-related. Focusing on lowering IT costs through self-guided service and minimizing over-capacity makes sense from an IT-perspective but neither of these guarantees that IT investments are focused on the "highest value" opportunities—the ultimate goal of demand management. In order to manage IT demand effectively, these tools must be accompanied by mechanisms that the group referred to as organizational enablers.

Key Organizational Enablers for Effective Demand Management

Members argued that IT demand management is not a single process that an organization can identify. That is, in response to the question "How do you manage demand?" no organization could say, "We use this process." Instead, the group suggested that demand management is a *developed organizational capability* that results from five key organizational enablers: strategic initiative management, application portfolio management, enterprise architecture, business–IT partnership, and governance and transparency. These key factors work synergistically with the tools previously described to enable effective demand management (see Figure 20.1). Having a successful application portfolio management (APM) initiative, for example, does not guarantee effective IT demand management, but the absence of APM would definitely jeopardize the efficacy of demand management. Each of these key organizational enablers is described below.

1. ***Strategic initiative management.*** Strategic initiative management is the organizational mechanism for prioritizing and funding IT investments at the *enterprise* level. Although the focus is primarily on large discretionary/strategic

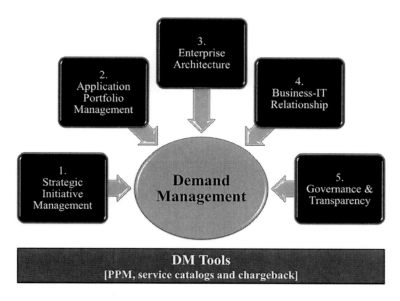

Figure 20.1 Tools and key enablers of demand management

investments, as the name implies, this process also adjudicates large infrastructure projects. One organization established a strategic project office (SPO) with a mandate to provide "governance and direction over enterprise-wide project approvals and planning to ensure these investments are aligned with the organization's core strategies." With a membership consisting of the head of each line of business plus the head of technology, the SPO meets monthly to review all projects exceeding $1 million that are unplanned,[3] as well as those with incremental annual operating expenses that exceed $500M. The SPO not only approves these projects, but also directly governs them through their life cycle.

The effective management of strategic initiatives is a crucial step for overall demand management. Without this capability, organizations are left with no structure for prioritizing IT funding opportunities at the enterprise level, and this leaves them unable to align their IT investments with corporate strategy. According to one manager, the absence of a strategic initiative management process results in a "siloed approach which results in ad-hoc decisions, increased cost and complexity, and redundancy of applications, all of which increase the overall demand for IT services." The cost of the legacy environment this creates further restricts the investment in new IT capabilities and innovation. The lack of this capability is a double-edged sword: it drives up the demand for IT resources while reducing the ability to conduct capacity planning to take advantage of a rationalized demand.

2. *Application portfolio management.* Unlike PPM that deals with future projects, application portfolio management (APM) focuses on existing applications, trying to balance expense against value (Caruso 2007). These applications may be assessed for their contribution to corporate profitability, and also on non-financial criteria such as stability, usability, and technical obsolescence. McKeen and Smith (2010) provide strategies for effectively implementing an APM initiative. The existing portfolio of applications (sometimes referred to as the asset portfolio) must be continually maintained in order to support the organization effectively. This need for continual maintenance creates demand for IT resources. Allowed to grow in response to the needs of separate lines of business, a legacy environment soon becomes highly complex, difficult to change, and expensive to maintain.

In one organization it was not until they had instituted an APM initiative that they discovered they had significant overlap and duplication across applications (e.g., 70 management-information systems, 51 order-management applications, and 27 regulatory-reporting systems). The costs of maintaining

---

[3] According to Gentle (2007), unplanned demand "corresponds to the huge amount of unpredictable work that IT does that is not contained in well-defined project structures. These include things like change requests, feature requests, and bug fixes, which arise from changing business and regulatory environments, changes in strategy, company reorganizations, mergers and acquisitions, and insufficiently tested systems."

this environment were driven up substantially and needlessly. Furthermore, their ability to deliver new applications was jeopardized due to the inherent complexities within the application portfolio itself.

With an effective APM initiative now in place, this same organization has reduced its technology-related operating costs and realized significant business value through reduced staff and maintenance requirements, reduced cycle times for process execution, a thorough rationalization of their application portfolio with a 40–50 percent reduction in size, and realized technology cost improvements through application retirement. Furthermore, the organization was able to re-orient their technology cost profile to value-creating activities and away from maintenance. Most significantly, resultant savings were applied to new initiatives without increasing the overall IT budget. This example demonstrates how APM can be effective at reducing overall demand as well as reshaping it.

3. ***Enterprise architecture.*** According to Wikipedia (2011), enterprise architects (EAs) "work with stakeholders, both leadership and subject matter experts, to build a holistic view of the organization's strategy, processes, information, and information technology assets. The enterprise architect links the business mission, strategy, and processes of an organization to its IT strategy, and documents this using multiple architectural models or views that show how the current and future needs of an organization will be met in an efficient, sustainable, agile, and adaptable manner. Enterprise architects operate across organizational and computing silos to drive common approaches and expose information assets and processes across the enterprise. Their goal is to deliver an architecture that supports the most efficient and secure IT environment meeting a company's business needs."

In this role, an EA is strategically placed to bridge the two worlds of business and technology. According to McKeen and Smith (2008), EAs are "able to take a view across business change programs, assessing their combined business and technical risk, overlap/dependencies, and business impact on the staff and customers of an organization." Over the years, the role of enterprise architecture has become even more business focused and this has drawn EAs into increasingly senior management discussions. The organizational advantages of this are immediate. It has enabled EAs to influence the demand for IT resources by vetting strategic choices in light of what is possible from a business *and* technical solution perspective. According to one manager, this allows his enterprise architecture group to "get ahead of the business which helps them to manage IT demand proactively."

The ability of EAs to shape demand depends on two leverage points. The first is the establishment of a "future state architecture blueprint" (McKeen and Smith 2006) that identifies the current architecture, the future architecture, and outlines a current-to-future transition plan. Combined with effective governance and transparency, this mechanism is highly effective at shaping

IT demand by ensuring that everything aligns with the architectural plan. At one organization it was their adoption of a common enterprise architecture that tightly integrated business and technology, enabling "informed enterprise-wide transformation planning and driving effective development across all business units."

The second key leverage point provided by enterprise architecture is the ability to promote enhanced business capability from a top-down perspective. Rather than depending solely on bottom-up demand from the lines of business, the enterprise architecture team at one organization was able to identify and champion enhanced business capabilities because of their ability to link the organization's technical architecture to business strategy. Deploying these two leverage points allows the IT organization to shape demand by aligning new initiatives with the architectural plan and by highlighting enhanced capabilities enabled by the same architectural plan.

4. *Busines–IT partnership.* Managing IT demand runs counter to the well-ingrained role of IT—to be an order taker, to do whatever the business needs and whatever is sent its way (Morhmann et al. 2007). For years the accepted wisdom has been, if the business wants it and is willing to pay for it, then it is not the role of the IT organization to question these decisions. Members of the focus group debated this issue. It was evident that no organization represented within the focus group subscribed faithfully to the "order-taker" role for IT; everyone felt that their IT organization needed to be more proactive in order to be most effective within their organizational service role. However, lively disagreement with regard to the degree of IT "proactiveness" emerged.

On one side of the issue, a manager adamantly stated, "IT should definitely take a leadership position in managing demand … and that IT was well positioned to identify, analyze, and recommend potential applications of IT to the business." At her organization the IT executive team had built strong relationships with their business partners over time, especially at the highest levels of the organization. Their CIO was a valued member of the executive committee, was requested to present to the board at every meeting for ten minutes (previously the CIO had presented once a year), and carried substantial influence in terms of the future application of IT in discussions about how best to leverage the business.

At another organization the relationship between IT and the business was not nearly as well established and lacked the requisite foundation of mutual trust (Smith and McKeen 2010). According to this manager, their IT organization was "struggling with the business to close knowledge gaps in terms of what the business was asking for and what IT was able to deliver." Some newly formed committees were in the "process of aligning IT with the business to enable prioritization of work across the different business units." A lack of business strategy and/or a clear understanding of business requirements had led to a vacuum that IT was attempting to fill. Demand management was described as the oscillation between "technology push" and "business pull," which produced a lot of business resentment. The lack of a mutual, trusting relationship clearly hampered the effectiveness of their demand management initiative.

A third organization suggested that value was driven at many levels within the enterprise, requiring alignment between IT and the business leadership on objectives, investments, and outcome. Her organization had articulated three levels of partnership required to effectively shape demand.

- The first level is as a utility partner focusing on table stakes; that is, keeping operations running as effectively as possible. The goal is competitive cost alignment and containment where IT partners with the business to reduce the operating costs of the business through such means as labor arbitrage and competitive sourcing.
- The second level is as a technology partner. The goal here is continuous improvement such as accelerated time to market through new or enhanced processes.
- The third level is as a business partner. This type of partnership is focused on business results through such mechanisms as improved market share, revenue growth, profit improvement, and cycle time reduction.

The group agreed that demand for IT resources does originate at different levels within the organization and therefore IT organizations must be effective at each of these different levels. In addition to senior IT executives, other key relationship players are business analysts, account/relationship managers, and business architects.

One organization mapped out a set of generic attributes for an effective IT–business partnership capable of shaping demand for IT resources. According to this manager, effective demand management requires the following:

- *Relationship management.* Collaboration and partnership are essential to identifying business capabilities and requirements. In fact, some have argued that relationship management has to transform into the role of demand management (Cameron 2006).
- *Leadership.* A technology manager's leadership style has significant implications for the success of the partnership; for example, is he or she driven by collaboration? Is the business a key partner or kept at arm's length?
- *Clear business requirements.* Without clear business requirements, the technology group will struggle. Even under the best of cases, high-level requirements may drastically change when digging into the details of business needs.
- *Marketing skills.* With the ever-changing technology landscape, marketing technology capabilities become critical. Thus instead of talking about technology, the conversation should be about business capability.

These partnership traits would take on different degrees of importance depending on whether the relationship called for a business partner, technology partner, or utility partner.

5. ***Governance and transparency.*** It is customary for organizations to have a process for vetting IT project proposals (i.e., a business case[4]). Furthermore, the
business is normally expected to pay for new development as well as a pro-rata
share of the technology costs to run the business (i.e., chargeback). Together
these two forms of governance shape the demand for IT resources. They do
this by encouraging and/or sanctioning investment behavior on the part of
the business. For example, we would expect that business managers would be
reluctant to request and pay for anything non-essential. Nevertheless, organizations find themselves having to manage IT demand. As a result, are we to
conclude that these governance mechanisms are inadequate? The focus group
made two arguments: first, they suggested that IT demand will always exceed
supply due to the myriad potential applications of information technology in
the workplace; and second, they felt that existing governance structures were
indeed lacking. We explore the latter of these two issues below.

Business managers continuously seek to leverage their business with technology,
whether that happens by streamlining processes, offering self-serve options, implementing enhanced information/reporting systems, or implementing dynamic pricing
systems. Provided they have the money, their only challenge is to win approval for the
requisite IT resources. IT managers are equally motivated to provide such systems
as are desired by the business. Specifically, delivering systems on time and within
budget rewards IT managers. Thus both parties are highly motivated to deliver new
capabilities to the business. The resulting effect, according to members of the focus
group, is encouragement to overstate the short-term benefits of delivering the desired
capability and to understate the long-term costs of maintaining it. Without a countervailing governance structure to reinforce different behavior, IT demand expands
to overwhelm supply.[5]

Recognizing the need for a remedial governance mechanism, two separate organizations adopted similar approaches. Both mandated the adoption of a standard
business case template combined with compulsory training for all business managers
in business case development. Both organizations also mandated that the finance
organization must sign off on the acceptability of benefits proposed in all business
cases. The third and arguably most important process change was to track the delivery of project benefits following implementation in order to hold business managers
accountable for realizing anticipated benefits. The combination of these three initiatives produced significant behavioral changes:

---

[4] Typical business cases require a business sponsor, risk analysis, architectural plan, business requirements,
detailed design, project management plan, vendor RFP (if applicable), work schedule, and project manager.
[5] From an economics point of view, a potential countervailing strategy would be a pricing mechanism. That is,
demand could be curbed by increased pricing of IT services. Although this might dampen demand in the short
run, according to the focus group, such a strategy would introduce so many new and different impediments to
the adoption of IT that it would be difficult to predict what long-term effects it might have on IT demand.

- Training business managers in the process of preparing business cases had the immediate effect of raising the overall quality of submitted business cases and sharpened the focus on benefits identification.
- Assigned accountability for realizing benefits countered the tendency to overstate benefits and understate costs.

All in, these governance procedures reduced overall demand for IT resources, but more importantly they focused limited IT resources on the "right" systems. Both firms expressed confidence that these were effective strategies for managing IT demand.

Transparency goes hand-in-hand with governance. A well-articulated process that is understood by everyone and adhered to by all managers is the goal. Information needs to be understood, consistently interpreted, and applied correctly for there to be any hope of effective decision making. A byzantine chargeback allocation algorithm, for example, provides little guidance in terms of appropriate action and usually fails to produce its intended behavioral effect. In like fashion, allowing "unplanned" or "off-plan" activity to enter the service queue undermines even the best demand management initiatives. One manager claimed unplanned demand is like "getting bitten to death by ducks"—no single bite will kill you but one thousand bites later and you are dead! As mentioned earlier, the solution adopted by one organization was to shuttle off all unplanned activity to their strategic project office in order to make it visible and force it to compete with other demands for IT resources, thereby ensuring an open and transparent process.

McKeen and Smith (2010) argue that effective application portfolio management can impact demand management due to the increased transparency provided by accurate information. In fact, providing information can on occasion make governance unnecessary. A vivid example of this was provided by one organization. Having made a significant investment in an application portfolio initiative to track IT expenditures, senior IT executives were able to present the following information to their senior business partners:

- The annual investment in systems designated as surplus by the business;[6]
- All investments to enhance these surplus systems;
- Annual investment in systems misaligned with overall strategy. For example, it was discovered that only 20 percent of their IT investment was directly focused on "improving the customer experience" and "driving revenue," despite the fact that these two areas were designated as the enterprise's top priorities.
- Investment in systems at odds with future state architecture.

Highlighting these expenditures resulted in almost immediate managerial action … something that had been lacking previously. Redundant systems were retired and investments in surplus systems were stopped. Of particular note is that these significant savings were obtained without the introduction of any additional governance mechanism. According to the focus group member, what called business

---

[6] This organization identifies all applications as "buy," "hold," or "sell." Surplus systems are those marked as "sell."

executives to action was seeing these numbers on the charts denoting unnecessary expenditures. She claimed that business executives simply "did not want to have their stuff in the red boxes."

Conclusion

While attention on supply side issues will continue (i.e., to ensure that the IT organization is run as efficiently as possible), future management activity must increasingly focus on the demand side to ensure that IT investments are made as effectively as possible. IT demand management, however, is not a single process but rather a "developed organizational capability." This capability requires basic tools (e.g., service catalog, chargeback, and project portfolio management) working in concert with five key organizational enablers (strategic initiative management, application portfolio management, enterprise architecture, business–IT relationship, and governance and transparency). Together these mechanisms enable organizations to allocate capital and human resources to the highest-value IT opportunities. Of equal if not greater benefit is that active demand management enables IT organizations to forge more effective working partnerships with the business. Instead of being relegated to the role of order-taker, IT organizations can now engage in proactive discussions with their business partners to establish a future agenda for IT. And because the supply side works in unison with the demand side, this enables enhanced capacity planning of benefit to both. For the first time many IT organizations will be able to get a step ahead of the business and build capability to enable new strategic business initiatives with shortened time to market. This has been a prized but elusive goal of IT. In organizations where IT is recognized for its strategic importance and/ or IT processes have reached a high level of maturity, managing IT demand has likely begun; for others, the time to manage IT demand has arrived.

Chapter Discussion Questions

1. Since IT organizations are most often "order takers," is it not arrogant of them to suggest that they will actually "manage demand"?
2. Suppose one of the five enablers of demand management in Figure 20.1 was totally absent. Describe the likely ramifications for the organization.

References

Betts, M. "Business Demand for IT is outstripping the budget." *Computerworld* Blogs, May 2009. https://blogs.computerworld.com/article/2481875/it-management/business-demand-for-it-is-outstripping-the-budget.html.

Cameron, B. "From Relationship to Demand Management: IT's Relationship Managers will be Focus for Aligning Business and IT." *Forrester Research*, October 2006.

Caruso, D. "Application Portfolio Management: A Necessity for Future IT." *Manufacturing Business Technology* 25, no. 10 (October 2007): 48.

Cramm, S. "Managing IT Demand 101." *CIO*, Article 32222, April 2004. www.cio.com/article/32222.

Gentle, M. *IT Success: Towards a New Model for Information Technology*. Hoboken, NJ: John Wiley & Sons, 2007.

Hackett Group Inc., "New Hackett Research Quantifies Growing IT Services Gap; Demand to Increase by 17% through 2010 as Budgets Remain Flat." Research Alerts #05122009, May 2009. www.thehackettgroup.com/about/alerts/alerts_2009/alert_05122009.jsp.

Hotle, M., J. Duggan, and J. Woods. "Drive Application Overhaul Efforts with a Portfolio Approach", Gartner Research Report, ID: G00205640, July 2010.

McKeen, J. D., and H. A. Smith. "Creating and Evolving a Technology Roadmap." *Communication of the Association of Information Systems* 20, Article 21 (September 2006): 451–63.

McKeen, J. D., and H. A. Smith. "The Emerging Role of the Enterprise Business Architect." *Communications of the Association for Information Systems* 22, Article 14 (February 2008): 261–74.

McKeen, J. D., and H. A. Smith. "Application Portfolio Management." *Communications of the Association for Information Systems* 26, Article 9 (March 2010): 157–70.

Morhmann, G., C. Schlusberg, and R. Kropf. "Demand Management in Healthcare IT: Controlling IT Demand to Meet Constrained IT Resource Supply." *Journal of Healthcare Information Management* 21, no. 3, (Fall 2007): 56–63.

Newscale, April 2010. http://www.newscale.com/solutions/IT_demand_management.

Potter, K. "IT Cost Optimization Round 2: Strategic Shifts and Doing Less with Less." Gartner Research Report, ID: G00205937, August 2010.

Smith, H. A., and J. D. McKeen. "Building a Strong Relationship with the Business." *Communications of the Association of Information Systems* 26, Article 19 (April 2010): 429–40.

Young, C. "ITSM Fundamentals: How to Construct an IT Service Catalog." Gartner Research Report, ID: G00210792, March 2011.

Wikipedia, definition of demand management. https://en.wikipedia.org/wiki/Demand_management (accessed March 2011).

Wikipedia, definition of enterprise architect. https://en.wikipedia.org/wiki/Enterprise_architect (accessed April 2011).

CHAPTER 21

Application Portfolio Management[1]

According to many industry assessments, the typical IT organization spends as much as 80 percent of its human and capital resources maintaining an ever-growing inventory of applications and supporting infrastructure (Serena 2007). Although no one argues about the importance of maintaining applications (after all, they do run the business), everyone is concerned about rebalancing the IT budget allocation to increase the discretionary spend by decreasing the maintenance spend, ensuring that the set of applications is well aligned with business needs, and positioning the organization technologically to respond to future initiatives. Collectively, this activity has come to be known as "application portfolio management" (APM).

Formally, APM is the ongoing management process of categorization, assessment, and rationalization of the IT application portfolio. It allows organizations to identify which applications to maintain, invest in, replace, or retire, and it can have significant impact on the selection of new business applications and the projects required to deliver them. The overall goal of APM is to enable organizations to determine the best approach for IT to meet business demands from both a tactical and a strategic perspective through the use of capital and operating funds allocated to building and maintaining applications. APM typically includes an analysis of operating and capital expenses by application, demand analysis (i.e., assessing business demand at the application level to determine its strategic and tactical business drivers), and application portfolio analysis (i.e., the current versus the desired state of the application portfolio in terms of both technology and business value).

Although APM is not a new idea, it may be one whose time has come. There are many espoused benefits of APM, including the following: reduction of the cost and complexity of the applications portfolio, reduction or elimination of redundant functionality, optimization of IT assets across different applications and functions, greater

---

[1] Excerpted from J. D. McKeen and H. A. Smith, "Application Portfolio Management," *Communications of the Association for Information Systems* 26, article 9 (March 2010): 157–70. Used with permission from Association for Information Systems, Atlanta, GA: 404-413-7444; www.aisnet.org. All rights reserved.

alignment with the business, better business decisions regarding technology, and an effective means of communicating the contribution of IT to the overall organization.

In this chapter we begin by examining the current status of IT applications in organizations. We then examine the notions of a portfolio perspective as it applies to applications (in contrast to a portfolio of financial assets) and outline the specific benefits of such a perspective. Implementing a successful APM initiative requires three key capabilities—strategy and governance, inventory management, and reporting and rationalization—which are described in detail. We conclude the chapter with some key lessons learned by organizations that have invested in APM.

The Applications Quagmire

Born of autonomous business-unit-level decision making and mergers and acquisitions, many IT organizations manage multiple ERP applications, knowledge management systems, and BI and reporting tools. All are maintained and periodically upgraded, leading to costly duplication and unnecessary complexity in IT operations. Left unchecked, the demands on the IT organization to simply maintain its existing inventory of applications threatens to consume the capacity to deliver new projects. (Serena 2007)

The proliferation of application systems within organizations is legendary. Built over time to serve an ever-changing set of business requirements, such systems span generations of technologies (e.g., hardware, software, systems, and methodologies), many of which are now obsolete and unsupported by the vendor community, are host to countless "workarounds," remain poorly documented, depend on the knowledge of a rapidly retiring workforce, and yet continue to support the key operations of the organization. Some (if not many) of these application systems have never been revisited to ascertain their ongoing contribution to the business. Based on decisions made by separate business units, many applications duplicate the functionality of others and are clearly redundant, and others have become unnecessary but have managed to escape detection. Accounts of organizations continuing to pay licensing fees for decommissioned software and supporting 27 different payroll systems all attest to the level of disarray that typically exists in large organizations. The full impact of such a quagmire becomes apparent either when the entire IT budget is virtually consumed by maintenance and/or when an organization attempts to integrate its suite of applications with those of an acquiring firm, whichever comes first.

Cause and effect are straightforward. The number of applications grows due to the practice of continually adding new applications without eliminating old ones. In the process, the number of interfaces increases exponentially as does the number of complex and often proprietary enterprise application integration (EAI) solutions to "bridge" these disparate systems. The combined effect is to increase the frequency of (and costs of supporting) redundant systems, data, and capabilities across the organization. As their number and complexity grow, so does the workload and, without expanding IT budgets and head counts commensurably, so does the portion of the IT budget devoted to maintenance and operations. From a management perspective, organizations are left with shrinking discretionary funds for new IT development and find themselves unable to assess the capability or measure the adequacy and value of current application support structures, track dependencies of business processes on applications, determine where money is being spent, and map IT investments to business objectives. Thus in many organizations the suite of IT applications has become unmanageable.

But while the cause and effect are identifiable, remedies are not easily obtained. The first obstacle is resources:

> The practice of continually adding to the IT burden while holding IT budgets and head counts relatively flat is obviously problematic. Yet that's exactly what many companies have done since the early 2000s. And this practice is one of the reasons why many CIOs feel that they simply don't have enough resources to meet internal demand for IT. (Gomolski 2004)

A second barrier is that few business managers want to give up any application once it's installed. In their minds, the agony of change is clearly not worth the rewards. "Some applications are so old that nobody remembers who ordered them" (Gomolski 2004).

The third impediment, and perhaps the most severe, is the fact that IT often lacks the political clout to make business managers engage in an exercise to rationalize applications across the enterprise in order to decommission some applications.

The Benefits of a Portfolio Perspective

A part of the application dilemma is the lack of a portfolio perspective. Historically, organizations have opted to evaluate applications exclusively on their own merits—a practice that can easily promulgate unique systems across any business unit that can justify the expense. One manager claimed that this practice results in "a stream of one-off decisions … where each decision is innocent enough but, sooner or later, you are in a mess … sort of like walking off a cliff using baby steps."

In contrast, adopting a portfolio perspective means evaluating new and existing applications collectively on an ongoing basis to determine which applications provide value to the business in order to support decisions to replace, retire, or further invest in applications across the enterprise. The portfolio approach is universal in finance and provides a point of comparison. Boivie (2003) presents the following analogy:

Just imagine you bought stock a decade ago for a lot of money, a good investment at the time, but then you did not review its value over the intervening years. Merely sitting on the stock may have been the right thing to do. Then again, you may have missed opportunities to invest more profitably elsewhere if the company was not doing well, or to invest more in the stock if it was profitable. Obviously this is not a wise way to handle your investment, but it's exactly what many companies are doing when it comes to investments in their IT applications!

Kramer (2006) concurs that application portfolio management is similar to the approach used by portfolio managers at money management firms where "investment officers continually seek to optimize their portfolios by assessing holdings and selling off assets that no longer are performing." It is suggested that "the same approach can be used by technology executives, especially when evaluating the applications in their portfolios and deciding which ones to continue funding, which to pull back on and which to sunset or kill." One firm highlighted the similarities between investment portfolio management and applications portfolio management (see Table 21.1) in order to advocate for adopting a portfolio approach for IT applications.

Table 21.1   Managing IT Applications as a Financial Portfolio

Investment Portfolio Management	Application Portfolio Management
Professional management but the client owns the portfolio.	Professional management but the business owns the portfolio.
Personal financial portfolio is balanced across investments in: • Equities • Fixed income • Cash	Application portfolio is balanced across investments in: • New applications • Currency (maintenance, enhancements, upgrades) • Retiring/decommissioning
Client directs investment where it is needed (e.g., 50% equities, 40% fixed, 10% cash).	Business directs investments where it is needed (e.g., 40% new applications, 30% currency, 30% decommissioning).
Client provides direction on diversity across investments (i.e., investment in one fund would exclude/augment investment in other funds).	Business provides direction on diversity of investment (i.e., investment in one business capability might exclude/augment investment in another).
Client receives quarterly updates on their portfolio health and an annual report.	Business receives quarterly updates on application portfolio health and an annual report.
New investments are evaluated on their impact on the overall portfolio as well as on their own merits.	New applications are evaluated on their impact on the overall portfolio as well as on their own merits.

The focus group suggested that the requirement for all new investments (i.e., IT applications) to be evaluated relative to all existing (past) investments within the portfolio is arguably the critical benefit provided by adopting a portfolio perspective. The group urged caution, however, due to the differences between a portfolio of financial assets (e.g., stocks and bonds) and one of IT applications. With the former, we assume a degree of independence among assets that rarely exists with applications. According to one writer (anonymous 2008), "While financial planners can sell an underperforming stock, CIOs will likely find it far more difficult to dispose of an unwieldy application." Applications are rarely stand-alone; business functionality is often delivered by an integrated web of applications that cannot be separated piecemeal. As a result, diversification strategies can be difficult where IT assets are highly interdependent and deliver returns only collectively (Kasargod and Bondugula 2005).

A portfolio perspective forces the linkage between the set of existing applications (i.e., the application portfolio) and the set of potential applications (i.e., the project portfolio). The linkage is bi-directional; that is, potential applications must be evaluated against existing applications and vice versa. Caruso (2007) differentiates these as follows:

- *Application portfolio.* The focus of the application portfolio is on the spending for established applications, trying to balance expense against value. These applications may be assessed for their contribution to corporate profitability and also on non-financial criteria such as stability, usability, and technical obsolescence.
- *Project portfolio.* Management of the project portfolio focuses on future spending, attempting to balance IT cost-reduction efforts and investments to develop new capabilities with technology and application upgrades.

The focus group suggested that organizations have focused most of their attention on new projects, which has in part resulted in the applications quagmire we have described. In our discussion in this chapter about managing the application portfolio, we argue that the effectiveness of the project portfolio can be enhanced substantially by managing the application portfolio much more judiciously. This linkage is made explicit later in the chapter.

The benefits to be realized by adopting an applications portfolio perspective are significant. The focus group was polled to solicit the benefits that their organizations had identified. These benefits were then grouped into the three categories, as suggested by Caruso (2007) and are presented in Table 21.2.

Table 21.2 A List of APM Benefits

1. Visibility into where money is being spent, which ultimately provides the baseline to measure value creation. a. Increasing the ease of determining which legacy applications are to be retired; b. Simplifying the technical environment and lowering operating costs; c. Reducing the number of applications and optimizing spending on application maintenance; d. Increasing the predictability of measuring service delivery for project selection; e. An enterprise view of all applications allowing for ease of reporting (i.e., How many applications use an ERP? How many systems support sales reporting?); f. A common view of enterprise technology assets improving reuse and sharing across the enterprise; g. Clarity over maintenance and support spending; h. Managing and tracking business controls and regulatory compliance of all applications.
2. Prioritization of applications across multiple dimensions, including value to the business, urgency, and financial return. a. Funding the right application effort by providing quick access to validated information in support of business cases for investment; b. Providing better project solutions by identifying available capabilities for reuse; c. Providing criteria to drive application rationalization and monitor impacts; d. Providing an "end state" view for all applications, which helps direct roadmaps and enables progress reporting; e. Expediting prioritization discussions and executive decision making; f. Driving IT refurbishment initiatives.
3. A mechanism to ensure that applications map directly to business objectives. a. Aligning business and IT efforts with business processes by providing, a) clarity of the application landscape leading to synergies across different business units and the pursuit of a global systems architecture, and b) insight into gaps or redundancies in the current portfolio, thereby enhancing the ability to manage risk effectively and efficiently; b. Enabling productive discussion with senior management regarding IT's contribution to business value; c. Identifying the strategic and high business value applications allows the redirection of some of the funding previously used for non-strategic applications; d. Enabling easy and effective analysis of impacts to applications from changing business conditions; e. Improving the focus and direction of investments; f. A vehicle to drive the technical portfolio to the "right" mix, based on strategy, architecture, TCO, and internal skill sets; g. Prioritizing efforts and focus for IT delivery; ensuring the right skills are in place to support business requirements.

The list of benefits is impressive. To put them into perspective, a number of comments are in order. First, if the benefits to be realized are this substantial, why haven't organizations moved more aggressively to enact APM practices? The short answer is that APM has been difficult to fund and, once funded, it represents an enormous management challenge. Second, the majority of these are "anticipated" benefits that have yet to be reaped by focus group firms. Third, APM requires the development of a number of related activities (described in the latter sections of this chapter). Although benefits are realized during individual activities, the most significant benefits are not realized until most, if not all, of these capabilities have been completed. Finally, APM involves a different way of approaching IT investments—a collective view of all IT applications across the enterprise—which has cultural and political ramifications for organizations. The good news is that those organizations that are well advanced in APM have realized significant benefits. We highlight one such firm in Table 21.3.

Table 21.3   An APM Case Study

Vision
• Reverse the rising tide of application maintenance costs;   • Fund strategic development efforts from reduced support and maintenance costs;   • Align IT with business goals.
Challenge
• Assess current portfolio of applications;   • Establish targets, savings strategies, and supporting plans;   • Data currency and accuracy.
Solution
• Identify redundant or obsolete applications and set end-of-year targets for retiring a committed percentage of the total;   • Classify applications by their strategic value and shift maintenance support focus to highly strategic applications;   • Rank applications with a quality score; applications failing to meet a baseline are selected for preventive maintenance, code simplification, maintainability;   • Migrate an increasing share of maintenance work to lower-cost geographies.
Value
• Cut applications by 70%;   • Established rigorous priorities; SLAs now vary based on objective business criteria;   • Re-engineered applications; defects down 58% and maintenance costs down 20%;   • Relocated work; significant maintenance is now performed in countries with costs 60–70% lower than previous.

Making APM Happen

Application portfolio management presents a significant management challenge and success requires the commitment of considerable organizational resources. The focus group suggested that APM involves the development of three interrelated capabilities. The first capability is the articulation of a strategy including goals, deliverables, and a set of governance procedures to guide the management of the application portfolio. Next is the creation of an applications inventory to monitor key attributes of existing applications. The third capability involves building an analysis and reporting capability in order to rationalize the applications portfolio according to the strategy established. These capabilities (depicted in Figure 21.1), although distinct, are closely

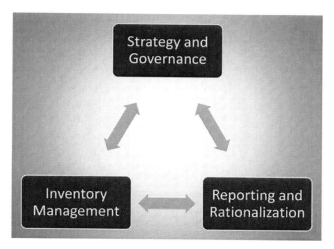

Figure 21.1 Key APM capabilities

interrelated and work synergistically.[2] To deliver value with APM, organizations must establish all three capabilities. Experience suggests that organizations typically start by inventorying applications and work from the middle out to refine their APM strategy (and how it is governed) as well as to establish efforts to rationalize their applications portfolio. As such, APM represents a process of continual refinement. Fortunately, experience also suggests that there are real benefits to be reaped from the successful development of each capability. These capabilities are described in detail below.

Capability 1: Strategy and Governance

There are many different reasons to adopt application portfolio management. At one firm, the complexity of the IT application portfolio had increased to the point of becoming unmanageable. The firm viewed APM as the means to gain some measure of control over a burgeoning collection of disjointed IT applications. Another firm had set an architectural direction and established an IT roadmap and viewed APM as a way to "put some teeth" into the enforcement of these policies. At a third firm, the manager of a strategic business unit was frustrated over escalating annual IT costs and the "pile of applications" that seemed to have "little connection to actual business services." A simple poll of the focus group, however, suggested that APM tended to be an IT-led initiative as opposed to a business initiative—a fact that has implications for launching and funding APM.

---

[2] The focus group did not see APM as a "stage" model where organizations advance through a prescribed set of stages. Instead they identified three highly interrelated "capabilities" that organizations need to establish in order to advance their application portfolio management.

To get an APM initiative underway, it is necessary to build a business case. How this is done depends on the firm's strategy. According to one manager, "If APM is positioned as inventory management, you'll never get the business to pay for it." In his organization, APM was promoted as a cost-reduction initiative focused on the elimination of unused (or underused) applications, unnecessary software licenses, duplicated data, and redundant applications. The business case included an aggressive schedule of declining IT costs to the business. In another organization, the APM initiative is supported internally by the IT organization and driven largely by the enterprise architecture group. In fact, the business is unaware of its APM program. In a third organization, APM was couched within the overall strategy of transforming the business. The argument was that APM could "reduce ongoing support costs for existing applications in order to re-direct that IT spend into business transformation." The business case included metrics and a quarterly reporting structure to ensure that savings targets were obtained. The conclusion reached by the focus group was that each organization is unique and, given the wide variety of potential APM benefits, the best strategy is to attach APM to a broader enterprise goal. They felt that if APM is attempted solely within the IT organization without business backing, it is less likely to produce the full range of benefits.

The strategy selected to launch APM has direct ramifications for the information collected about each application (i.e., the second capability—inventory management) as well as what information is reported and tracked by senior management (i.e., the third capability—reporting and rationalization). In the next section of this chapter, we present a comprehensive set of information that could be collected for IT applications within the portfolio. Organizations, depending on their APM strategy, may focus on a subset of this information and develop a reporting and rationalization capability built on this information.

APM strategy and governance are linked; if strategy is the destination, then governance is the map. According to one manager, governance is "a set of policies, procedures, and rules that guide decisions and define decision rights in an organization." Application portfolio governance answers three questions:

1. *What decisions need to be made?* This addresses the types and/or categories of decisions often referred to as decision domains. It also links the decisions with the processes that are needed to manage the application portfolio.

2. *Who should make these decisions?* This addresses the roles and accountabilities for decision makers (e.g., who provides input, who approves and has final authority). This links the decisions to be made (the "what") with the decision makers (the "who").

3. *How are these decisions made?* This addresses the structures and processes for decision making (e.g., the architecture review board). This links the decisions to be made (the "what") with the people/roles (the "who") involved in decision making with the timelines and mechanisms for making those decisions (the "how").

On an ongoing basis, organizations introduce new applications and (infrequently) retire old applications. The key difference with APM is that these applications are managed holistically across the enterprise on a much more formalized and less piece-meal basis. The goal is to discover synergies as well as duplication, alternative (and less costly) methods for providing business services, and rebalancing (or rationalizing) the portfolio of applications with regard to age, capability, and/or technical health. This represents a significant organizational change that impacts governance procedures directly. According to one IT manager, "No longer can business units acquire an IT application that duplicates existing functionality without scrutiny by the APM police." With the adoption of APM governance procedures, such actions become visible at high levels within the organization.

How new governance procedures are actually implemented varies by organization. The focus group suggested that effective APM governance must be both free-standing (in order to have visibility and impact) as well as closely integrated within the frame-work of existing governance mechanisms (in order to affect the status quo). As an example, the IT project selection committee must consider the impact of prospective IT projects on the existing portfolio of enterprise applications if the organization is to achieve its APM rationalization goals regarding architecture and/or functionality. That is, the APM governance processes must leverage existing organizational gov-ernance processes, including architectural reviews, exception process handling, IT delivery processes, strategic planning and annual budgeting, and technology reinvest-ment and renewal. One manager shared his enterprise IT governance framework to demonstrate where and how APM was situated within other established processes (see Figure 21.2).

Effective governance starts with ownership, which entails responsibilities and accountabilities. At a tactical level, each IT application should have an owner. This individual is held responsible for the ultimate disposition of the application; that is, when it is enhanced, refurbished, or decommissioned. The sense of the focus group was that the application owner should be a business manager, except for internal IT applications. Each application should have a business owner, and it is common to also appoint a custodian whose key duty is to keep the information current. Given the technical nature of the application information (see Appendix A), the custodian is typically an IT employee, perhaps an account manager or someone within the enterprise architecture group.

With stewardship (i.e., owner and custodian) assigned for major application, the next level of governance is the portfolio level. A management committee com-prised of application owners, senior enterprise architects, and IT planners/strategists should meet regularly, perhaps quarterly, to make decisions regarding the disposition of applications within the overall portfolio. This committee would report to the senior executive on portfolio activities, performance toward goal achievement, and estab-lishment of linkages to fiscal planning and strategy. In very large organizations an additional committee of portfolio owners might also be required.

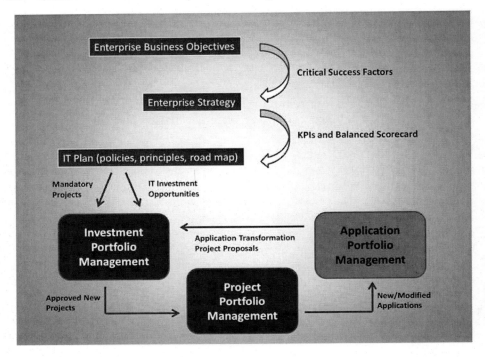

Figure 21.2 Positioning APM within an enterprise IT governance framework

Effective governance is critical for overcoming a number of problems common during the initial phases of APM. Some of the challenges experienced by the focus group included the following:

- Application owners are accountable to execute the process, but no one has defined who (or what body) is accountable for the process itself or what governance practices should be applied to make it happen.
- Managing applications requires additional maturity for defining a roadmap for the portfolio. Without this, some applications are well planned while the overall portfolio is not.
- The classification criteria for applications are in flux and lack an executive process for validating the ratings.
- Application assessments are not taken seriously by executive owners ("Everything is critical"), which erodes the credibility of the process and the overall value of the exercise of managing applications as a portfolio.
- Business managers lack awareness and accountability.
- There is difficulty from the "supply" side; for example, reluctance to take ownership of the data to ensure its integrity, quality, and timeliness.
- Demand-side aggression pushes for more and more application attributes.

The focus group felt that each of these problems requires effective governance procedures. But like all organizational initiatives, changes to existing routines and methods take time to mature.

Capability 2: Inventory Management

Before building an inventory of applications, organizations first need to know what applications they are going to inventory. One firm started by defining an application as a computer program or set of computer instructions that allows end users to accomplish one or more specific business tasks and is able to operate independently of other applications. An application can also be a distinct data store used by multiple other applications. Examples include commercial off-the-shelf packages; applications written in Excel that perform specific business functions; custom-developed computer software programs; a data warehouse and/or the reporting applications accessing it; and/or modules, services, or components, either purchased or custom built to perform a specific business function. This definition excludes system software or platform software (e.g., operating systems, device drivers, or diagnostic tools), programming software, and user-written macros and scripts.

What is most important is that organizations identify which specific applications will be included in the portfolio to be actively managed. One firm excluded all applications not explicitly managed by IT (e.g., Excel spreadsheets developed by managers for analytical purposes). Another focused only on major applications according to size. A third firm only included "business-critical" applications. This decision has direct implications for the size of the APM effort. The organization that limited its portfolio to business-critical applications reduced the portfolio to 180 applications from 1,200—a significant reduction in the amount of effort required. The organization's decision to limit (and therefore focus) its application portfolio depended on the strategy outlined in Step 1 above.

With inclusion criteria established, organizations must then identify what specific information about applications will need to be captured. A list of possible information items gathered from the members of the focus group is presented in Appendix A. These items are categorized according to the following five headings:

- *General application information* is the information used to explicitly and clearly identify an application—distinct from all other applications—and provide a basic understanding of its functionality.
- *Application categorization* is the information providing criteria used to group applications for comparison and portfolio management purposes (e.g., business capability provided, life cycle status).
- *Technical condition* provides the overall rating of the technical quality of the application, including various elements of risk (e.g., development language, operating system, architecture).
- *Business value* provides an overall rating of the value of the application to the business (e.g., business criticality, user base, effectiveness).

- *Support cost* captures the order of magnitude of the overall cost of an application after deployment. It includes maintenance and support costs (including upgrades) but not the initial purchase, development, or deployment costs.

The focus group could not overstate the importance and criticality of selecting the information to be maintained as part of the application inventory as this information dictates the types of analyses that can be performed after the fact (as outlined in the next section). Once selected, the task of capturing application information and keeping it current is a monumental effort. Without clear ownership of the information and assigned responsibilities for a custodial function, attempts at application portfolio management typically falter. One of the key motivations for establishing a strict information regime is the delivery of demonstrable benefits from the exercise. These are discussed in the next section.

Capability 3: Reporting and Rationalization

With an application inventory established, a set of standard parameter-driven reports can be produced to monitor the status of all existing applications so management can readily ascertain the health of any specific application or the overall health of the portfolio of applications. One firm has a collection of standard reports that analyze the number of applications and their costs, how business capabilities are supported and where duplication exists, breakdowns of annual application costs, application life cycle patterns, and reuse options for future projects. One widely adopted report compares applications on the basis of business value, technical condition, and cost (see Figure 21.3). As depicted, this chart helps organizations rationalize their IT application portfolio by tracking applications over time as they become less important to the business and/or lose technical currency. One organization found that eliminating those applications in the bottom left of the quadrant—which provide limited business benefit, often at a significant cost—can be a "combination of quick hits and longer-term initiatives." Even managers reluctant to retire a business application can be convinced with evidence of the full support costs.

Once the application inventory is assembled, the number of ways to "slice and dice" the information is unlimited and the value obtained is commensurate. One manager claimed that for the first time her organization is able to answer questions such as "How many applications use a particular technology?" and "How many systems support sales reporting?" The provision of ad hoc reporting capability is a quick way to discover the number of current licenses with a specific vendor and/or to assess the costs of providing specific business services. Ultimately, organizations need to know their true costs of doing business in order to explore options for providing different customer services. The information produced by analyzing the IT application portfolio takes organizations a huge step closer to this level of understanding and optimization.

The information needs supported by an application inventory vary by stakeholder. The IT organization wants to map business functionality against applications; the risk, audit, and security teams are most interested in regulatory compliance and a

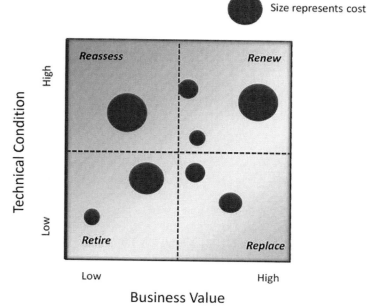

Figure 21.3 Application portfolio highlighting business value, technical condition and cost

risk management perspective; and business teams are interested in understanding the costs and business value of the applications they use. Even within IT, different groups (e.g., solutions delivery, information security, production support, executive management, business continuity, regulatory compliance, infrastructure, architecture, and planning) have information needs that are unique from the application portfolio. For this reason, most firms mandate a single application portfolio capable of supporting many different views at different levels as well as a composite view of the entire portfolio. One manager explained this by claiming that although different views of the portfolio satisfy individual groups within her organization, the "consolidated view ultimately demonstrates the effectiveness of monitoring and tracking business performance of the assets across the entire IT application portfolio."

Key Lessons Learned

The following represent some of the lessons learned based on the collective experience of the members of the focus group:

- **Balance demand and supply.** Managers tend to push for the inclusion of more and different application attributes as well as more reports of infinite variety (the "demand" side) while balking at assuming ownership of this data in order to ensure its integrity, quality, and timeliness (the "supply" side). When launching an APM initiative, clear procedures should be established to govern regular enhancements and releases for APM reporting.

- *Look for quick wins.* Gaining awareness and acceptance of an APM initiative can be an uphill struggle. This effort is aided greatly by capturing a number of "quick wins" early on. For example, organizations should look carefully at the possibility of decommissioning applications as a ready source of immediate and visible wins that impact the bottom line directly. Reuse provides midterm wins, and rationalization provides longer-term wins.
- *Capture data at key life stages.* It is a mistake to wait to capture data when applications are already in production. Data should be captured at multiple stages—when an application is first approved, when in testing, when promoted to production, during significant modifications, and when retired. As soon as data are captured and made available, the organization can benefit. For example, knowing the attributes of applications under development can be valuable for planning/budgeting purposes and ultimately enables better project solutions.
- *Tie APM and TCO initiatives together.* If a total cost of ownership (TCO) initiative is underway, ensure that the APM is closely tied to the TCO initiative. Much of the information captured as part of the APM initiative will support the TCO initiative, and vice versa. Knowing this relationship in advance will ensure that the data are captured to facilitate both purposes. The long-term savings can be significant.
- *Provide an application "end-state" view.* It is important to provide current information about applications, but it is equally important to provide an end-state view indicating the application's future trajectory. This facilitates a planned and orderly evolution toward retirement for applications as well as key information for business planning (e.g., roadmaps, gap reporting, and progress reporting).
- *Communicate APM benefits.* Gaining awareness and acceptance of an APM initiative is a constant struggle. Organizations must seek opportunities to communicate why this initiative is underway, what results have been realized, and what the next stages to be accomplished are. Effective communication is even more important in situations where the APM initiative is being driven internally by the IT organization.

Conclusion

This chapter provides guidance to those investigating APM and/or planning to launch an APM initiative. Application portfolio management promises significant benefits to adopting organizations. Obtaining those benefits, however, requires the development of three mutually reinforcing capabilities. The first capability is the development of an APM strategy buttressed with governance procedures; the second is the creation of an application inventory; and the third is a reporting capability built to align the application portfolio with the established strategy. Each of these capabilities provides stand-alone benefits, but together they enable an organization to optimize its IT application assets, reduce the cost and complexity of its portfolio, reduce or eliminate redundant functionality, facilitate better business decisions regarding technology, and effectively communicate the contribution of IT to the overall organization.

Chapter Discussion Questions

1. Given the extensive list of benefits derived from APM, how do you explain why most organizations do not manage their applications as a portfolio?
2. Describe the likely outcome of an organization that fails to manage its application portfolio effectively.

References

Anonymous. "Maximizing IT Investment." *Wall Street & Technology*, April 2008.

Boivie, C. A. "Taking Stock of Your Portfolio: Do You Have a Good Idea of the Value of Your IT Applications, Both Old and New?" *CIO Canada* 11, no. 10 (October 2003).

Caruso, D. "Application Portfolio Management: A Necessity for Future IT." *Manufacturing Business Technology* 25, no. 10 (October 2007): 48.

Gomolski, B. "Cleaning House." *Computerworld* 38, no. 51 (December 2004).

Kasargod, D., and K. Bondugula. "Application Portfolio Management." *Infosys* (April 2005): 1–8. Originally published in *www.gtnews.com*. http://www.gtnews.com.

Kramer, L. "CIO Challenge: Application Portfolio Management." *Wall Street & Technology*, May 2006.

Serena Software Inc. "Application Portfolio Management (APM): Solving the Challenges of APM with Serena." www.serena.com/docs/repository/products/mariner/datasheet-apm-mariner.pdf, accessed March 12, 2011.

Appendix A

Application Information

A) *General application information* is the information used to explicitly and clearly identify an application—distinct from all other applications—and provide a basic understanding of its functionality.
   - Name—the name that uniquely identifies the application;
   - Short name—an abbreviation or acronym that is likely a unique identifier of the application and is used for reporting when there is not room to use the application's full name;

- Description—a more extensive description of the application typically focusing on its functional scope;
- Portfolio owner—the title of the portfolio owner of the application and the name of the person currently filling that role. (The portfolio owner is typically filled by someone at VP level or higher.)
- Stakeholders—key people (by name and title) who could have been identified as a portfolio owner if multiple portfolio owners were allowed;
- Application owner—the title of the portfolio owner's delegate (if there is one) and the name of the person currently filling that role. (The application owner is typically someone reporting to the portfolio owner and empowered to make decisions relating to the ongoing use and evolution of the application. The application owner role is typically filled by someone below the VP level.)
- Business consultant—the name of the IT-business liaison. (This person is part of the IT organization but is responsible for the relationship with the business unit.)
- Internally versus externally developed—states whether the application was developed internally (by any business or IT organization) or whether it was purchased from an external vendor;
- Vendor—the name of the vendor that owns the application. (For internally developed applications this should be the business unit or IT unit that is responsible for maintaining the application; i.e., that provides the resources and funding.)
- Product name—the name of the product. (Only required when a product has an explicit name that is not the vendor name.)
- Version number—the complete version number of the application that is in production;
- Current version—the most current version number in full release by the vendor;
- Implementation date—the year and month that the solution went into production;
- Last major upgrade—the year and month that the last major upgrade went into production. (Major upgrades typically require a project approach, explicit funding, training, and planning to avoid downtime, etc. This field is blank if there has not been a major upgrade after the implementation date.)
- Last minor upgrade—the year and month that the last minor upgrade went into production. (Minor upgrades are typically upgrades that can be performed during regularly scheduled maintenance windows and can be performed as part of routine application maintenance. This field is blank if there has not been a minor upgrade after the last major upgrade, such as point releases, security patches.)

- Next scheduled review—the year and month that the application profile should next be reviewed. (By default, this should be one year from the current review, but will be updated as assessment schedules are developed.)

B) *Application categorization* is the information providing a variety of criteria/data used to group applications for comparison and portfolio management purposes.
  - Application scope—identifies the breadth of use of the application across the organization (e.g., enterprise, multidivisional, divisional, multidepartmental, departmental, individual users);
  - Life cycle status—identifies the life cycle stage that the application is in (e.g., emerging, standard, contained, retirement target, retired);
  - SBUs used by—a choice of one or more business divisions that use the application;
  - SBUs used for—a choice of one or more business divisions that the application is used on behalf of;
  - Application capability—broad categories of capability that applications provide (e.g., supply chain management [SCM] planning, SCM execution, SCM procurement);
  - Application subcapabilities—subcapabilities of functionality that applications provide. (A single application will often provide functionality covering multiple subcapabilities.)
  - Support organization—identifies the organizational support for the application (e.g., IT organization, third party, business unit);
  - Recoverability—the requirement to be able to recover the application in the event of a disaster and the ability to perform that recovery;
  - Application type—a general categorization of the application's use of data (e.g., analytical/reporting, transactional, collaborative, hybrid);
  - Application profile—a general categorization of the application's functional profile (e.g., suite, best of breed, in-house);

C) *Technical condition* provides the overall rating of the technical quality of the application, including various elements of risk.
  - Development language—the programming languages that the application is developed with. (The language element should address programming code running on the server, client, database, middleware, etc.)
  - Operation system(s)—the operating system(s) required for all layers of the application where there are application-specific requirements. (This can be applied to the server, database, middleware, client, etc. This evaluation categorization does not address the Web browser in a Web-based application.)
  - Hardware platforms—the hardware platforms required for all layers of the application where there are application-specific requirements. (This can be applied to the server, database, middleware, client, etc.)

- Database/data model—the database platform and database model (i.e., data architecture) that the application is tied to (or built on);
- Integration—the integration tools and model used to integrate the applications with other applications. (The "model" aspect of this criterion is closely related to the overall architecture of the systems but specifically looks at the framework/approach used for integration.)
- Architecture—the application architecture, technology patterns, etc., that define "how" different elements of technology were put together to create the application, such as NET, J2EE, J2SE, OO, Client/Server, Web-based, thin-client, etc. (This criterion also addresses the extensibility of the application—the ability of the applications to be modified to meet future/changing functional requirements.)
- Security—the capability of the application to 1) limit access to data and functionality to specific users and/or groups, and 2) provide audit information related to functions performed (or attempted to be performed) on the data viewed (or attempted to be viewed) by specific users. (This metric addresses the application's native capabilities, the specific implementation/ modification of those capabilities, and the security requirements of the organization.)
- Vendor viability—the likelihood that the vendor will remain strong in the relevant application market and industry vertical;
- Vendor support—the ability and commitment of the vendor to provide support for the applications. (This includes the ability and commitment to provide new releases and patches to the application.)
- Key abilities: 1) availability of the application relative to user requirements identified in service level agreements (SLA), 2) scalability of the application to meet current and future user and transaction volumes, and 3) performance of the application in starting, retrieving information, and performing transactions;
- User interface—the overall usability/intuitiveness of the application's interface. (This is often reflected by training requirements, support requirements, online documentation, etc.)

D) **Business value** provides an overall rating of the value of the application to the business.
  - Competitive advantage—the extent to which the application enables a capability that 1) increases revenue, 2) lowers cost, or 3) differentiates the company in the marketplace;
  - Business criticality—the extent to which the application materially affects the company's ability to conduct core business processes such as sell, deliver, close financial books. (This includes the ability to meet regulatory requirements.)

- User base—the number and variety of users who use the application. (This measure is adjusted to reflect the difference between causal/occasional users and power users, as well as internal versus external users. This measure also includes transaction volumes that the application performs to account for essential applications with few users but large transaction volumes that the business is dependent on.)
- Current effectiveness—ability of the application to meet current business requirements within the scope of the functionality it was intended to provide;
- Future effectiveness—ability of the application to meet future business requirements within the scope of the functionality it was intended to provide and logical/reasonable extensions of that functionality.

E) **Support cost** captures the order of magnitude of the overall cost of an application after deployment. It includes maintenance and support costs (including upgrades) but not the initial purchase, development, or deployment costs.
  - Elements included—license maintenance, other licensing fees, vendor/external support, internal support, and hardware;
  - Elements not included—PCs, network, telephony, or other shared services; end-user costs, such as time lost to support calls, downtime, etc. (Typically these data are not readily available at the level of granularity required.)

Project Management at MM[1]

"We've got a real 'warm puppy' here," Brian Smith told Werner McCann. "Make sure you make the most of it. We could use a winner."

Smith was MM's CIO, and McCann was his top project manager. The puppy in question was MM's new venture into direct-to-customer marketing of its *green meters*—a product designed to help better manage electrical consumption—and the term referred to the project's wide appeal. The strategy had been a hit with analysts ever since it was revealed to the financial community, and the company's stock was doing extremely well as a result. "At last," one analyst had written in his popular newsletter, "we have a company that is willing to put power literally and figuratively in consumers' hands. If MM can deliver on its promises, we fully expect this company to reap the rewards."

Needless to say, the Green project was popular internally, too. "I'm giving it to you because you have the most project management experience we've got," Smith said. "There's a lot riding on this one." As he walked away from Smith's office, McCann wasn't sure whether to feel complimented or terrified. He had certainly managed some successful projects for the company (previously known as ModMeters) over the past five years but never anything like this one. "That's the problem with project management," he thought. "In IT almost every project is completely different. Experience only takes you part of the way."

The Green project was different. It was the first truly enterprise-wide project the company had ever done, and McCann was having conniptions as he thought about telling Fred Tompkins, the powerful head of manufacturing, that he might not be able to have everything his own way. McCann knew that to be successful this project had to take an outside-in approach—that is, to take the end customers' point of view on the company. That meant integrating marketing, ordering, manufacturing, shipping, and service into one seamless process that wouldn't bounce the customer from one department to another in the company. MM had always had separate systems for each of its silos, and this project would work against the company's traditional culture and

---

[1] H. A. Smith and J. D. McKeen, "Project Management at MM," #1-L05-1-009. Smith School of Business at Queen's University, November 2005. Reproduced by permission of Queen's University, Smith School of Business, Kingston, Ontario, Canada.

processes. The Green project was also going to have to integrate with IT's information management renewal (IMR) project. Separate silos had always meant separate databases, and the IMR project was supposed to resolve inconsistencies among them and provide accurate and integrated information to different parts of the company. This was a huge political challenge, but if it didn't work, McCann couldn't deliver on his mandate.

Then there was the issue of resources. McCann groaned at the thought. MM had some good people but not enough to get through all of the projects in the IT plan within the promised timelines. Because of the importance of the Green project, he knew he'd get good cooperation on staffing, but the fact remained that he would have to go outside the company for some of the technical skills he needed to get the job done. Finally, there was the schedule that had to be met. Somehow, during the preliminary assessment phase, it had become clear that September 5 was to be the "hard launch" date. There were good reasons for this—the fall was when consumers usually became concerned with their energy consumption—but McCann worried that a date barely twelve months from now would put too much pressure on his team. "We've got to get in there first, before the competition," Smith had said to him. "The board expects us to deliver. You've got my backing and the support of the full executive team, but you *have* to deliver this one."

Six Weeks Later

It was full steam ahead on the Green project. It's *amazing* what a board mandate and executive sponsorship can do for a project, thought McCann, who knew how hard it usually was to get business attention to IT initiatives. He now had a full-time business counterpart, Raj Sambamurthy. Samba, as he was known to his colleagues, had come out of Tompkins's division and was doing a fantastic job of getting the right people in the room to make the decisions they needed to move ahead. The Green steering committee was no Mickey Mouse group either. Smith, Tompkins, and every VP affected by the project were meeting biweekly with him and Samba to review every aspect of the project's progress.

McCann had pulled no punches when communicating with the committee. "You've given me the mandate and the budget to get this project off the ground," he had told them. "But we have to be clear about what we're trying to accomplish." Together, they had hammered out a value proposition that emphasized the strategic value of the project and some of the measures they would use to monitor its ultimate success. The requirements and design phase had also gone smoothly because everyone was highly motivated to ensure the project's success. "Linking success to *all* our annual bonuses sure helped *that!*" McCann had remarked wryly to Samba.

Now McCann was beginning to pull together his dream team of implementers. The team had chosen a package known as Web-4-U as the front end of the project, but it would take a lot of work to customize it to suit their unique product and, even more to integrate it with MM's outmoded back-end systems. The Web-4-U company was based in Ireland but had promised to provide 24/7 consulting on an as-needed basis. In addition, Samba had now assembled a small team of business analysts to work on the business processes they would need. They were working out of the firm's Cloverdale office, a thirty-minute drive from IT's downtown location. (It was a shame they couldn't all be together, but space was at a premium at headquarters. McCann made a mental note to look into some new collaboration software he'd heard about.) Now that these two pieces were in place, McCann felt free to focus on the technical "guts" of the system. "Maybe this will work out after all," he said.

Three Months to Launch Date

By June, however, McCann was tearing out what little hair was left on his head. He was seriously considering moving to a remote Peruvian hamlet and breeding llamas. "*Anything* would be better than this mess," he observed to Yung Lee, the senior IT architect, over coffee. They were poring over the project's critical path. "The way I see it," Lee stated matter-of-factly, "we have two choices: We can continue with this inferior technology and meet our deadline but not deliver on our functionality, *or* we can redo the plan and go back to the steering committee with a revised delivery date and budget."

McCann sighed. Techies *always* saw things in black and white, but his world contained much more gray. So much was riding on this—credibility (his, IT's, the company's), competitiveness, stock price. He dreaded being the bearer of this bad news so he said, "Let's go over this *one* more time."

"It's not going to get any better, but here goes," Lee took a deep breath. "Web-4-U is based on outmoded technology. It was the best available last year, but *this* year the industry has agreed on a new standard, and if we persist in using Web-4-U, we are going to be out of date before Green even hits the street. We need to go back and completely rethink our technical approach based on the new standard and then redesign our Web interface. I know it's a setback and expensive, but it has to be done."

"How come we didn't know about this earlier?" McCann demanded.

Lee replied, "When the standard was announced, we didn't realize what the implications were at first. It was only in our quarterly architecture meeting that the subject came up. That's why I'm here now." The architects were a breed apart, thought McCann. All tech and *no* business sense. They'd lost almost three months because of this. "By the way," Lee concluded, "Web-4-U knew about this, too. They're scrambling to rewrite their code. I guess they figured if you didn't know right away, there would be more chance of you sticking with them."

The chances of *that* are slim to none, thought McCann. His *next* software provider, whoever that was, was going to be sitting right here under his steely gaze. Seeing an agitated Wendy Chan at his door, he brought the meeting to a hasty close. "I'm going to have to discuss this with Brian," he told Lee. "We can't surprise him with this at the steering committee meeting. Hang tight for a couple of days, and I'll get back to you."

"OK," said Lee, "but remember that we're wasting time."

Easy for *you* to say, thought McCann as he gestured Chan into his office. She was his counterpart at the IMR project, and they had always had a good working relationship. "I just wanted to give you a heads-up that we've got a serious problem with IMR that will affect you," she began. Llamas began prancing into his mind's eye. "Tompkins is refusing to switch to our new data dictionary. We've spent months hammering this out with the team, but he says he wasn't kept informed about the implications of the changes, and now he's refusing to play ball. I don't know *how* he could say that. He's had a rep on the team from the beginning, and we've been sending him regular progress reports."

McCann was copied on those reports. Their pages of techno-jargon would put *anyone* to sleep! He was sure that Tompkins had never got past the first page of any of those reports. His rep was a dweeb, too, someone Tompkins thought he could live without in his daily operations.

"Damn! This is something I *don't* need." Like all IT guys, McCann *hated* corporate politics with a passion. He didn't understand them and wasn't good at them. "Why hadn't Samba and his team picked up on this? They were plugged into the business. Now he was going to have to deal with Chan's problem as well as his own if he wanted to get the Green project going. Their back-end processes wouldn't work at all unless everyone was using the same information in the same format. Why couldn't Tompkins see that? Did he *want* the Green project to fail?"

"The best way to deal with this one," advised Chan, "is to *force* him to accept these changes. Go to John Johnson and tell him that you need Tompkins to change his business processes to fit our data dictionary. It's for the good of the company, after all." Chan's strong suit wasn't her political savvy.

"You're right that we need Tompkins on our side," said McCann, "but there may be a better way. Let me talk to Samba. He's got his ear to the ground in the business. I'll speak with him and get back to you."

After a bit of chitchat, Wendy left McCann to his PERT chart, trying again to determine the extra cost in time if they went with the new technology. Just then the phone rang. It was Linda Perkins, McCann's newly hired work-at-home usability designer. She was one of the best in the business, and he was lucky to have snagged her just coming off maternity leave. His promise of flexible working hours and full benefits had lured her back to work two months before her year-long leave ended. "You've *got* to do something about your HR department!" Perkins announced. "They've just told me that I'm not eligible for health and dental benefits because I don't work on the premises! Furthermore, they want to classify me as contingent staff, not managerial, because I don't fit in one of their petty little categories for employees. You promised me that you had covered all this before I took the job! I gave up a good job at LifeCo so I could work from home."

McCann had indeed covered this issue in principle with Rick Morrow, IT's HR representative, but that had been almost eight months ago. Morrow had since left the firm. McCann wondered if he had left any paperwork on this matter. The HR IT spot had not yet been filled, and all of the IT managers were upset about HR's unreceptive attitude when it came to adapting its policies to the realities of today's IT world. "OK, Linda, just hang in there for a day or two and I'll get this all sorted out," he promised. "How's the usability testing coming along?"

"That's *another* thing I wanted to talk with you about. The team's making changes to the look and feel of the product without consulting me," she fumed. "I can't do my job without being in the loop. You *have* to make them tell me when they're doing things like this."

McCann sighed. Getting Perkins on the project had been such a coup that he hadn't given much thought to how the lines of communication would work within such a large team. "I hear you, Linda, and we'll work this out. Can you just give me a few days to figure out how we can improve things?"

Hanging up, he grabbed his jacket and slunk out of the office as quickly as he could before any other problems could present themselves. If he just kept walking south, he'd make it to the Andes in three, maybe four, months. He could teach himself Spanish along the way. At least the llamas would appreciate his efforts! MM could take its project and give it to some other poor schmuck. *No way* was he going back! He walked furiously down the street, mentally ticking off the reasons he had been a fool to fall for Smith's sweet talk. Then, unbidden, a plan of attack formed in his head. Walking always did the trick. Getting out of the office cleared his head and focused his priorities. He turned back the way he had come, now eager to get back in the fray. He had some things to do right away, and others he had to put in place ASAP.

Discussion Questions

1. Some organizational factors increase a project's likelihood of success. Identify these "facilitators" for the Green project.

2. Other organizational factors decrease a project's likelihood of success. Identify these "barriers" for the Green project.

3. Outline the things that McCann needs to do right away.

Working Smarter at Continental Furniture International[1]

Joel Parsons hurried down the hall to the monthly executive committee meeting doing a mental checklist of all the things he was responsible for: sales analysis—check; marketing stats—check; quarterly and YTD financials—check; operating statistics—check; trends in each of these areas—check. Parsons was right-hand man to the President of Continental Furniture International (CFI) and his primary job was to collect, analyze, and interpret any and all information the President needed to run the company. Joel had joined CFI a year ago from a similar job as Manager of Data Analysis, assisting the Vice President of Operations at UPS, where he had been involved in implementing some of the world's most sophisticated delivery scheduling and package flow technology. "I could use a bright young MBA here with me to shake things up at CFI," the President, Alan Chambers, had told him during his interview. "We need better business intelligence if we're going to be better than our competition."

"*That* was a laugh," thought Joel as he took his place beside Chambers and flipped open his laptop. These days he lived on Excel. This company thrived on its spreadsheets and Joel was responsible for digesting everyone else's data and packaging it for the President so he was always up to speed. Sure, they also had computer reports and even a financial "dashboard," thanks to the company's new ERP system, but the business world was changing and these canned reports only scratched the surface of what the President needed to know.

The next hour was a typical executive meeting, with each VP reporting on his or her progress and the President grilling them on *exactly* what was going on. To keep everyone on their toes, he always liked to have a few facts at his fingertips. At this meeting, there seemed to be a theme. "How much do we spend to heat our Andover warehouse?" he inquired of the VP of Operations. "Why are our delivery costs rising so quickly?" "What are we doing to make sure our drivers are following all our safety

[1] H. A. Smith and J. D. McKeen, "Working Smarter at Continental Furniture International," #1-L10-1-002. Smith School of Business at Queen's University, February 2010. Reproduced by permission of Queen's University, Smith School of Business, Kingston, Ontario, Canada.

protocols?" Occasionally, he would turn to Joel to check a fact or a trend, but he had done his homework and wanted everyone to know it. Joel watched the VPs squirm with discomfort as they tried to dig through their own spreadsheets to find the information Alan was demanding.

As they moved through the agenda, Joel was happy he wasn't on the hot seat. The last to report was the CIO, Cheryl Drewry. A long-serving executive, Drewry was tough, spoke her mind, and delivered what she promised; it was the reason she'd been around so long. After listening to Cheryl's report on the progress of their major IT projects, Alan paused and all heads looked up expectantly.

"I asked you all to clear an extra hour for this meeting for a reason," he stated. "We're doing well as a company but we need to do better. Our ERP system has got us part of the way. We now have good, common processes and some common data and consistent functionality. In short, we've picked all the low-hanging fruit. Now I'm worried about what's next. We can't afford to be complacent. *Everyone* has an ERP these days—even those guys at WWF. Everyone grinned at the nickname of World Wide Furniture, CFI's archrival for many years. The two companies had seesawed back and forth at the No. 1 and 2 positions in the furniture industry. Right now, CFI was No. 1 and it was Alan's job to keep it that way.

Alan continued, "What we now need is a way to work *smarter*—a way to leverage the information we've got and use it more effectively. There are lots of things that we could do but my first priority is to use information to enable CFI to *Go Green!*" He paused dramatically, while the VPs took a deep breath wondering what it was going to mean for their divisions. "Cheryl and I have discussed this and we feel there is enormous potential to use information, IT systems, and our great people to become more productive and more profitable and to reduce costs, while saving energy. This is truly a win-win for everyone!"

The room burst into sustained applause. The idea was a winner to be sure. How could you not like it? But Joel knew the hard work that it took at UPS and he wondered if these guys knew what they were in for. Alan turned the floor over to Cheryl who gave a brief overview of what they were planning.

"First, we are going to give each of you a set of data analytics tools so that you can explore our data warehouse yourselves. We want you to start thinking about ways you can use data differently. Second, we are going to establish an energy informatics team, composed of some business and IT people. They are going to examine any and all opportunities for using information to save energy anywhere in our company by working smarter. Third, we want your ideas and support to make this a corporate showcase."

Alan stood up. "This is an exciting and very strategic initiative for our company. It's a chance to be both socially and fiscally responsible and to lead in our industry. The Energy Informatics function is going to be crucial to its success so I'm personally going to be monitoring our progress by having this team report directly to me, with a dotted line to Cheryl. And fortunately, we've got just the right person to lead it." He gestured at Joel.

"Joel Parsons has several years' experience doing just this type of work at UPS. He helped them implement package flow technology that enabled the company to shave 30 million miles off its daily delivery driving two years ago. This has saved more than 3 million gallons of fuel annually—benefiting both the company and the environment. Take a bow, Joel."

Totally dumbfounded, Joel stood up and bowed dramatically and the meeting broke up a minute later, with everyone shaking his hand and congratulating him on his new appointment. Gathering his papers and laptop, he felt a hand on his shoulder. It was Alan.

"Sorry for the surprise, Joel, but this was super secret and I knew you would love a chance at this job. You've been suggesting we improve our analytic capabilities ever since you got here."

That was true, but delivering these capabilities was going to be a serious challenge. While he knew what the goal was, getting there was going to be a project of a nature few companies had tried. It was going to take it all—business smarts, technology, data, people's commitment at every level and processes. Somehow, they ALL had to tie together effectively to deliver real business and environmental value.

"I'll do my very best for you sir," he replied. "Give me a few weeks to get my thoughts together and to speak with Cheryl and the other VPs and I'll outline how I suggest we implement this strategy." With a curt nod of his head and a clap on his back, Alan left the room, leaving Joel with a million thoughts swirling in his head.

Over the next few weeks Joel had meetings with every one of the VPs to assess the scope of the opportunities involved; identify issues, concerns, and potential obstacles; and quietly evaluate who was *really* on board with the Green strategy.

In addition, he met individually with the two IT members of his team who had been hand-picked by Cheryl. "She's chosen good people," Joel thought. Susan Liu was a data warehouse specialist. She understood what data the company was already collecting from its various systems, how "clean" it was, and what types of analyses were being done at present.

Mario Fortunato was an analyst who had helped implement the company's ERP system, which was now its processing backbone. "He was a good choice," thought Joel, "because he has an excellent overview of the entire company's operations from suppliers to consumers." Joel had asked Alan to hold off appointing the last business member of the team until he better understood the business expertise that might be needed.

In their first team meeting, Joel outlined their mandate as he saw it. "Going green is both a huge opportunity and a huge challenge. So far, we've never used our data and systems to help us use energy more effectively. While we've had some energy-saving initiatives at CFI, these have been entirely initiated by our building maintenance group doing generic things like installing energy-efficient light bulbs and such. What we need first is a 'quick hit' so that everyone in the company can see what we're trying to do and why."

Susan jumped in. "We could start with our data centers. There seem to be lots of ways to save energy there."

"You're right of course, Susan," said Joel. "We should be doing this and I'll make sure that Cheryl has this in her plans. But what we need here is a much more visible way to demonstrate the business value and energy efficiency of this initiative."

Mario looked thoughtful. "I'm not sure if this is what you mean but we know how much each of our buildings, offices, and warehouses across the continent use in electricity, water, and heating and cooling. Our ERP system gathers this information from the utility bills that are sent to us electronically. Each building is considered a separate unit for billing purposes and has a separate set of metering. Could we run a contest that would post each building's energy usage each month and provide prizes when they reduce their usage relative to their previous three-year average?"

"*That* is an absolutely brilliant idea, Mario!" Joel exclaimed. "It's quick—at least I think it is; it's visible; it uses data we already have; and it involves everyone. And best of all, we can run with it while we work on a more comprehensive energy informatics strategy."

Joel was right on all counts. Three months later, the team launched the "Great Green Challenge" with an energy utilization dashboard on everyone's desktop as well as on special monitors in the warehouses. This showed each building's utilization of the three main resources and enabled staff to understand their usage not only in comparison to previous years but by time of day and month. They could also compare their usage against other similar buildings. Each building had a "green committee," which collected employee suggestions and worked with the appropriate people to implement them. Prizes would be awarded in various categories such as, biggest percentage monthly decline in usage, most innovative suggestion, and largest annual cumulative percentage decrease. The team also posted the most effective ideas on its collaboration site so others could see them. Prizes were small—coffee and donuts for all staff, movie passes, and virtual gold stars—but the contest gave the whole company a focus for its efforts to reduce its carbon footprint and its staff clear information about how they could work to save energy. Everyone was motivated by this program and within a few months after the launch, utility bills were reflecting small but significant declines. Alan even dropped by to congratulate the team on its success.

Success gave the team, which had now grown by two new members, further ideas for other energy informatics projects, so Joel called a strategy meeting to help chart out their next move.

"What if we were to tap into the computers in our trucks?" asked Menakshi Deena, who had joined them from the Operations Division. "They collect lots of data about everything from seatbelt use to oil pressure to the amount of time spent idling. Since we have thousands of trucks, we could really save a bundle if we could figure out how to use them more efficiently and safely."

They hashed the idea around, growing more and more positive about it. "I like it!" Joel said at last. "Let's make Energy Telematics our next major Green team initiative."

After running the idea by Alan, who gave it the go-ahead, the team started into the project in earnest. Sue and Menakshi were put in charge of data collection.

"We can get more than 200 vehicle-related elements from every truck," Sue reported. "If we put a GPS chip in each truck, we can collect data on what the trucks and the drivers are doing at every stop in their route. We can then use this data to optimize all sorts of energy use."

"But we're going to need to develop some software to help us analyze and report all this data," said Mario, doing some rapid calculations. "There will be literally thousands of data points every day for every truck."

It took a lot of work to figure out all the technical details. The company's trucks contained a variety of different hardware and software platforms, and daily data collection and standardization routines had to be developed. Then the team had to develop algorithms to analyze what was collected in order to determine where problems were occurring. Ted Prior from Logistics helped design a pilot test with fifty trucks in their Omaha depot, flying out personally to be there when the data receivers were installed.

"They work great," he reported Friday afternoon just before flying home. "We only had a few glitches but otherwise, when the trucks pull in at the end of the day, the drivers simply push a transmit button on their dashboards and all the data is transmitted. We're going to be up and running in no time!"

Monday morning Joel arrived bright and early to find an urgent voicemail from Alan's EA. "He wants to see you *immediately!*" said the message. Hurrying up to the executive suite, Joel wondered what the problem could possibly be. Everything was on track and running smoothly as far as he could tell. Alan's face told a different story. "Sit down," he barked, when Joel peered in the doorway. "I've just heard that our drivers in Omaha are threatening to strike," he said as Joel took his seat. "They think you're going to use your system to monitor their behavior. What's going on?"

"I have no idea, sir," Joel stammered. "We've just done a technical pilot."

"Well, I've told them out there that the pilot has been suspended indefinitely," Alan said. "Clearly, you haven't been careful about the impressions you're giving so you'd better go back to the drawing board."

Back in the team room, Joel called an urgent meeting to explain the situation. "We've done a lot of work to collect this data and it could have a huge impact on our costs, energy efficiency, and safety record," he noted. "But we will not get a chance to prove this if we don't figure out how to get the drivers onside. We didn't need to 'sell' the Great Green project, but this hostile reaction suggests that we may have some selling to do with other parts of the organization as well as our truck drivers. Anybody got any other ideas about what could go wrong?"

"Well, our front-line operations managers are super busy," said Menakshi. "We'd better be careful how we present this program to them or it could be seen as a lot of extra work."

"Our mechanics should be involved as well," said Ted. "They seemed quite interested in the information we could pull off the trucks. They could be quite helpful if we get them involved."

"We've got all this great data," said Sue, "but how are we going to get the drivers to *act* on it? Just collecting this information isn't enough."

"We've also got to consider how to roll this project out across the company," said Mario. "If the drivers can get this upset about a simple technical pilot, what are they going to do when they see the information we're planning to collect!"

The team fell silent and Joel turned all these thoughts over in his mind. He knew his future at CFI depended on what they did next. They'd barely started this project and it was already in trouble.

"Okay," he said. "We've hit a snag so now we've got to find a way to get Energy Telematics back on track. I told Alan we'd work up a plan and if he likes it he'll unsuspend the project. Who's got some ideas?"

Discussion Questions:

1. Why was Joel's team caught off guard by the hostile reaction of the truck drivers to the "technical" pilot of the Energy Telematics project at the Omaha depot?

2. Why did the "Great Green Challenge" succeed while the Energy Telematics project hit road bumps right out of the gate? What are the lessons learned for Joel and his team?

3. Develop a plan for Joel and his team to get the Energy Telematics project unsuspended. The plan will need details of who, what, when, where, and why.

Introducing Agile Development at American Attire

"Welcome to American Attire," said CEO Lisa Ross with a smile, warmly shaking her new CIO's hand. "We're glad you're here. The sooner you can get IT whipped into shape, the better. The competition's killing us!" Gene Engler smiled broadly back at her, more to reassure the room full of senior execs gathered to meet him than to communicate any positive message to Lisa. More than anyone, Lisa knew what a challenge she had given him. When he'd been recruited, she had been blunt. "Our IT project spending is too high and projects are taking too long to complete," Lisa had said. "The retail world is changing rapidly and everything that can change is becoming visual or interactive content. This is not a world where we can take several years to develop an IT project."

American Attire is a chain of clothing stores that had started as clothes for work-men—such things as boots, overalls, heavy-duty shirts, socks, and gloves—that was now trying to morph into a "business casual" clothing store for both men and women. "Our growth strategy is to attract more women and to stock more attractive and functional casual clothing that will appeal both to working men and women across a broad range of occupations, and to these same people on their days off," Lisa had told Gene in his interview. "But to do this, we need to revamp our systems to further enable our marketing capabilities and introduce next generation e-tail technologies to the company. You'll find some of us are skeptical that IT can do this so it's going to be up to you to 'show them the money' and prove that IT can deliver the goods. I'm hearing a lot of muttering that we should outsource the whole IT function."

Over the next few weeks, Gene made a point of sitting down with his business colleagues to get the lay of the land before launching into any changes. Their com-plaints were pretty consistent: "We need to improve our time to market," and "We shouldn't take so long to deliver our IT projects." Turning to his IT direct reports in their first group meeting with him, he asked, "How long did it take us to deliver our last three large projects?" After some meaningful looks between them, the Director of the Project Management Office, Caroline Taylor, spoke up. "They each took more than a year to implement," she stated. "But you have to understand that a significant part of this time was taken up documenting system requirements and objectives and more time was taken up dealing with scope creep because the business kept adding new things that they couldn't live without."

Gene frowned, absorbing this information. "So are you saying that it's the business' own fault or that IT takes too long to do these things?" "It's a bit of both, I'd say," said Brian Brophy, Director of Application Development. "Part of it is our methodology, which requires us to dot every 'i' and cross every 't' before we can move ahead. The procedures and paperwork can be onerous, especially for the business. But part of it is how we work with the business. We often have to hunt people down to help us with the requirements and then they don't do their homework and forget things that come back to haunt us. Sometimes it takes *weeks* to get them to sign off on their requirements and we're left to take the blame."

"I agree with Brian," said Caroline. "But you have to remember that our methodology was put in place for a good reason. We need controls for all sorts of reasons—to ensure privacy, security, financial transparency, risk management, and effective operations—just for a start. Our systems are so central to the company that any mistake could cost us big time! Just look at the data breaches that have been in the media or the recent bank systems crash. These things are front-page news. We need to be careful!"

"You're absolutely correct about that, Caroline," said Gene, "yet the fact remains that we need to do *something* to speed things up. Sounds like you are still developing systems using the traditional waterfall method. Other companies are managing to work more quickly and responsively so we *have* to start delivering more, faster, or Lisa will find someone else who will. Who's got some ideas?"

For the next hour or so they debated how to streamline their methodology, improve governance processes, and increase outsourcing. "It looks like there's some value in doing all of these things," Gene concluded. "But it also looks like you've done a pretty good job in most of these areas already."

"We *have*," agreed Brian. "But we still waste a lot of time getting requirements done, getting the right business people involved, and then doing the testing." Everyone in the room groaned at the word "testing." "Testing takes between 20 and 40 percent of the development effort," Brian added. "We have three levels of testing: first by the development team, then by a separate quality assurance (QA) team, and finally by the business users. These last two groups take their own sweet time because they follow their own processes and don't understand the impact they have on the progress of an individual project or on the business as a whole."

Gene looked around at the earnest faces at the table. "You're a good team and you've done well holding the fort since last year when George Nichols retired." George had been the company's long-serving CIO who understood the *old* ways of doing things at American Attire perfectly, but who had been reluctant to introduce much change in his final years of service. "But I was brought in with a mandate from Lisa to shake things up," he continued. Seeing their apprehensive faces, he hurried on.

"That doesn't mean people are going to be losing their jobs. There will be some restructuring but, as I said, we have a good group here. We just need some refocusing on how to deliver more value faster to the business. I'd like us to consider agile development."

A hush fell across the room as they all considered this idea. This would *never* have been considered when George "Keep the Lights On" Nichols was CIO. He had spent years putting structured development practices and governance in place to provide company systems and guarantee operational stability. And these had served the company well … in their time. Projects were delivered on schedule and on budget and operations barely hiccupped. The problem was that the business needed more, faster.

"How would that work?" asked Caroline. She, like her colleagues, knew about agile development from trade publications and conferences, even if they'd never used it. "It's a big change and as I understand it, it would affect most parts of IT in some way or another."

"You're right, Caroline," said Gene. "Agile works differently and we don't have all the capabilities in place to go full speed with agile right now, but I want to undertake a pilot project that will help us learn, work out the kinks, and demonstrate that we *can* be a more flexible, responsive, and business-centric IT function that can meet the needs of our business. Let's think about what we'll need and put some thought and effort into making it work. The first steps will be choosing the right pilot project and team and then getting everyone some training in agile development principles. What type of project do you think we should be looking for?"

"The project we choose shouldn't be overly complex or too dependent on integration with existing systems," suggested Brian.

"We would need to ensure we have a cooperative sponsor," offered Philip Hayhoe, Director of Relationship Management. "As I understand it, an agile development project needs more or less full-time business participation."

"What about operations participation?" asked Joe Pereira, the Infrastructure Director. "An agile project has new implementations every two weeks or so, correct? So we need direct involvement."

"I think you're both right with these ideas," concluded Gene. "And I think we should get QA involved as well. I also know someone who would be a great agile coach for our first project. Let me speak with him and work with Caroline and Phil to find the right project. I've already got Lisa's mandate to get started, so in the meantime think about what else we'll need to do to make this pilot successful. We need to all pull together to make this project a showpiece of what IT can do."

Over the next few weeks, with some major participation from Gene, the pieces fell into place. Gene sold the idea to the senior business managers by telling them, "We could spend six months documenting detailed requirements with the traditional method *or* we could spend two weeks and deliver something functional that everyone can see." He got their approval for two pilot projects. "We'll take what we learn from the first and apply it in the second," he told his team. "Then, after that, the company will make a decision about future developments." In the meantime Brian explored agile tools and processes so that when the approval came to test the concept, IT would be ready.

The first project was well defined and the sponsor was willing to act as a guinea pig for the new process. The challenge was that the system had to be fully functional and implemented by November—less than four months away. AssortAA was a product that would assist buyers in better predicting assortments across the country—in sizes and styles—according to previous patterns of purchases, integrating these with industry demographic data, and then dynamically adjusting them as needed. The reason for the deadline was that buyers and store operations all met at headquarters in November to finalize the spring orders and the date couldn't be changed.

Brian had selected a development team and appointed a scrum master from among his top performers, and QA and Operations had each appointed a person to work with them on a dedicated basis. A project room had been organized so that everyone could sit together. The sponsor had agreed to send someone to the training session. So far, so good.

The first glitch came late in the first sprint. "Our business rep, Cathy Jang, won't make any decisions," complained Vic Robeznieks, the scrum master. "She says she's got to take all decisions back to *her* boss and then takes a few days to get back to us. And she's hardly ever in the project room with us. She says most of what we're asking her to do isn't her job!"

"I'll talk to Phil right away about this," promised Brian.

Phil and Brian discussed this matter. "There's a lot of confusion in the business about what their roles and responsibilities are for this project," said Phil. "Ken, our sponsor, wants to be involved in making all the decisions about this project but obviously he can't be there all the time. Cathy's too junior to be given full decision-making authority, and she's only been allocated to this project part-time."

"That's ridiculous!" fumed Brian. "We told them we needed full-time participation right up front! The only way this is going to work is if they understand what they're supposed to do and put the right people in place. I think we need to escalate this to Gene."

While Gene worked on getting the right level of business participation and educating Cathy and her boss about their roles and responsibilities, fresh problems emerged as they neared the end of the second sprint. "We've way overestimated what we can do in this sprint," Vic told Brian, Caroline, and their agile coach, Mike Khan. "Everyone's asking for changes after the last sprint and we need to do a better job of prioritizing them."

"You're right," said Mike, "You want to ensure that key changes are made but not get distracted from your main goal of getting this project done. That's the job of your product owner. He or she needs to make these decisions and keep the big picture of the product in view. And Vic," Mike continued, "make sure you and your team follow the 80:20 rule when deciding what gets done."

Turning to Brian and Caroline, Mike said. "You two may also need to work more closely with the team to help them get their user stories right. Estimation is still difficult with agile and sprints often end up too big and this can be discouraging. You need more consistency of delivery so that your clients can see progress."

"Wow," Caroline said to Brian when they were alone. "I didn't realize we had to be *this* involved with agile. I wonder how it will work if *all* our projects are delivered this way?

Not long after this, there were grumblings from the project team, which had been set up in a converted meeting room. Brian dropped in on Gene midway through the fourth sprint. "Our guys have now been at it flat out for almost two months and the backlog of changes is growing even while they're trying to get out new functionality. There's hardly room to swing a cat in the team room and while it's nice being co-located with everyone so that we can get answers when we need them, people need their space and they're getting on each other's nerves. The noise is irritating some people, and others feel that their personal work styles are not supported. And there's absolutely *no* privacy!"

"I'm not sure what I can do in the short term," said Gene, "but your concerns are noted." He knew what Brian was talking about. The project room was cluttered and smelly from various takeout meals. There were constant interruptions and very little room to spread out papers or take a break. But space was at a premium.

At about the same time, Ethan Matthews, Director of IT Architecture, ran into Vic in the hall. "How's AssortAA going?" he asked casually.

"It's going well," said Vic enthusiastically. "We're getting some better support from the business now that they can see what we're delivering and how it's working. They *love* the graphical interface we've given them."

"That's great," said Ethan, "but what are you doing about our traditional consultations, like those with architecture, to ensure that the bigger picture is taken into consideration? It seems like architecture and portfolio management and some higher-level objectives have been left out of project planning. We haven't even *seen* the graphic package you implemented."

Vic nodded. "You're absolutely right. We just went into the development with only a sketch of an idea. We're under the gun here and don't have the time to get into all that big picture stuff, reviews, stage gates, and sign-offs. We're lucky if we get home after a twelve-hour day! If you want more process, you're going to have to take it up with Gene."

Ethan nodded thoughtfully as Vic hustled off toward the project room. This was definitely an issue that needed to be raised with Gene, and right away. Something needed to be done about this cowboy mentality unless the company wanted to go back to the "bad old days" when systems were developed *ad hoc* and without regard to the overall technical direction and operational sustainability of the infrastructure and applications.

By the beginning of the fifth sprint, it had become clear that more resources were needed. Vic, Caroline, and Brian conferred and agreed that they needed to bring in some staff from their offshore outsourcer in India. "I think if we can turn over two user stories to them over the next two sprints, we can finish on time," said Vic.

"Can they handle this?" asked Caroline.

"They assure us that they can handle this new methodology," said Brian. "My idea would be to act as the manager of the whole portfolio while Vic manages the team here, and we have another scrum master in India for that team. I'd help them with coordination and guidance and get them another ops person and QA tester. I'll also speak with Gene about how we get more business participation for this team."

By the end of this sprint Gene felt that he should install a revolving door on this office. The head of QA had just left after complaining that the Indian team had not interpreted "agile" as tested code but merely as developed code. "It's *not* our job to do these tests or to make sure that the new code integrates with the old," she'd told him. "You need to do a better job educating these people about our standards."

Gene couldn't disagree and he picked up the phone to get Brian and Mike together for an impromptu meeting to see how they could best do this. He got an earful from Brian. "We need better tools to coordinate with India," he complained. "I can't do my job when they're working completely opposite hours from me and I can never get them and Vic's team together to talk. Can we get some better video and collaboration in here?"

"I'll add it to the list," sighed Gene.

At the beginning of the sixth sprint, Gene dropped into the team room to rally the troops for the final effort. "You've all been great!" he said enthusiastically. "I'm getting lots of positive feedback from the business because you're actually showing them what we're delivering and giving them a chance to give you feedback and correct misunderstandings. Everyone's looking forward to the great unveiling of the fully tested and implemented system at the buyers' meeting in a couple of weeks." After some enthusiastic clapping, the team got back to work, and Brian walked out into the hall with Gene.

"Thanks for the pep talk," Brian said. "People really appreciated it. Some of them are having a tough time with this new way of working. You know, many IT people aren't really 'people-people.' Now they're asking if they can do some of their work from home and I don't know what to say. Mike told us we really need daily attendance to make agile work."

Gene looked thoughtful. "Apart from that, how are you managing?"

"You've given me a first-class team for this pilot and they've worked really hard," said Brian. "But I'm not sure if we have the skills as an organization to do this all the time with all our projects. We're asking a lot of them. And the operations and QA people feel the same way. They're proud of what we're all accomplishing with AssortAA but they feel like they're in a pressure cooker all the time. And very few of our people feel comfortable working so closely with the business. They don't have the business knowledge or skills to interact easily with business people outside the team. That's always been the job of the relationship managers."

"I know," said Gene. "But that's going to have to change. IT's too important to the business for there to be an 'us' and 'them' mentality. Business and IT are each business people first and foremost and everyone has to be an equal stakeholder in our projects."

"But I do hear what you are saying, Brian," added Gene. "You've all done a terrific job and gone the extra mile to get this project off the ground. It's been a heroic effort. Once AssortAA has been delivered, I want to get everyone together again to look at what we've accomplished and what needs to be done for the second pilot to make agile development a more repeatable, sustainable methodology for all our work. We've had some major kudos from the business and Lisa tells me she's hearing lots of positive buzz about IT, so I think we're on the right track."

Two weeks later, Brian and Vic and their team realized the extent of their accomplishments when they stood on the stage of the auditorium and accepted the applause of a couple of hundred buyers and store operations people who had been blown away by the AssortAA live demo.

"We really did it!" Vic whispered to Brian. "I didn't think we could actually get this done in just four months, but we *did!*" The pride of the team was undeniable. There was no way anything in IT had *ever* generated such a positive response.

As the team gathered together in the local watering hole for a well-deserved celebration, Brian and Vic's phones pinged simultaneously with identical emails from Gene. "Congratulations on your success! Can you meet me at 3 p.m. to start planning the second pilot? It's bigger and much higher profile so I want you to help me figure out what we need to do better and how to do it. Cheers!"

Discussion Questions

1. What are the criteria Caroline and Philip should use to select the second pilot?
2. List the lessons learned from the first pilot for the benefit of the agile team assigned to the second pilot.
3. Outline how the agile team assigned to the second pilot should manage their relationships with other key stakeholders, such as the architecture group, the privacy and security people, quality assurance and testing, and the regulatory compliance group.

Index

Note: page numbers in *italics* refer to a figure or a table.

account managers, 21, 25
agile methodologies, 185, 196, 200, 277–78, 282, 291
  mini case example, 347–53
agility lack, 57
alignment, strategic, 17
analytical technologies, 30–31. *See also* technology and technologies
analytics, 32, 33, 35, 36, 41, 46, 185, 202, 214, 238, 241
anthropomorphism, and artificial intelligence, 243
API economy, 226–27. *See also* application programming interfaces (APIs)
application portfolio diagram, *329*
application portfolio management (APM), 316–17, 330–31
  application information
    application categorization, 332–33
    business value, 334
    general application information, 331–32
    support cost, 335
    technical condition, 333–34
  applications quagmire, 317–18
  benefits of, 318–22, *321*
  case study, *322*
  and demand management, 308–309, 313
  governance, 323–24
    challenges addressed by, 326–27
    and ownership, 325
    questions answered by, 324
  implementation of, 322–23
  IT applications as financial portfolio, 319–20, *319*
  key capabilities, *323*
    inventory management, 327–28
    reporting and rationalization, 328–29
    strategy and governance, 323–27
  key lessons, 329–30
application programming interfaces (APIs), 222–23, 233–34. *See also* API economy
  algorithm APIs, 224

business APIs, 224
  for continuous platform innovation, 225–26
  defined, 223–24
  doing business with, 230
  experience APIs, 224
  frameworks for, 227–30, *229*
    closed API market; broad API use, 229
    closed API market; limited API use, 228
    open API market; broad API use, 229
    open API market; limited API use, 228
  getting started
    adopting new tools and capabilities, 232
    build APIs first, 232
    change how you think, 231–32
    connecting APIs to business metrics, 233
    develop API governance, 230–31
    ensuring control, 233
    exposing and addressing risks, 233
    identify sources, 230–31
  for improvement, 225
  for interorganizational innovation, 225
  for leveraged products and services, 225
  mediation, 224
  portal, 224
  portfolio, 224
  system APIs, 223
  tools for use with, 224
  value of, 225–26
architecture, 29. *See also* enterprise architecture
  data, 34
  flexible, 48
  governance of, 86
Architecture Builder, 134
artificial intelligence, 236–37
  defined, 237–38
  management of
    business value, 241
    cognitive ergonomics, 242
    data management, 240
    digital transformation, 240
    role of IT in, 241–42
    skills development, 241

testing and audit, 242
open (open AI), 244
preparing for, 244–45
recommendations for managers
ask bigger questions, 242–43
beware of anthropomorphism, 243
build multiple work models, 244
consider open AI, 244
developing trust, 243–44
use in organizations, 238–40
automated controls, 116
Automated Identification System (AIS), 68–69, 71
AVP Data Strategy, 34

backup and recovery services, 61, 62
big data, 29, 41, 43, 196, 238, 240, 241, 248, 250.
See also data
budget allocation, 21–22
budget cycles, rolling, 24, 103
budgetary practices, 26. *See also* IT budgeting
accessing actual IT spending, 101
corporate fiscal policy, 98
fiscal IT budgets, 93, 101
functional IT budgets, 94, 101
importance of, 95–97
and IT planning, *98*
IT spending levels, 99
strategic goals, 98–99
business
enabling, 22
improvement, 22
innovation, 56
knowledge, 124–25
models for, 4, 20
multichannel, 42
new directions for, 42
opportunities, 23
partners, 311
requirements, 311
risk, 115
strategy (and IT strategy), 16, *17*, 18–19
structure (digital), 45
transformation, 16
unit applications, 7
unit governance, 87
business value
and application portfolio management, 334
and artificial intelligence, 241
and customer experience, 210–12
developing IT strategy for, 16–17
and ET adoption, 272
mini case example, 167–71
business–IT relationship, 120–21
assumptions regarding, 122

characteristics of, 123
and demand management, 310–11
elements of a strong relationship, 122–23
foundation of, 123–24, *124*
competence, 124–26
credibility, 126–27
interpersonal interaction, 127–28
trust, 129–31
guidelines for, 134–35
interaction of people and processes, 121–22
lack of clarity in, 122
nature of, 121–23
Business-process-as-a-service (BaaS), 54–55
buy-in, and system development, 284–85

capital expenditures, 93
change
metaphor for, 43
resistance to, 11, 296
chargeback, 306
Chief Data Officer, 34
Chief Enterprise Architect, 156–58
CIOs
challenges for, 26–27
role of, 44
cloud computing, 52–53, 187, 188
for business innovation, 56
Business-process-as-a-service (BaaS), 54–55
cost of, 54
for cost saving, 56
current reality, 53–55
for data storage, 56
for development support, 55
for expertise, 56
for infrastructure, 55
Infrastructure-as-a-service (IaaS), 54
for integration, 56
mobile apps for, 54
Platform-as-a-service (PaaS), 54
pressure to utilize, 53–54
security statistics, 57
Software-as-a-service (SaaS), 54
strategy for, 52–53, 55–56
for usage management, 56
value of, 54
cloud computing challenges
adjustments in IT practices, 59
changes in IT knowledge and skills, 59
compliance and regulatory risk, 56
data risk, 56
external risks, 56–57
increased cost, 57–58
integration challenges, 58–59
internal risks, 57–59

IT governance, 58
  lack of agility, 57
  lack of cloud readiness, 58
  loss of control, 58
  security breaches, 57
  supplier risk, 57
  third-party applications, 58
cloud ecosystems, 58
cloud vendor selection and management, 88, 196
  backup and recovery services, 61
  framework for evaluation, 63, 65
  functionality, 61
  issue clarification, 60–62
  maintaining competitive environment, 59–60
  negotiation, 60–61
  outages and uptime, 61
  preparation for, 60
  price caps, 61
  vendor management, 61–62
codes of conduct, 150
cognitive ergonomics, 242
collaboration, 48, 136–37, 151
  characteristics of, 141–43
  components of
    people, 143–44
    platforms, 145
    processes, 145
    program, 144–45
  and development, 275
  difficulties with DevOps, 297
  facilitating, 148–50
  focus of, 142–43
  locations for, 143
  mass, 142
  methods of, 143
  moving beyond the firewall, 150
  participants in, 142
  plan for adaptation, 149
  principles of behavior, 150
  range and scope of, *141*
  rationale for, 137–41
  role of IT in, 146–48
  services, 53
  and shared vision, 149
  starting with specific fundamentals, 149–50
  and system development, 285–86
collaboration services, 53
commercial ecosystems, 46. *See also* ecosystems
common systems, 7
communication(s), 44–45, 90, 116, 126
  of APM benefits, 330
  and collaboration, 143, 146
  electronic, 143
  in experimentation, 203, 206
  lack of, 282

  nontechnical, 127
  unified, 139
  working with DevOps, 298
communities of practice, 285
community engagement, 44
competence
  and execution, 125
  and expertise, 125
  and financial awareness, 125
  in IT organizations, 124–25
  and the need for business knowledge, 124–25
  ways to strengthen, 125–26
competitive advantage, 30, 99
complexity, reducing, 284
compliance issues, 56, 57, 65, 84
conferencing, 146
  electronic, 143
conflict, 128–29
conflict-resolution skills, 128
consumer technologies, 266. *See also* technology and technologies
content management, 140, 143, 144, 145, 147
conversion
  best practices in, 10–11
  from idea to reality, 9–10
costs
  allocation of, 94–95
  efficacy of, 83
  increases, 57–58
  of operations, 94
  reduction projects, 22
  savings, 4, 56, 139
credibility, 126–27
cross-functional teams and systems, 19, 205–206, 299
culture, 150
  and collaboration, 143–44
  supportive, 47
customer experience, 196, 209–10, 218–19
  and business value, 210–12
  consistency and reliability, 212
  dimensions of, 212–14, *213*
  essentials for IT
    customer focus, 216
    data management, 217
    delivery, 217–18
    designing for utilization, 216–17
    visioning, 215–16
  improving, 218–19, 294
  innovation, 213
  knowledge and data, 212
  role of technology, 214–15
  timeliness, 213
customer involvement, 85

data. *See also* information
    big data, 29, 41, 43, 196, 238, 240, 241,
       248, 250
    classification of, 62
    definitions of, 36
    integrity of, 36
    and IT governance, 86, 89
    key assets, 34, 36
    life cycle of, 34
    loss of, 60
    management of, 217, 240
    master, 29
    meta-, 32
    new types of, 31
    quality, of, 36
    storage of, 56
data and analytics strategy, 46
data architecture, 34
data ecosystem, 34, 35, *35*
data journey, 35–36
    developing engagement, 36–37
    improving data quality, 36
    setting priorities, 37
    working on data definitions, 36
data processing (DP), 29
data risks, 32, 57
data strategy, 29–30, 196
    action-oriented, 32
    data classification, 62
    defined, 32–34
    development of, 38
    need for, 30–32
    operations, 33
    policy, 33
    post-industrial, 32
    pragmatic, 32
    risk-oriented, 32
    standards, 34
    stewardship, 33–34
    where it fits in, 34–35
decentralization, 154, 267
decision-making, 63
    fact-based, 89
    impact of, 97
    improvement of, 4, 43
    rapid, 272–73
demand management, 302–303, 314. *See also* IT
    demand
    economics of, 305
    key organizational enablers
       application portfolio management (APM),
         308–309
       business-IT partnership, 310–11
       enterprise architecture, 309–10

       governance and transparency, 312–13
       strategic initiative management, 307–308
    tools for, 305–307, *307*
       chargeback, 306
       project portfolio management (PPM),
         305–306
       service catalog, 306
development productivity, 275–76
development support, 55
device ecosystems, 47. *See also* ecosystems
DevOps, 49, 179, 185, 196, 200
    benefits of, 293–94
    challenges
       collaboration difficulties, 297
       inadequate fundamentals, 297–98
       integration of service providers, 297
       lack of budgets, 296
       lack of management support, 295
       lack of skills, 297
       organizational constraints, 295
       organizational structure, 295
       resistance to change, 296
       tools for use with, 296–97
    characteristics of, 293
    defining, 292–93
    getting started with, 298, 300
       allocating time and money, 299
       coaching, 299
       communicate and educate, 298
       consult, 298
       developing cross-functional teams, 299
       don't get carried away, 299
       establishing foundational elements, 299
       taking incremental steps, 298
    problems solved by, 291–92
    transforming to, 290–91
digital business structure, 45
digital experience
    design, 45
       reinforcing, 42
digital operating model, 45
digital platform assessment, 45
digital strategy, 196
    complexity of, 40
    components of a mature strategy, 45
    connecting internal and external audiences, 43
    creating and evolving, 39–40
    defined, 40–41
    developing and implementing, 43–45
    and exploration, 41
    holistic orientation of, 41
    importance of, 41
    a mechanism for thinking about new
       directions, 42

as metaphor for change, 43
as overarching view of multichannel business, 42
reinforcing physical and digital experience, 42
scope of, 41
supporting, 45–50
    data and analytics strategy, 46
    flexible architecture, 48
    improved measurement, 49
    new capabilities, 47–48
    pervasive relationship management, 46–47
    rapid development and implementation, 48–49
    support for experimentation, 48
    supportive culture, 47
    unknown aspects of, 40
    value of, 42–43
digital transformation, and artificial intelligence, 240
Director Data Services, 34
disaster recovery planning, 139
disruption
    due to artificial intelligence, 236
    first steps for IT managers, 192–93
    and the future of IT, 188–90
    and IT, 187–88
    management of, 184–85, 192–94
        in IT, 190–91
    in organizations, 185–87
    sources of, 186
disruptive innovation, 186. See also innovation
document management, 147
document sharing, 285

ecosystems
    cloud, 58
    commercial, 46
    data, 34, 35, 35
    device, 47
    innovation, 46
    innovation in, 229
    interest, 46
    maritime transport, 66–72
    platform, 46
efficiency, improving with DevOps, 294
electronic communication, 143. See also communication
electronic conferencing, 143
emerging technologies (ETs), 196
    addressing uncertainty
        economic uncertainty, 270
        market uncertainty, 269
        technological uncertainty, 269–70
    assessing, 267–69

in business today, 265–66
identifying, 267
management of, 265, 270–72, 273
    addressing uncertainty, 273
    assigning as a job, 272
    educating others, 272
    go with the energy, 272
    rapid decision making, 272–73
    tie ET adoption to business value, 272
employee engagement, 36–37, 43
enterprise application integration (EAI), 317
enterprise architects (EAs), 309–10
enterprise architecture, 24, 275, 309–10
    mini case example, 154–59
    redesigning, 192–93
enterprise funding models, 103
enterprise IT governance, 86
enterprise resource planning systems (ERPs), 275
enterprise transformation, mini case example, 246–51
estimated time of arrival (ETA), 68
evolutionary system development, 277
executive leadership, 5, 19, 20–21, 311
experimentation, 48, 207
    with artificial intelligence, 239–40
    behavior change, 199
    business model, 199
    culture of, 196–97
    customer, 198
    data, 198
    definitions of, 197–98
    funding and governing, 206
    getting started with, 205–207
    and innovation, 197–98
    intra-company, 199
    and IT
        architecture, 200
        capabilities, 202
        development, 200–201
        strategy, 199–200
        structure, 201–202
    life cycle of, 202–203, 203
        defining experiment and success criteria, 204
        find sponsors, 203–204
        learning and evaluation, 204–205
        proof of concept, 204
        set the culture, 203
    opportunistic, 198
    strategic, 198
    and value delivering, 13
expertise, 56

failure, rethinking, 206
feedback, 23, 43, 49, 126, 142, 158, 181, 198, 204, 240, 259, 352
    from customers, 213–14
file-sharing services, 53
fiscal policy, 98
flexibility, 18, 48, 140–41
    in system development processes, 283–84
function points, 275
funding
    different "buckets" for, 24–25
    models for, 26

global logistics, mini case example, 66–72
global sourcing, 22
going green, 342–46
governance. *See also* IT governance
    API, 230–31
    application portfolio management, 323–24
        adopting more flexible processes, 283–84
        challenges addressed by, 326–27
        and ownership, 325
        questions answered by, 324
    architecture, 86
    board, 86
    business unit, 87
    in demand management, 312–14
    enterprise IT, 86
    local, 87
    of operations, 86
    and risk management, 110
    of security and privacy, 86
    of strategic projects, 86
    supportive structure for, 26

hazards, and risk management, 109

Identity and Authorization Management (IAM), 64
image recognition, 238
information. *See also* data
    accessibility of, 140
    access and collaboration, 146–47
    management and collaboration, 146–47
    risks, 110
information security management systems (ISMS), 63
information systems (IS), 29
information technology (IT), 29
infrastructure, 7
    cloud for, 55
    initiatives, 8, 23
    technologies, 266
Infrastructure-as-a-service (IaaS), 54

innovation, 18, 102–103, 175, 190, 192, 196
    continuous platform, 225–26
    and customer experience, 213
    disruptive, 186
    in an ecosystem, 229
    improvement of, 43
    interorganizational, 225
    mini case example, 253–58
innovation ecosystems, 46
integrated systems, 19
integration, 30, 56
    challenges, 58–59
    improvement of, 43
    in system development, 278
    of technology, 148
interest ecosystems, 46
Internet of Things (IoT), 196, 222
interoperability, 83
interpersonal interaction
    management of politics and conflict, 128–29
    nontechnical communication, 127
    professionalism, 127, 129
    social skills, 128
    strengthening, 129
ISO 27001, 63
ISO 27017, 63
IT. *See also* IT budgeting; IT demand; IT governance; IT strategy and planning; IT value
    bimodal, 191
    and collaboration, 146–48
    internal practices, 10
    investments, 6, 77–81
    processes, 99–101
    risk management, 116–17
    role in artificial intelligence management, 241–42
IT budgeting, 73, 75, 77–81, 92–93
    appointing IT finance specialist, 102
    enterprise funding models, 103
    fiscal, 93, 101
    functional, 94, 101
    key concepts, 93–95
    and the planning process, 97–101
    practices that deliver value, 102–103
    rolling budget cycles, 103
    separating operations from innovation, 102–103
    using tools and methodologies, 102
IT demand. *See also* demand management
    management of, 302–303
    understanding, 303–305
IT finance specialist, 102
IT governance, 58, 83, 130–31
    and cloud computing, 58
    components of, *87*

elements of, 85–87
evolution of, 87–89
increasing importance of, 84–85
promotion of effective, 89–91
and trust, 130–31
IT managers, and disruption, 192–93
IT strategy and planning, 97–101
  and budgeting, 98
  and business strategy, 16, 17, 18–19
  corporate processes, 97–99
  critical success factors, 20–21
  development of, 17
    account or relationship managers, 25
    barriers to, 27
    different funding "buckets," 24–25
    enterprise architecture, 24
    prioritization rubric, 25
    rolling planning and budget cycles, 24
  dimensions of, 21–23
  implementation of, 16–17
  initiatives for
    business enabling, 22
    business improvement, 22
    business opportunities, 23
    infrastructure initiatives, 23
    opportunity leverage, 23
  mini case example, 73–76
IT transformation, mini case example, 160–65
IT value. See also IT value proposition; value
  best practices in identifying potential, 8
  best practices in understanding, 7
  defined, 3–4
  locating, 5
  measuring, 4
  modes of delivery, 5, 6
  realizing, 5
  three classes of, 7
IT value profiles
  Architecture Builder, 134
  Partner, 134
  Project Coordinator, 133–34
  Systems Provider, 134
  Technological Leader, 134
IT value proposition
  delivering, 2–3
  three components of, 7, 7
  understanding, 3
IT-based risk. See also risk management
  holistic view of, 107–110, 109
  management of, 106–107
iterations, 90, 114, 204, 206, 242, 291
iterative system development, 277

joint ownership of initiatives, 13

knowledge sharing, 285. See also collaboration

laws, compliance with, 56, 84
leadership, 311
  executive, 5, 19, 20–21
legal issues, and risk management, 109
lines of business (LOBs), 201
local governance, 87

machine learning, 237. See also artificial intelligence (AI)
management. See also application portfolio management (APM); demand management; risk management
  of content, 140, 143, 144, 145, 147
  data, 240
  of disruption, 184–85, 190–94
  document, 147
  electronic, 143
  of emerging technologies, 265, 270–73
  Identity and Authorization (IAM), 64
  inventory, 327–28
  portfolio, 13
  project, 336–40
  relationship, 46–47, 311
  strategic initiative, 307–308
  usage, 56
  vendor, 61–62
managers
  advice to, 37
  IT, 192–93
  recommendations for, 62
  relationship, 7, 25
  senior, 20–21
Maritime Transport Ecosystem, 66–72
marketing skills, 311
mass collaboration, 142. See also collaboration
master data, 29. See also data
metadata, 32. See also data
microservices, 223, 231. See also application programming interfaces (APIs)
migration strategy, 65
mini cases
  Consumerization of Technology at IFG, 259–63
  Delivering Business Value with IT at Hefty Hardware, 167–71
  Enterprise Architecture at Nationstate Insurance, 154–59
  Enterprise Transformation at Trustworthy Insurance, 246–51
  Global Logistics and the Maritime Transport Ecosystem, 66–72
  Innovation at International Foods, 253–58

Introducing Agile Development at American
  Attire, 347–53
IT Investment at North American Financial,
  77–81
IT Planning at ModMeters, 73–76
Project Management at MM, 336–40
Transforming IT at Global Digital Imaging,
  160–65
Working Smarter at Continental Furniture
  International, 341–46
mission statement, 162
mobile technologies, 54, 88, 169–70
monitoring, 90
multichannel business, 42

natural language processing, 237. *See also* artificial
  intelligence
neural networks, 237. *See also* artificial intelligence
new ideas, 44. *See also* innovation

operating expenses, 93
opportunities
  identification of, 7–9
  leveraging, 23
organizational chart, 162
outages and uptime, 61
outsourcing, 22, 59, 85, 88, 90, 94, 133, 136,
  163, 184, 187, 188, 189, 193, 219, 272, 275,
  280, 304

Partner IT function, 134
partnership, between IT and business, 21–22
pattern identification, 237, 238
people risks, 110
physical experience, reinforcing, 42
pilot studies, 13. *See also* experimentation
planning cycles, rolling, 24
planning practices, 26
planning support, 65
platform ecosystems, 46
Platform-as-a-service (PaaS), 54
platforms, for collaboration, 145
"plug-and-play" dynamics, 39
politics, 128–29
portfolio management, 13
positioning, strategic, 4
pragmatic, 37
price caps, 61
prioritization, 37, 110–11
  rubric for, 25
privacy issues, 84, 86, 150
process risks, 110
productivity, increased, 4

professionalism, 127, 129
Project Coordinator, 133–34
project management, mini case example, 336–40
project portfolio management (PPM), 305–306
project portfolios, 320
prototypes, 62
pull technologies, 267
push technologies, 267

quality assurance, 83

rapid application development (RAD), 275, 277
rapid development, 48–49
rapid implementation, 48–49
regulatory environment, 99
regulatory issues, 56, 84, 109
regulatory risks, 57
relationship management, 46–47, 311
relationship managers, 7, 25
release valves, 90–91
relevance, 190
reporting and monitoring, 65
resistance to change, 11, 296
return on investment (ROI), 4
risk
  aversion to, 83
  compliance, 57, 65
  concerns regarding, 31
  cultural, 110
  data, 32, 57
  external, 56–57
  internal, 57–59
  IT-based, 106–10, *109*, 116–17
  people, 110
  regulatory, 57
  supplier, 57
  technical, 115
risk management, 85, 106–107, 110, 116–17, 191
  and APIs, 233
  and collaboration, 147
  and criminal interference, 110
  expecting change, 111–12
  holistic portrait of, 110–12
  improving capabilities, 115–16
  internal and external components, 109–10
  of IT risk, 116–17
  multiple perspectives, 112
  potential risks to enterprise, 109
  and priorities, 110–11
  risk classification schemes, 118–19
risk management framework (RMF), 112–15
  policies and standards, 113
  risk categories, 113
  risk mitigation, 114

risk ownership, 114
risk reporting and monitoring, 114–15
risk types, 114
risk reduction, using DevOps, 293
risk taking, 48
and experimentation, 197
robotics, 237. *See also* artificial intelligence
rolling budget cycles, 24, 103

security issues, 65, 84, 86
breaches, 57
cloud computing, 57
and collaboration, 147
and governance, 86
senior management, 20–21
service catalog, 306
service improvement, 4
service level agreements (SLAs), 60–62, 65
service providers
cloud, 63–65, 88, 196
integration of, 297
shared services, 22
skills
and artificial intelligence, 241
business, 219, 241, 273
collaboration, 143
communication, 156, 283
contract negotiation, 60
decision-making, 176
development of, 241, 296–97
flexing, 149
of IT staff, 40, 59, 122, 129, 189, 194, 202, 219, 280
of leaders, 47, 156, 176
marketing, 311
new, 10, 23, 59, 63, 184, 198, 210, 271, 297
relationship management, 271
research, 271
service management, 228
social, 128
soft, 47–48, 129, 176
strategizing, 26–27
technical, 156, 241, 273, 280, 337
for thought leadership, 179–81
visionary, 202, 271
SOA, 223. *See also* application programming interfaces (APIs)
social networking technologies, 139, 143
social skills, 128
soft skills, 47–48, 129, 176
software, for communication and collaboration, 146
software-as-a-service (SaaS), 22, 54, 187
speed, 18

spiral system development, 277
staff augmentation, 90
strategic initiative management, 307–308
strategic project office (SPO), 308
strategy and strategizing, 26–27
alignment with execution, 85
goals, 98–99
implementation, 16–17, 96–97
investments, 94–95
project governance, 86
themes, 20
supplier risks, 57
synchronization of capabilities, 21
system development, 275
anti-waterfall methods, 277
improving productivity, 282, 287
addressing bottlenecks, 286
adopting more flexible processes, 283–84
clarifying roles and responsibilities, 286–87
creating a smarter development environment, 285–86
educating perceptions, 285
enhancing success metrics, 284–85
focusing on outcomes, 286
monitoring performance, 285
optimizing the bigger picture, 283
promoting desired behavior, 285
reducing complexity, 284
simplifying testing, 287
simplifying the development environment, 287
incremental, 277
obstacles to improving productivity, 280–82
analysis, 281
business involvement, 281
testing, 281
problem with, 276–77
trends in
adopting new approaches, 277–78
changing resourcing strategies, 280
composition, 278
enhancing waterfall methodology, 278–79
improved governance, 279–80
integration, 278
waterfall method, 276, 277, 278–79
system prioritization, 275
Systems Development Lifecycle (SDLC), 271
Systems Provider, 134

technical risk, 115
Technological Leader, 134
technology and technologies. *See also* artificial intelligence (AI); IT

analytical, 30–31
  consumer technologies, 266
  consumerization of, 259–63
  and customer experience, 214–15
  decentralized, 267
  infrastructure technologies, 266
  pull, 267
  push, 267
  social networking, 139, 143
technology integration, 148
technology partners, 311
technology renewal funds, 8
third parties, and risk management, 109
third-party applications, 58
thought leaders, 173
  characteristics of, 177–79
  defining, 174–75
  distinguishing features of, 177
  and IT, 175–77
thought leadership, *178*, 181, 196
  fostering, 179–81
  in an IT function, 179
topline value, 16, 138–39
total cost of ownership (TCO) initiative, 330
transparency, in demand management, 312–14
trust
  and artificial intelligence, 243–44
  in the business–IT relationship, 129–31
  and IT governance, 130–31

uncertainty
  addressing, 273
  economic, 270
  market, 269
  technological, 269–70
usage management, 56
utility partners, 311

value. *See also* business value; IT value; IT value
  proposition

  and accessibility of information, 140
  and accessibility of people, 139–40
  chunks of, 12
  conversion, 7, 9–10
  and cost savings, 139
  delivering, 12–14
  and flexibility, 140–41
  of IT, 2
  and IT effectiveness, 139
  as many-layered concept, *4*
  models of, 19
  new types of, 31
  opportunities, 7–9
  perceptions of, 6
  realizing, 7, 10–11
  sources of, 196
  topline, 16, 138–39
vendors
  already serving enterprises like yours, 64
  certified, 62
  changing management process, 65
  locking in, 60
  meeting current requirements and future
    roadmap, 64
  meeting service-level agreements (SLAs), 65
  pricing, 65
  reporting and monitoring, 65
  responsiveness of, 65
  security and compliance, 65
  strong technology stack, 65
  third-party, 88
Vessel Traffic Service (VTS), 68–70
video conferencing, 143
virtual interaction, 138
vision, 37

"W" effect, 5, *6*
waterfall methodology, 266, 277, 278–79
Watson computer, 239
working smarter, mini case example, 341–46